SUPERHEROES

JOE KUBERT'S WONDERFUL WORLD OF COMICS

To Muriel

Thank you for your inexhaustible patience and understanding

ACKNOWLEDGMENTS

I thought this book was going to be easy. After all, I've been a comic book cartoonist most of my life. Who would know the subject better? I've learned, however, that doing a book and doing a comic book are two different things. My sincerest appreciation is hereby tendered to Sylvia Warren, the editor, who is responsible for the form and readability of this book. Our relationship was, for me, a positive learning experience.

First published in 1999 by Watson-Guptill Publications
1515 Broadway
New York, NY 10036
Copyright © 1999 by Joe Kubert
ISBN 0-8230-2561-6

Library of Congress Cataloging-in-Publication Data

Kubert, Joe, 1926-
        Superheroes : Joe Kubert's wonderful world of comics / Joe Kubert
            p.   cm
        Includes index.
        ISBN 0-8230-2561-6
        1. Comic books, strips, etc.—Authorship. 2. Heroes—Comic books, strips,
    etc.—Authorship. 3. Cartooning—Technique. I. Title.

    PN6710.K83 1999
    808'.066741 21—dc21
                                                99-045930

Manufactured in the United States

First printing, 1999

2 3 4 5 6 7 8 9 / 07 06 05 04 03 02 01 00

CONTENTS

BACKGROUNDS

TELLING THE STORY
PROCEDURE AND TOOLS

THE CREATIVE PROCESS
RAGMAN STORYBOARDS

FOREWORD

I have been drawing since I was two years old, which is when I first learned which end of the pencil made the mark. I have been a professional cartoonist from the age of twelve. At this writing, I am seventy-two years old and still working in the profession I've always loved. Hopefully, this book will extend the pleasure and diminish the frustration that others experience in attempting to draw in a comic book mode.

The main subject is a character type who helped turn the wonderful world of comic books into a multimillion dollar industry—the superhero. The first superhero made his appearance in the mid-1930s. Though sales of superhero comics have had their ups and downs since then, today's superheroes are a presence to be reckoned with: in cinema, television, Web sites (forgive the pun, Spidey), newspaper syndication, clothing, toys, and much, much more.

I'm assuming that you have purchased this book because you have an interest in drawing in general and cartooning and superheroes in particular. (For some unexplainable, inexplicable reason, you and I enjoy an involvement with cartooning and comic book superheroes. Seeing them come alive in movies and on T.V. doesn't diminish that interest, does it?) The six sections of this book were designed to help you gain the insight and skills necessary for you to put your interest and ideas into graphic cartoon form, to enable you to take your interest to the ultimate. As you will find, although my emphasis is on superheroes, most of the techniques covered here could be used to create any type of comic book character—in any type of story.

Part One is a portfolio of heroes and superheroes across millennia. Part Two takes you through some basic skills, and Part Three suggests ways to use skills + imagination + research to create your very own superoriginal pantheon of superheroes—whether human, robot, android, or animal. Part Four shows a gallery of styles and superhero characters. Part Five covers location, the backgrounds for your creations. Part Six puts it all together, how to use what you've learned to tell a story—sequencing, script, layout, thumbnails, from roughs to final drawings, inking and lettering. The last section of the text shows how a comic book artist goes from script to storyboard—using actual storyboards for Ragman, a superhero character that I helped create in the early 1970s.

Finally, there are two bonus sections. The first describes the basic tools of the trade (pencils, pens, paper, etc.), which you can turn to at any time if you're in doubt about what equipment you need. The second deals with potential career paths for anyone who is serious about becoming a comic book artist.

So, work along with me. Get yourself some paper and a pencil. Don't forget an eraser. None of us are perfect, y'know, and mistakes are the way we all learn. Then, start to draw. It should be obvious, but for some reason it isn't: *The only way anybody learns to draw (and I believe anybody can draw!) is by drawing.* By doing a lot of drawing. Your improvement in drawing, how quickly you learn and how well you do, is directly related to the amount of time you spend drawing. So turn the page and let's get started!

HEROES AND SUPERHEROES
FROM PREHISTORY TO FUTUREWORLDS

Thousands and thousands of years before the dawn of written language, human artists drew, carved, and painted complex, often mysterious images of their worlds. The oldest of these ancient pictures are mostly of animals, like this large black bull painted on the walls of Lascaux Cavern, France, but there are also images of people (perhaps shamans, or sorcerers), weapons (at first spears and later bows and arrows), handprints, and symbols.

A modern artist who wants to create a hero or superhero based on our prehistoric ancestors must imagine the lives and backgrounds of those early humans. Look at the artwork shown here and think about what it must have been like to be one of the people who created or were fascinated and thrilled by these drawings. Why were they done? Were these millennia-old "cartoons" a magical way to transmit superpowers to the hunters of the tribe? What were the values of the tribespeople? How did they get their food? What were their attitudes toward each other? Toward neighboring tribes? Anwers to such questions, however conjectural, are a way to get "inside" your prehistoric hero, to endow him (or her) with believable traits.

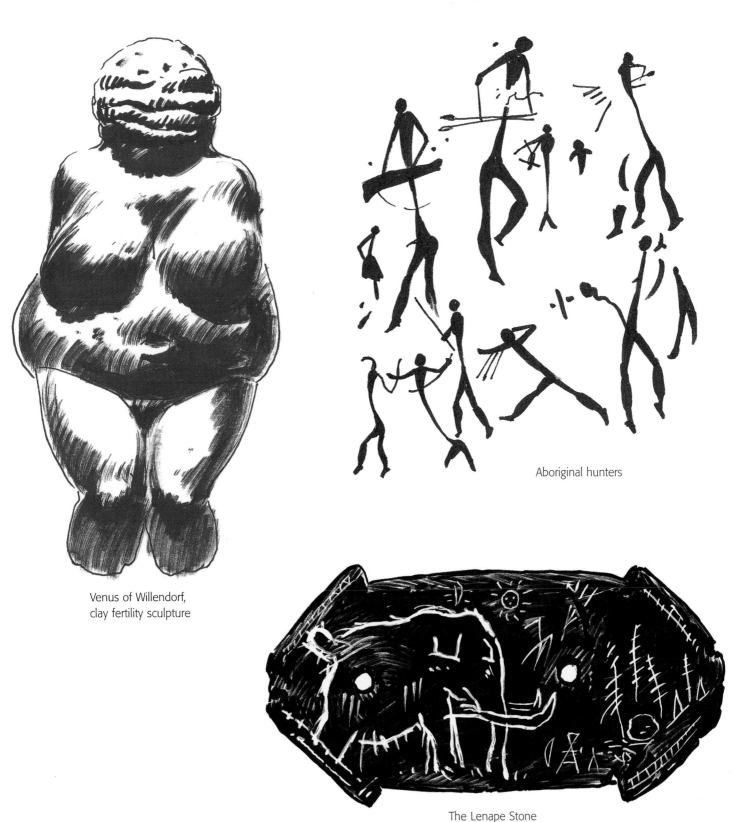

Venus of Willendorf,
clay fertility sculpture

Aboriginal hunters

The Lenape Stone

A PREHISTORIC SUPERHERO

Tor, the superhero caveman, differs physiologically from his modern counterparts. Note the heavy brow and strong jaw. I envisioned him as a skillful hunter, whose broad nose is highly adapted to pick up a scent. Short hair in front does not obstruct sight, while thick hair in back protects his neck. Fur and lizard skin protect his wrists, torso, and legs. He is heavily muscled, but success in his daily life depends on a combination of brain and brawn.

Tor walks with a heavy stride, leaning forward. He's no lightweight. His shoulders move in rhythm with his steps—right foot forward, right arm back; left foot back, right arm forward. He grips his spear firmly, fingers comfortably encircling the shaft. He stares ahead, but he is conscious of everything around him. That's how I felt Tor should be, and that's how I drew him.

Of course, Tor's three-dimensional qualities are also the result of tried and true techniques. A standing figure composed mainly of horizontal and vertical lines, without twist and foreshortening, would have seemed stiff and lifeless.

Practice drawing your heads from every angle. Notice how the relative proportions of the features change depending on the angle of view.

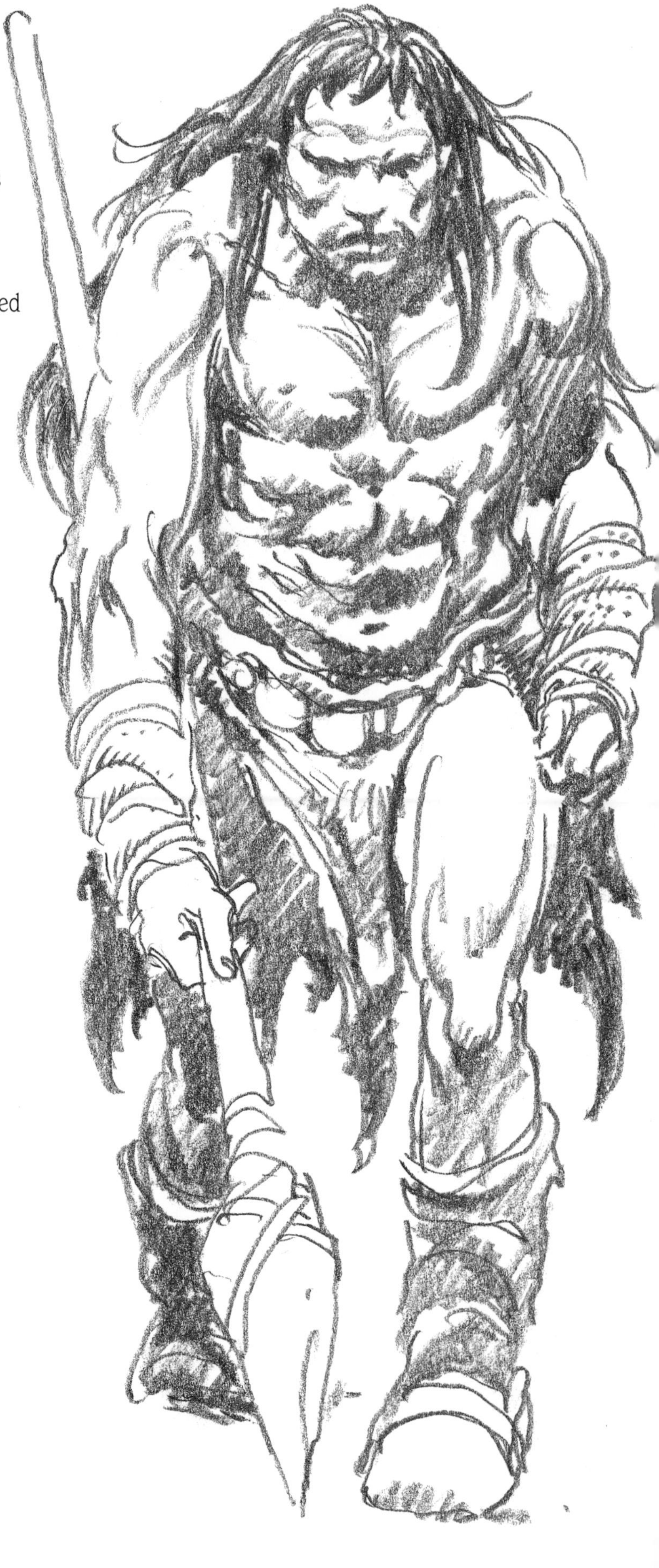

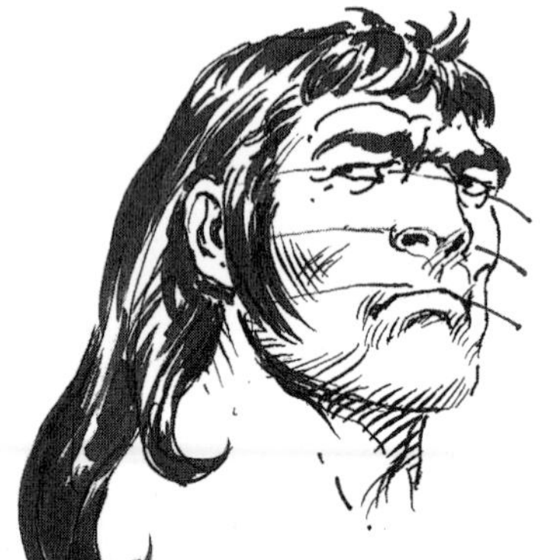

3/4 up

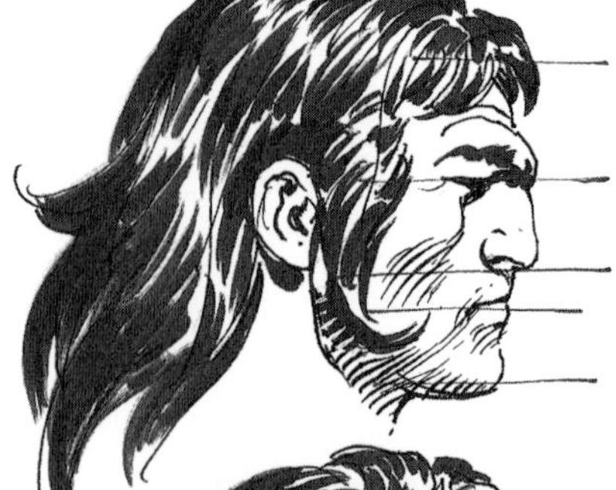

Profile

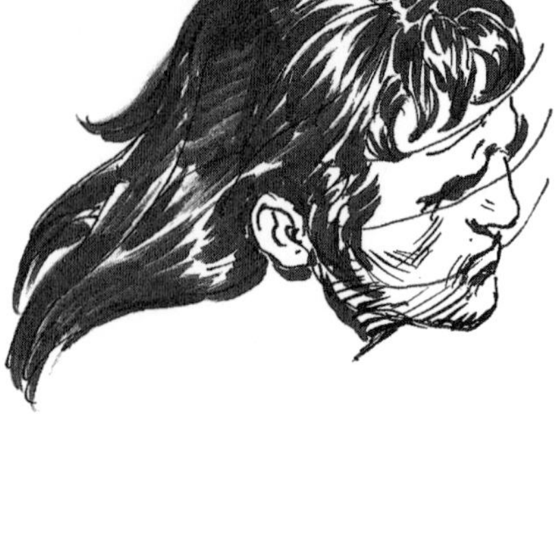

Down

By combining geological research and findings of prehistoric fossils and cave drawings, we cartoonists can achieve a clearer concept of what now-extinct animals looked like many thousands (and even millions) of years ago. Once you create historically accurate creatures, you can mix and match them any way you want in your comic book sequences. A recent series of sci-fi novels pictured great dinosaurs dominated and controlled by humans living in teeming metropolises. These stories "work" because the illustrations seem to make such an anomaly believable. The backgrounds are based on photographic references and the dinosaurs look alive because they are founded on paleontologists' and artists' recreations of these ancient beasts.

As a cartoonist, you bring to your art knowledge and experience. Add a soupçon of dramatics and emotion. A lively mix. The more appropriate your references, the more impact your drawings will have. Visit your local museums. Read, read, read. Collect pictures.

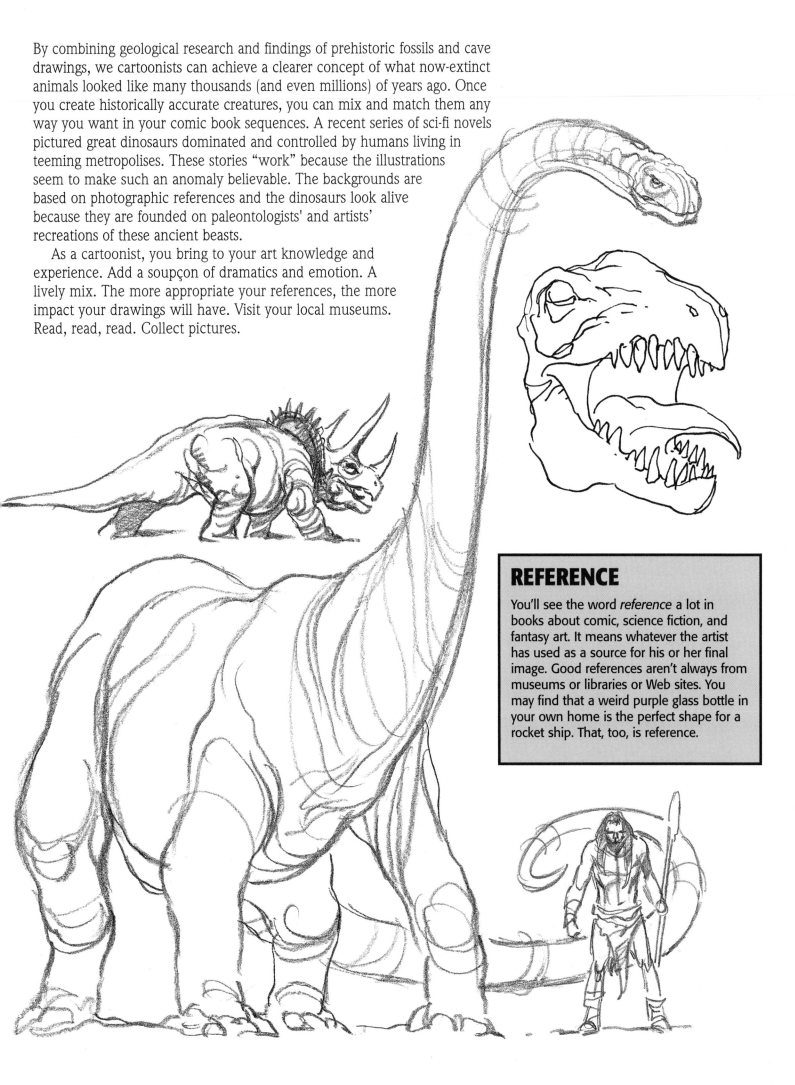

REFERENCE

You'll see the word *reference* a lot in books about comic, science fiction, and fantasy art. It means whatever the artist has used as a source for his or her final image. Good references aren't always from museums or libraries or Web sites. You may find that a weird purple glass bottle in your own home is the perfect shape for a rocket ship. That, too, is reference.

A SUPERHERO WITH COPTIC COOL

Egypt was the home of one of the world's earliest great civilizations. Like the art and captions in today's comic books, the paintings and heiroglyphics that adorn the tombs of the pharaohs tell stories in pictures. Not that you would want to copy them for your own characters—they lack depth and dynamism—but you can use them to create a superhero with a Coptic slant and an awesome costume.

The sarcophagi, or coffins, found in ancient Egyptian tombs are fabulous sources of information about what the people looked like, how they dressed, and what ornaments they wore. The death mask of the young king Tutankhamen, who ruled almost 4000 years ago, shows the young king's eyes and eyebrows heavily outlined with makeup, perhaps with kohl (made with powdered antimony, burnt almonds, black copper oxide, and brown ocher). The Eyptians were masters of makeup—for both sexes.

Design a superhero with an Egyptian likeness. Before you start, collect references for various objects, like wristbands, headdress, scepter, sandals, etc. Any one of these may be a source of power for your superhero. (The Internet has a wealth of sites about ancient Egypt, with text, pictures, and even short videos.) Use your imagination, but base your ideas on historical fact. Often, professional cartoonists will spend more time on a search for good reference than they will on an actual drawing.

In the process of creating a new character, cartoonists often make up what is known as a *character sheet,* which consists of a series of schematic drawings showing the person in a variety of positions (as here) and facial close-ups (as in the drawings of cavemen's heads on page 10). Doing character sheets is a good way to get to "know" your hero, so that you can draw him (or her) from any angle. (The horizontal lines on these drawings are done as a way to maintain correct relative proportions no matter what angle the figure is viewed from. Proportionality grids are discussed in detail in the next section.)

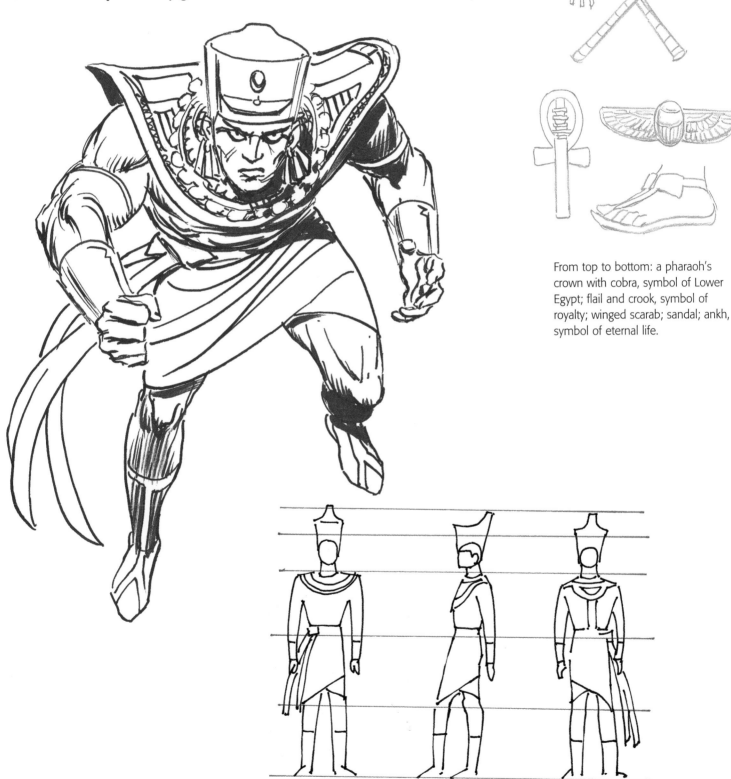

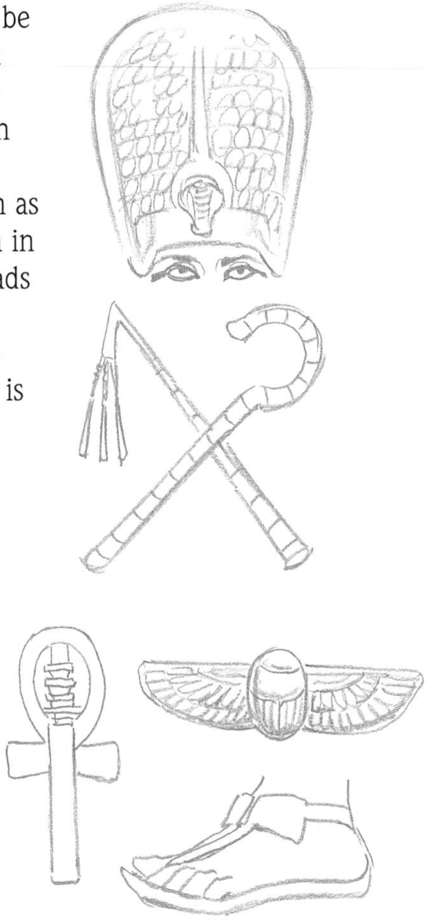

From top to bottom: a pharaoh's crown with cobra, symbol of Lower Egypt; flail and crook, symbol of royalty; winged scarab; sandal; ankh, symbol of eternal life.

MEDIEVAL MAN

Medieval knights were mounted on horses when they fought dragons and other evil-doers. So—you must learn how to draw horses. If you've never tried to draw a horse, let me be the first to tell you that they're not easy to draw. In lieu of bringing one into your room, visit your library and borrow a book with pictures of this beautiful animal. Copy and trace them. Work on the details, such as hooves, legs, and musculature. Get pictures of horses in motion. Study the muscles of a racehorse. Draw the horse's head from every angle. Pay attention to the saddle, stirrups, bridle, and reins.

Do rough sketches first, then draw in the details.

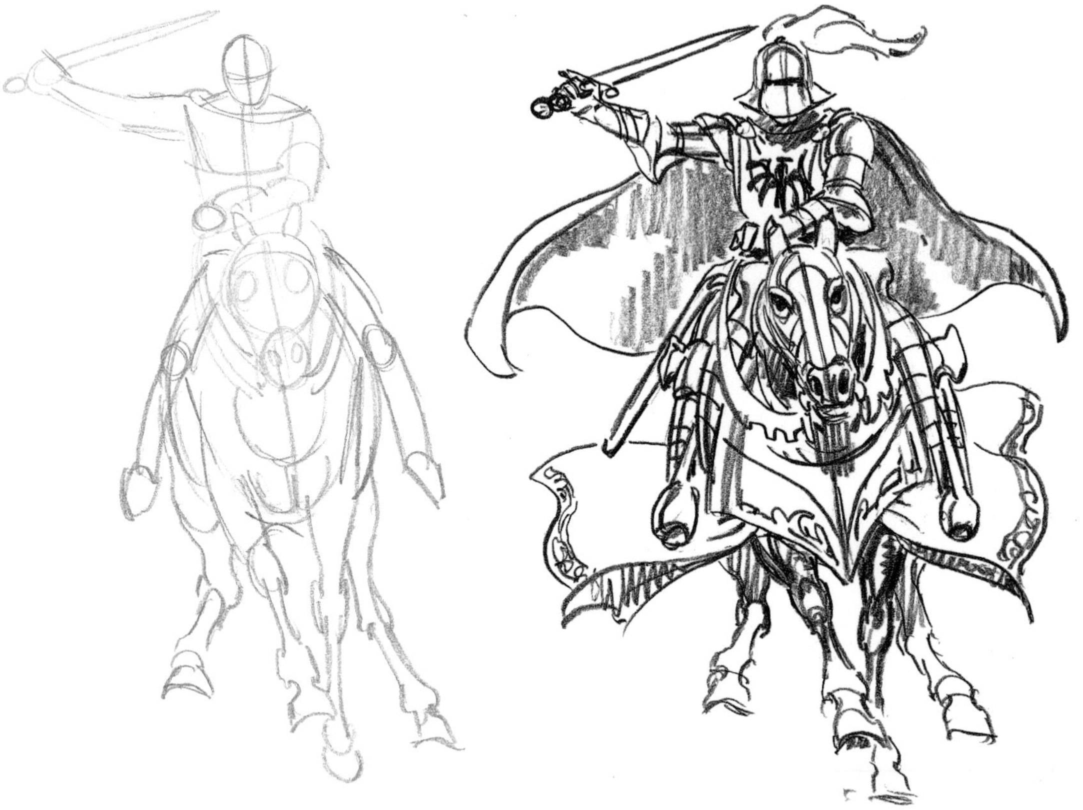

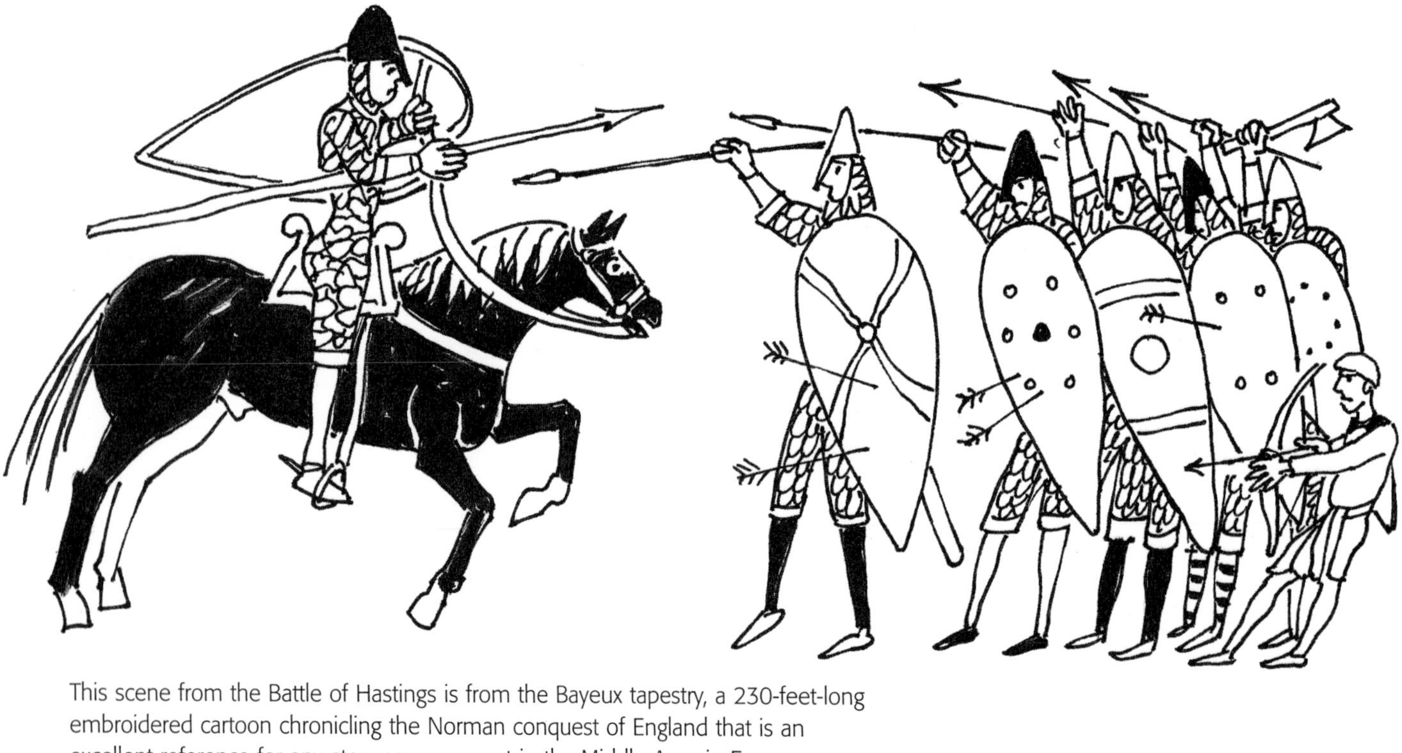

This scene from the Battle of Hastings is from the Bayeux tapestry, a 230-feet-long embroidered cartoon chronicling the Norman conquest of England that is an excellent reference for any story sequence set in the Middle Ages in Europe.

Armor circa 1400

The days of chivalry and knights in armor have inspired countless tales of heroes and their adventures—and may well be just what it takes to spark your creative imagination. As always, it's essential to collect references and do research. The credibility of your character (hero or superhero) is built from authentic details. The four helmet types shown here, copied from authentic pieces in museum collections, were all in use during the Middle Ages, yet each has a distinctive look.

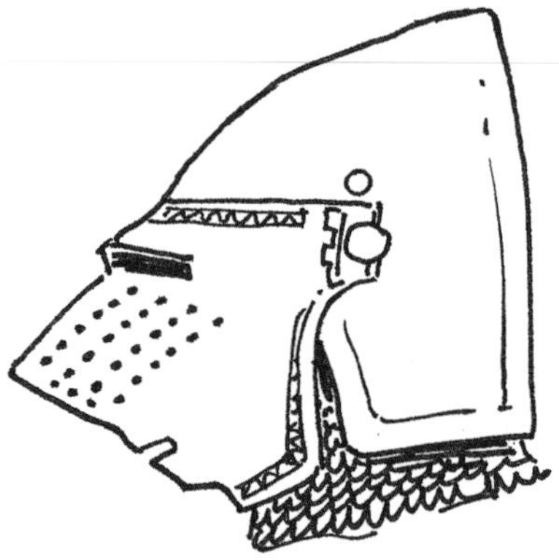

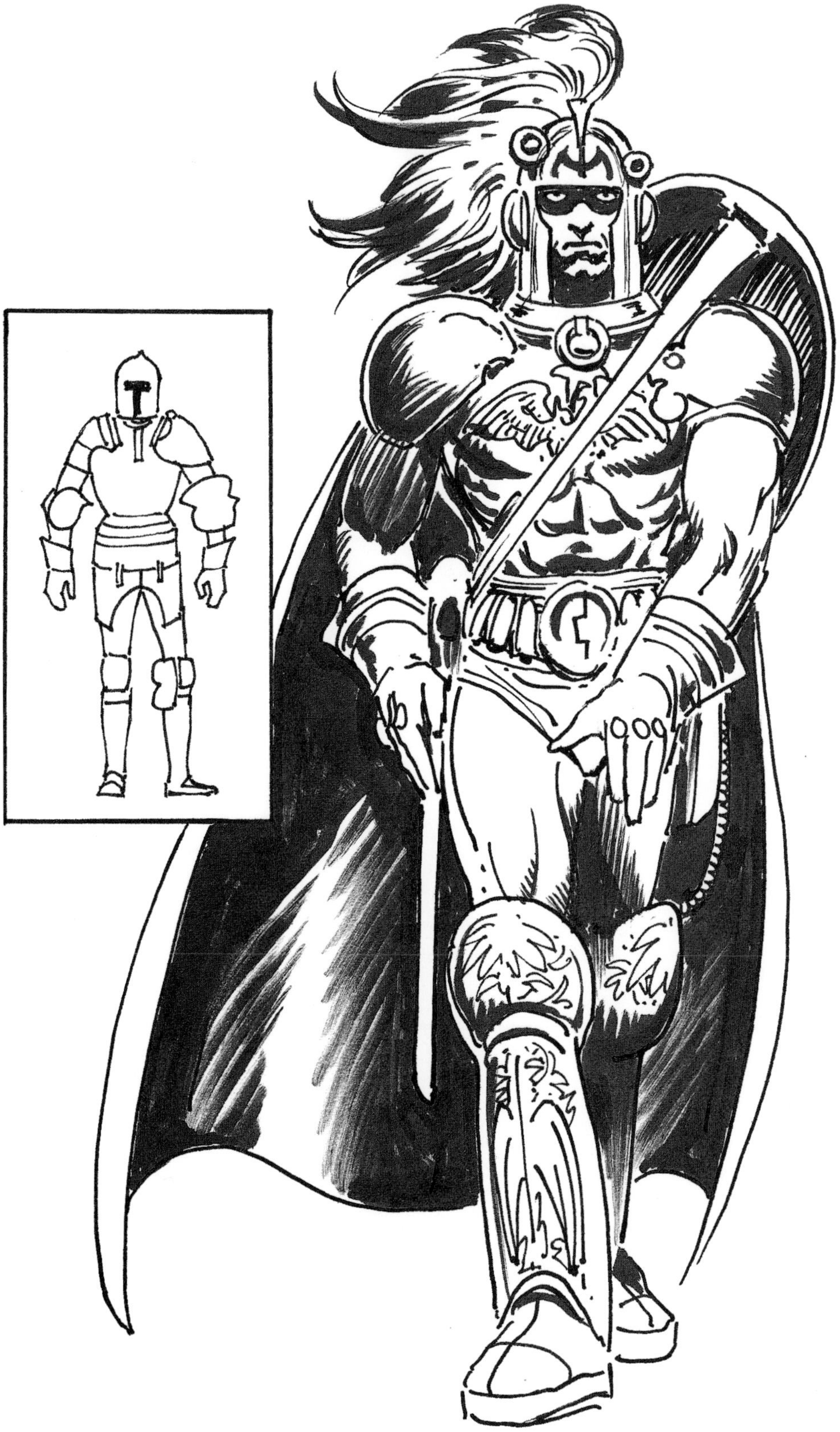

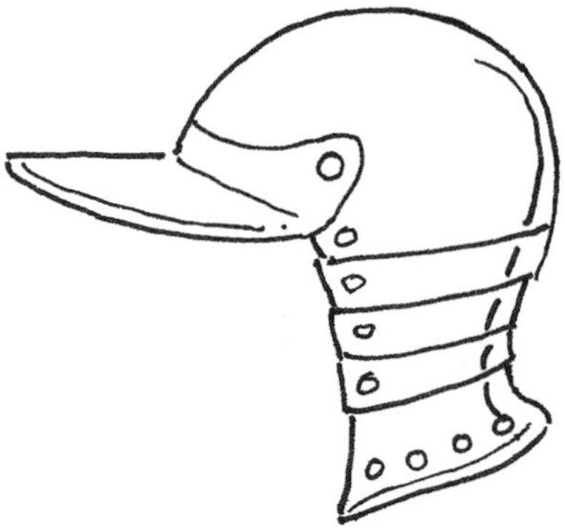

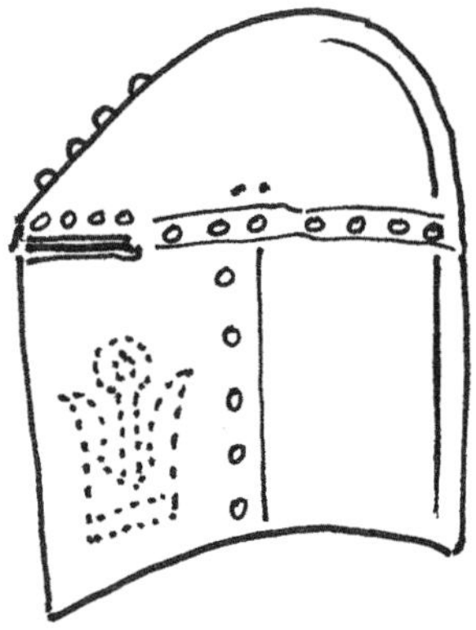

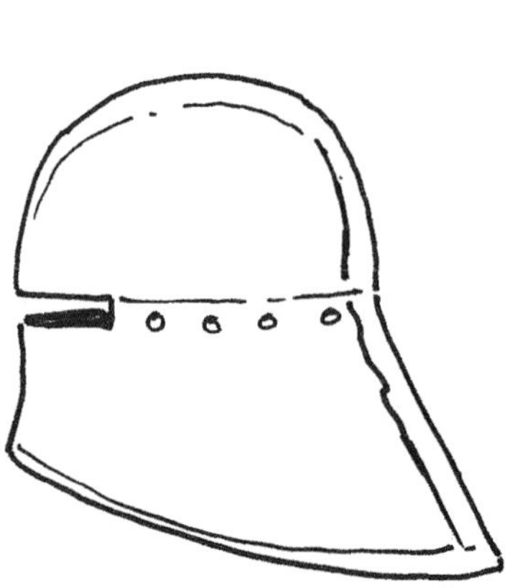

From top to bottom: sugarloaf helm; lobster tail helm; spangenhelm; sallet.

HEROES FROM AMERICAN HISTORY

Native Americans

Many thousands of years before European explorers reached the shores of North America, the land was occupied by widely dispersed Native American nations, comprised of hundreds of different tribes. These indigenous peoples were physically quite different from one another, spoke different languages, and dressed differently. The rich history of pre-Columbian Americans offers a motherlode of material for cartoonists who want to create a superhero character. A Native American superhero? Sounds exciting, doesn't it? Hold on—you'll have to do your homework first.

Reference. Research. Reading. The three "R"s that will put Reality into your cartoons.

For practice, design a costume for a Native American superhero by placing a piece of tracing paper over the first figure at the bottom left of the page. Now, using your own ideas, draw a costume. Feel free to adopt parts of the costumes I've drawn. Don't be afraid to make mistakes. Some of your most valuable learning experiences come from not being afraid to make mistakes, recognizing them, and then correcting them. And all it takes to correct a mistake you've made on a piece of tracing paper is another piece of paper.

You'll probably want your superhero to have a weapon of some sort. Base your creation on history, on the real things used by real tribes. A bow and arrows. A tomahawk. A war club. A knife. What kind of futuristic weapon can you design based on the real things? What can these new weapons do? Are they electronically driven or radar-targeted? You're the designer. You're the boss. You decide.

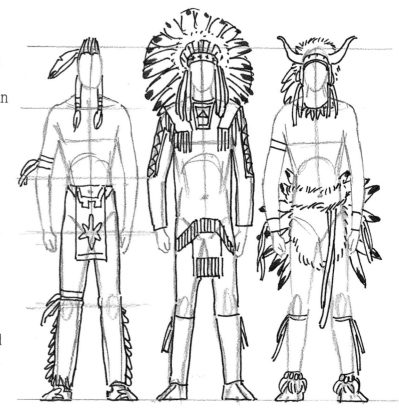

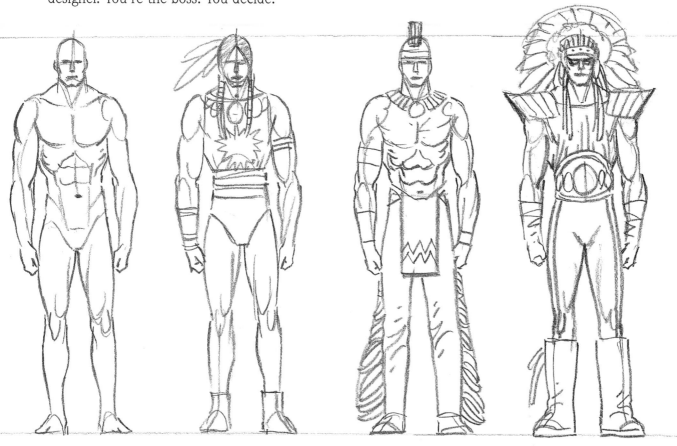

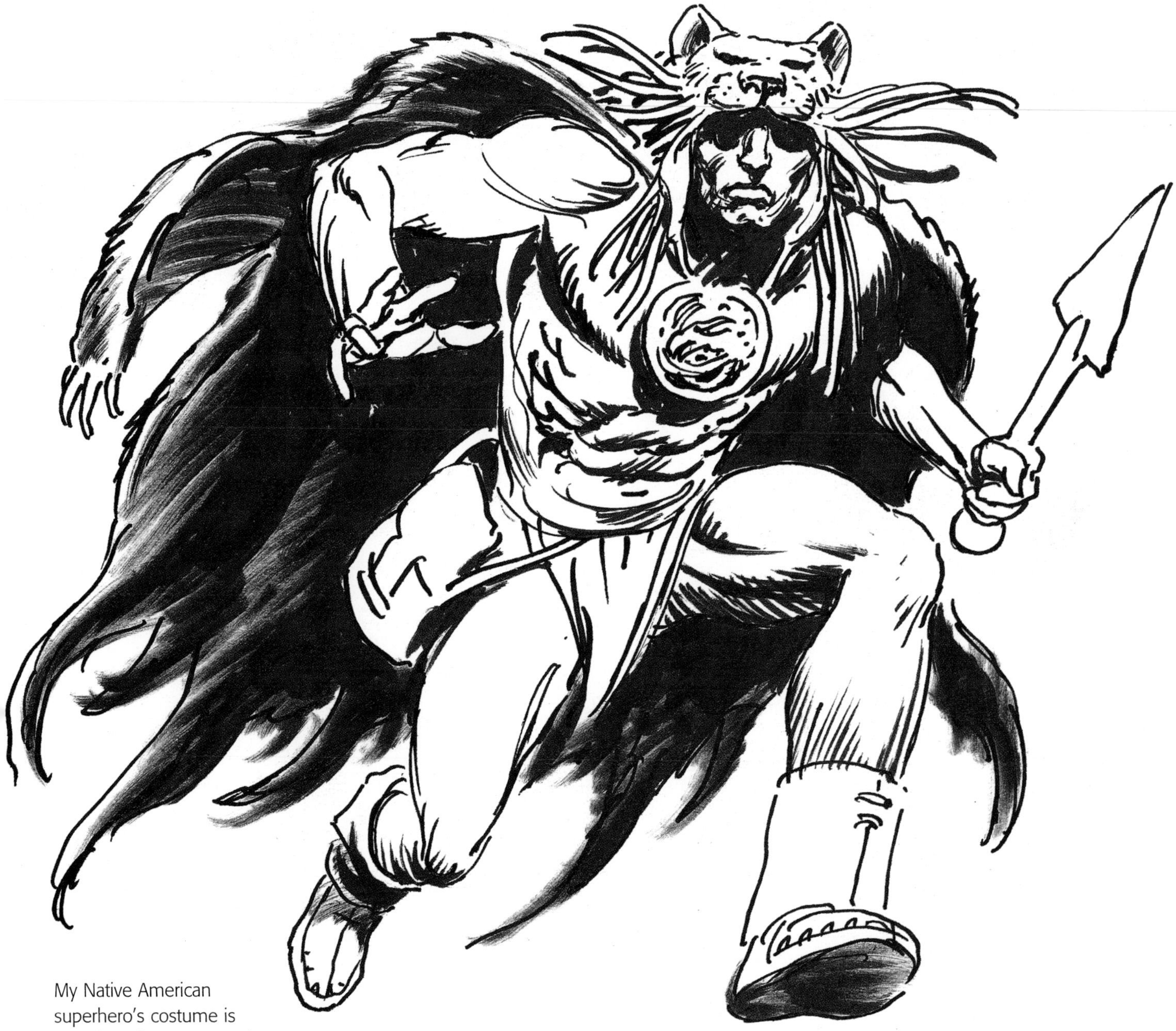

My Native American superhero's costume is based on the ceremonial dress worn by a Blackfoot medicine man.

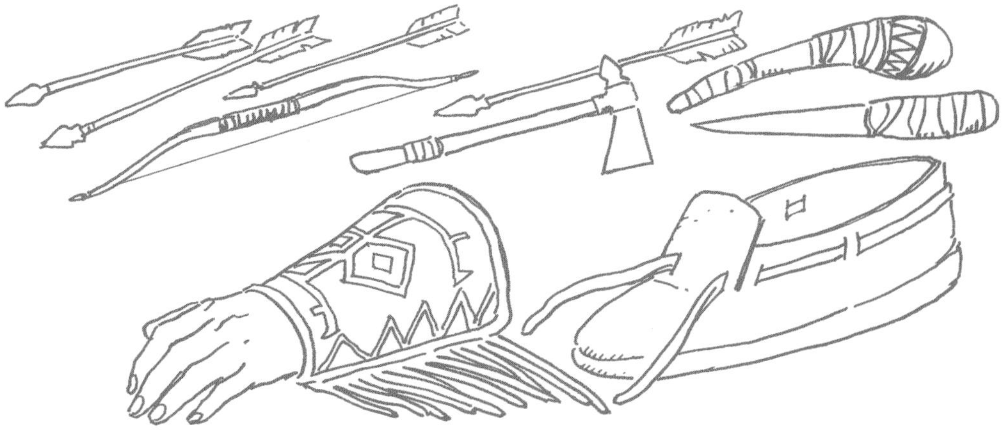

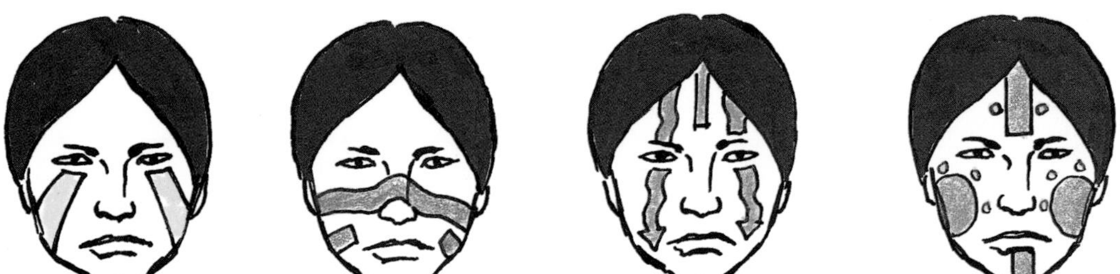

The Wild, Wild West

Cowboy heroes, fictional and real, have been a staple in comic books and syndicated newspaper comic strips from the very beginning. Red Ryder, Tom Mix, Buffalo Bill, Wyatt Earp, and Billy the Kid are only a few of the larger-than-life westerners who have become part of our country's folklore. Even before the appearance of the comic strip, western heros like Buffalo Bill were lionized in "penny dreadfuls," pulp fiction for the masses. For decades, these graphic tales of western heros bore little resemblance to reality. Most, in fact, were figments of the imaginations of writers and artists who had never been further west than Buffalo.

In the last twenty years, however, newspaper and photo archives and oral histories have illuminated the real world of the old west, and have provided a foundation for historically accurate movies, television, novels, paintings, illustrations, and comic books. Take advantage of these sources of information to create your own western hero.

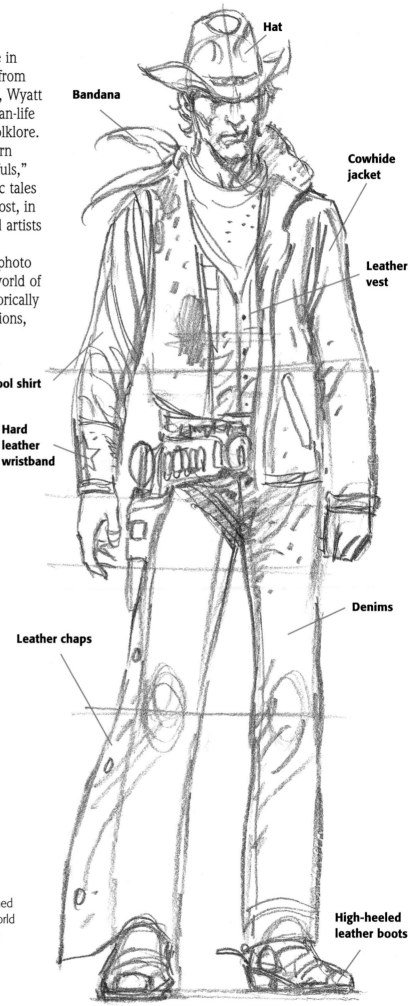

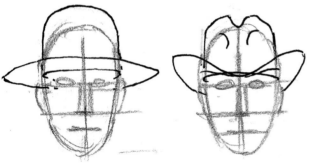

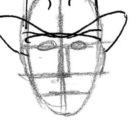

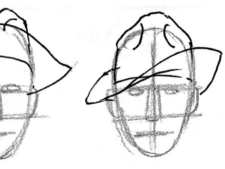

Here's a tip on drawing a cowboy's hat. Start with a wide-brimmed tall crowned hat. Make sure the hat fits on the head, not sits on top of it. Then style your hat. You can bend the brim and crease the crown, push the front brim way up, draw a cool tilt. Once you've got the basic hat shape fitting as it should, the possibilities are endless.

Hat
Bandana
Cowhide jacket
Leather vest
Wool shirt
Hard leather wristband
Denims
Leather chaps
High-heeled leather boots

A cowboy's clothes were designed for maximum protection in a world where both weather and terrain could be harsh and unforgiving.

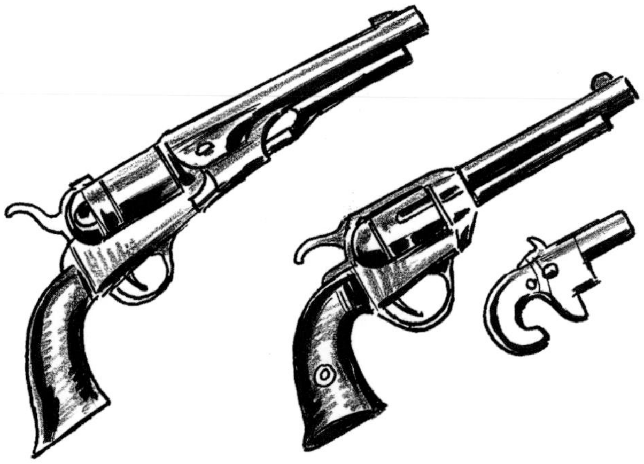

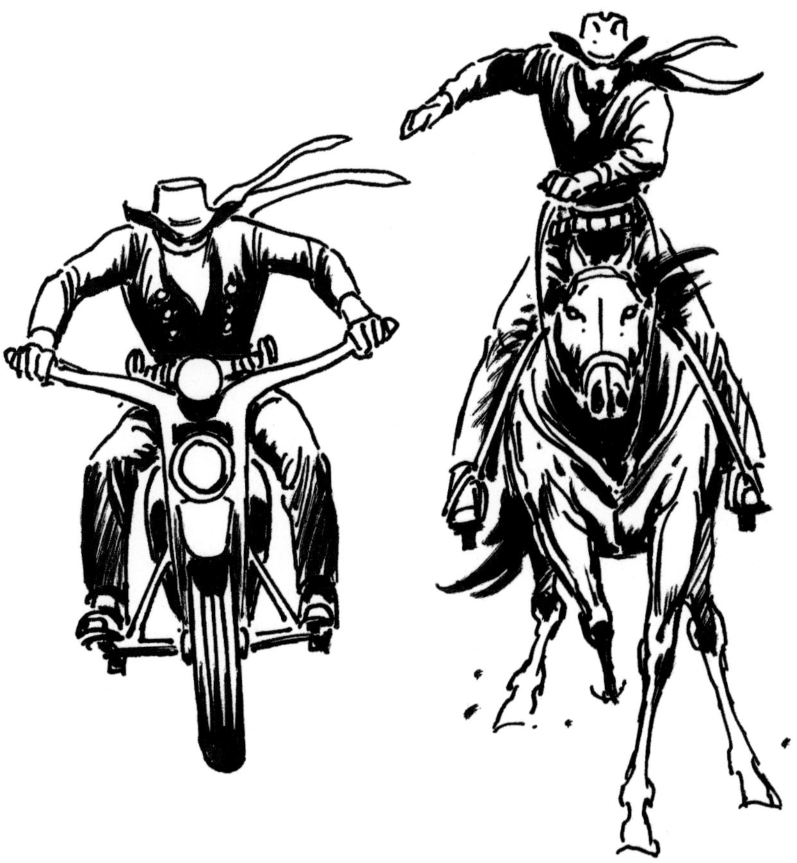

Guns were a part of the cowboy's costume. Like spears and knives and lances, guns come in a wide variety of types. The single-shot handgun that was used during the Civil War was quite different from the automatic six-shooter, although they appeared only a few years apart. And the baby derringer was a product of its time, when gamblers hid more than aces up their sleeves. I didn't draw these guns from memory, I used r-e-f-e-r-e-n-c-e.

A popular version of a western comic book superhero was one of a cowboy riding a motorcycle instead of a horse. A reasonable change, since the action took place in a contemporary urban city instead of the wild west. It made for interesting pictures. Besides, motorcycles are easier to draw than horses.

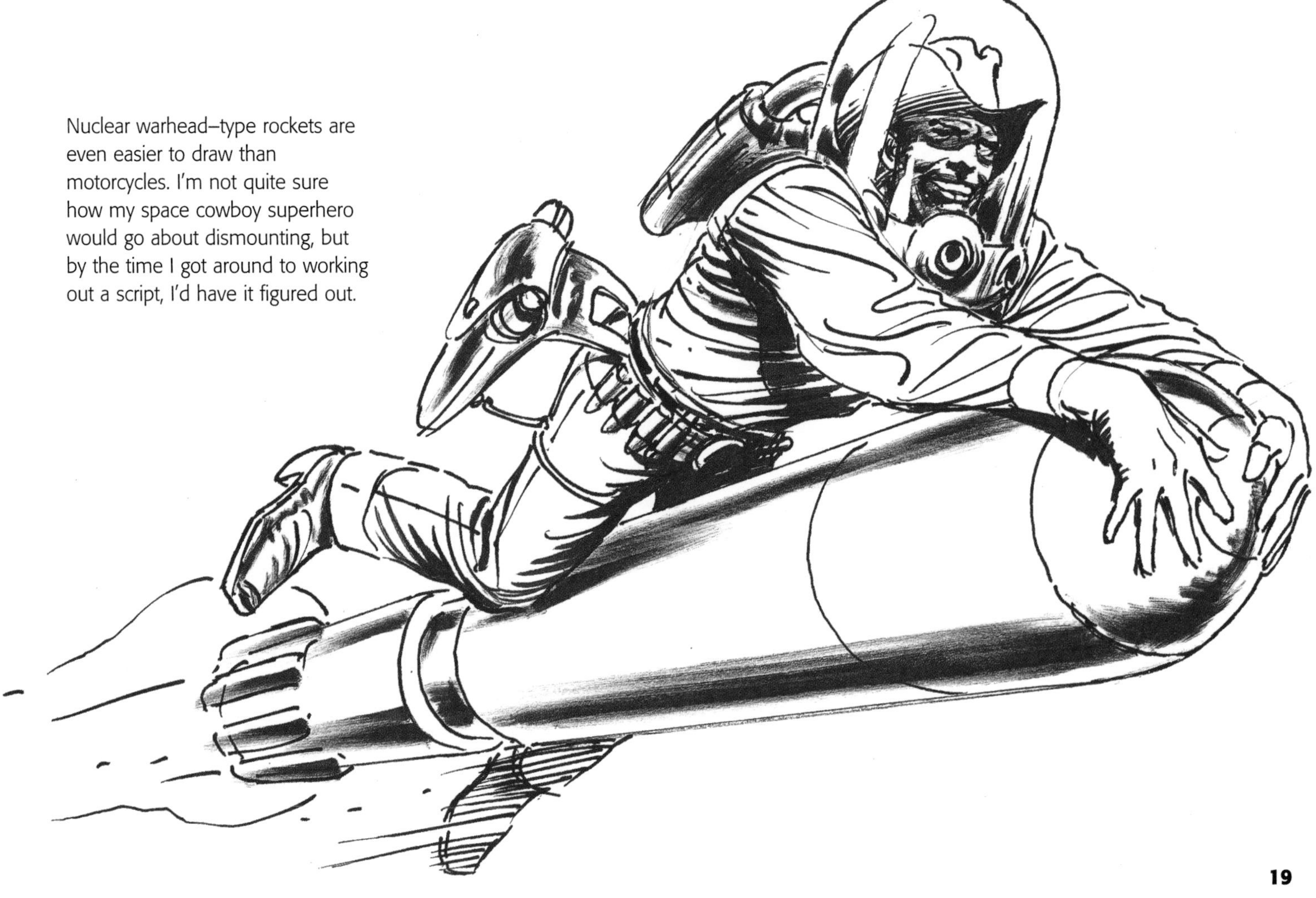

Nuclear warhead–type rockets are even easier to draw than motorcycles. I'm not quite sure how my space cowboy superhero would go about dismounting, but by the time I got around to working out a script, I'd have it figured out.

WAR HEROES AND SUPERHEROES

Obviously, there is a relationship between heroes, superheroes, and soldiers. The designation of "hero" has been accompanied by medals in armed forces around the world. So it's not surprising that the costumes of comic book superheroes often have a military flavor, even when the character is a civilian.

Military dress has changed over the decades and differs from country to country. Again, it's important for all you aspiring comic book artists to collect information and illustrations whether you want to draw a G.I., create soldiers from the future, or just want your superhero's costume to have a military look.

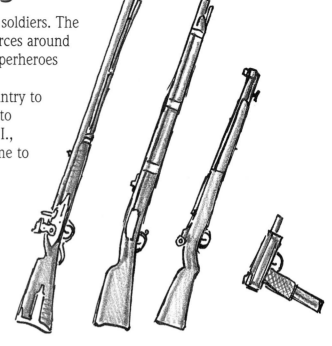

The weapons used by the men who fought in the Revolutionary War bear little resemblance to today's automatic handguns. From left to right: muzzle-loading ball-and-powder musket used in the Revolutionary War; Springfield rifle (World War I); M-30 (World War II); 9mm Uzi pistol capable of firing 32 rounds without reloading.

During the Revolutionary War, few nonofficers wore formal uniforms. This solider in buckskin might have been one of Ethan Allen's Green Mountain Boys.

As the armed forces became more regulated, so did their uniforms. A variety of uniforms were issued during the Civil War, including the famous "Blue" and "Grey," the colors of the armies of the North and the South, respectively.

World War I Army uniforms were cotton, not wool, and tan, not blue. Note the knee to ankle wraps, called puttees.

Designed for maximum protection without sacrificing mobility, World War II uniforms offered many advantages over their predecessors.

Heroism in war has been the subject of countless comic books. World War I (1914–1917) and World War II (1941–1945) are the most popular time periods for these stories. A testimony to the genre's popularity is the 30-year uninterrupted run of Sgt. Rock, a DC Comics character with which I was involved in an editorial, writing, and drawing capacity.

While drawing the Sgt. Rock character, I learned a great deal about the importance of information, research, and reference. If Sgt. Rock was to be credible and believable to my reader audience, then I had to pay attention to details. How did helmets differ in different armies and different wars? Despite soldiers' uniforms being similar, how did they wear them in distinctive ways? What did their boots look like? What did soldiers wear in cold weather as opposed to summer heat and the tropics? The anatomy and basic uniform of the four soldiers below are the same, but minor changes in details are enough to give them a different look.

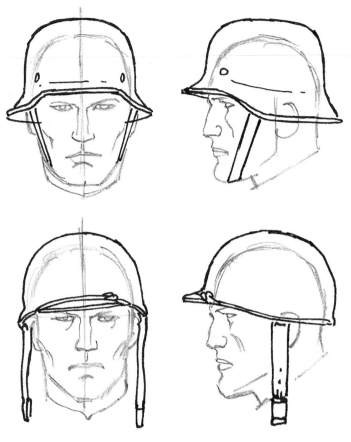

World War II helmets. Top, German model; bottom, United States issue.

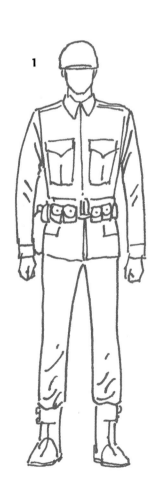 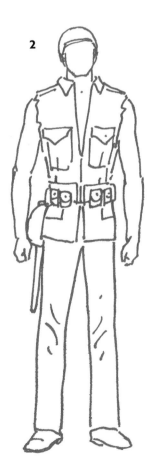 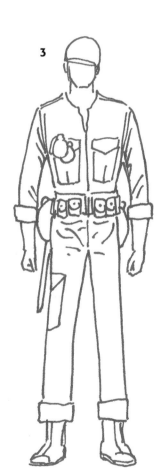 

These four G.I.s—all World War II soldiers—are distinguished by detail. (1) The basic uniform; (2) a distinct tough-guy look--torn sleeves (definitely nonregulation), open shirt, helmet tilted back; (3) yet another variation--rolled sleeves (to mid-forearm), helmet tilted sideways, grenades, rolled-up pants, collarless shirt, pocket on trousers, second canteen; (4) ready for jungle duty--sleeves rolled up all the way, ammo belt, shirt open to waist, trousers bloused low, helmet straps hanging.

My World War II corporal, like the other heros and superheroes in this portfolio, has a life and personality of his own, not just because of my penciling and foreshortening techniques but *because all the details are researched and right!* Nothing in this portrait is accidental:

1. Two chevrons designating rank (corporal).
2. Open shirt, no T-shirt.
3. Dents on helmet.
4. Loose straps on helmet.
5. Torn sleeves.
6. Cuffs rolled on forearms.
7. Grenades.
8. Double ammo belts.
9. Carries an automatic weapon.
10. Two canteens.
11. Bayonet.
12. Pants are loose, not "bloused."
13. Regulation boots, well-worn.

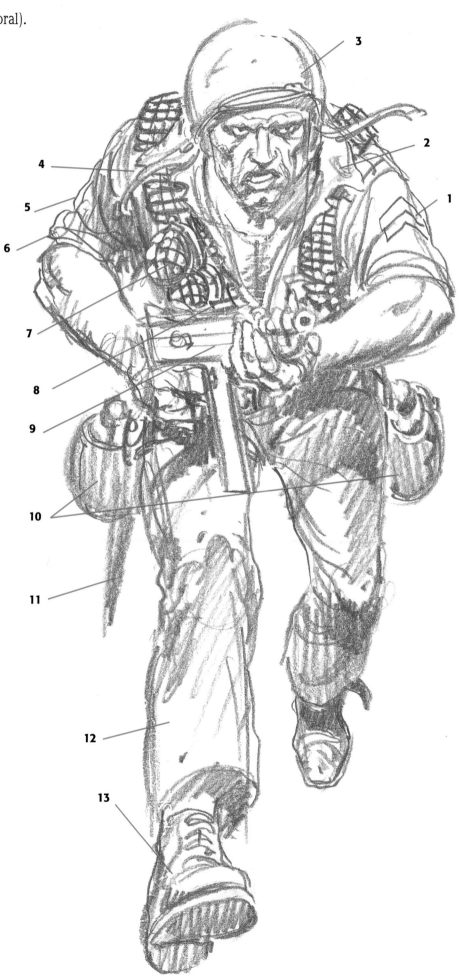

I've updated and incorporated many military elements for my superhero soldier of the future concept. Try designing your own character. Would your superhero have the ability to fly with the help of a back-mounted jet pack? How would you design the headgear? Or the backpack?

What would he (or she) look like? Think about his (or her) face. These faces are all meant to be of soldiers, but I envision them fighting in very different armies.

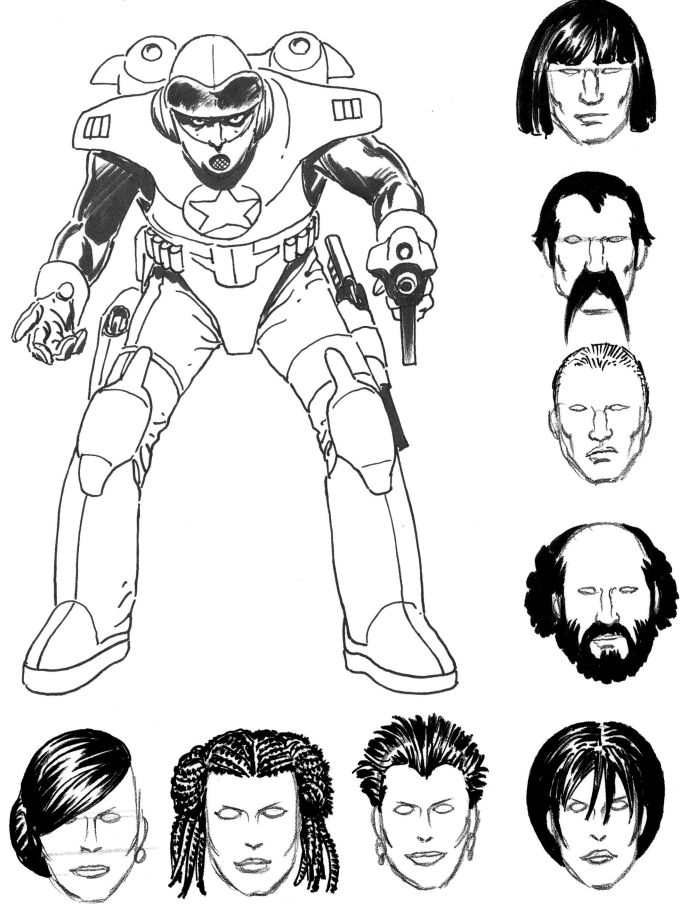

FUTUREWORLDS

Projections of futureworlds have always been fascinating subjects for scientists, writers, and artists.

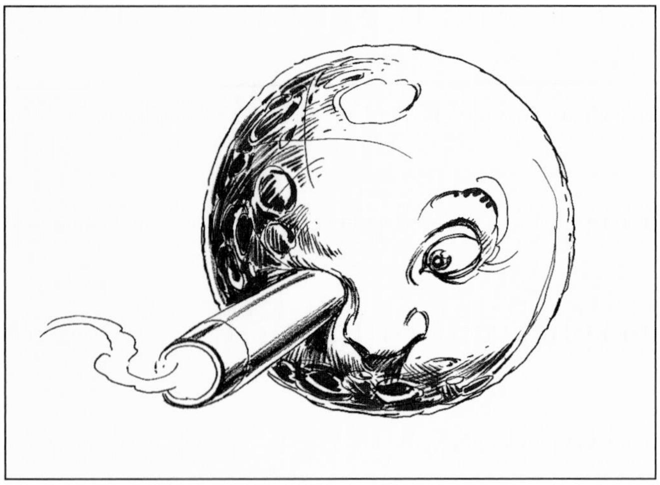

A copy of a frame from French director Georges Méliès's 1902 film *A Trip to the Moon.* During this special effects sequence from what film historians cite as the world's first sci-fi flick, a rocket ship shot from a giant cannon on earth crashes into the right eye of the "man in the moon."

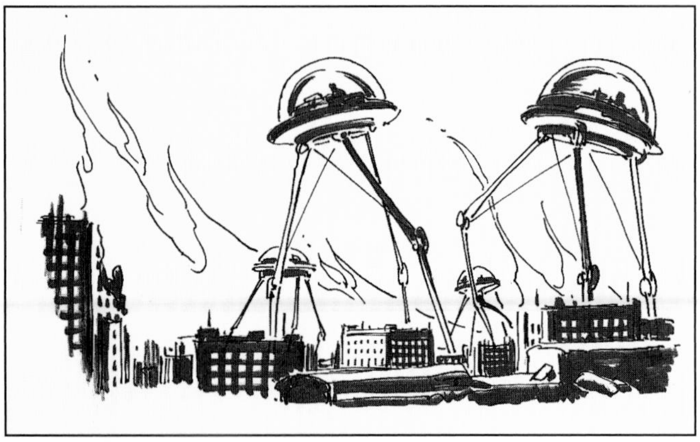

Although the artist who created the moon rocket scenario obviously thought the whole idea was pure fantasy, by the time that film appeared the genre of science fiction was already firmly established. In 1870 Jules Verne wrote *20,000 Leagues Under the Sea,* and H. G. Wells' 1898 novel *The War of the Worlds,* a scene from which is shown here, vividly described a Martian attack on Earth. Proof positive that even the most fantastic concepts can be credible if treated realistically enough was the impact of a 1939 radio drama, conceived and directed by Orson Welles, based on the Wells novel. Listeners, who truly thought that Earth was being invaded by aliens, were frightened into mass hysteria.

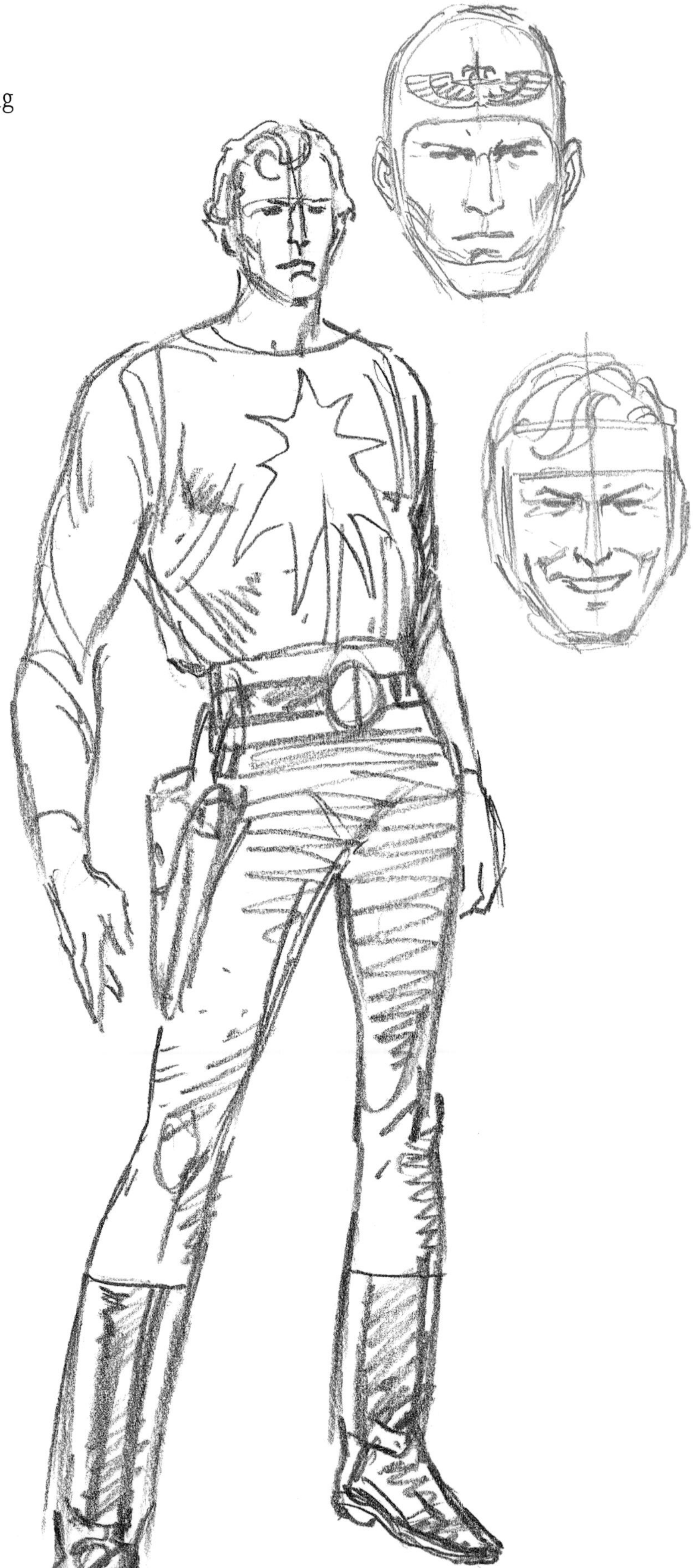

Many early comic strips appearing in newspapers based their ideas on books and novels. Although the cartoonists' worlds existed only in their imaginations, their drawings made the stories believable. The hero's costumes were dashing . . . and effective. The ray guns looked like they might really work.

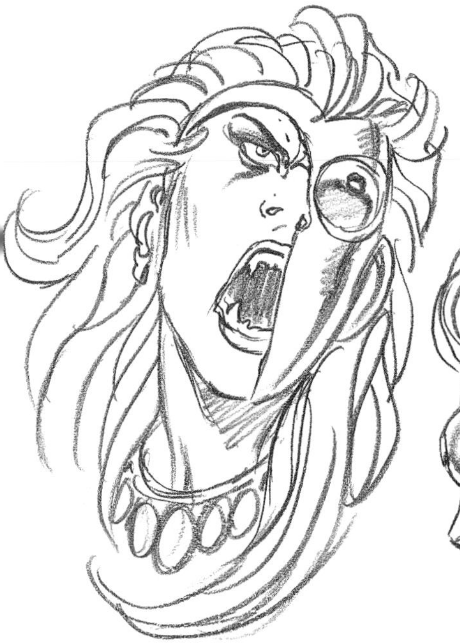

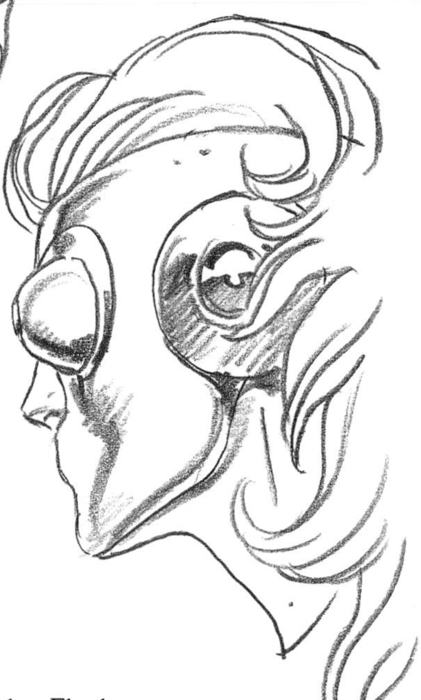

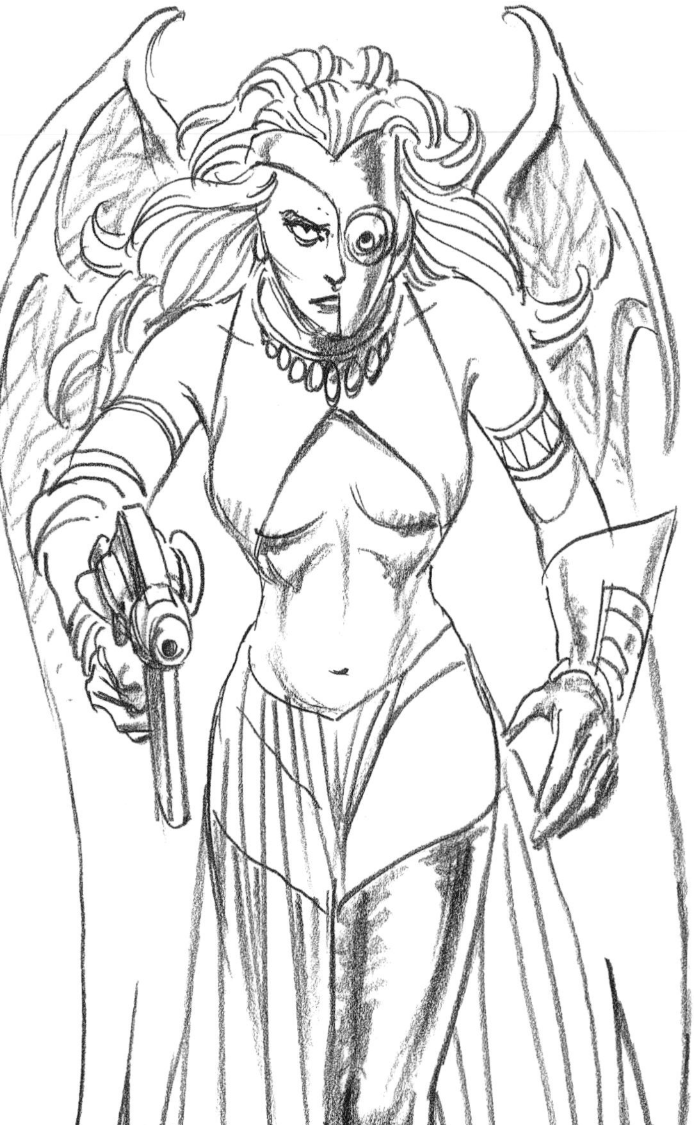

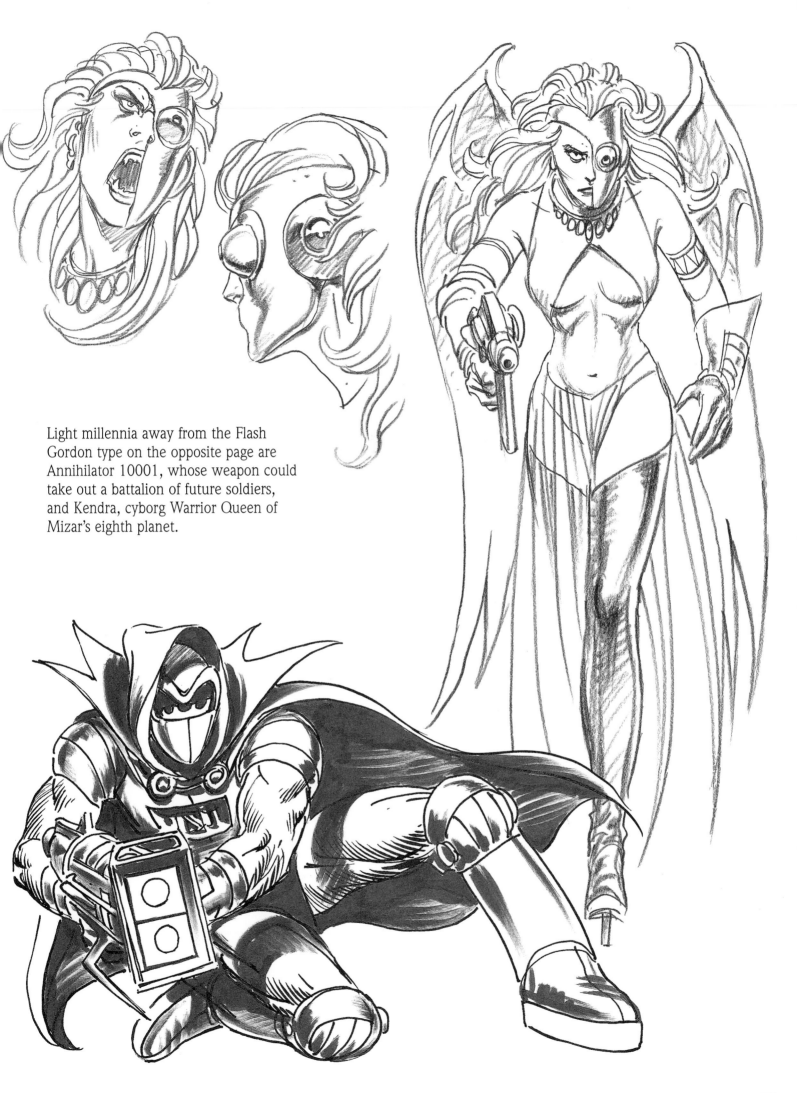

Light millennia away from the Flash Gordon type on the opposite page are Annihilator 10001, whose weapon could take out a battalion of future soldiers, and Kendra, cyborg Warrior Queen of Mizar's eighth planet.

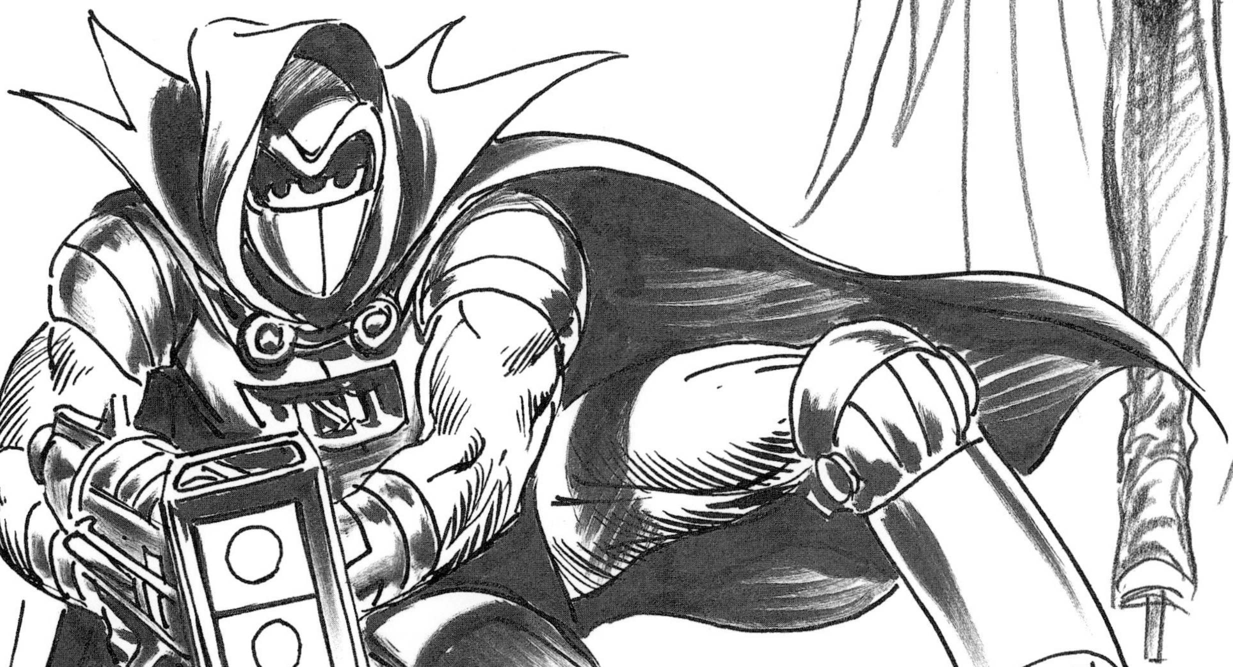

SUPERHEROES IN THREE DIMENSIONS

The best cartoonists, like the best artists in other media, are illusionists. They create fully realized worlds that invite us to suspend our disbelief, to be caught up in the lives of the people who inhabit those worlds, to delight in every detail. Part One was all about accuracy of reference as a foundation for credibility. Part Two goes into the actual "how to's" of creating the illusion of depth and dimension when you are drawing superhero bodies. It also offers some very important guidelines on getting details and proportions right—from hair to toes.

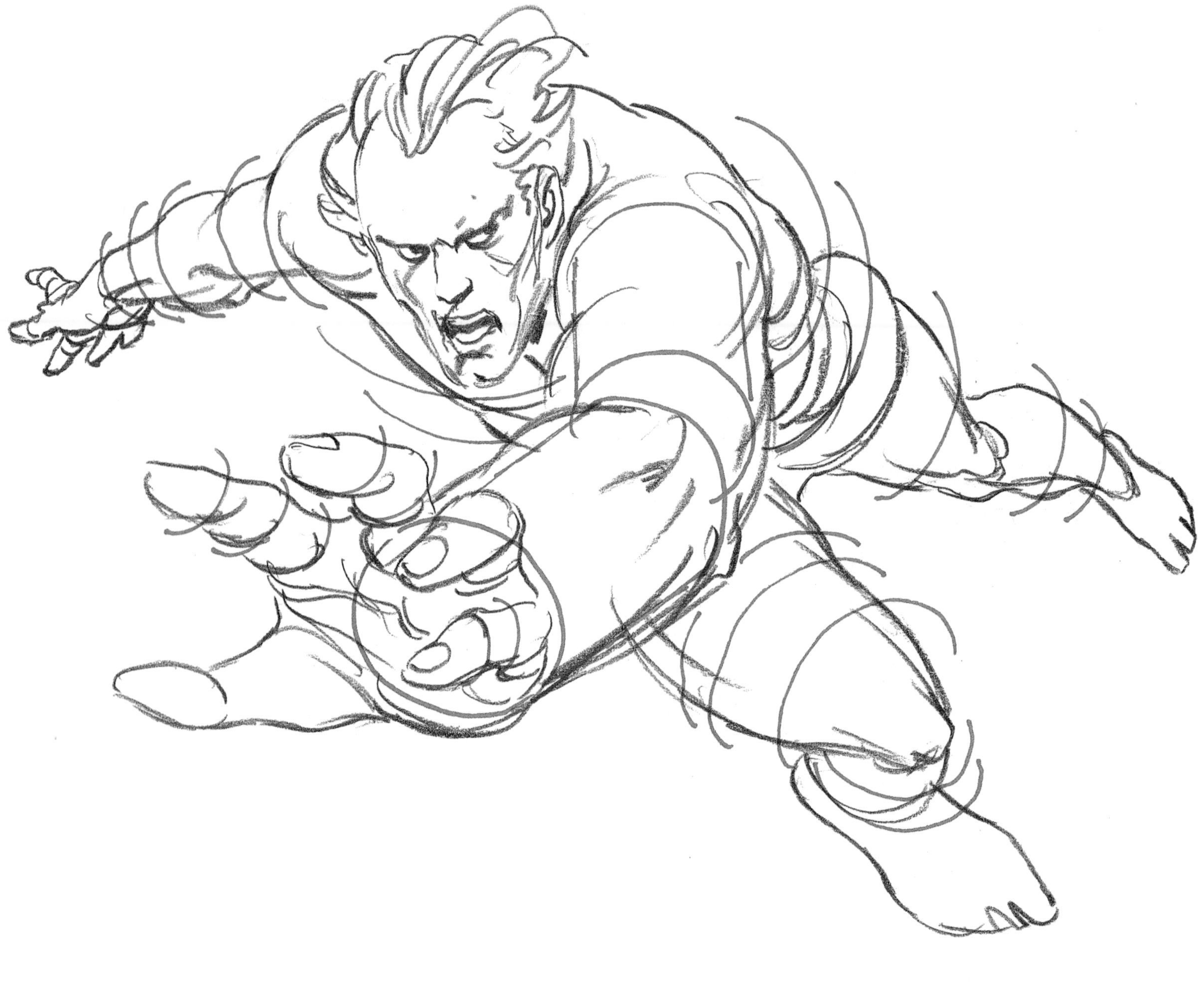

An understanding of how to use foreshortening is essential for comic book artists. You can draw figures that have a three-dimensional quality without relying on foreshortening, but you can't make them look as if they were leaping right off the page. Both drawings on these pages show foreshortened figures. Look at the sketch on the opposite page. The body parts farthest away are *shorter* than the ones closest to us. They are also smaller in diameter, as indicated by the circular sections I have sketched curving around the legs, arms, and fingers. The circles around the fingers of the left hand—the body part that seems to project out of the picture plane—are at least three times the size of a circle that could be drawn around the fingers of the right hand! Since many cartoonists like to start out by drawing limbs as tubular shapes, I also sketched tube outlines for the left arm. Check out the humongous relative size of those tubes!

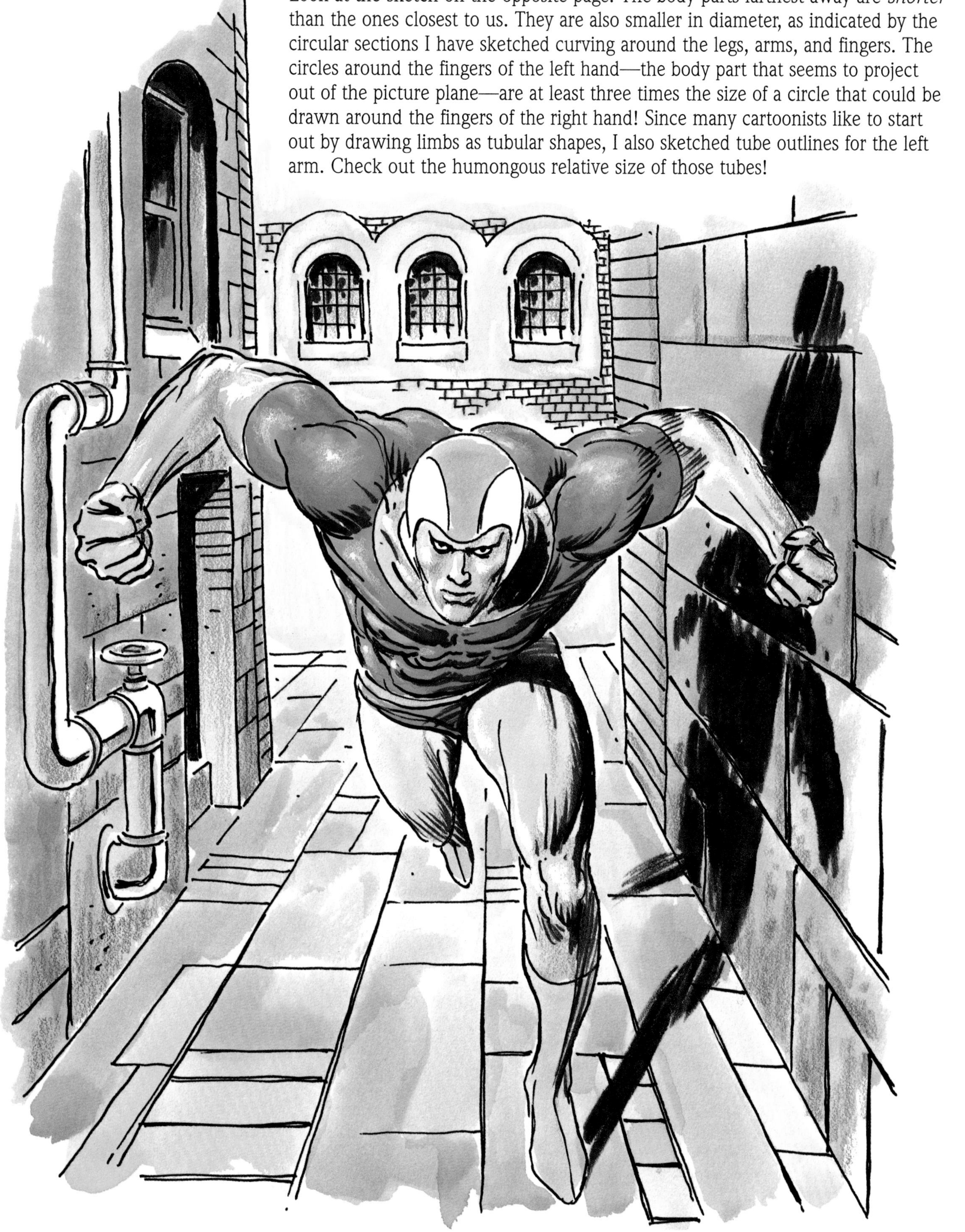

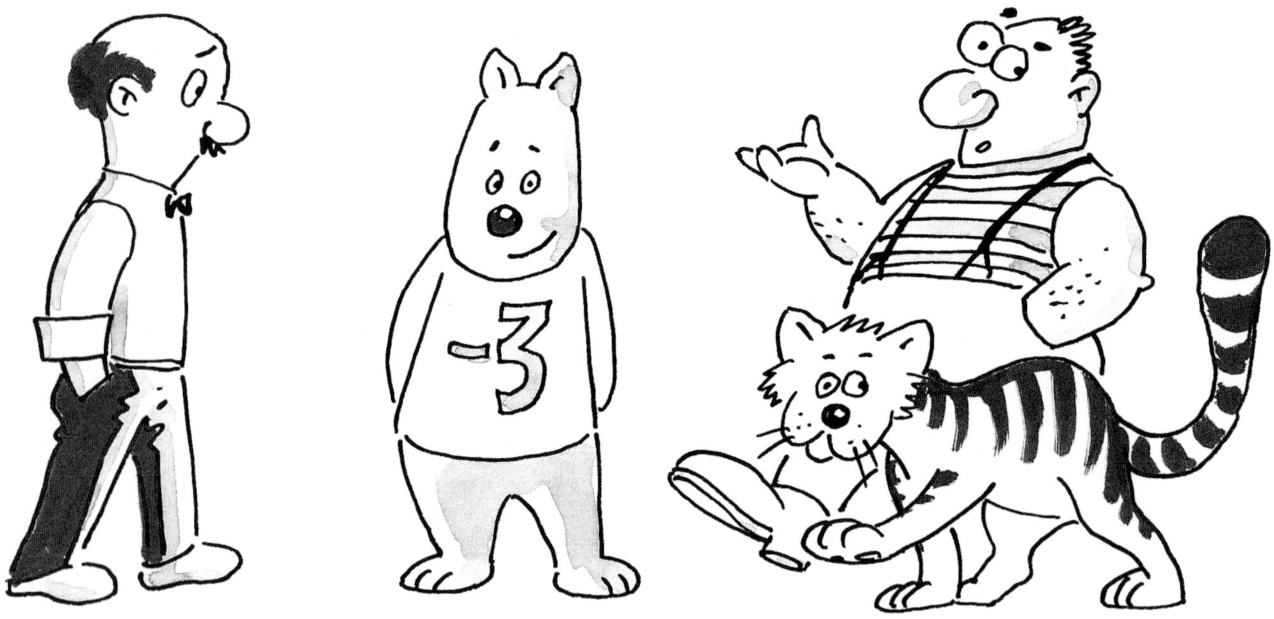

Examine the cinematic animation in any well-done film cartoon. Despite the simple, linear outlines, the figures and objects have incredible dimensionality. A roundness. A solidity. Even the slightest hint of another side to a figure endows the drawing with a fullness, a thickness, a three-dimensional quality. And remember this simple trick: placing one object in front of another creates depth.

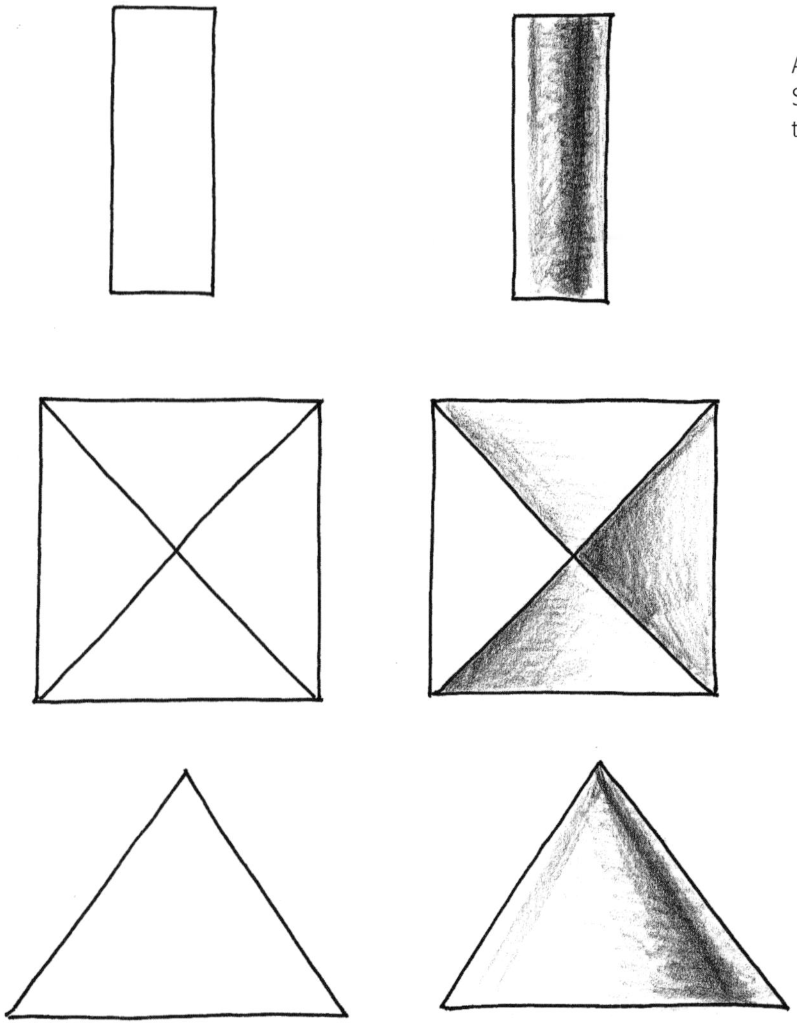

Another component of dimensionality is shading. Simply adding shading to these outlines turns them into three-dimensional objects.

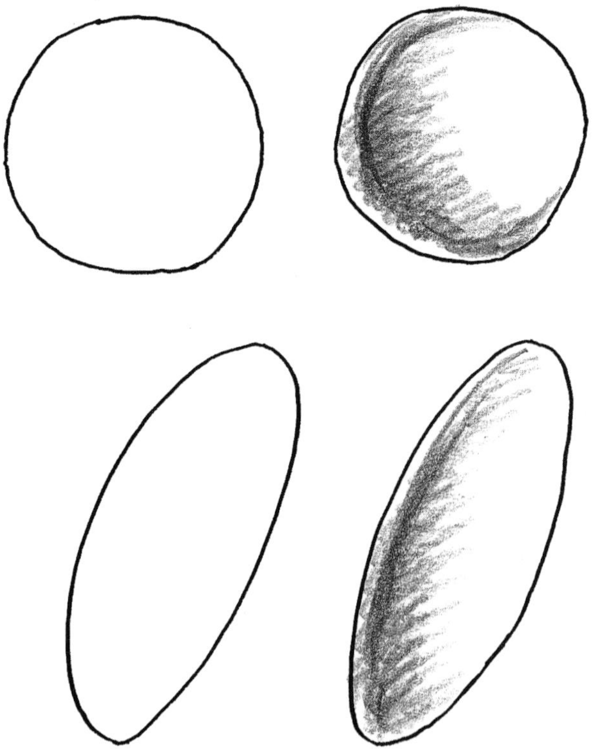

Achieving a correct sense of perspective in an illustration is not just a matter of applying what you may have learned in drawing class or read in books about ruled horizon lines and specific vanishing points. For me, drawing comic art according to rigid rules tends to stiffen the drawing and reduce, not enchance, space, depth, and dimension.

Drawing a picture with depth is like drawing the human figure in three dimensions. All artists learn the basic proportions and how to use foreshortening, but no two artists will draw a superhero in exactly the same way. An artist will depart from the rules—will exaggerate—when the artist feels exaggeration is necessary. If the drawing doesn't look right, the artist may refer back to the basics to find and correct the error. But the final criterion for judging any piece of art is, Does it *look* right? If it looks right, it is right. And if it looks wrong, it is wrong, even if it has been done according to the book.

Similarly, the correct use of T-squares, rulers, and triangles for drawing perspective may result in a formally perfect drawing that is at the same time perfectly boring!

A drawing may have more than one vanishing point. Lines of perspective may curve a bit as they recede toward the horizon. The objects meant to be closest to the viewer may not conform exactly to existing perspective lines. There may be variations and, yes, exaggerations.

It takes a lot of practice to acquire the kind of hand-eye coordination necessary to create a drawing with believable, effective dimensionaltiy. First, try your sketches freehand. If they look wrong, use your straightedges to check and correct. But don't be a slave to your tools. Your tools should work for *you.*

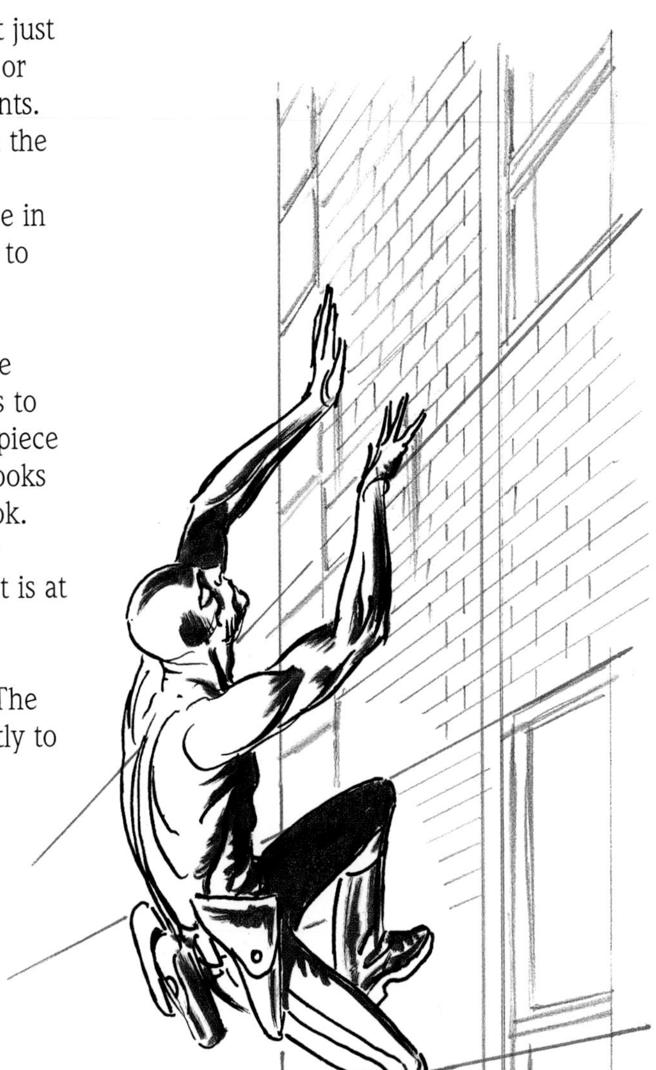

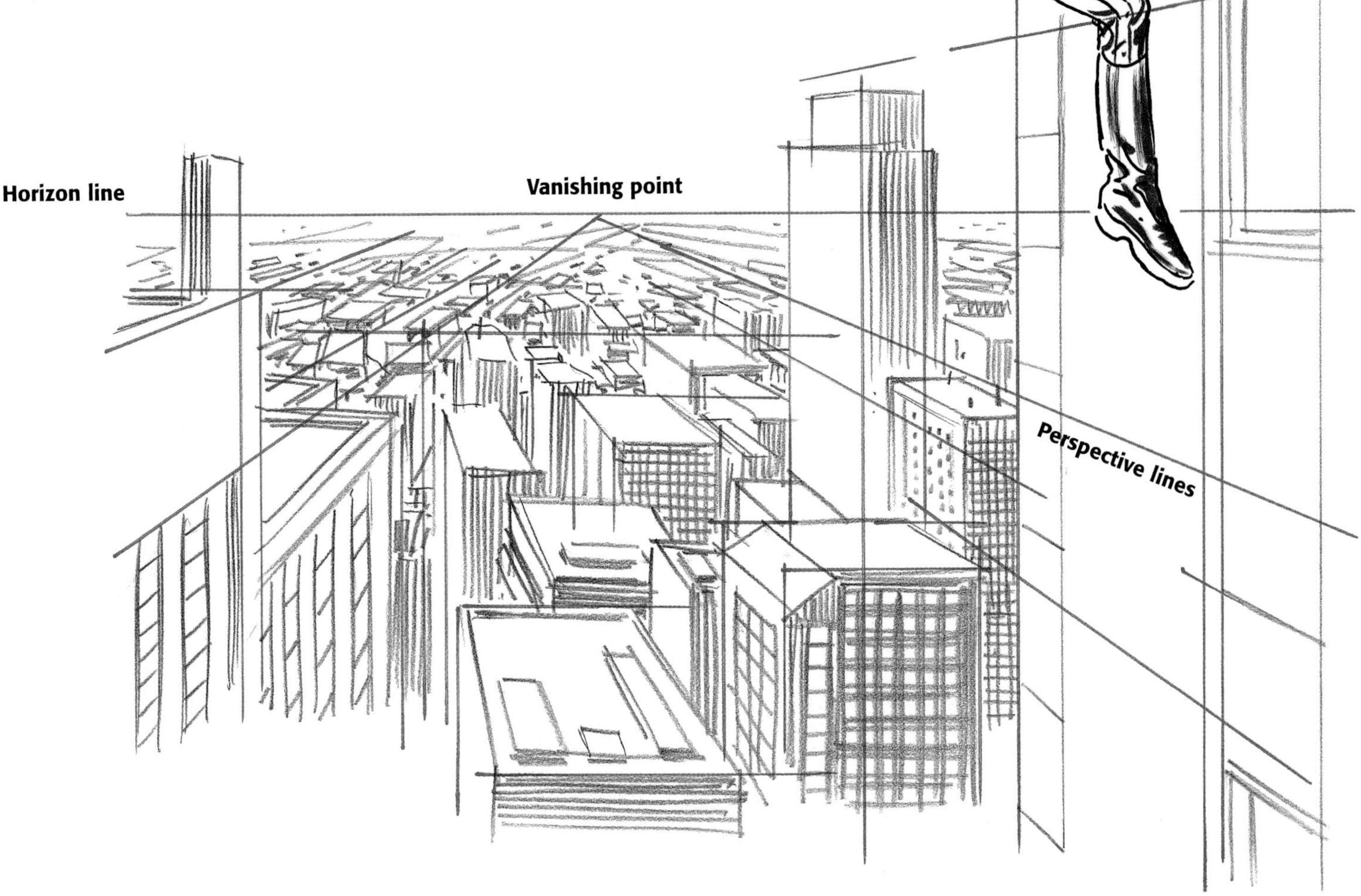
Horizon line
Vanishing point
Perspective lines

ANATOMY IN PERSPECTIVE

The best way to learn to draw any part of the human body, male or female, superhero or otherwise, is to draw from life. A live model is a three-dimensional form with a front, back, and sides. The artist can *see* foreshortening, perspective, and proportion. Many local colleges and universities offer classes in life drawing to the general public. If taking a class isn't possible, try sketching family members. Or check out some of the many art instruction books on anatomy written especially for artists.

THE HEAD OF A HERO

Cartoonists learn early on that the most successful drawings of the human figure—at least in terms of reader reaction—are those with the best-drawn heads and hands. If the head and hands are drawn correctly, the drawing will more readily be accepted, even if there are certain disproportionate variations in the rest of the figure. But don't let this principle lull you into thinking that it isn't important to draw the total human figure correctly. A good drawing is the sum total of all its well-drawn parts.

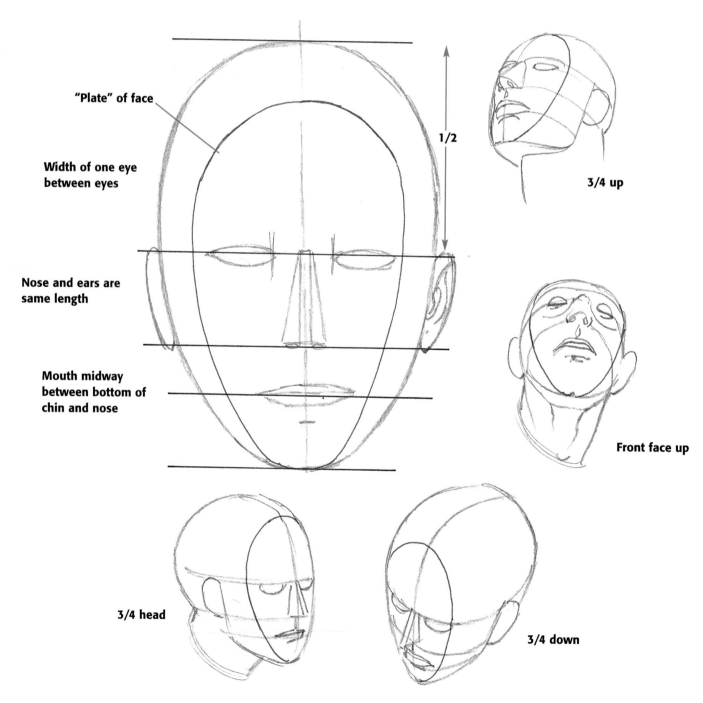

"Plate" of face

Width of one eye between eyes

Nose and ears are same length

Mouth midway between bottom of chin and nose

1/2

3/4 up

Front face up

3/4 head

3/4 down

These are the general basic proportions of the human head. With slight variations, they work for male and female alike—and for superheros or "normal" characters. Practice drawing heads from all angles. Don't worry about hair yet. We'll get to that.

The plate of the face extends from where the brow recedes to the tip of the chin

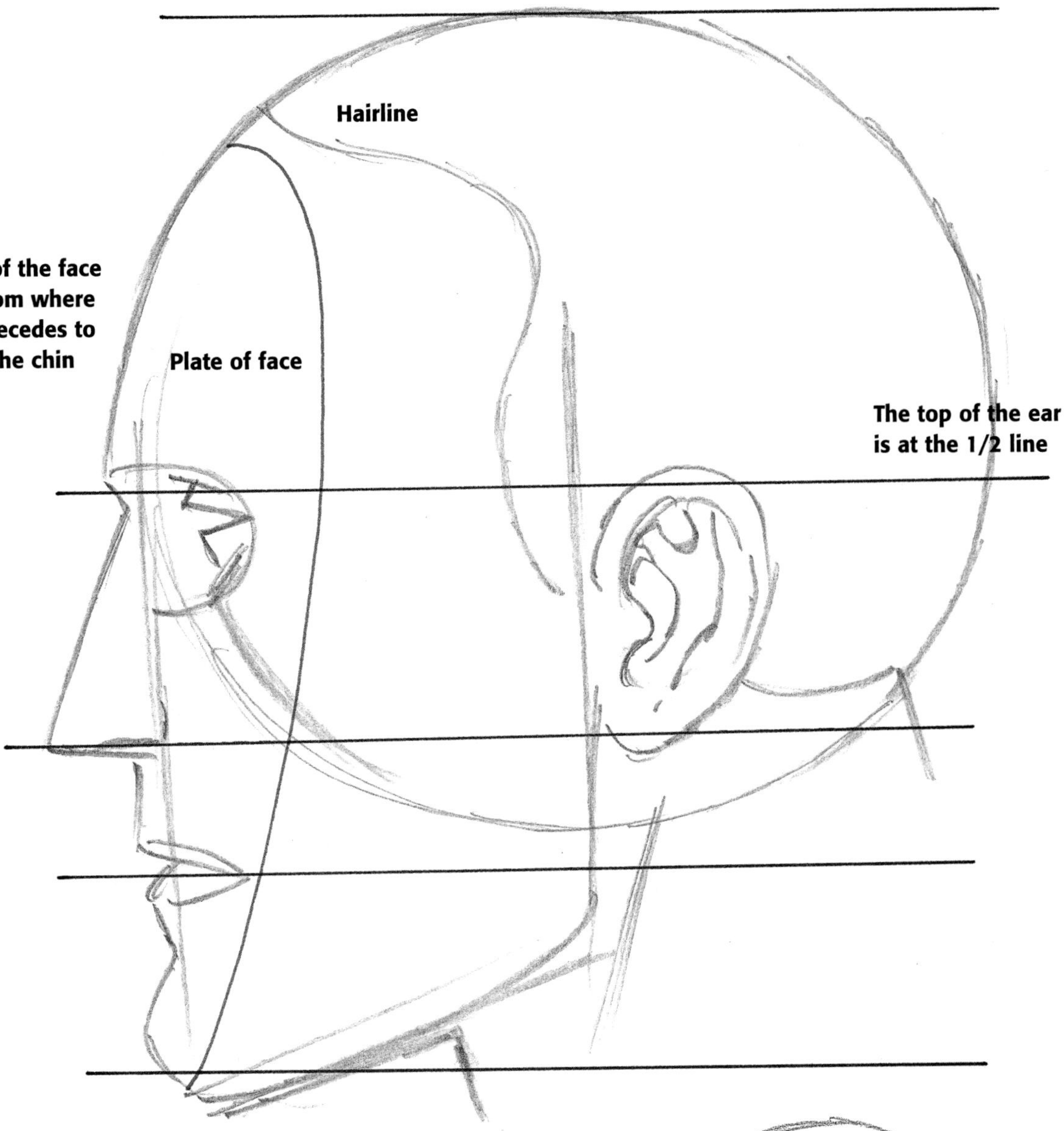
Hairline
Plate of face
The top of the ear is at the 1/2 line

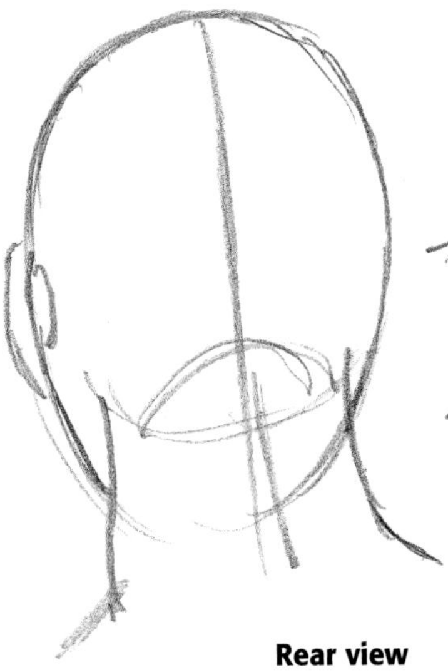

Rear view

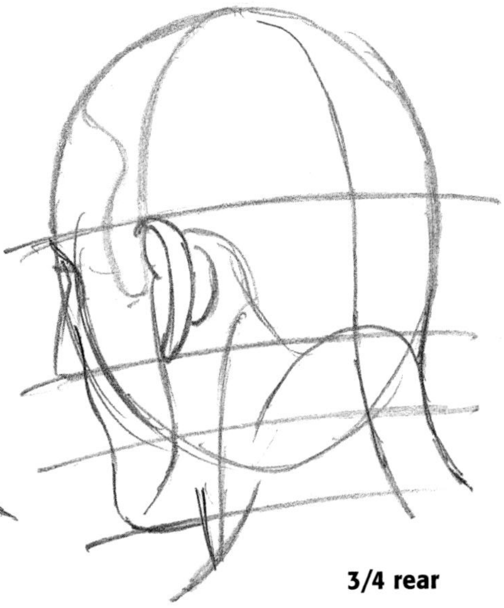

3/4 rear

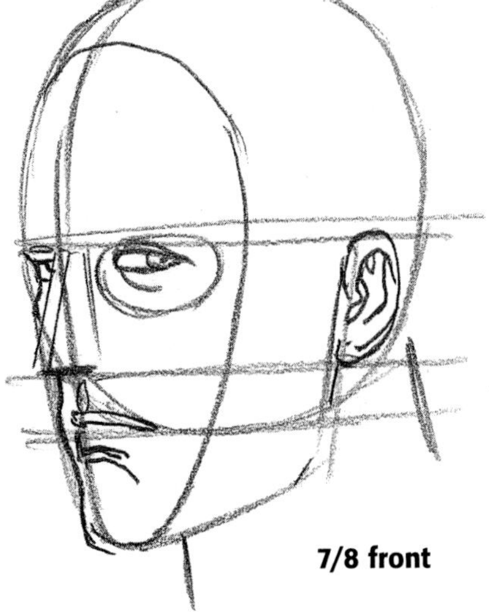

7/8 front

Another way to think about the human head and face is as the exterior of the human skull. The basic shape of our heads, including forehead width, cheekbones, chin, etc., is determined by the shape of our skull. But skulls are expressionless. You can draw a realistically shaped human head by superimposing your drawing over the outline of a skull, but the head will remain anonymous until you add features. It is the variety of facial features that distinguishes one character from another. A character with tiny jet-black eyes, a long nose, thin lips, and a full head of hair will look very different from a bald character with a broad forehead and full lips. The double chin of an obese person is a graphic detail that separates that character from a thin individual with a pronounced adam's apple. But before you can imagine or copy features, you need to get the basic shape right. If you practice drawing the human skull devoid of features, you will gain a better sense of where and how the eyes are set and how the teeth and jaws actually work.

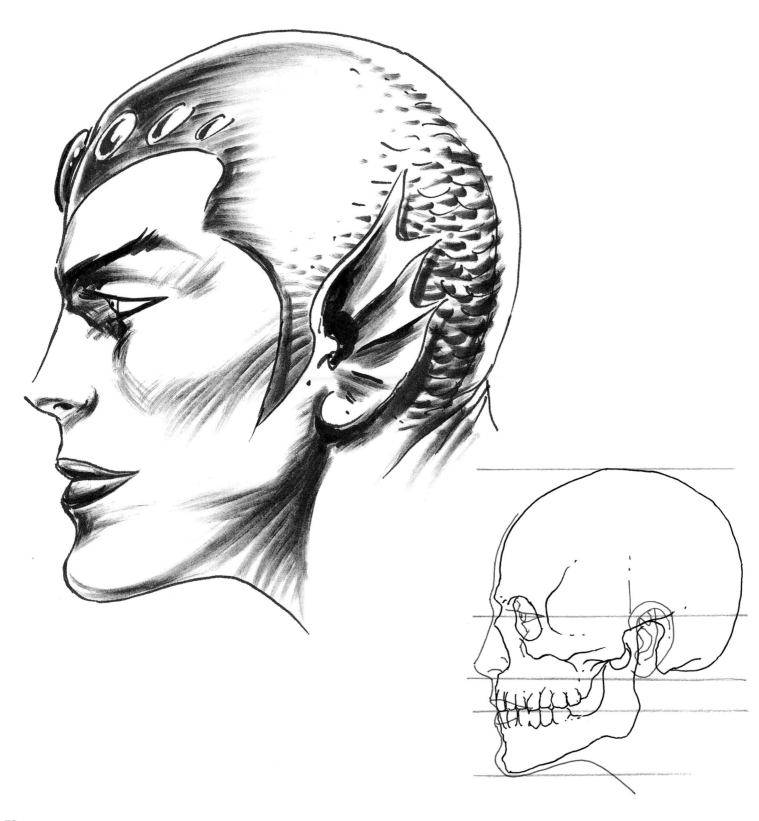

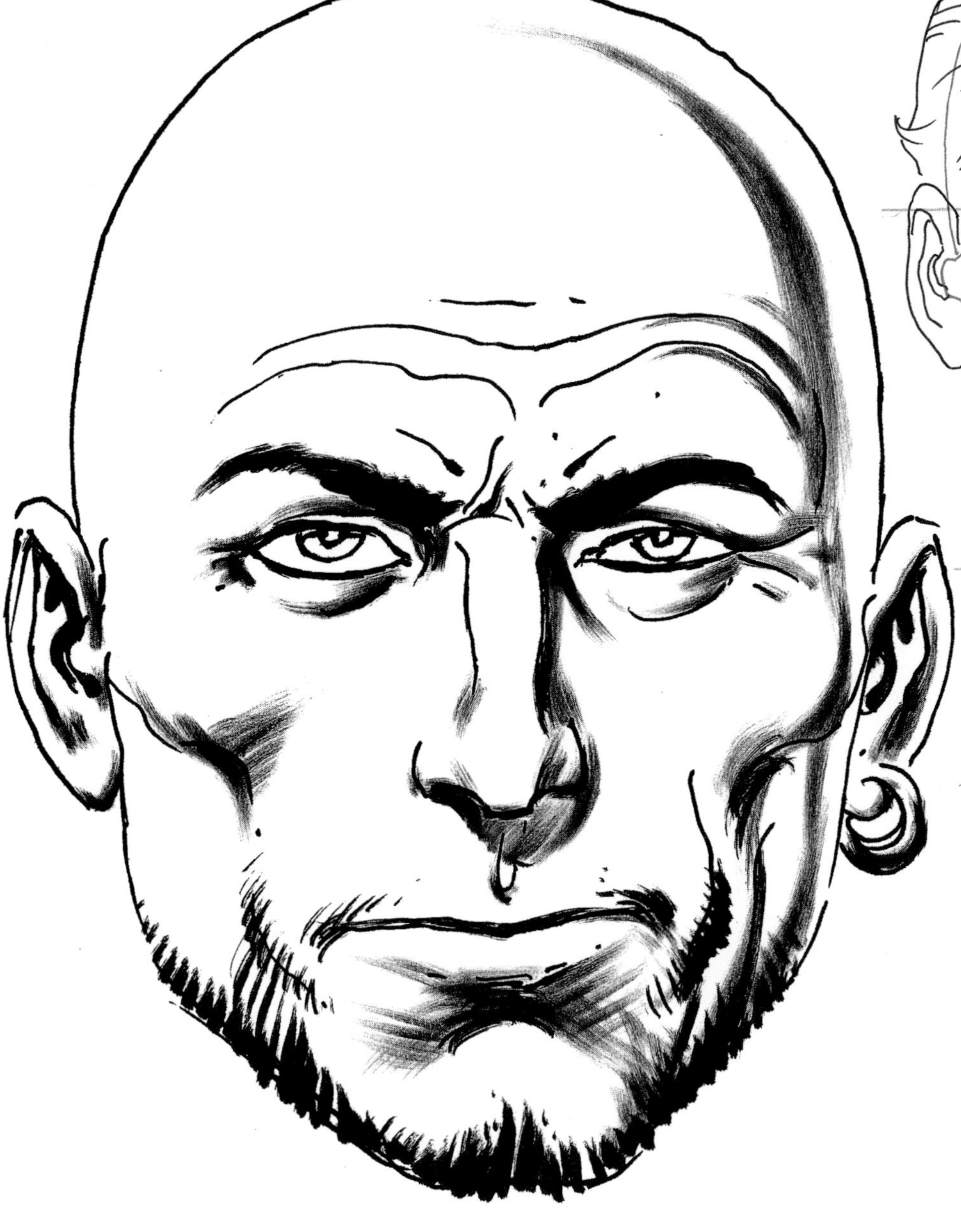

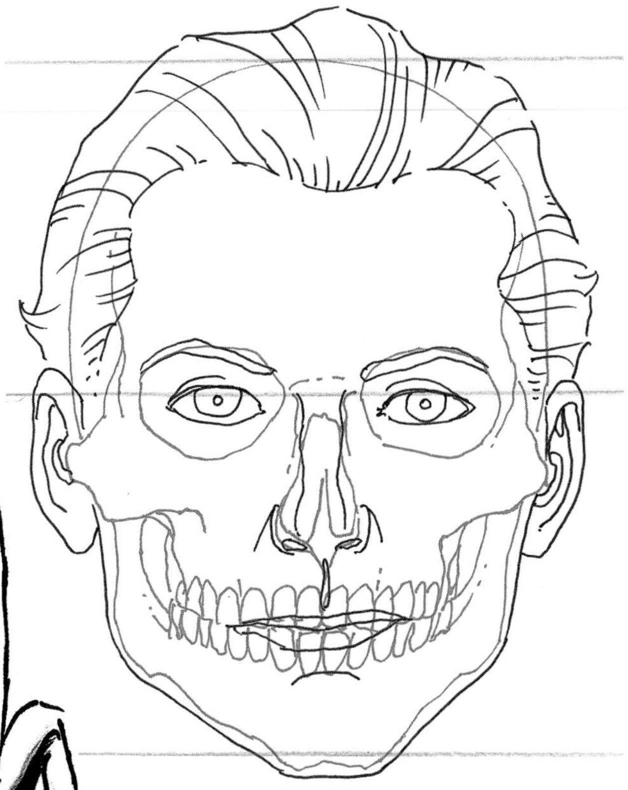

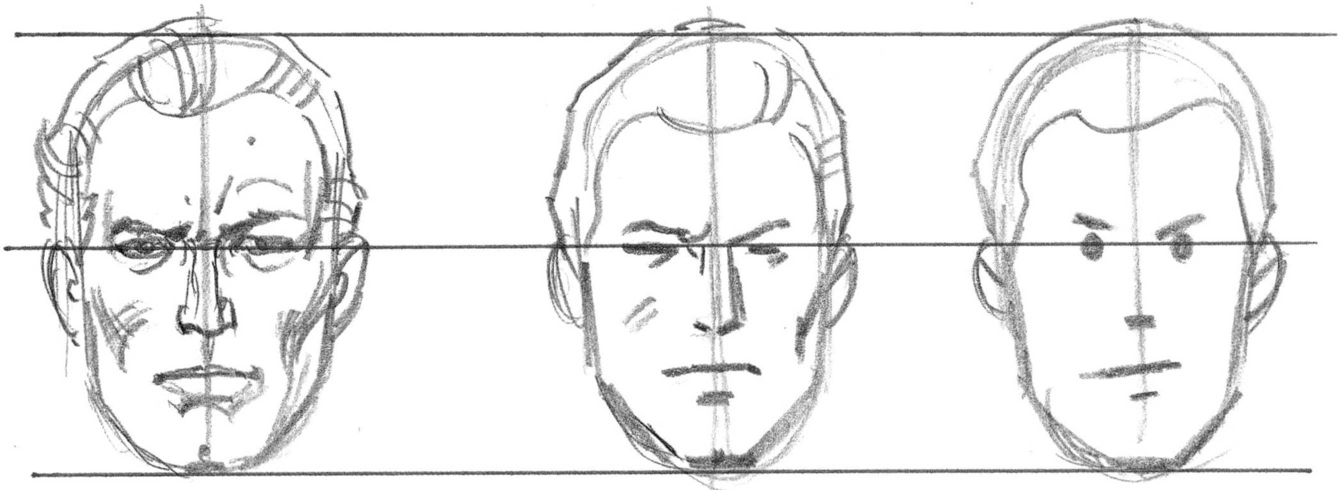

Cartoonists who use a simplified style must nonetheless base their drawings on tried and true precepts of good proportion. Many young novice cartoonists have the mistaken idea that "simple" means neglecting basics. Knowing what to leave out of a drawing is often more difficult than knowing what to put into it.

THE MALE SUPERHERO

The exaggerated anatomy of a superhero must be based on good old mundane, *un*exaggerated, generally accepted rules of proportion. Therefore the first step in drawing superheroes—whether face-on, twisted, tilted, or foreshortened—is to acquire the ability to draw the human figure according to those rules. Your ability to do this and your degree of success depend on the amount of time you spend at drawing. The more you draw, the more you will improve. Don't worry about making mistakes. We all do. Just keep that eraser handy and keep on drawing.

The graph, or proportionality grid, shown here is my system for checking and determining the correct proportions of the average male figure. This becomes very useful when I draw a figure that doesn't look quite right. By comparing lengths of limbs to torso to head, I can usually spot where I have made an error in proportion.

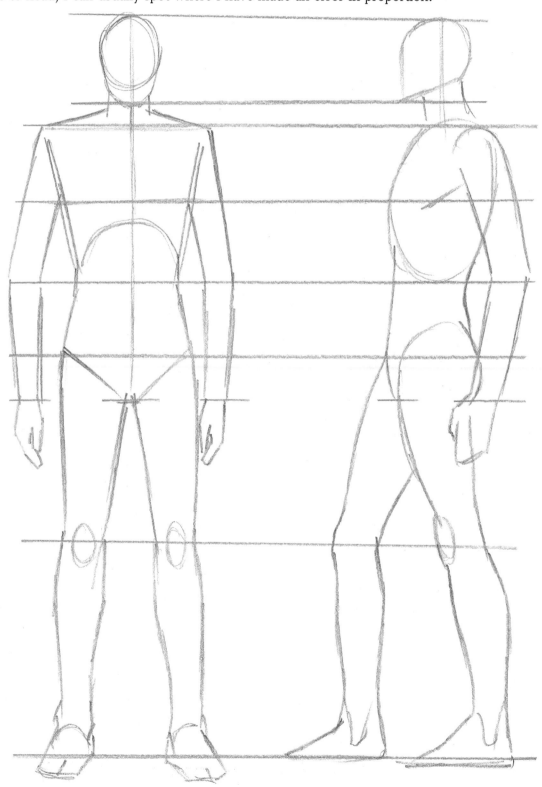

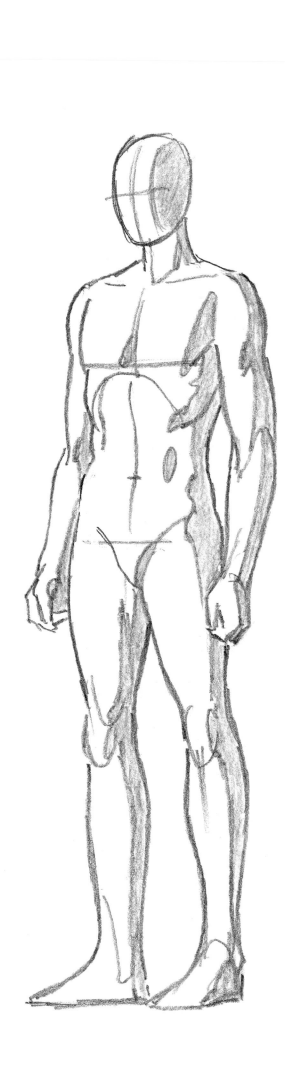

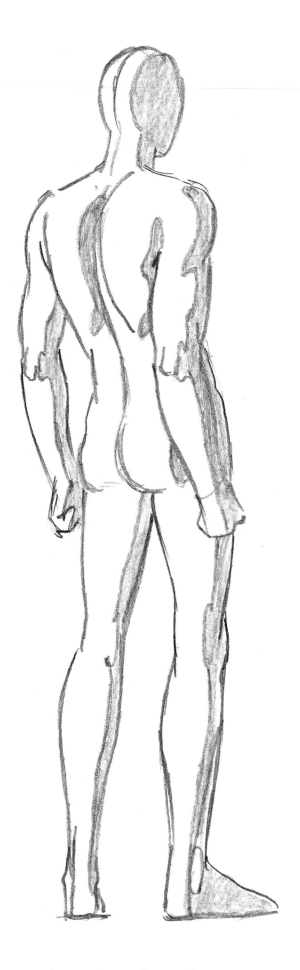

The proportions on the more three-dimensional figures here are the same as those on the facing page.

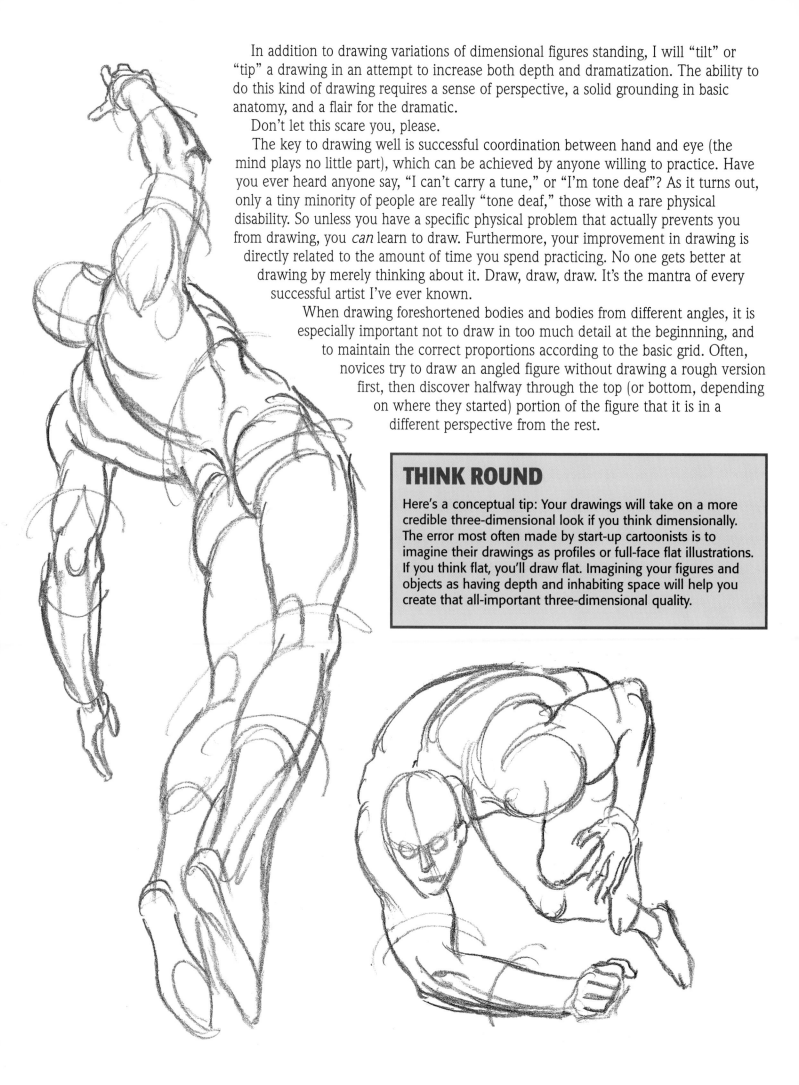

In addition to drawing variations of dimensional figures standing, I will "tilt" or "tip" a drawing in an attempt to increase both depth and dramatization. The ability to do this kind of drawing requires a sense of perspective, a solid grounding in basic anatomy, and a flair for the dramatic.

Don't let this scare you, please.

The key to drawing well is successful coordination between hand and eye (the mind plays no little part), which can be achieved by anyone willing to practice. Have you ever heard anyone say, "I can't carry a tune," or "I'm tone deaf"? As it turns out, only a tiny minority of people are really "tone deaf," those with a rare physical disability. So unless you have a specific physical problem that actually prevents you from drawing, you *can* learn to draw. Furthermore, your improvement in drawing is directly related to the amount of time you spend practicing. No one gets better at drawing by merely thinking about it. Draw, draw, draw. It's the mantra of every successful artist I've ever known.

When drawing foreshortened bodies and bodies from different angles, it is especially important not to draw in too much detail at the beginnning, and to maintain the correct proportions according to the basic grid. Often, novices try to draw an angled figure without drawing a rough version first, then discover halfway through the top (or bottom, depending on where they started) portion of the figure that it is in a different perspective from the rest.

THINK ROUND

Here's a conceptual tip: Your drawings will take on a more credible three-dimensional look if you think dimensionally. The error most often made by start-up cartoonists is to imagine their drawings as profiles or full-face flat illustrations. If you think flat, you'll draw flat. Imagining your figures and objects as having depth and inhabiting space will help you create that all-important three-dimensional quality.

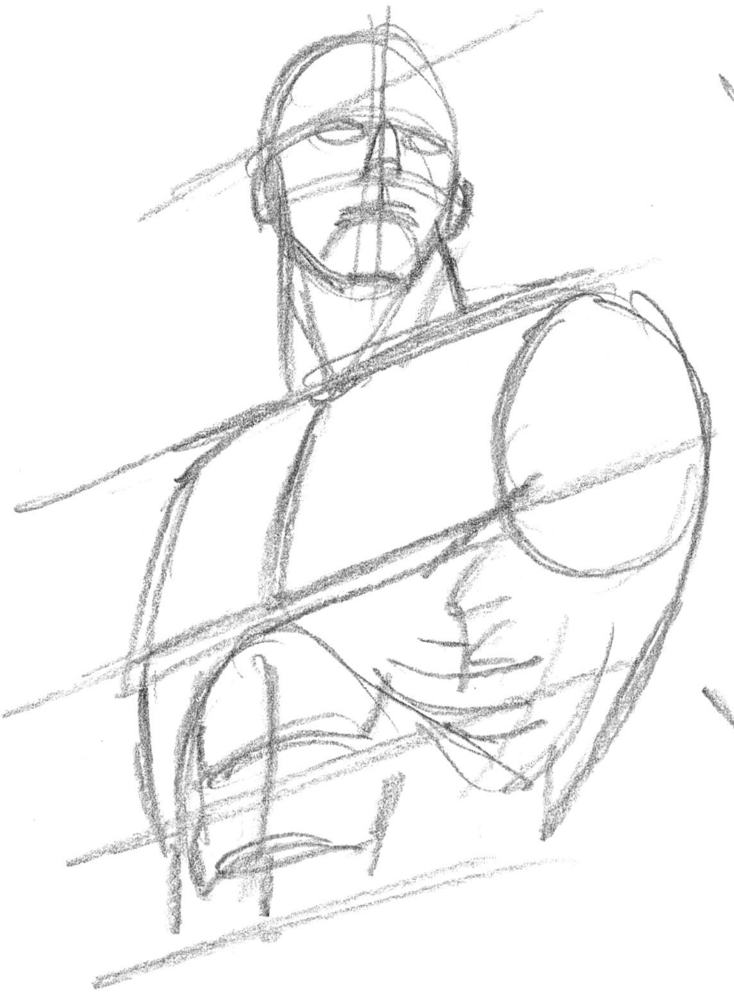

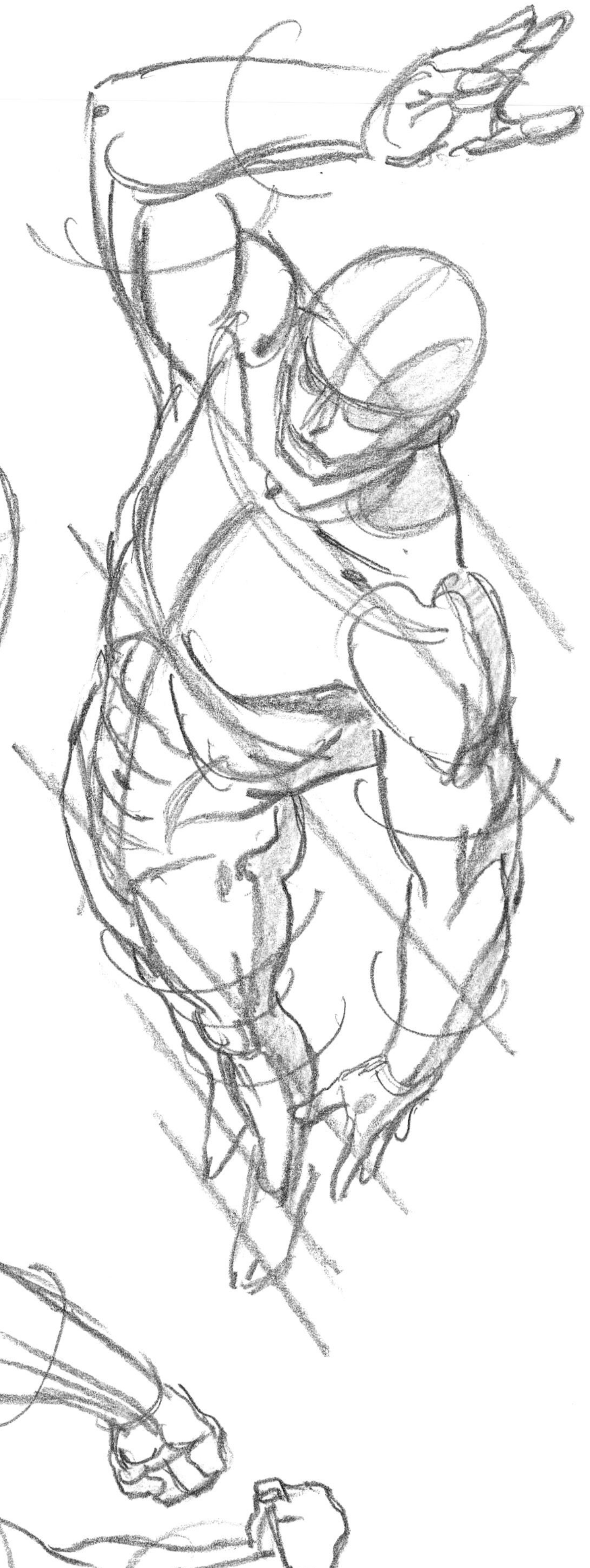

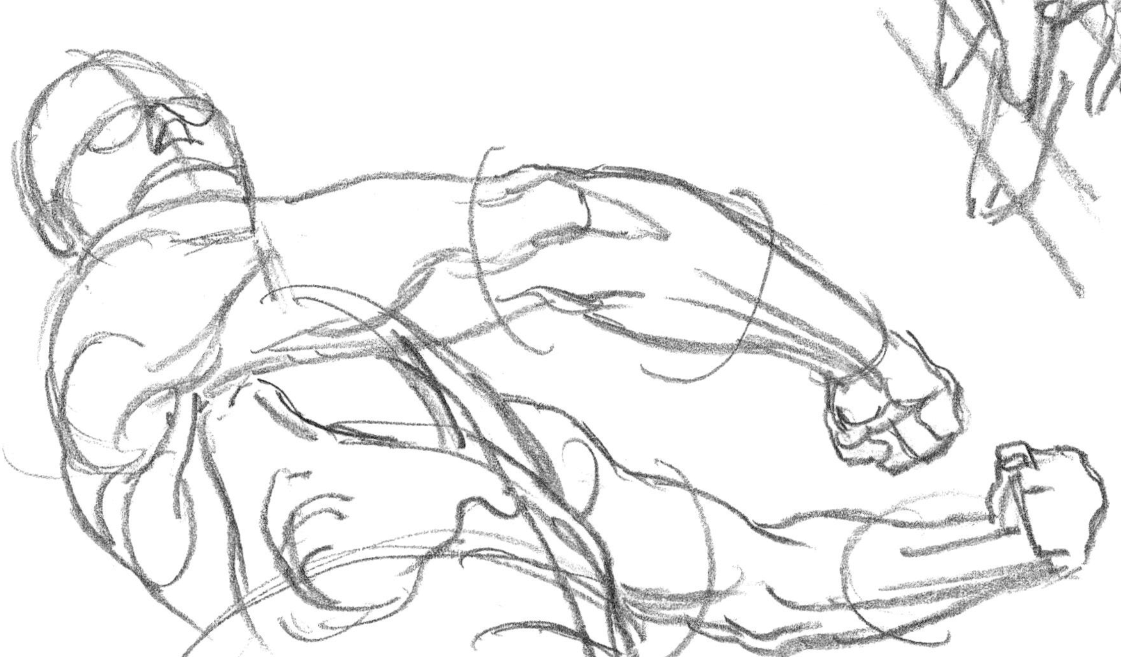

Exaggerating Musculature

In constructing a superhero character, make sure that every part of the anatomy contributes to the overall effect of power and strength. Exaggeration of muscles endows the character with a physique that identifies the superhero. But never abandon your foundation: the "normal" physique. Think of what you are doing as *enhancing* the normal form. If the various body parts of the superhero are disproportionately exaggerated or distorted, the figure will seem funny, peculiar, or bizarre. The drawings on these pages show the right degree of exaggeration from "normal" to "super." Notice that the superhero's hands and feed are *not* exaggerated.

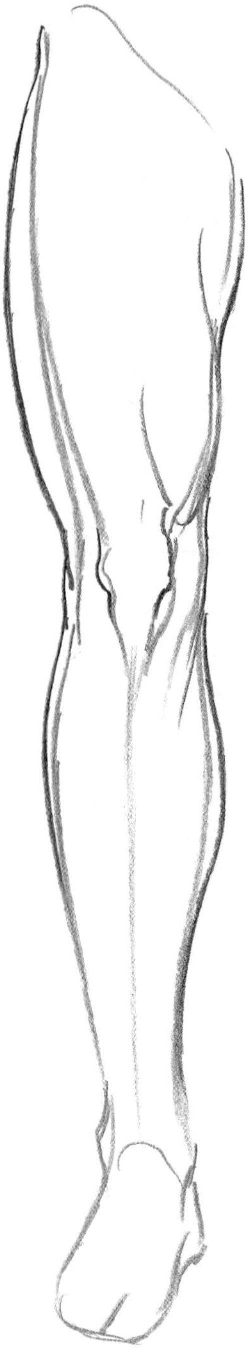

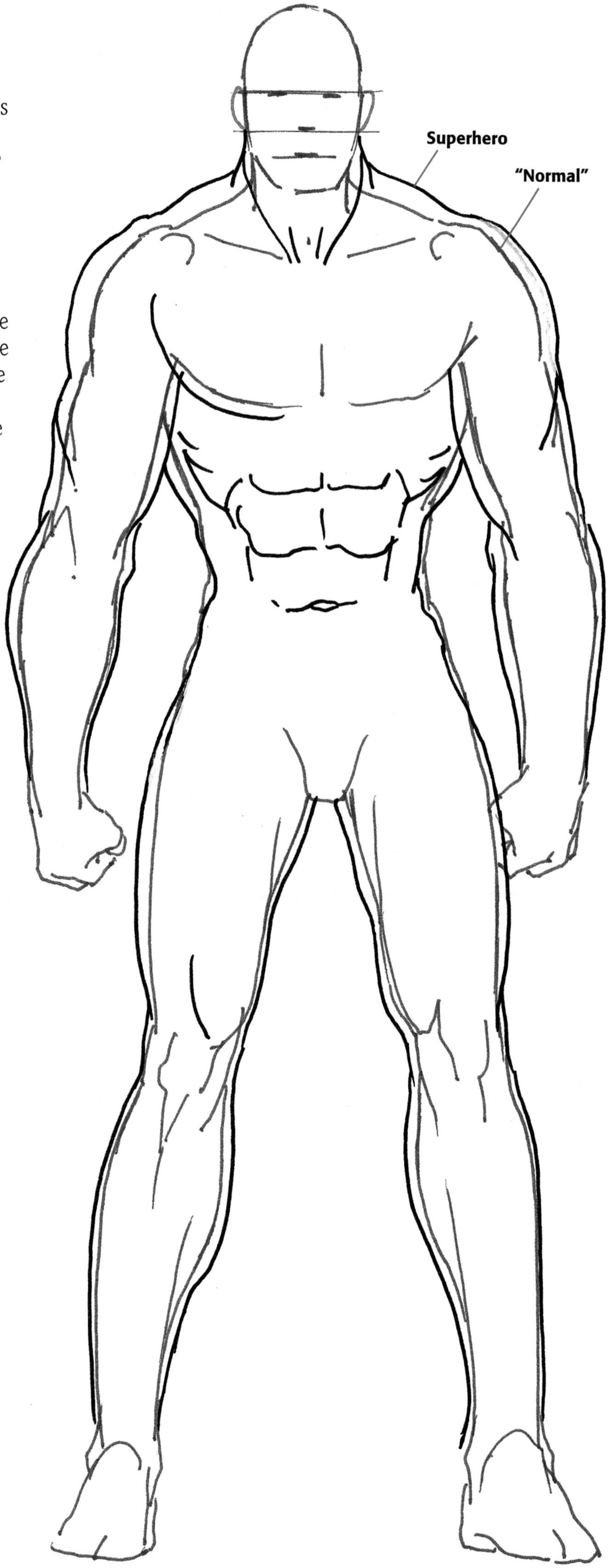
Superhero
"Normal"

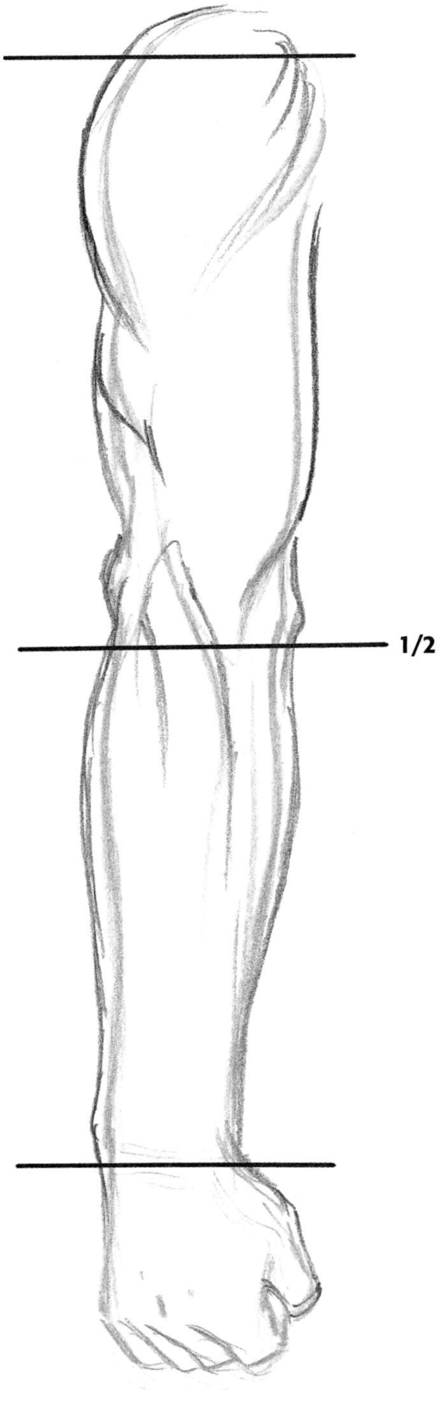
1/2

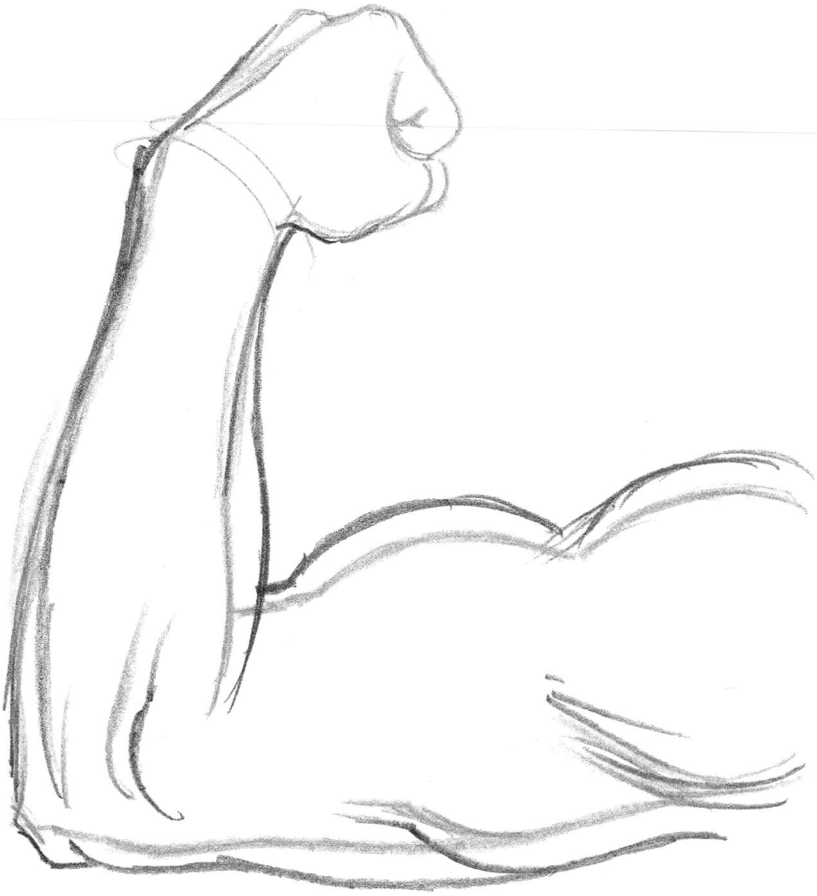

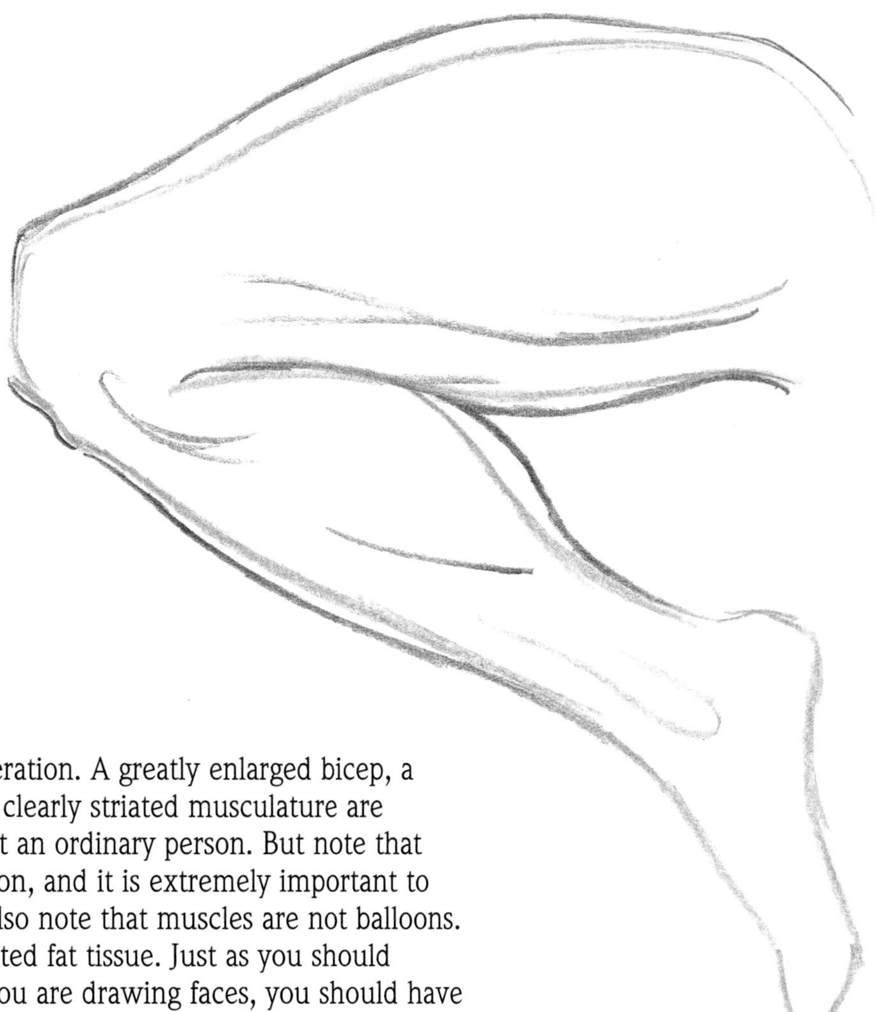

Superhero drawing is founded on exaggeration. A greatly enlarged bicep, a powerfully thickened thigh, a forearm with clearly striated musculature are signals that the character is a superhero, not an ordinary person. But note that exaggeration magnifies mistakes in proportion, and it is extremely important to maintain the correct *relative* proportions. Also note that muscles are not balloons. They are made of fibers and cords, not inflated fat tissue. Just as you should visualize the skull beneath the skin when you are drawing faces, you should have a clear picture in your mind of what bare muscle tissue looks like when you are drawing biceps, triceps, quadriceps, lats, or any other muscle group.

The detailed drawings of musculature on these two pages, with the "normal" figure inked in black and the superhero exagggeration inked in red, are here for reference. In most illustrations, only those muscles reacting to movement or stress should be delineated in such a detailed fashion.

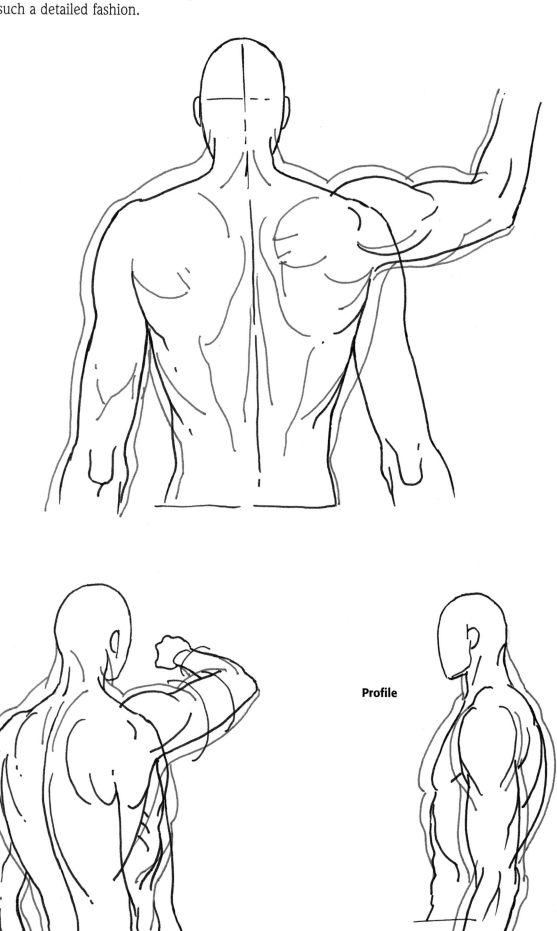

3/4 rear

Profile

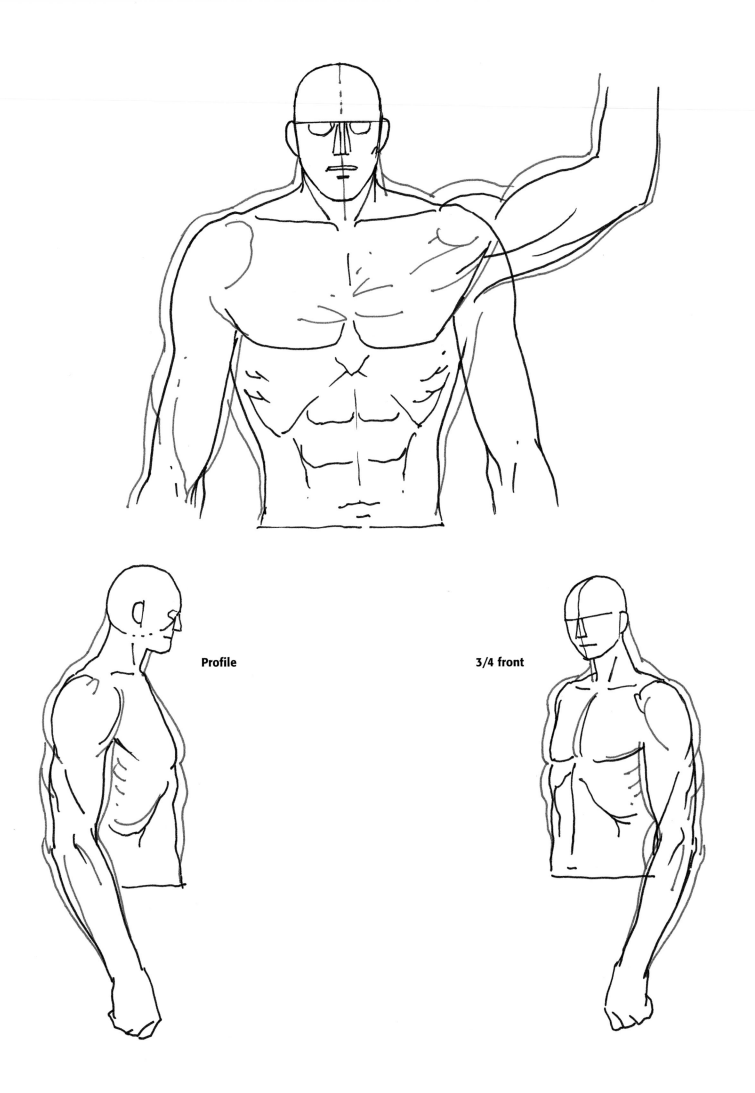

Profile

3/4 front

Muscles Under Stress

There *are* times when you will need to show your superhero performing a feat that takes big-time muscle strength. Short of taking your sketchpad to a body-building gym, how are you going to draw those stressed-out supermuscles? Try this: Imagine yourself as the superhero. Which muscles come into play when you pick up something heavy from the ground? When you lift it over your head? When you flex your bicep? When you flex your leg? When you twist your body? Maintain a weight-lifting exercise regimen and check out what you are doing in front of a mirror. The muscles that you are using for a particular task are the same muscles that will be used by your superhero.

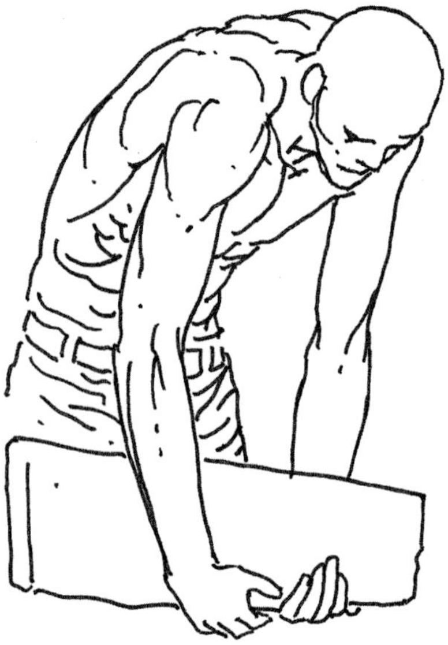

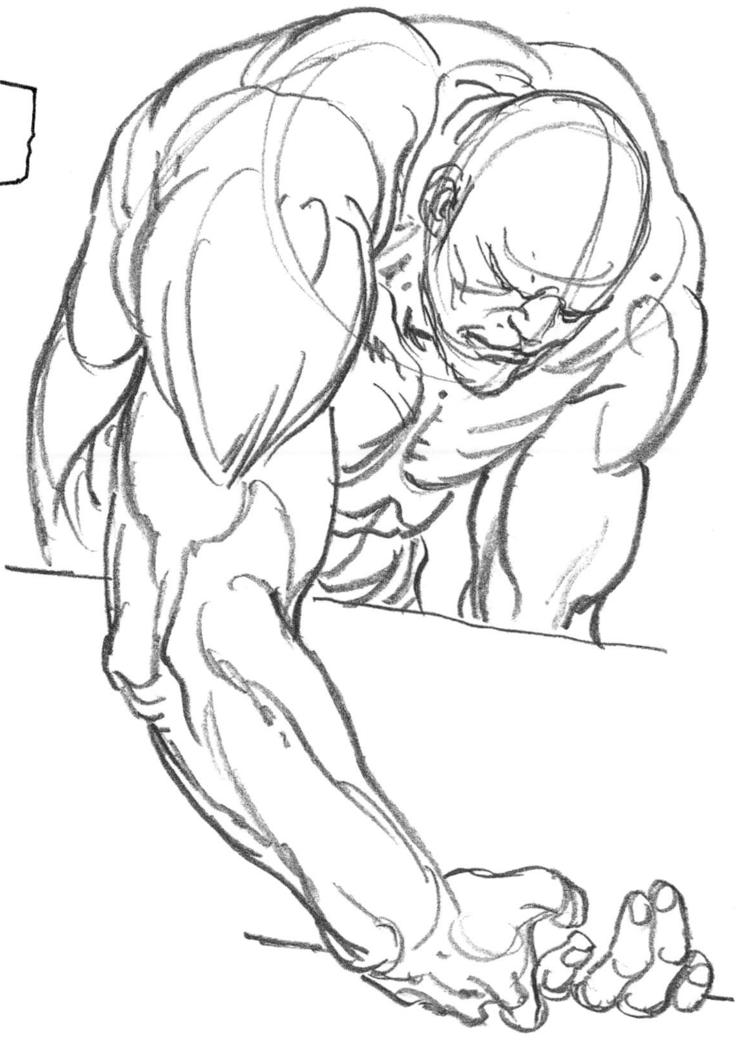

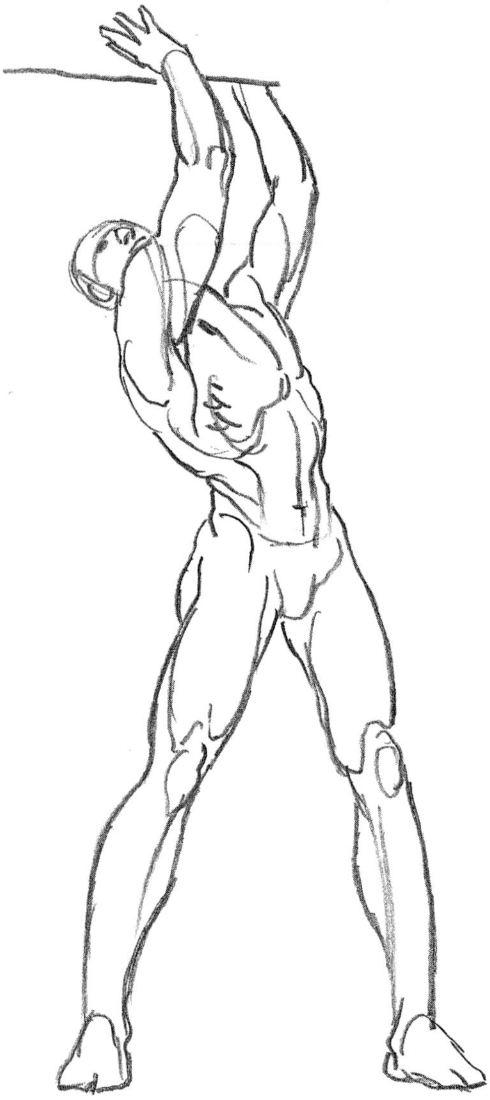

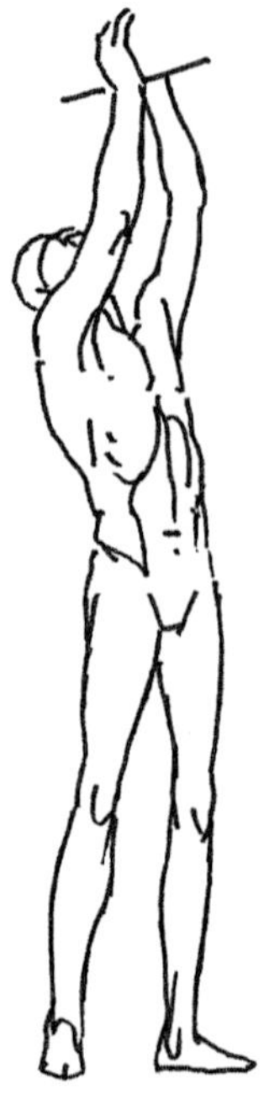

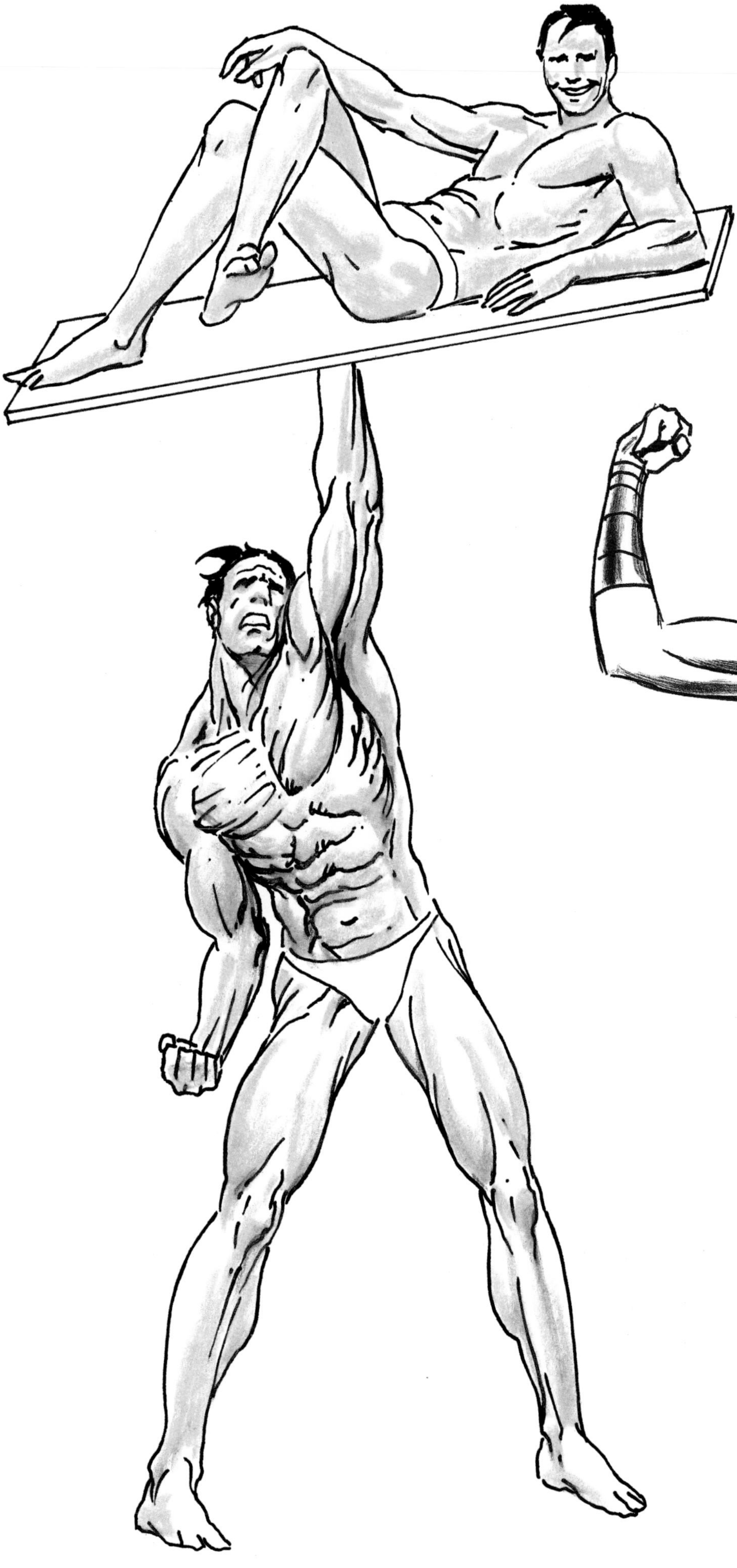

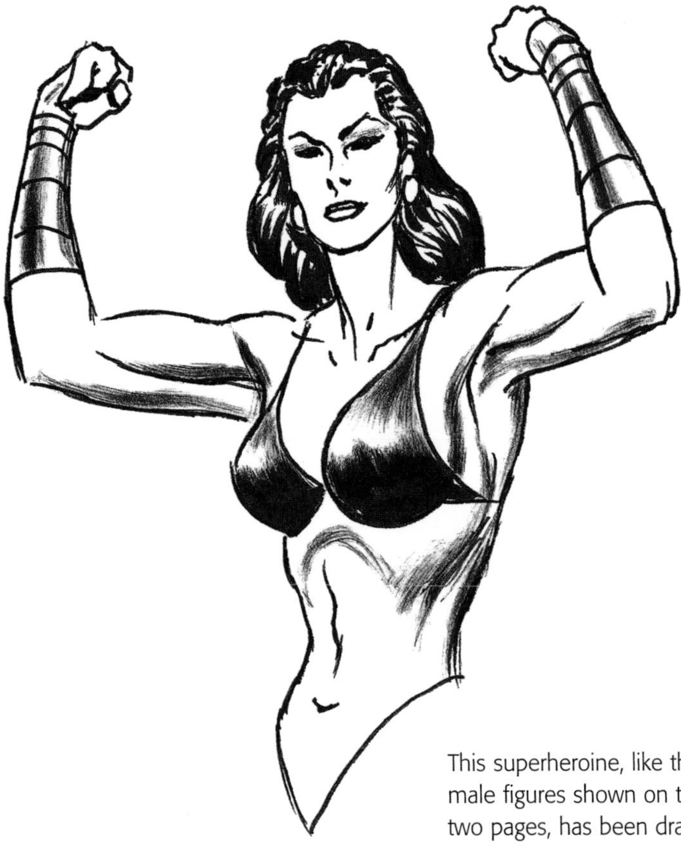

This superheroine, like the male figures shown on these two pages, has been drawn to emphasize her super-muscles, but she remains quintessentially female.

Not even superheroes walk around constantly flexing their muscles. (Besides looking peculiar, it would be extremely tiring.) From the standpoint of storytelling, the most effective use of strained or stressed muscles is to convey that the superhero is making an extra physical effort to accomplish a particular task.

SUPER EXTREMITIES

If we look closely, we find that at the extremities of arms and legs we have hands and feet. The difficulty in drawing these appendages is that each is comprised of fingers and toes. Usually, five per unit.

The sketches on these pages are examples of my approach when drawing these parts of the human figure. Drawing hands and feet correctly is more than just a matter of anatomical accuracy. Hands and feet can also reflect a character's internal emotions.

For most artists, hands and feet are particularly difficult to draw. Drawing foreshortened hands and feet is especially difficult. It's helpful to think of the palm as a paddle, which tapers out from the wrist. The fingers are jointed tubes which fan out like the ribs of a fan.

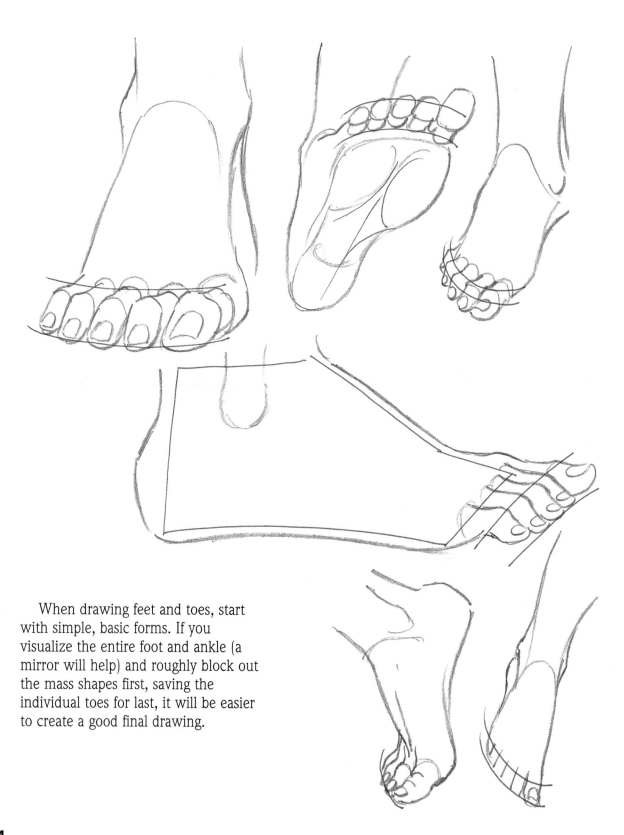

When drawing feet and toes, start with simple, basic forms. If you visualize the entire foot and ankle (a mirror will help) and roughly block out the mass shapes first, saving the individual toes for last, it will be easier to create a good final drawing.

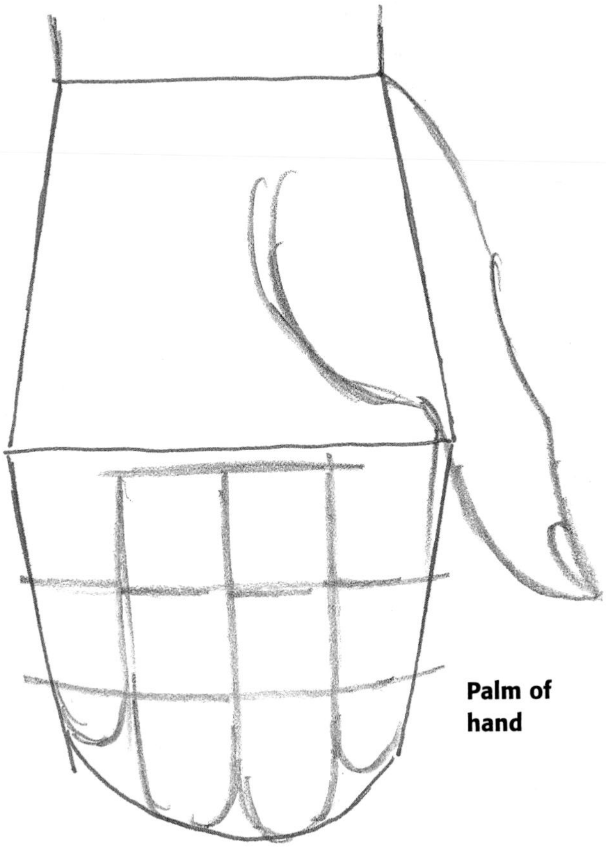
Wrist tapers
Palm of hand

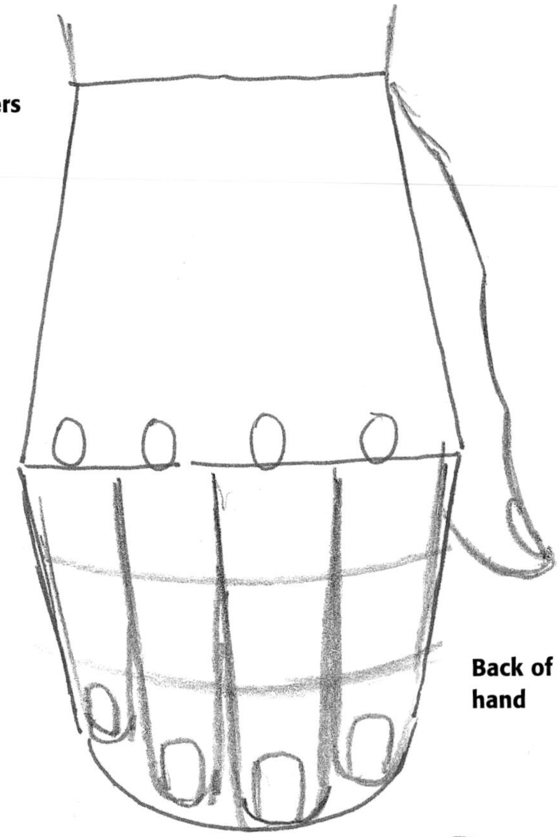
Back of hand

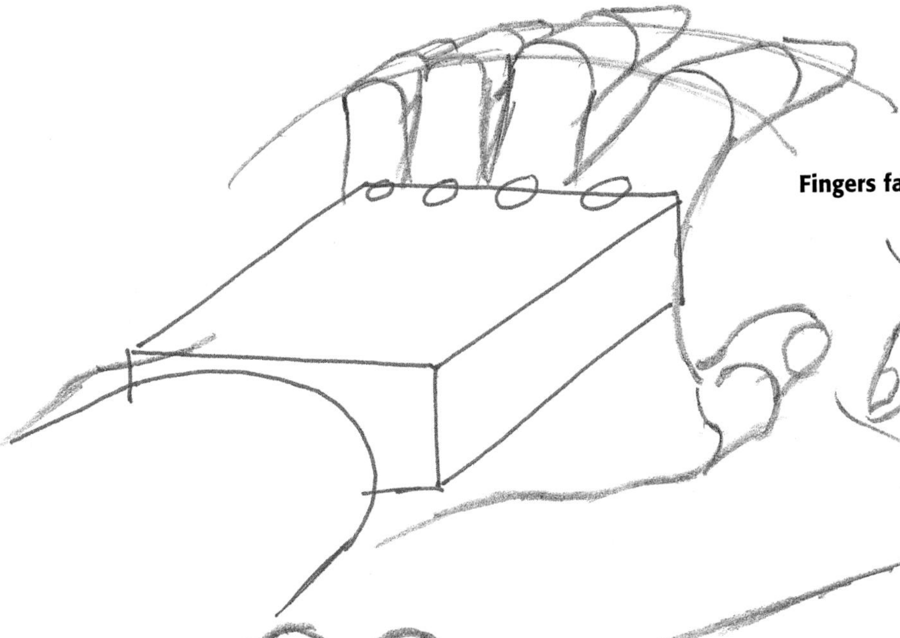
Fingers fan out

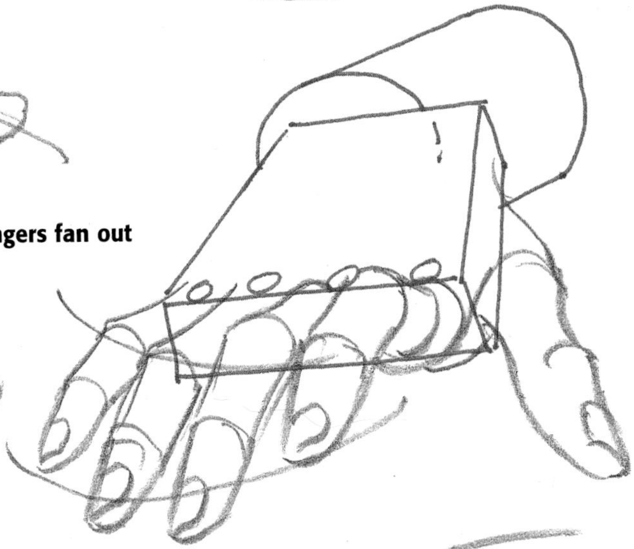

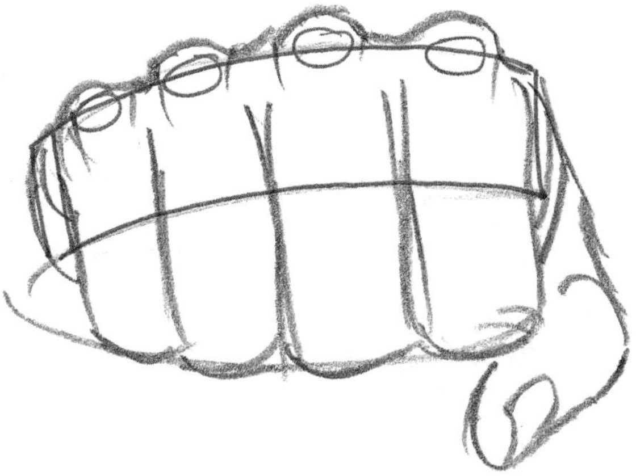

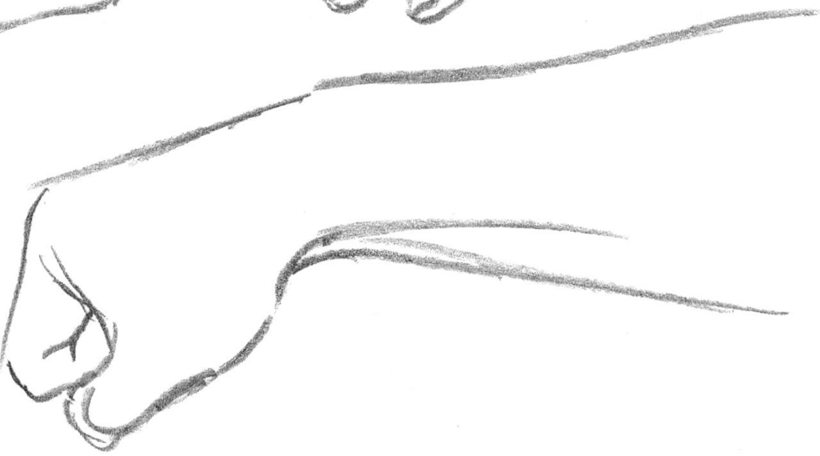

Beginners tend to draw hands in stiff, inflexible positions with little sense of dimension. Hands, however, are capable of remarkably expressive movement and possess weight and density.

Practice by drawing your own hand from a variety of positions. Be sure to include the wrist, both to "anchor" the hand and to convey a sense of movement and foreshortening.

THE FEMALE SUPERHERO

It has been my experience that novice cartoonists often have difficulty drawing the female figure. Conversely, female cartoonists have problems drawing a truly "masculine" male figure. One approach to overcoming these gender-related shortcomings is not unlike the way a method actor gets "inside" a new role.

Start with the premise that you, the cartoonist, are first and foremost a storyteller and therefore must have a sensitivity to characters and characterization. When you are drawing an evil, villainous character, you should start by conceptualizing what makes the character evil, what villainous acts he might be capable of. In essence, you act the part internally in order to convey these characteristics graphically.

Similarly, the male cartoonist drawing a female character must think about the whole person, not just the typically female attributes, such as large breasts and hips. Overendowment is a common mistake.

Another remedy, one I have repeated often in this book, is to return to the basics. To start with the unexaggerated female form.

The parallel lines in these drawings show the basic relative proportions of the female body.

Hip joint at 1/2

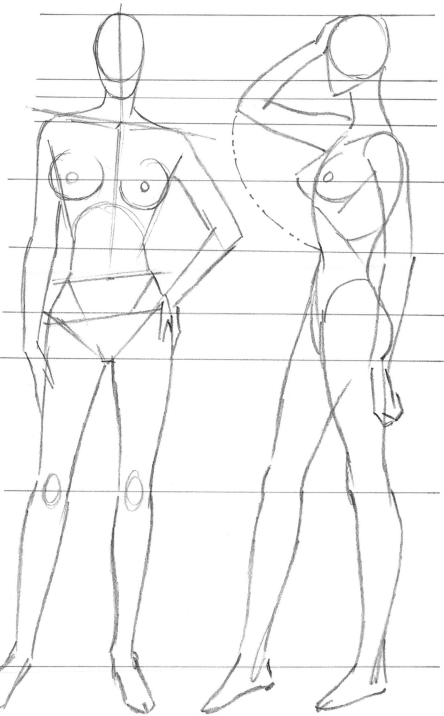

Female superheros, like male superheros, have a front, sides, a top, and a bottom. They are not flat paper cutouts. Sometimes adding a bit of shading to your figure drawings will create the dimensionality you are after.

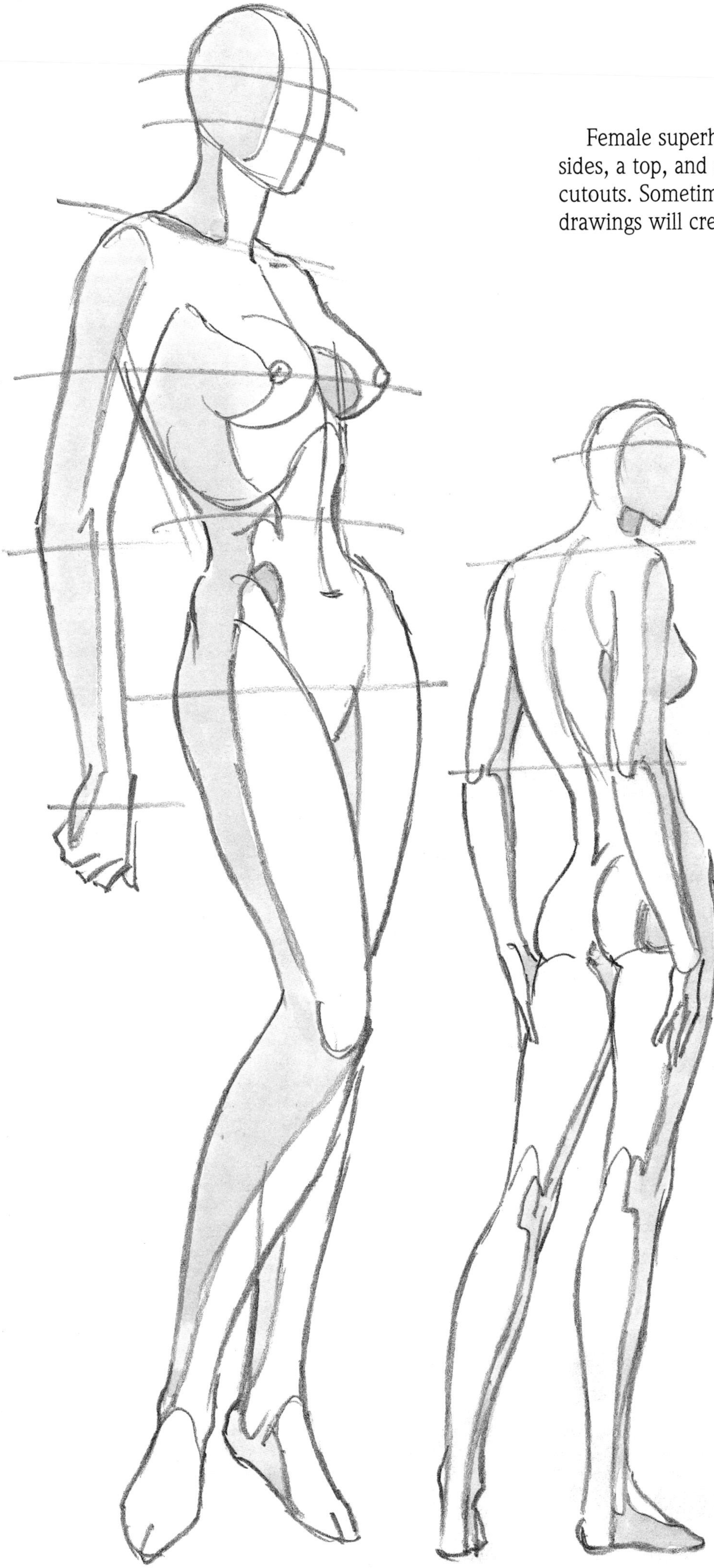

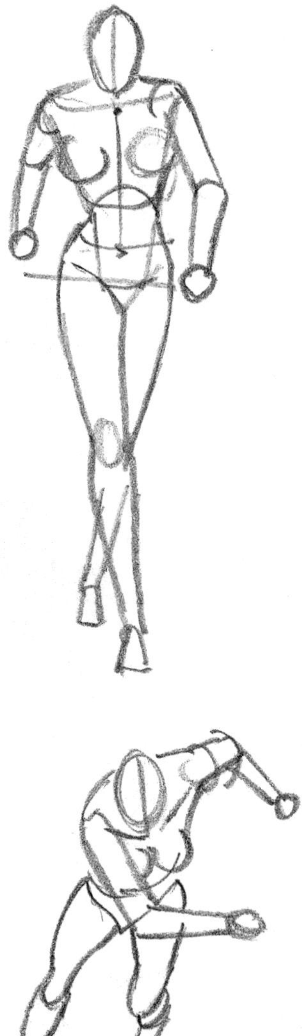

Drawing the female form in a cartoon style for comic books presents a unique set of problems. Adding "superheroine" to the mix brings additional complications. Depending on the characterization, the female superheroine is probably endowed with enormous strenth, yet must remain feminine, attractive, and alluring. Retaining the feminine is difficult to accomplish when your superheroine is battling a dozen villains at once, or tearing down the facade of a building.

Posture and attitude are important. A masculine pose detracts from a character's "femaleness."

As always, when drawing twisted and foreshortened figures, start out with rough sketches, and use the basic proportion grid.

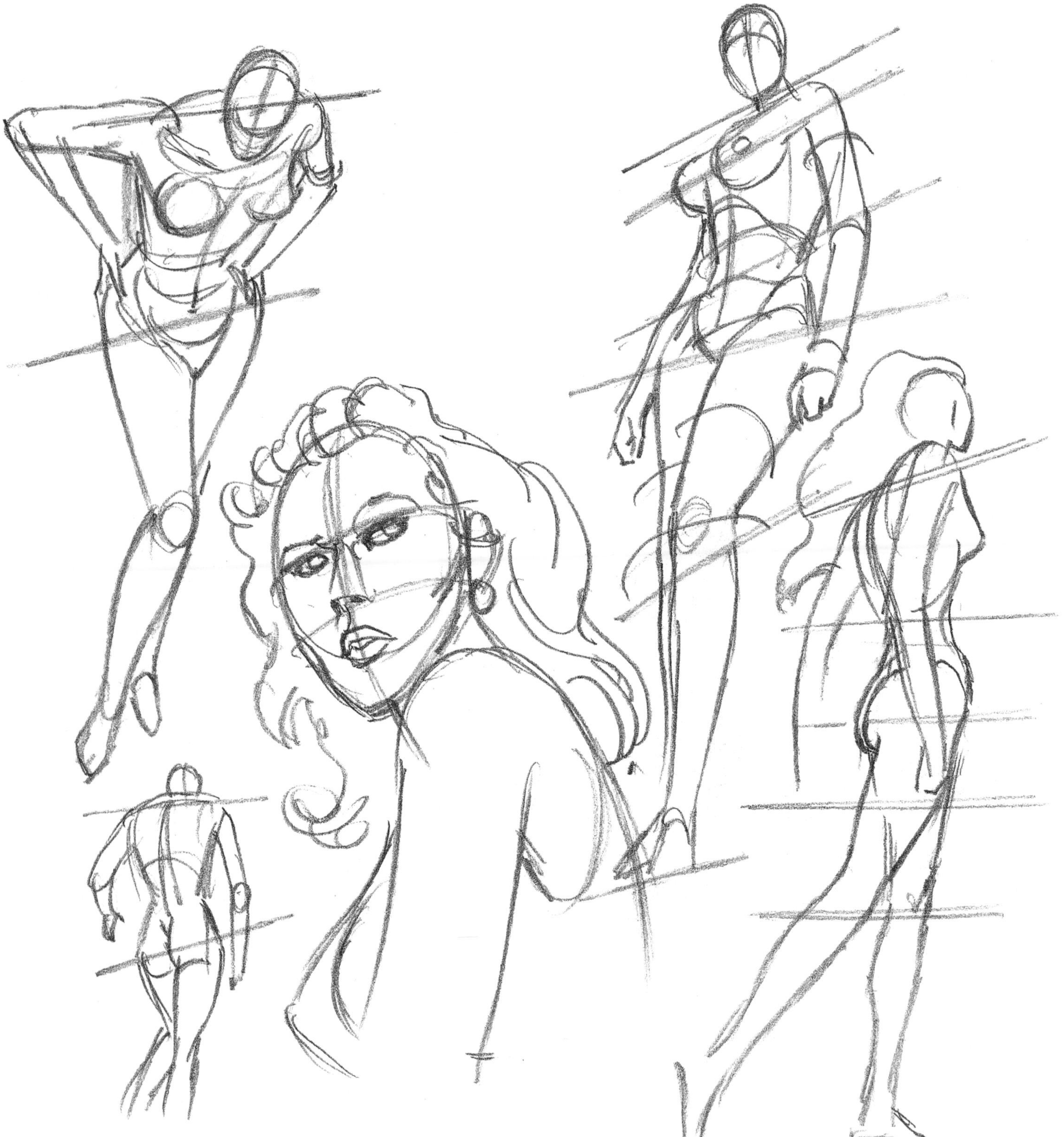

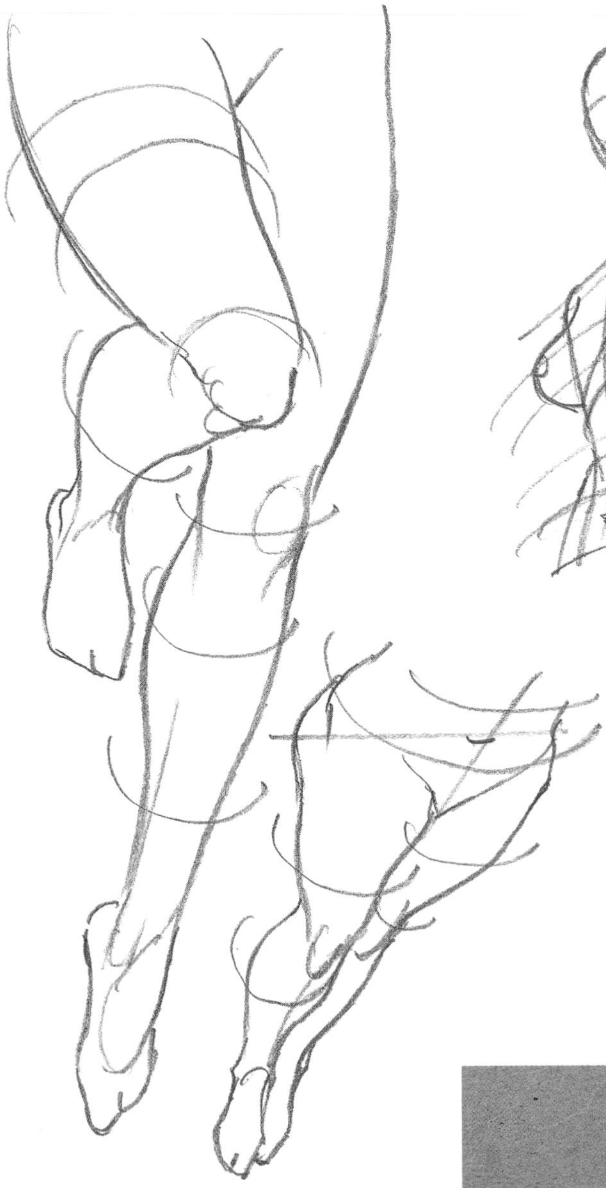

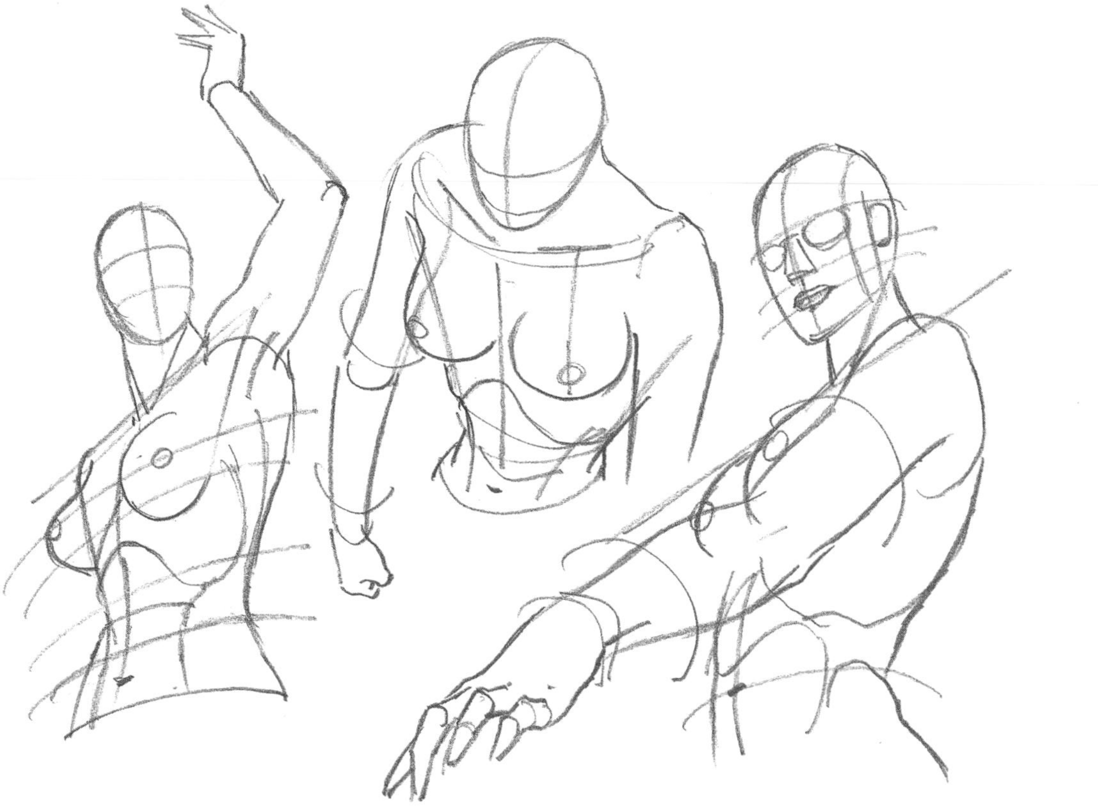

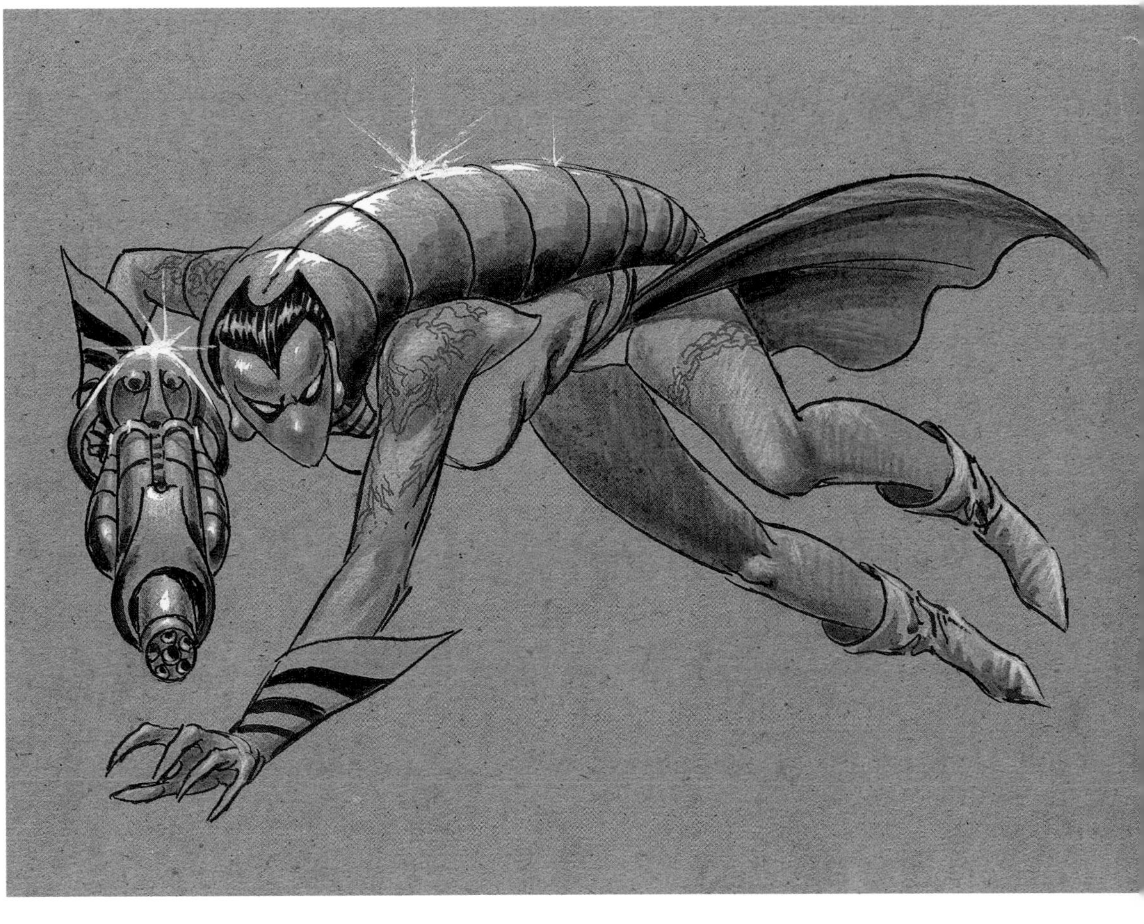

Here's a humanoid superheroine (or supervillain) who doesn't need giant muscles to get what she wants. Note the series of bulbous forms extending from the back of her head down her spine. Is this where she carries her eggs, or do these sacs contain deadly poison? She breathes through her skin and communicates through mental telepathy—hence no need for mouth or nose. She has the strength-for-size power of an insect, making her capable of incredible physical feats. How do I know all this? Because I thought about her *before* I started drawing. Do you have some ideas for a superheroine or supervillain? Bring them to life in your drawings.

Superheroine—Not Super Body Builder

The most successfully drawn superheroines are those without enormous or distinctly rendered muscles. Instead, the arms and legs should give an impression of form and weight. A sense of solidity rather than muscularity.

Although the basic structure of the female skeleton is like the basic structure of the male skeleton, it is generally accepted that a longer, tapering leg is more typical of the female skeleton. Similarly, the bones of the female arm taper to a more delicate wrist.

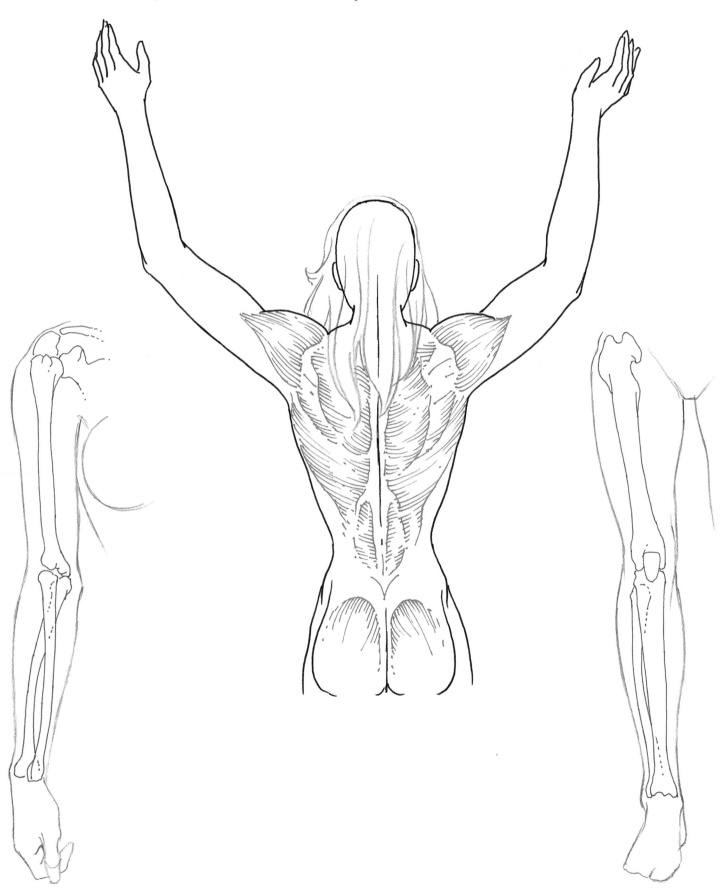

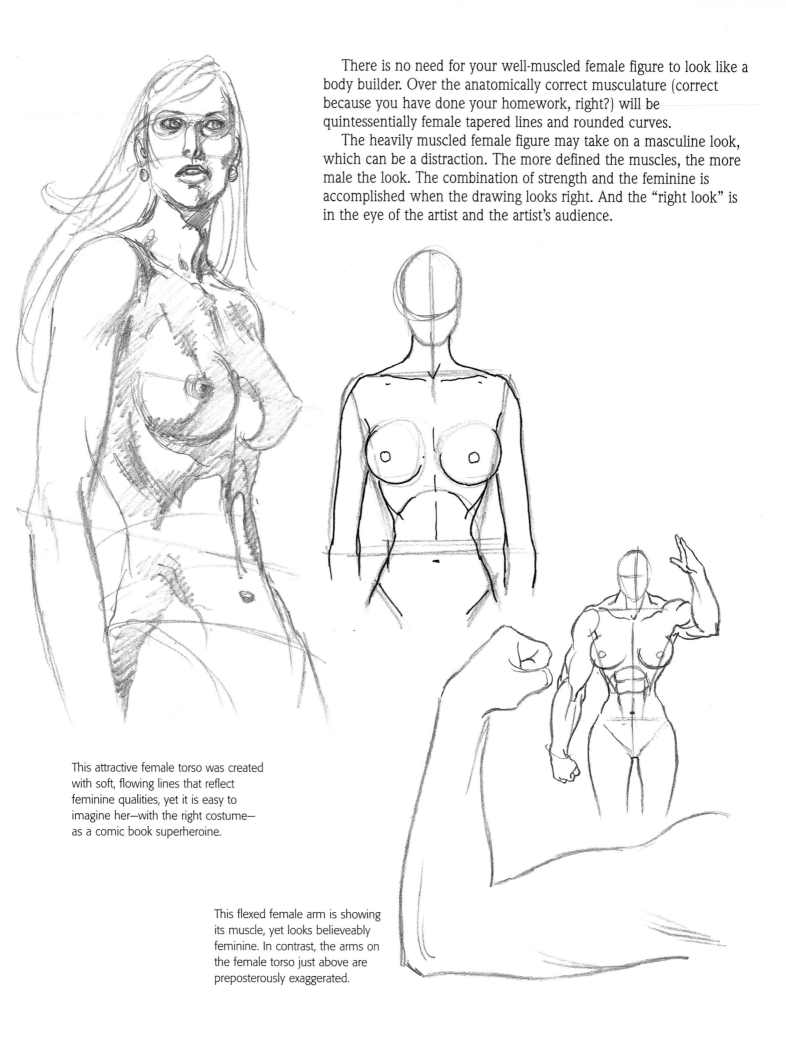

There is no need for your well-muscled female figure to look like a body builder. Over the anatomically correct musculature (correct because you have done your homework, right?) will be quintessentially female tapered lines and rounded curves.

The heavily muscled female figure may take on a masculine look, which can be a distraction. The more defined the muscles, the more male the look. The combination of strength and the feminine is accomplished when the drawing looks right. And the "right look" is in the eye of the artist and the artist's audience.

This attractive female torso was created with soft, flowing lines that reflect feminine qualities, yet it is easy to imagine her—with the right costume—as a comic book superheroine.

This flexed female arm is showing its muscle, yet looks believeably feminine. In contrast, the arms on the female torso just above are preposterously exaggerated.

Feminine Hands and Feet

The bone structure of hands and feet is virtually the same for both male and female, but the female's hands and feet are generally smaller and the bones are on a smaller scale. When drawing the superheroine, it's important to let the gender be obvious in all the details. If the body is recognizably a woman's but the hands and feet seem masculine, the drawing will not be effective.

The female hand and foot are best illustrated with flowing lines. Extended fingernails and adornments (like bracelets and rings) also enhance the feminine appearance.

Boots and gloves should also be designed to reflect the superheroine's femininity. The woman's boot has a high heel and she may wear a ring on her gloved figure or bare toe.

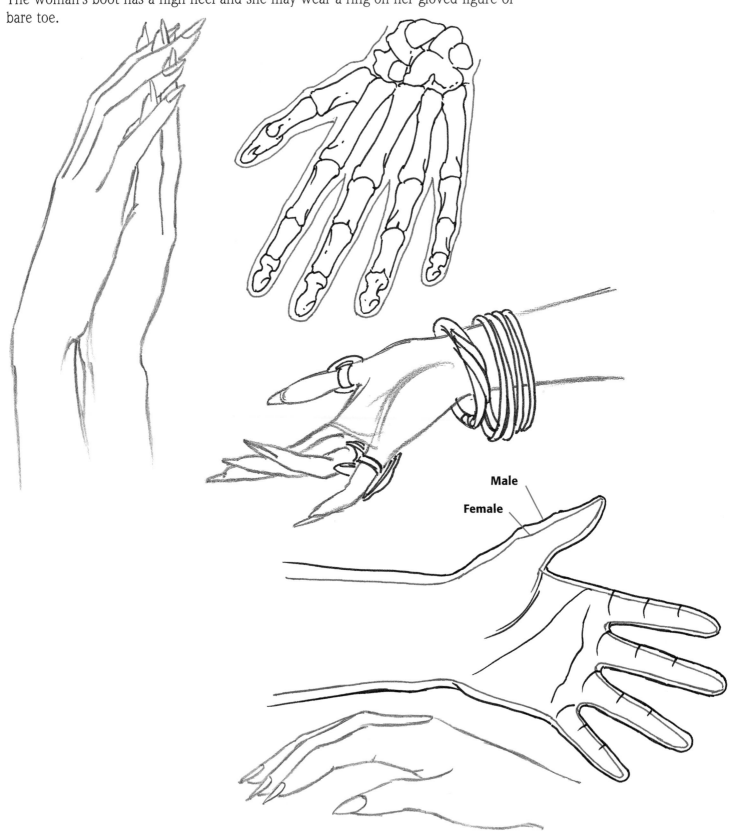

Male

Female

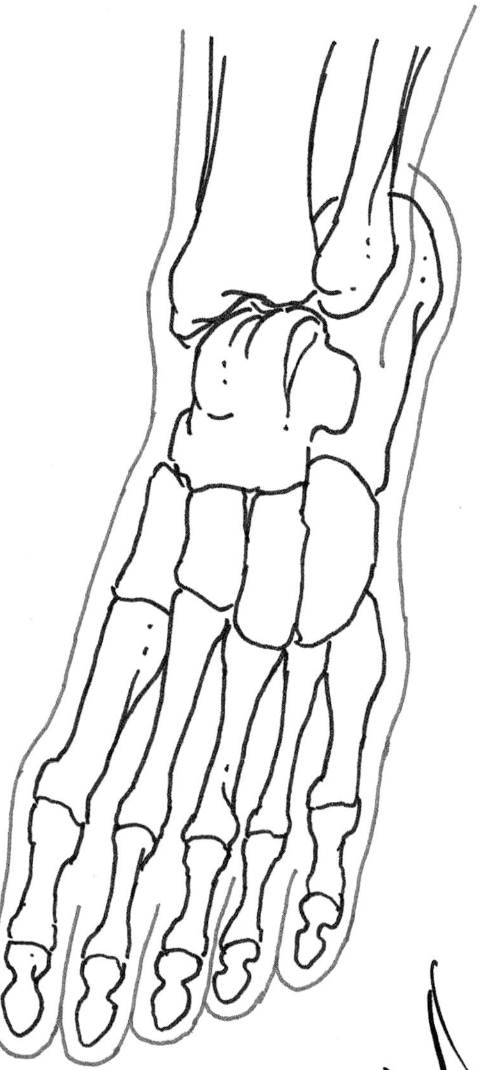

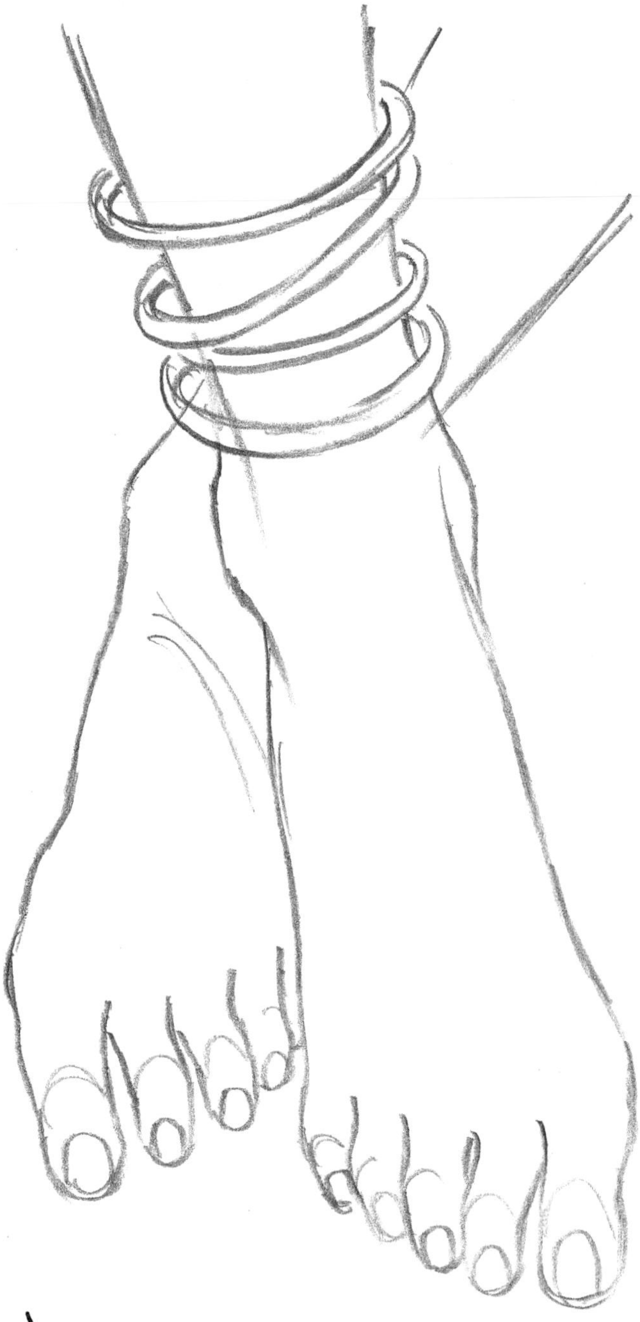

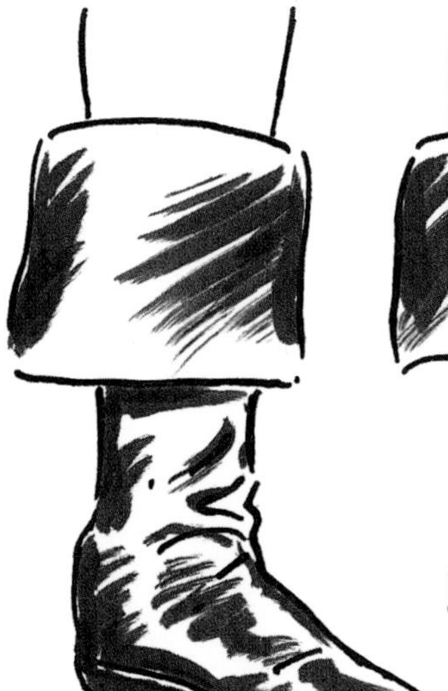

Male

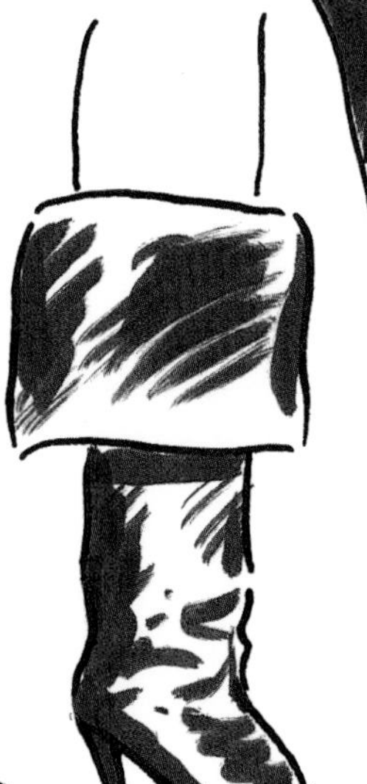

Female

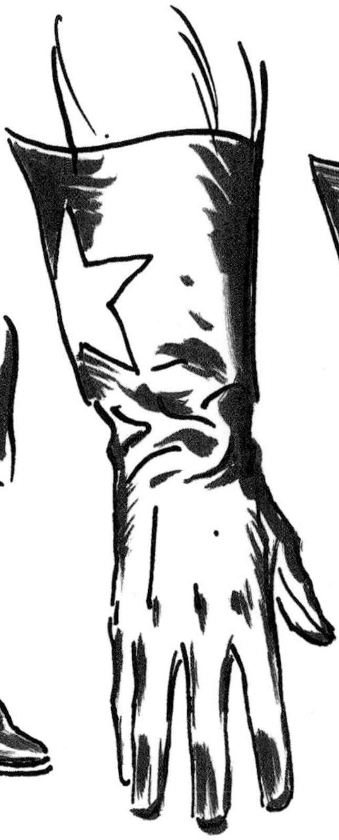

Male

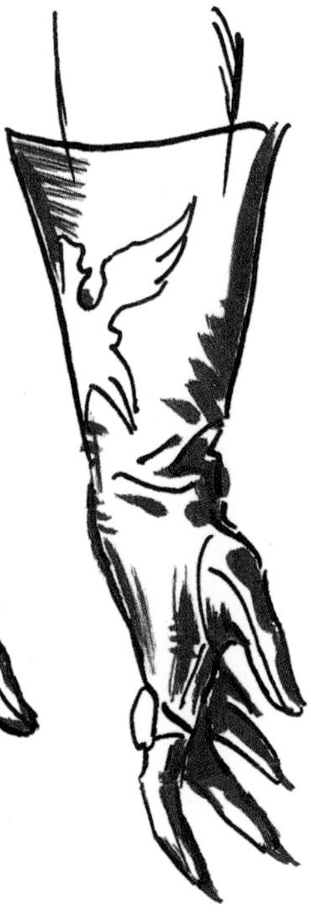

Female

Hair

In my years as a professional cartoonist I've been asked by many young aspirants, "How do you draw hair?" The following suggestions, which were given to me by artists I respected when I was just starting out, have been helpful to me throughout my career.

- Human hair is part of the head, but it doesn't "sit up" on top of the skull. It conforms to the curves of the skull.
- Hair is composed of fibers, like fine or coarse threads, which have a flow and movement of their own, almost like liquid. The cartoonist uses lines to suggest the flow of hair (short or long, straight or curly) and to convey the sense that hair is composed of individual filaments. It's not necessary to draw every strand to achieve the desired effect.
- Figuring out where the light source is and making sure the highlights are consistent with that source also help to suggest texture, form, and movement.
- A character's hair can be a clue to character and personality, so practice drawing a lot of different hairstyles.

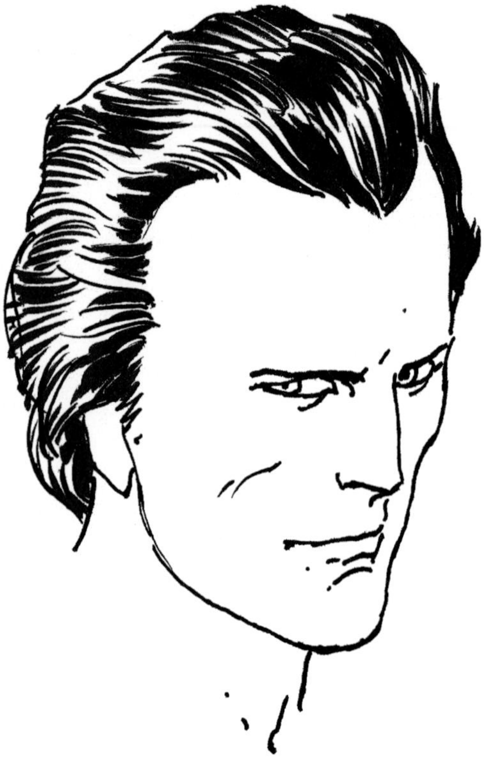

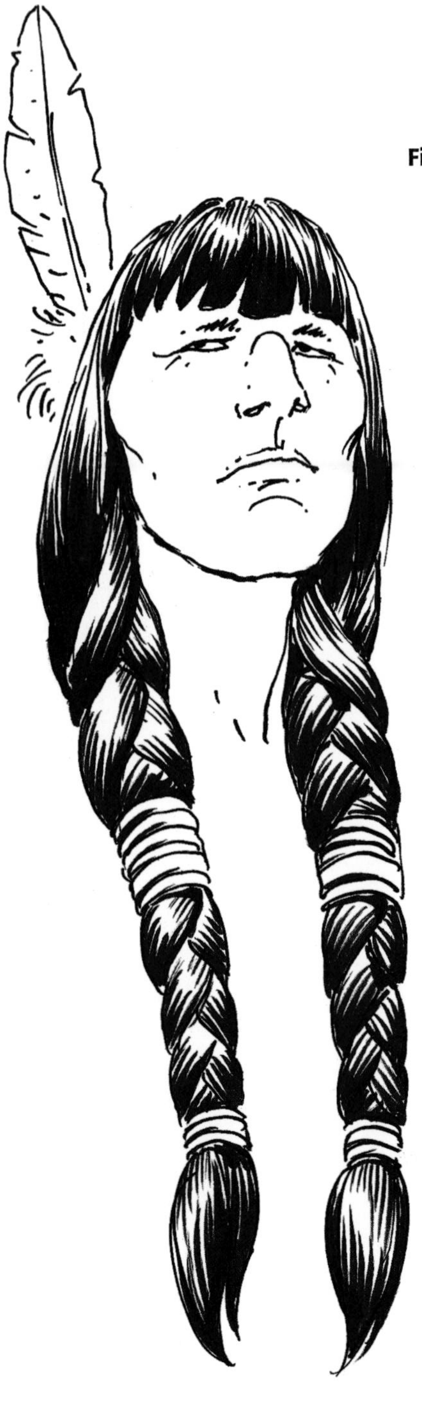

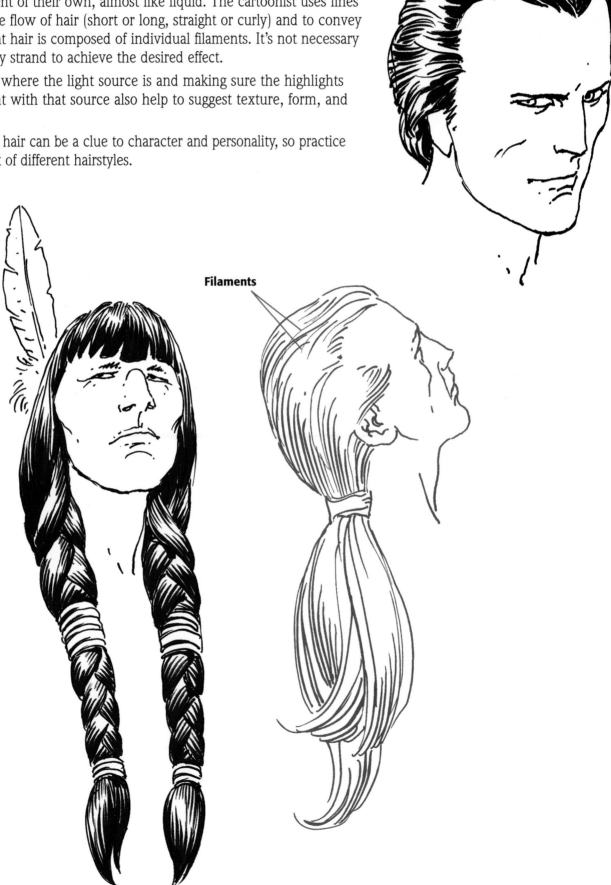

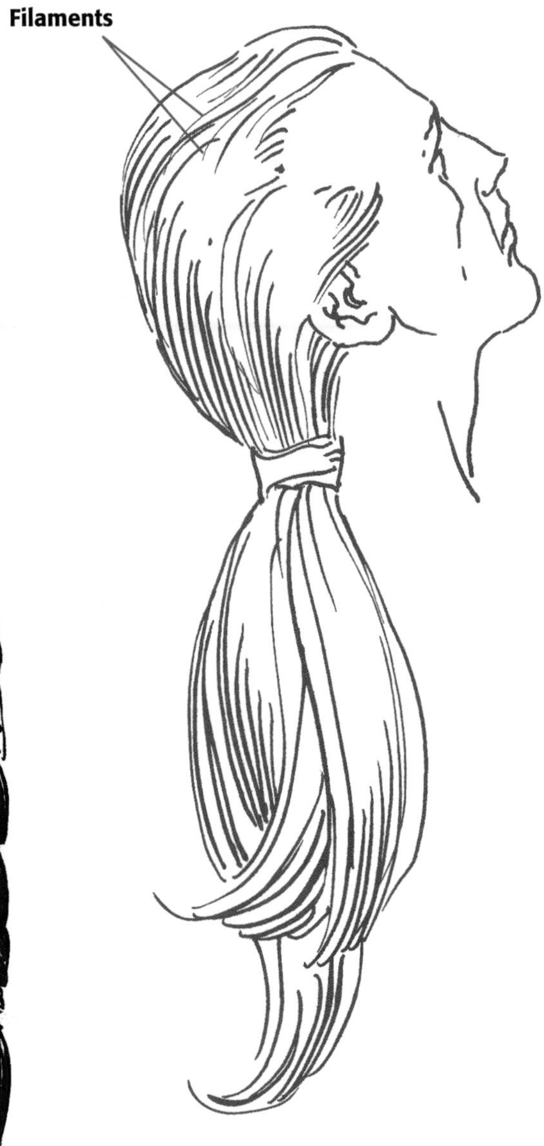
Filaments

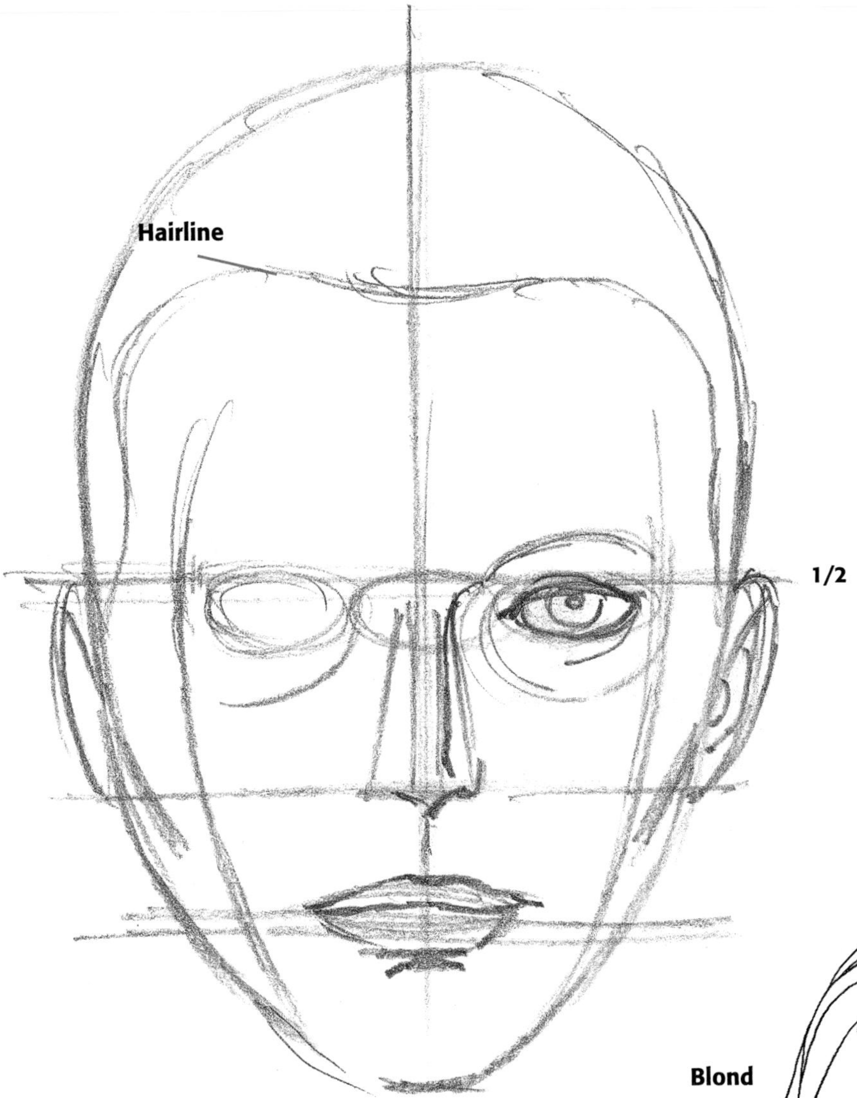
Hairline
1/2

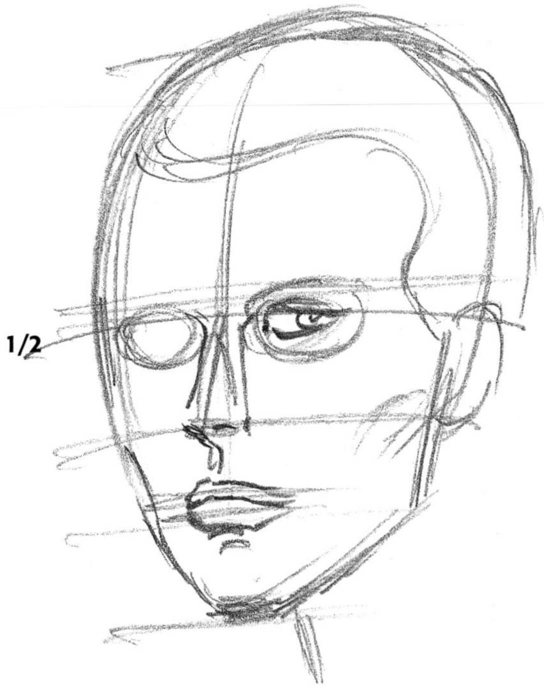
1/2

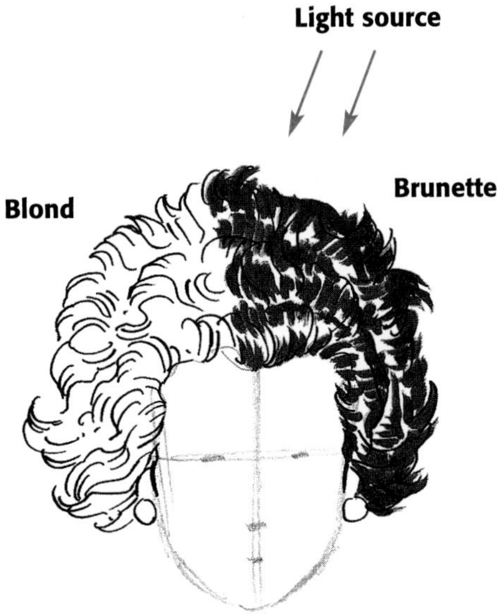
Light source
Blond
Brunette

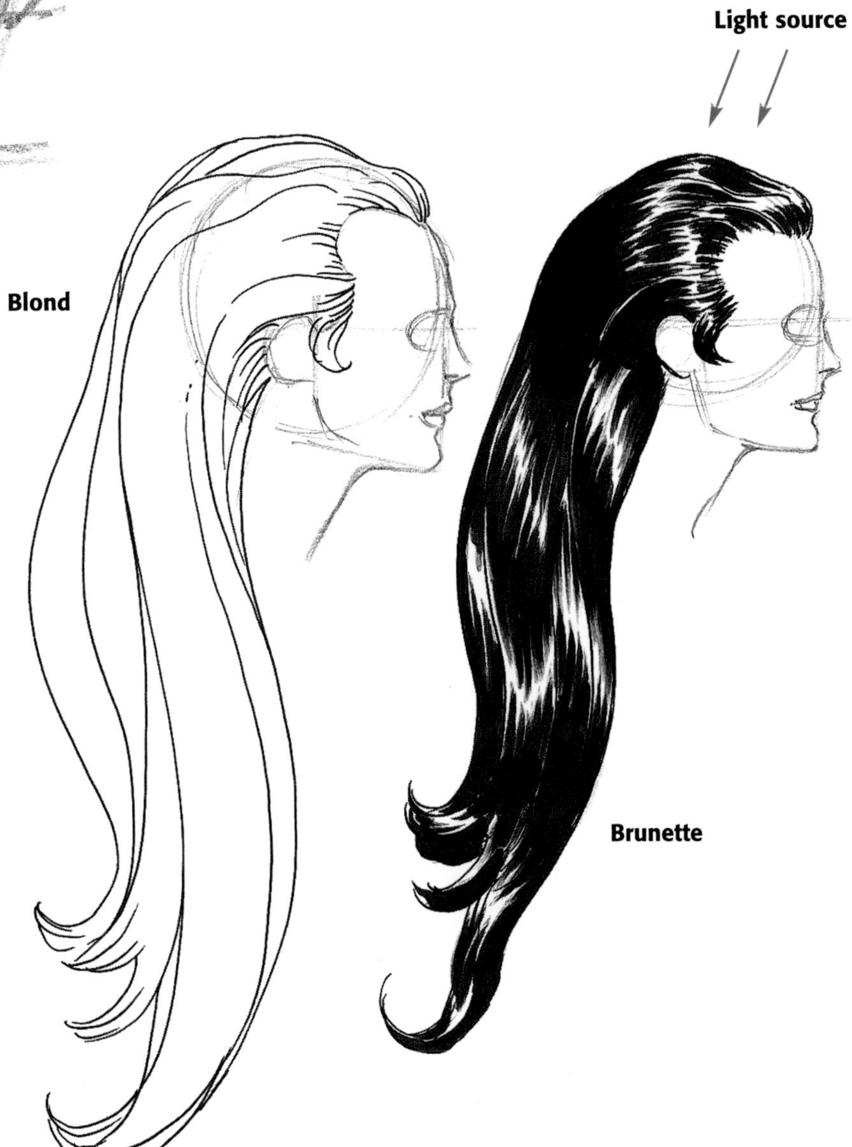
Light source
Blond
Brunette

The location at the top of the forehead from which hair emanates, the *hairline,* is the same for both men and women (at least for young men and women). The differences lie in textures, colors, and lengths.

EMOTION AND MOTION

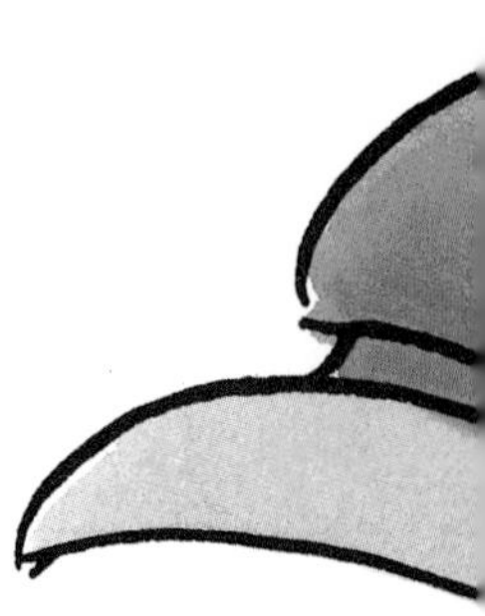

This section is all about how to show emotion—the feelings our superheroes have—and motion—how to show them moving in space. In fact, emotion and motion are closely related. An angry person expresses rage not only through facial expressions, but through body language. And whether you are drawing humorous figures, superheroes, or animals, the basic rules for drawing characters whose emotions are crystal-clear to the viewer are the same. Take anger, an emotion which can be seen in every species of animal capable of expression and which affects four-legged and two-legged animals in similar physical ways. Anger seems to concentrate itself at the center of the face. The eyebrows pull together as the nose wrinkles up. The open mouth tends to pull the upper lip upward. The eyes lower under drawn lids. The stare becomes intense as nostrils flare and lips draw down and back. Teeth are bared.

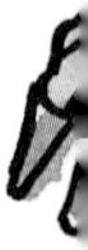

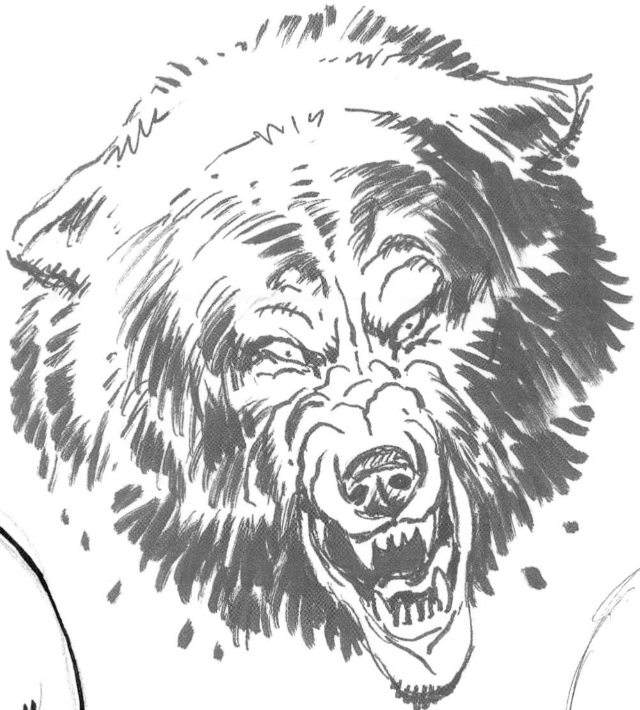

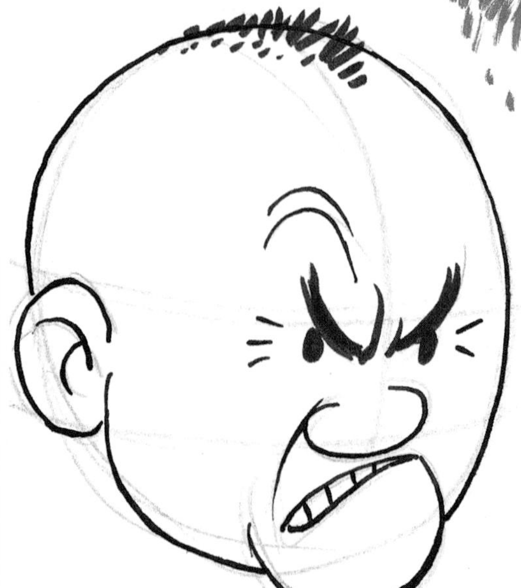

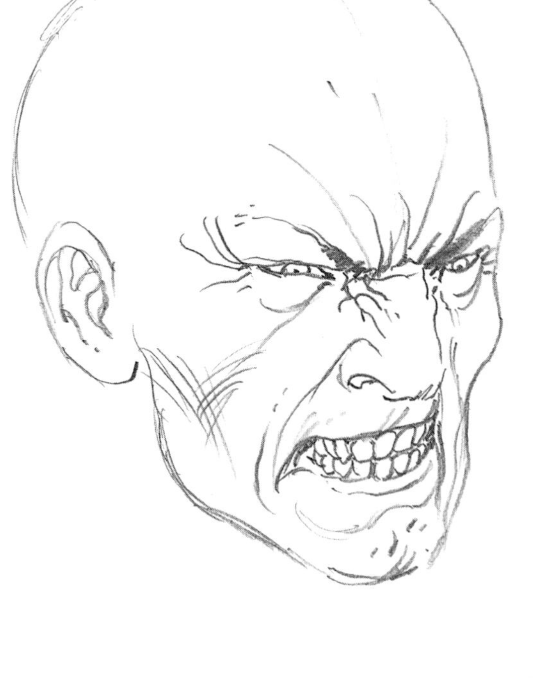

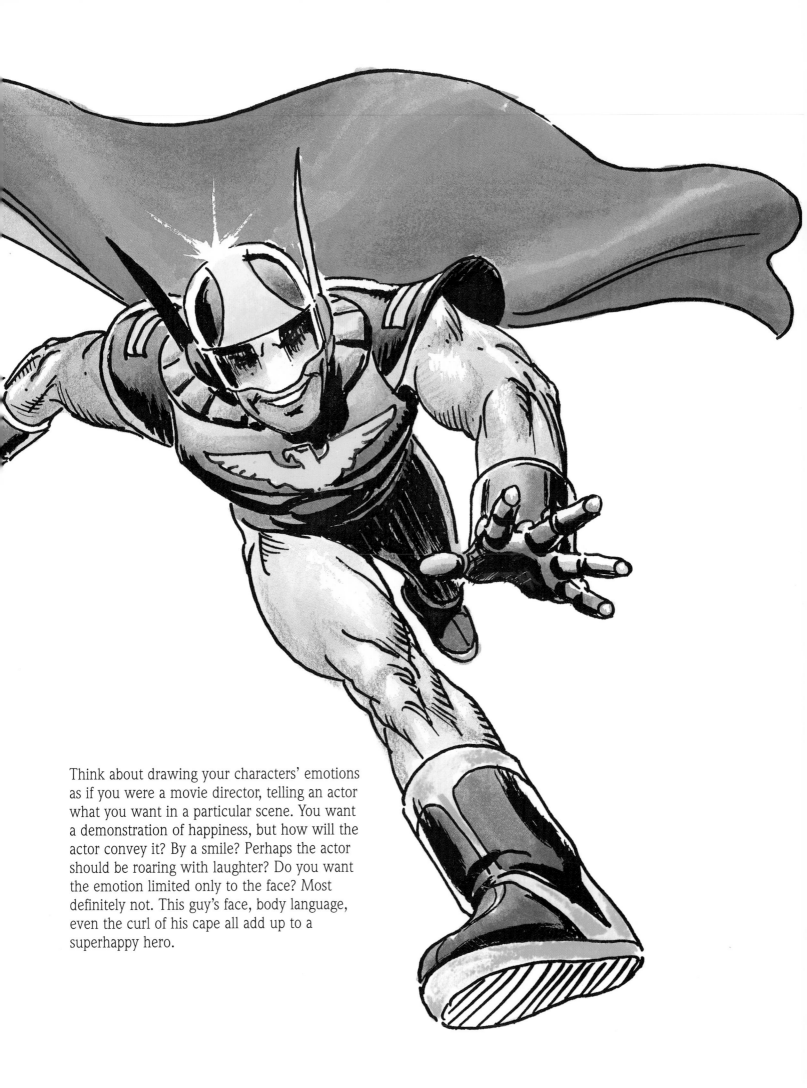

Think about drawing your characters' emotions as if you were a movie director, telling an actor what you want in a particular scene. You want a demonstration of happiness, but how will the actor convey it? By a smile? Perhaps the actor should be roaring with laughter? Do you want the emotion limited only to the face? Most definitely not. This guy's face, body language, even the curl of his cape all add up to a superhappy hero.

WHO SAID SUPERHEROES DON'T HAVE FEELINGS?

Happiness

What makes the "happy face" happy? It's just a yellow circle with wide open eyes and an upturned mouth. In fact, that ubiquitous symbol is a good object lesson. Just as you started out simple when drawing your superheroes' bodies, so your first efforts at drawing emotion should begin with basic shapes and curves. Remember: whatever emotion you want your character to express, be sure the body language works with the face.

These twelve sketches, which pair six features-only faces with six body poses, go from mild contentment to raucous laughter.

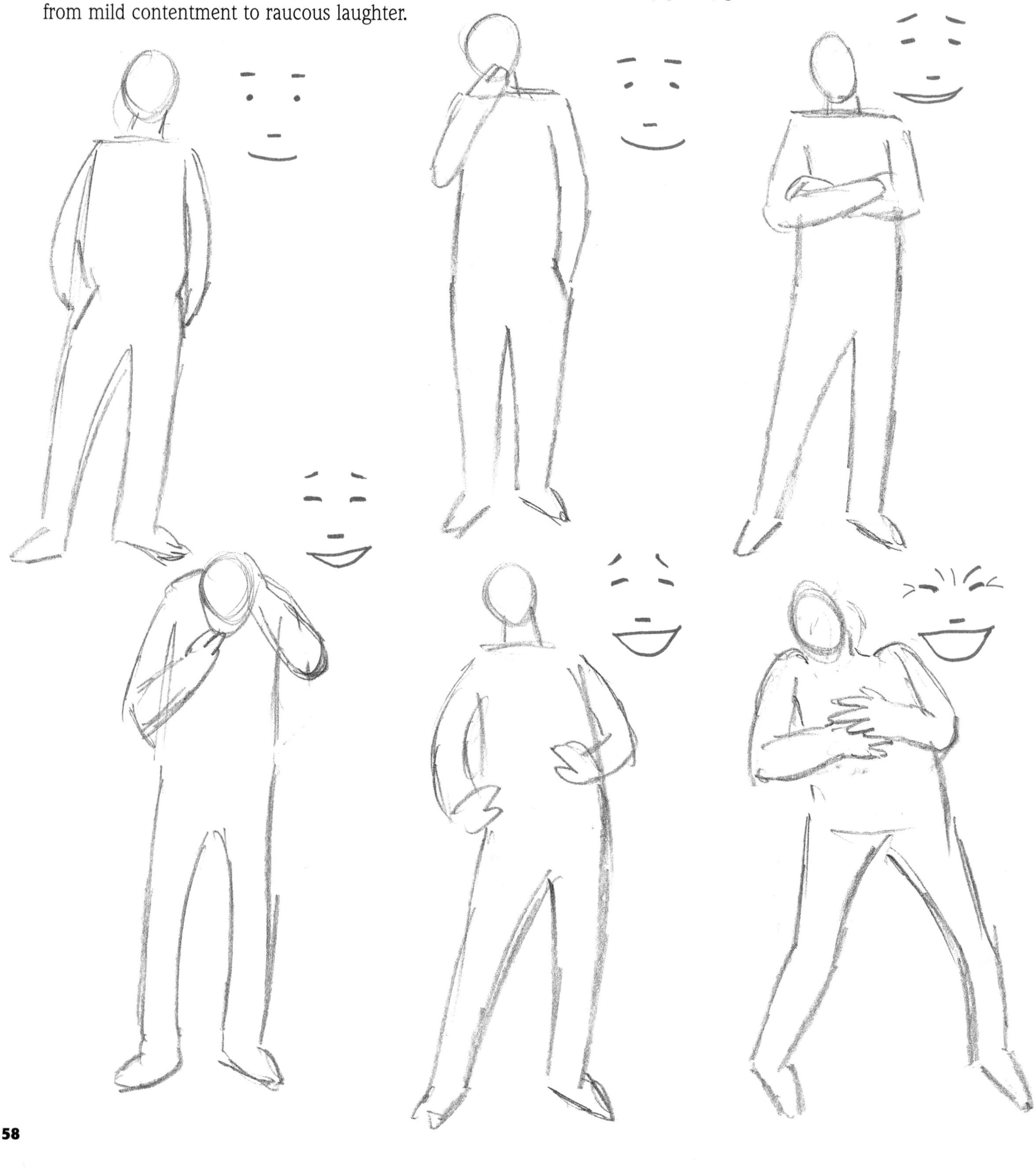

Sadness

Beginning cartoonists tend to show that their character is sad by drawing tears streaming down its face. Never mind that the face is expressionless, the tears will suffice to show the emotion. Wrong! Certainly people often cry when they are sad. But tears alone will not do it. A downward curve of the mouth, a downward slant of the eyebrows, a narrowing of the eyes (an attempt to blink back or generate tears) and a slack, open mouth combine to show sorrow. Sometimes pain and weariness are there as well.

Human sadness expresses itself in many ways.

The phrase "carrying the weight of the world on your shoulders . . ." perfectly expresses the debilitating effect sadness or sorrow can have on the human body. Extreme sorrow may even render a person incapable of motion.

Note that I did these sketches simply in an attempt to capture this sometimes elusive emotion. I'm concentrating on the emotional aspects of the illustration, not the details. I'll build the details once I feel that I've captured the emotion.

Try it yourself. Pick an emotion—anger, say—-and draw a series of sketches starting with the mildest form of the emotion and ending with the extreme. Leave out details of clothing and anatomy. Concentrate on the emotion you want to show. Draw in your own style, humorous or representational. The emotion is the same in all cases.

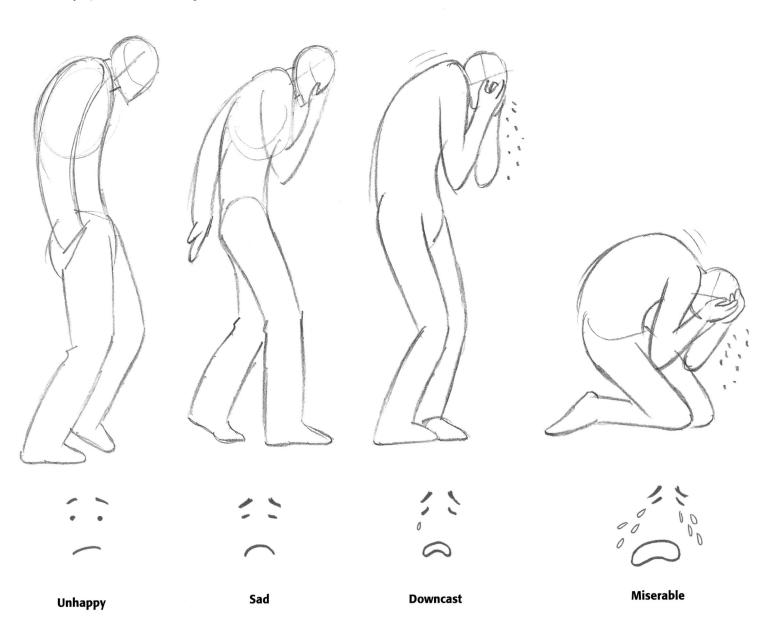

Unhappy   **Sad**   **Downcast**   **Miserable**

Pain

You have a sudden excruciating pain in your chest. A punch to the solar plexus? A knife wound? A bullet wound? Your shoulders hunch up. Your head goes down in your attempt to quell the pain. You grab your midriff, clawing at the pain inside. Your knees come together. Your legs buckle, as you attempt to keep your balance. You don't want to fall.

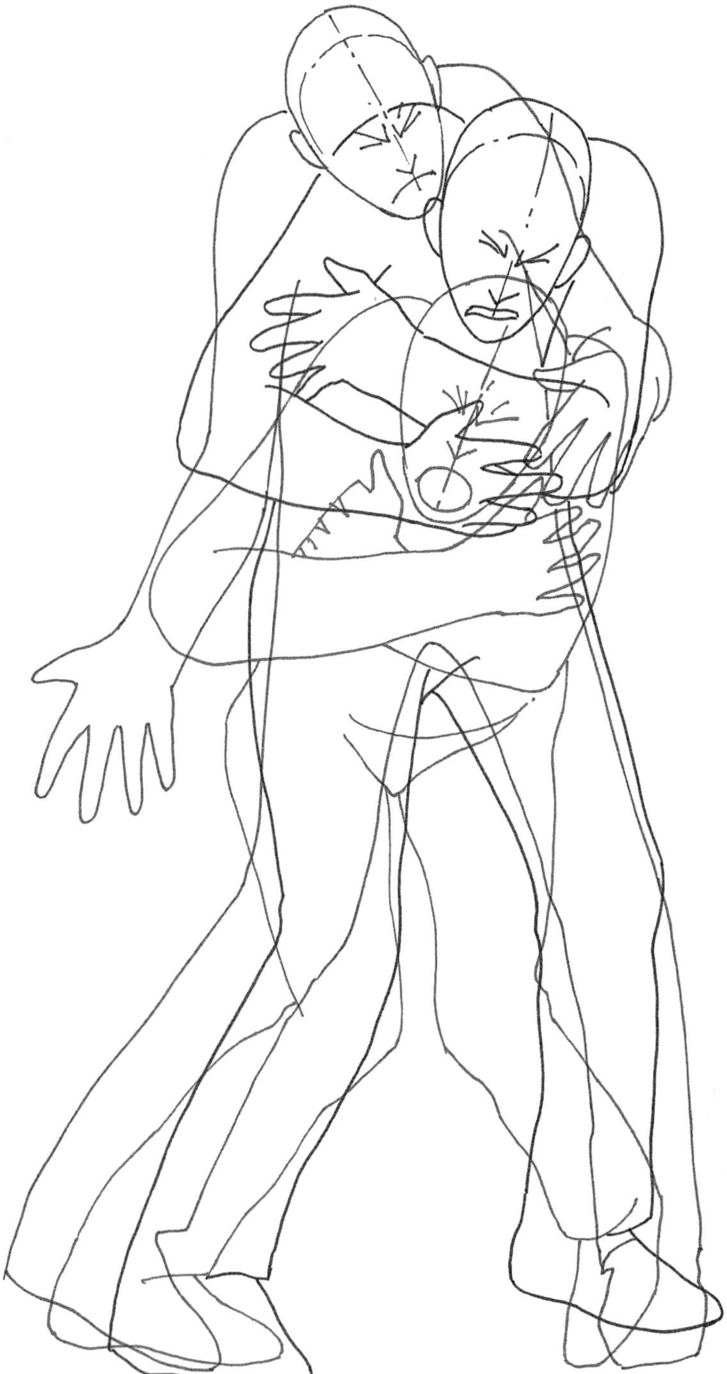

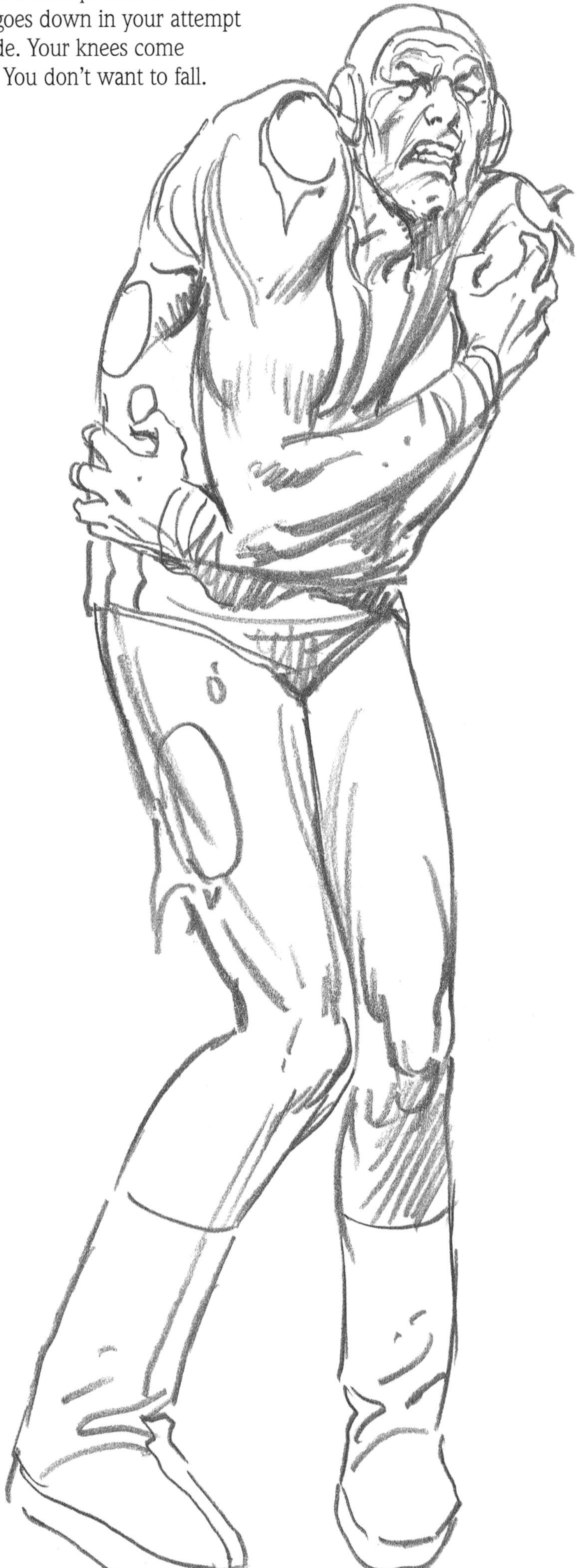

I have never experienced this sort of intense pain, but in order to draw a picture of a superhero in extreme pain, I must imagine how it would feel. Only then will my drawing be accepted in a story line that requires a character to show such pain.

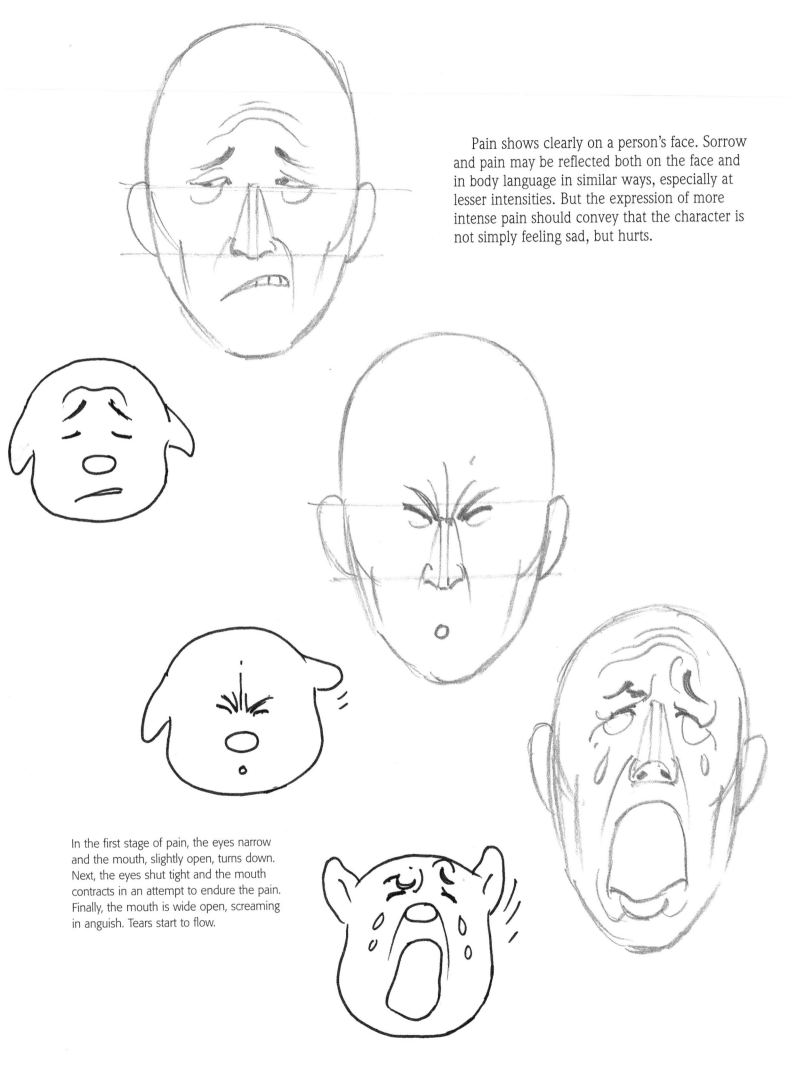

Pain shows clearly on a person's face. Sorrow and pain may be reflected both on the face and in body language in similar ways, especially at lesser intensities. But the expression of more intense pain should convey that the character is not simply feeling sad, but hurts.

In the first stage of pain, the eyes narrow and the mouth, slightly open, turns down. Next, the eyes shut tight and the mouth contracts in an attempt to endure the pain. Finally, the mouth is wide open, screaming in anguish. Tears start to flow.

Combining Facial Expressions and Body Language

Before you start to draw, concentrate on the emotion you intend to illustrate. How intense is it? The terrified character on this page has basically the same features as the frightened character, but he is sweating and his mouth is wide open, perhaps screaming. A few minor line changes can completely alter the graphic intensity of a given emotion.

Concern

Mild trepidation: Uh, oh, is that who I think it is?

Definite worry: It is. It's him!

Fear: Omigod, he's seen me!

Terror: I'm doomed!

You might not agree with the way I have labeled these simple drawings of different types of body language, but I believe they demonstrate an important principle. A few minor line changes can suggest a completely different emotion.

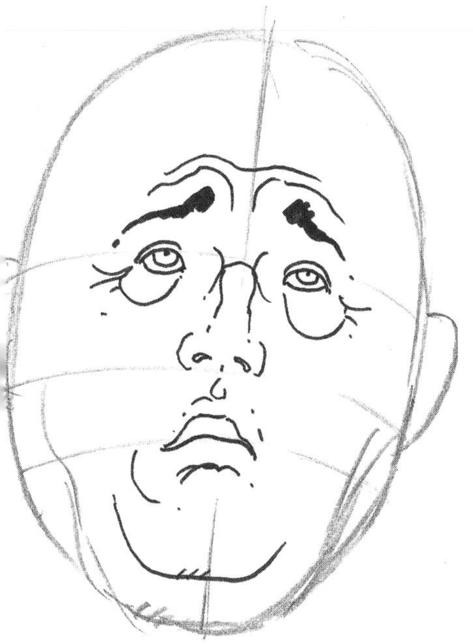

Worry

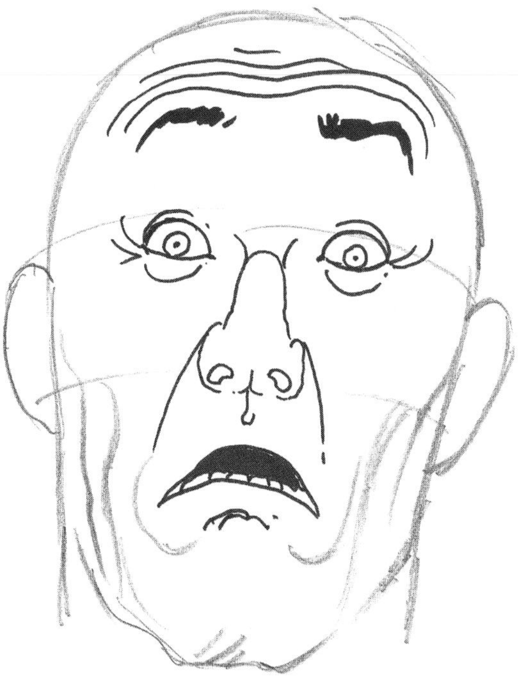

Fear

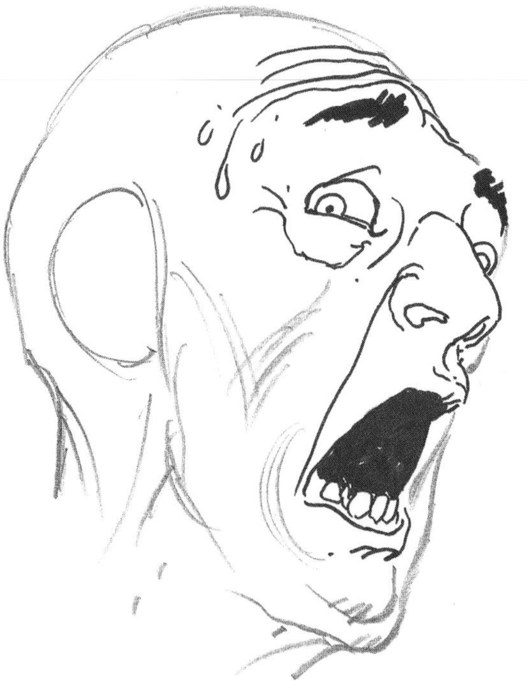

Terror

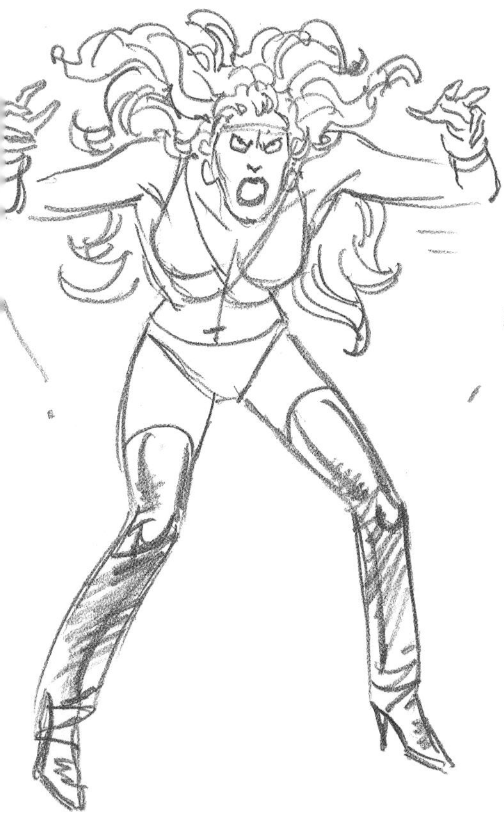

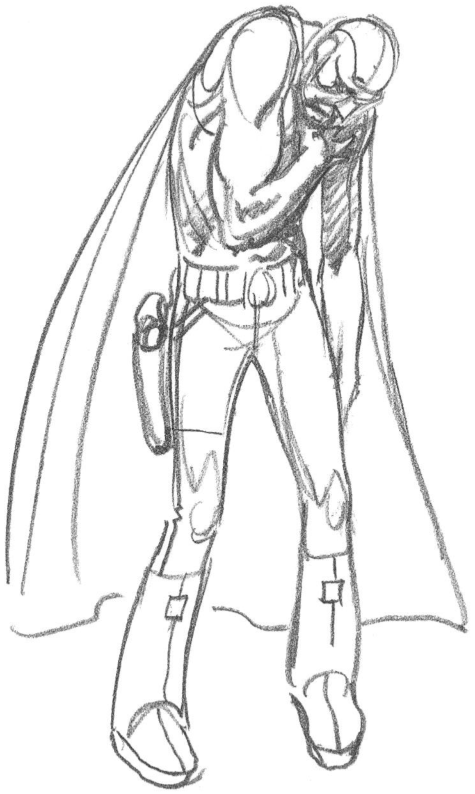

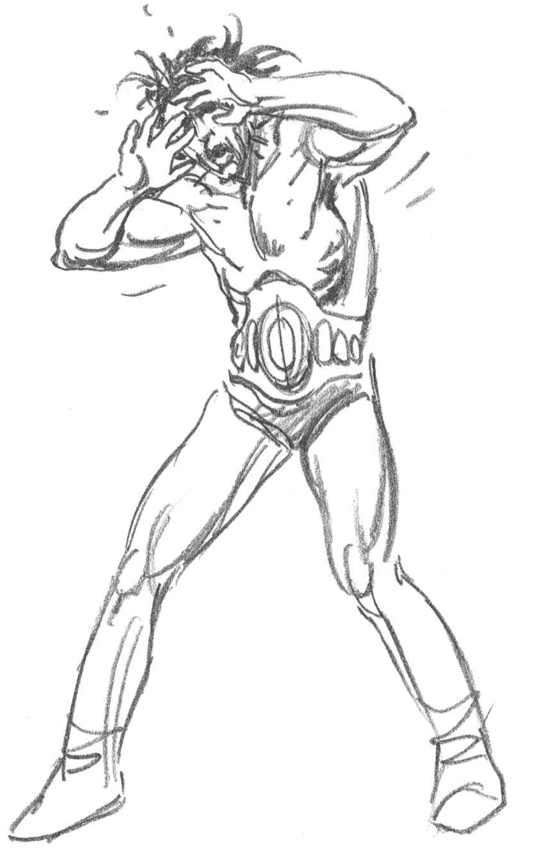

When the coordination between body language and facial expression works, the viewers will believe in the character's emotion.

SUPERHEROES IN ACTION

Even the simplest of cartoon interpretations of characters in motion rely on a thorough knowledge of basic art precepts. To draw characters who convey a sense of action and motion, cartoonists, like film animators, must spend a lot of time observing what happens when real people move.

Practice by finding photographs of people in motion—walking, running, jumping, playing basketball. Place tracing paper over those photos and simplify the figures.

Notice how wrinkles in fabric form at body joints like elbows, shoulders, and knees because of the tension created in the fabric by movement of the body.

Think about how we move. In order to maintain balance, arms and legs must act in coordination. Right leg forward, left arm forward and right arm back. Right leg back, left arm back and right arm forward. We do this automatically when we walk, to maintain balance.

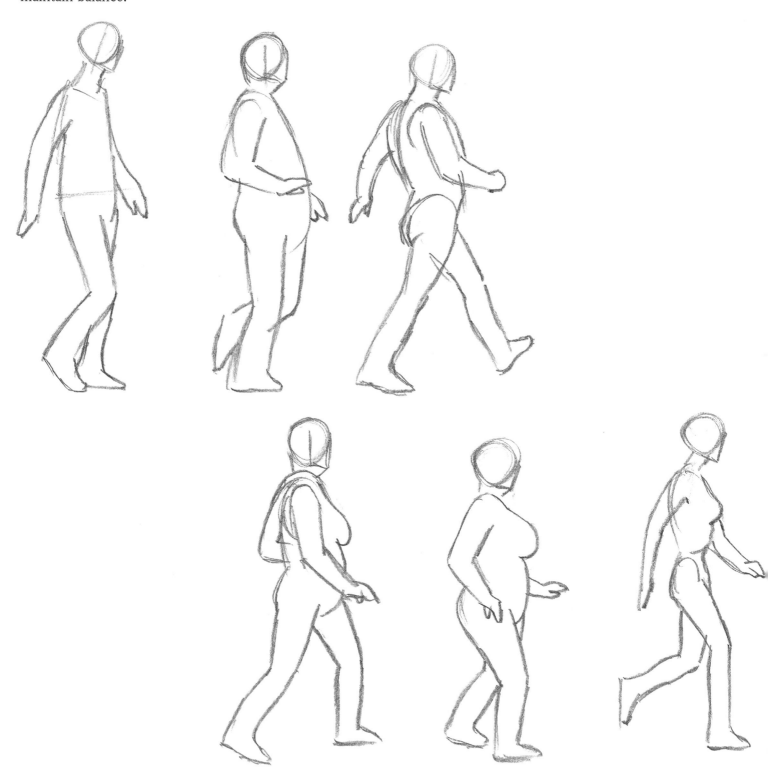

When you are doing your own sketches of superheroes in motion, keep in mind the basic principles of proportion and perspective. Start out with an idea of the shape of the space your moving superhero will inhabit. Build your drawing using the techniques discussed previously: foreshortening, grid lines, circles, and, if you like, tubes.

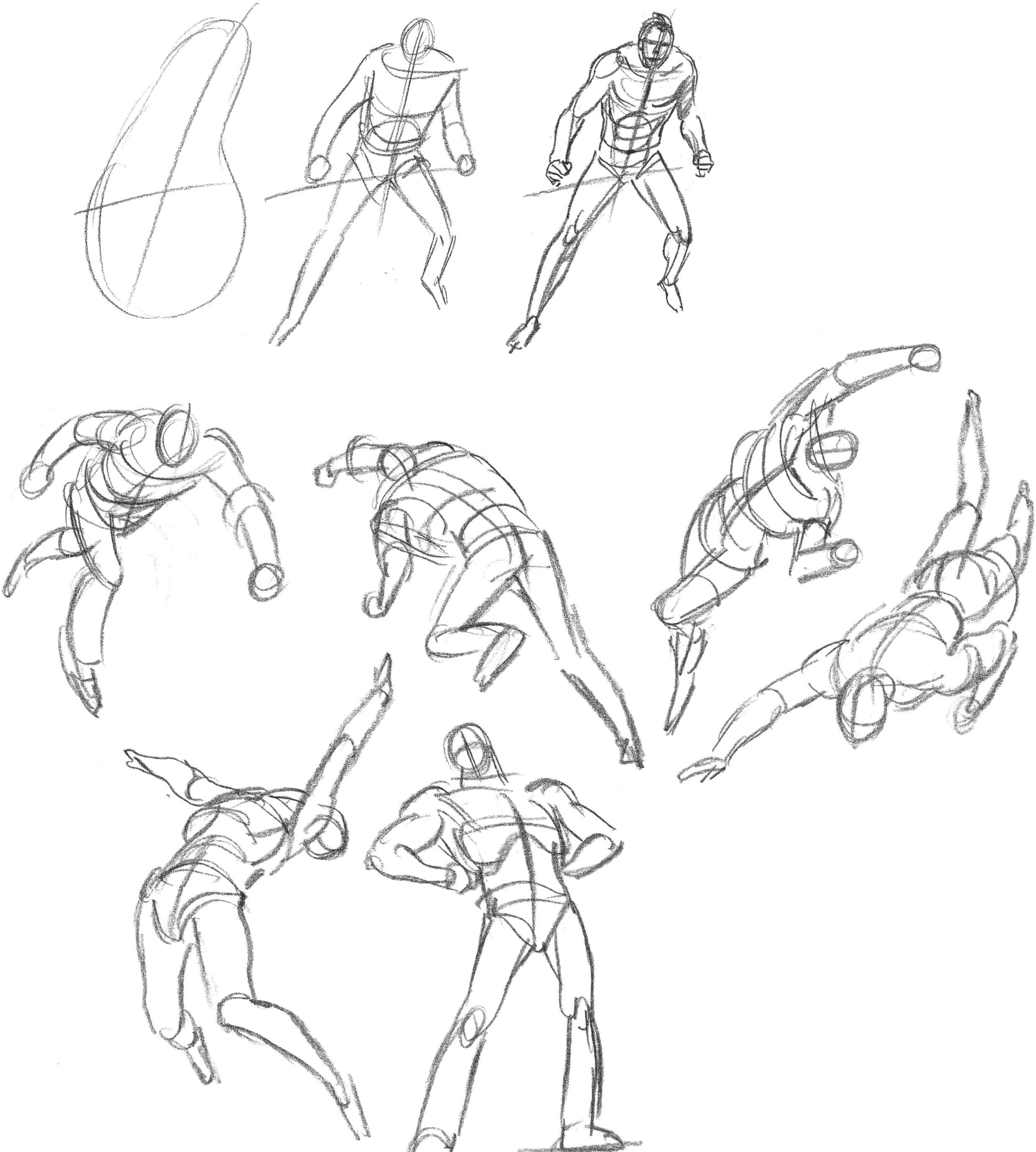

Starting an illustration with details is a common drawing error made by novice cartoonists. How many of you start drawing a face by first drawing an eye or a nose? Or start the drawing of a figure with the head, or an arm or a leg, assuming that you'll get the whole drawing on the paper? And how many times have you run out of space for a hand or a foot? Starting with details can be even more of a disaster when you are trying to draw an action figure.

Here's another good reason for doing rough sketches of the space your character will occupy before drawing in details. If you end up by really liking the detailed part of your drawing even though it doesn't "work" as part of the total composition, you may be reluctant to erase and start over. You may be afraid that if you lose your cool details, you will not recapture the essence of your character. It is fears like that which inhibit learning and prevent improvement. Once the basic figure is blocked into the right space, you can add the details—and the costume.

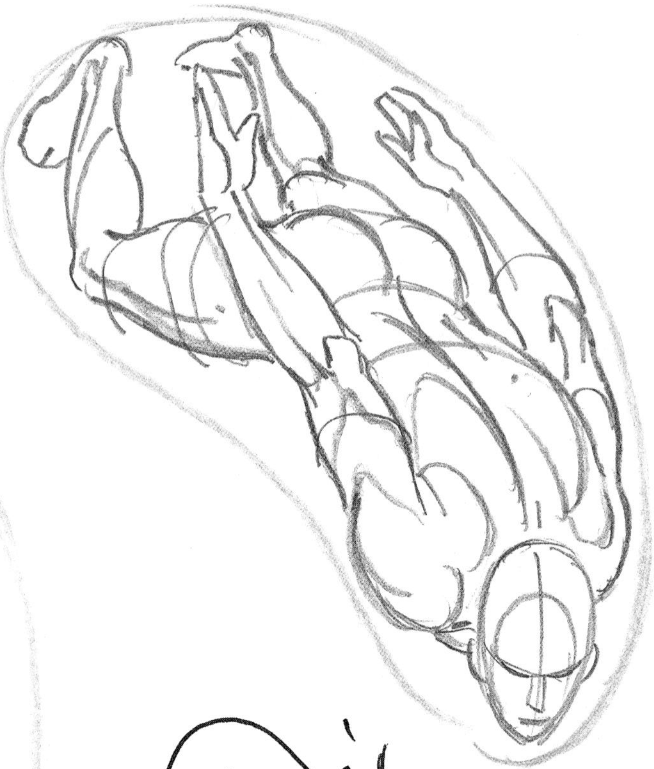

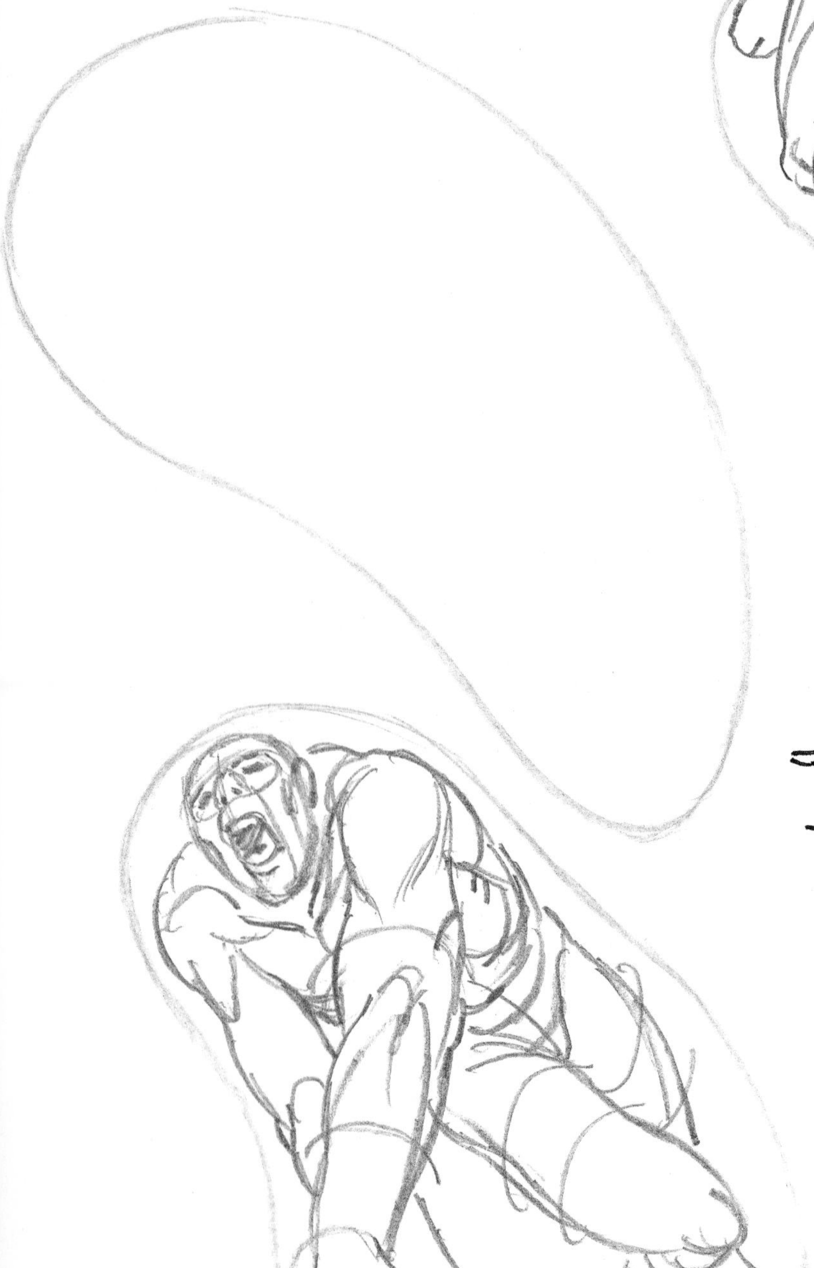

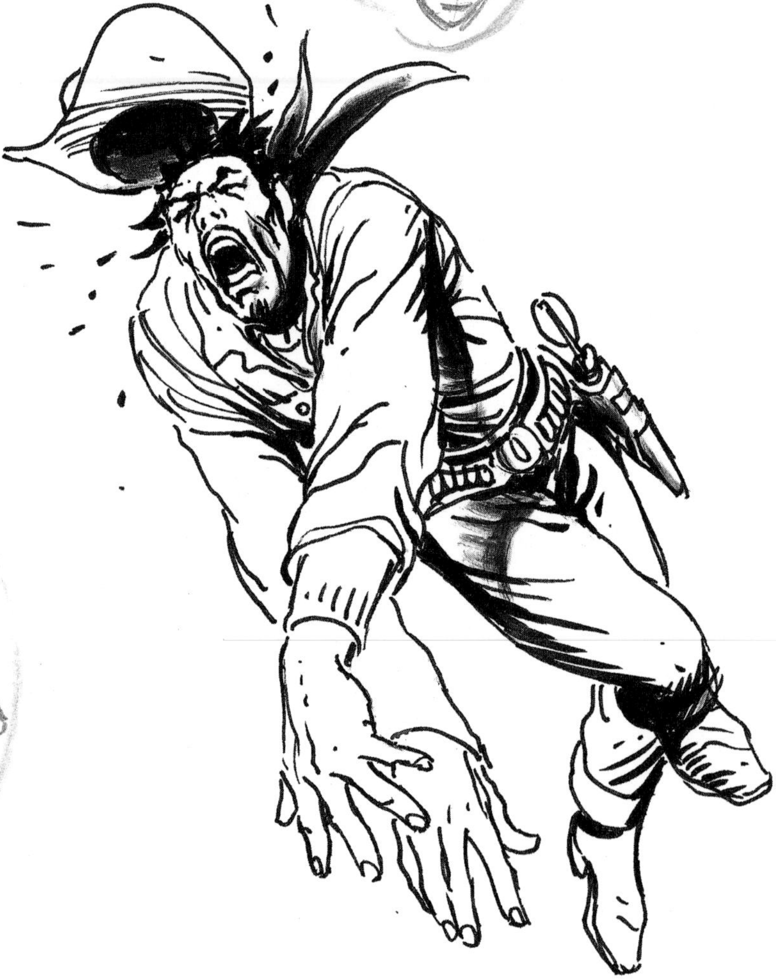

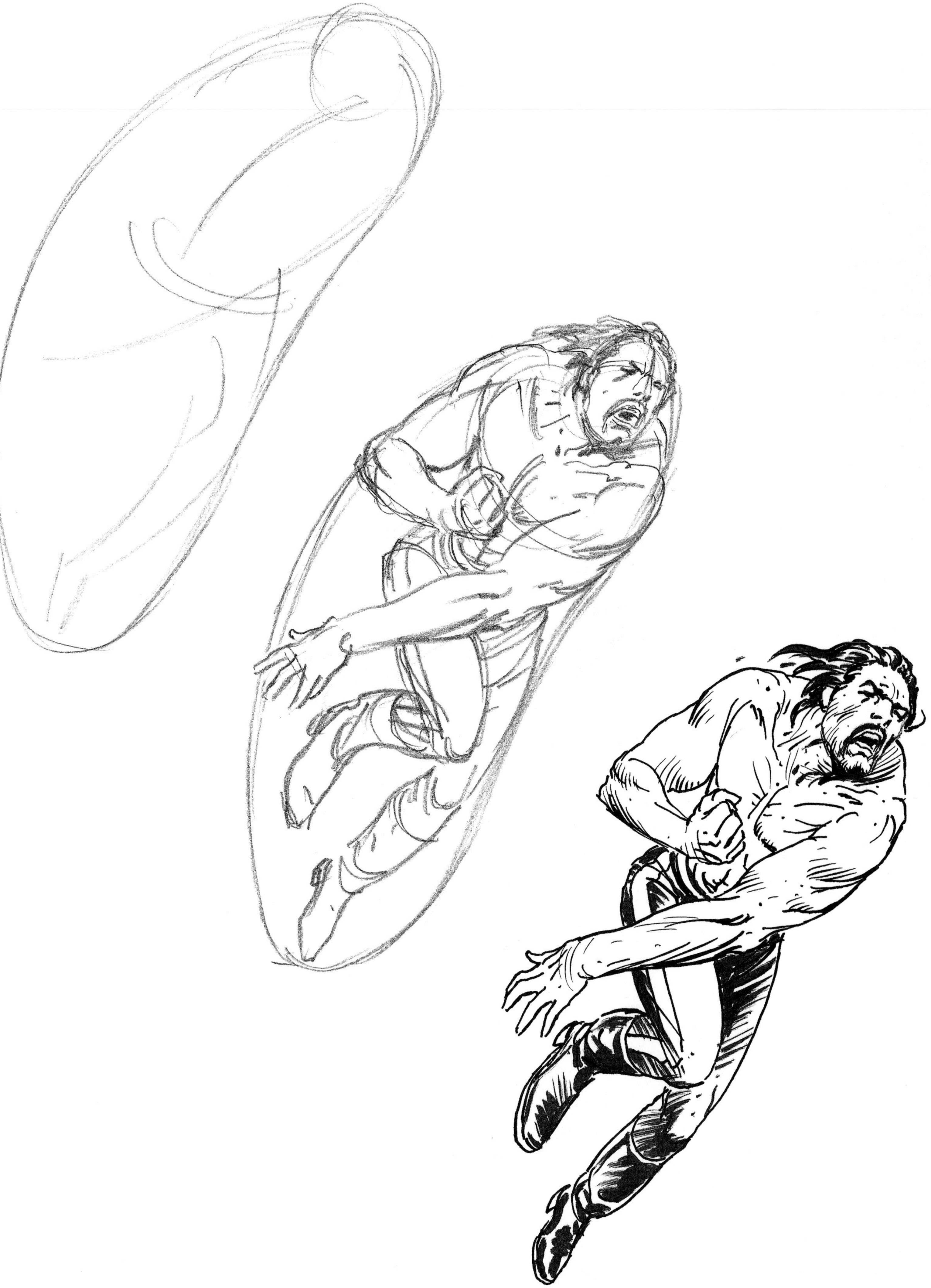

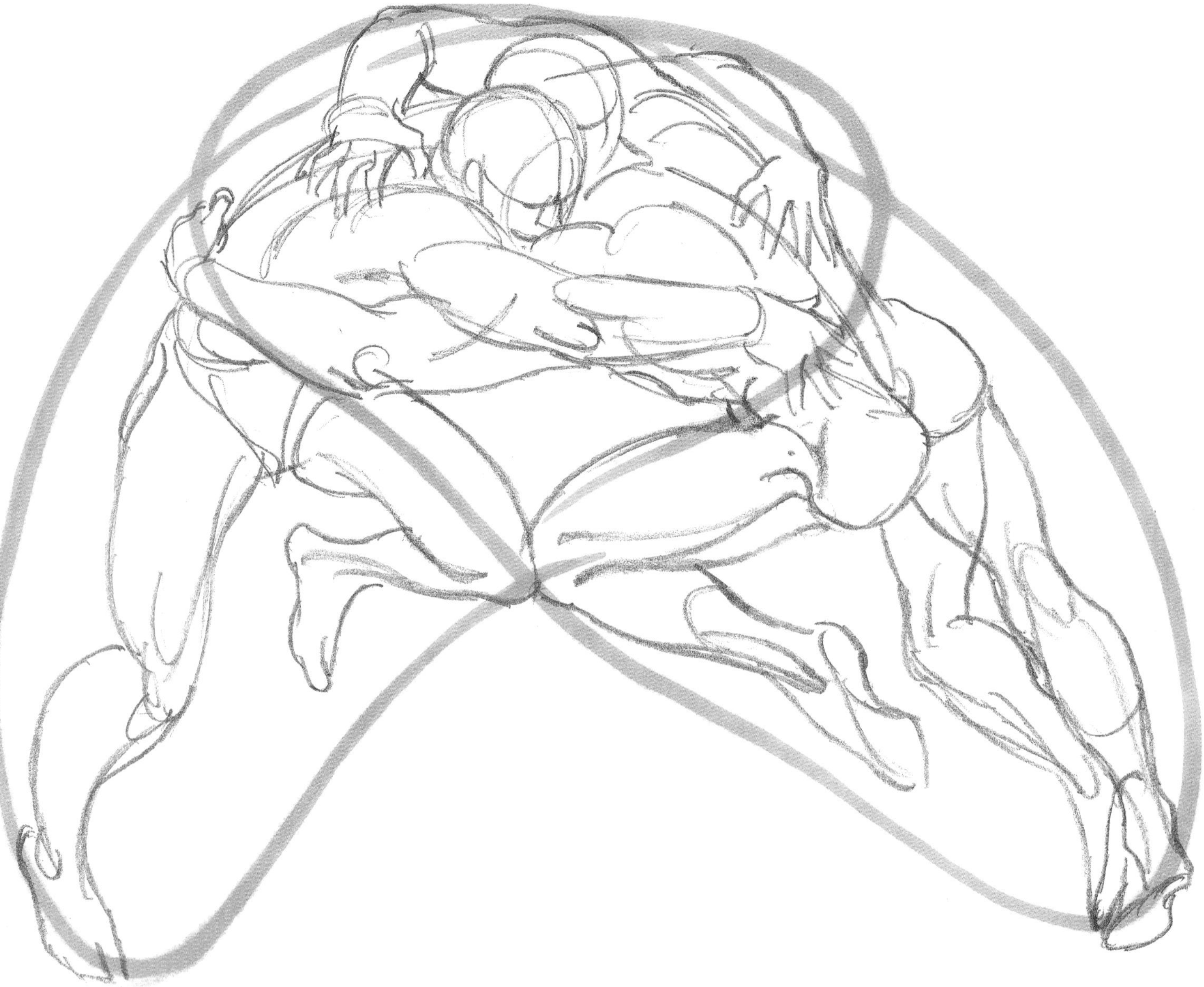

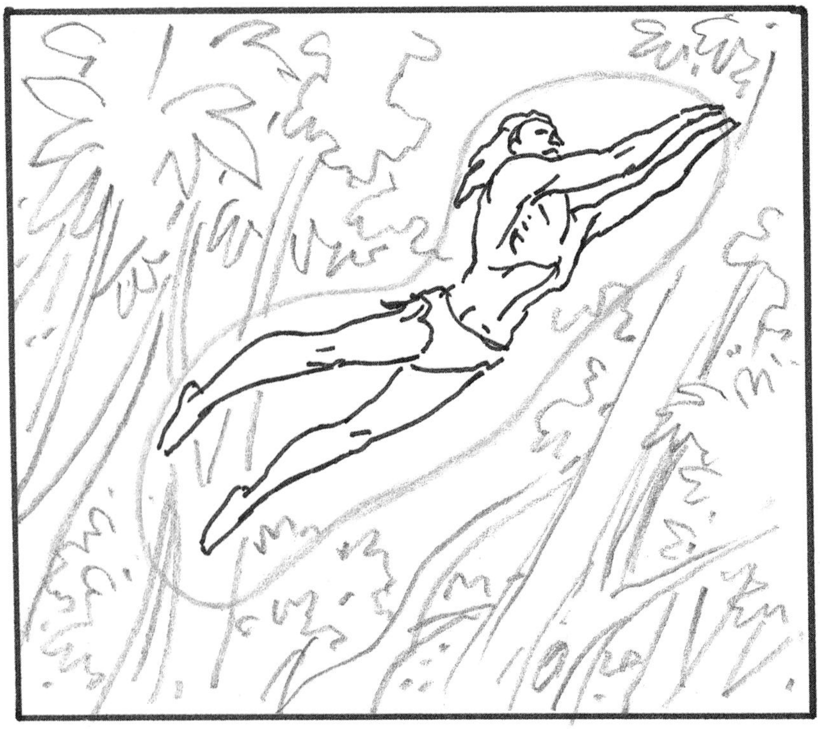

Starting your drawings of figures in action with amorphous shapes works not only for single figures, but for two or more figures interacting and for figures within a panel.

In both of the sequences shown on the opposite page, I planned and roughed in the composition before adding any details. The cartoonist's goal is to design every panel to enable the reader audience to follow the story. If any part of a figure is left out, or if any background information necessary for understanding the action is not included, the panel will lack impact and may even be confusing.

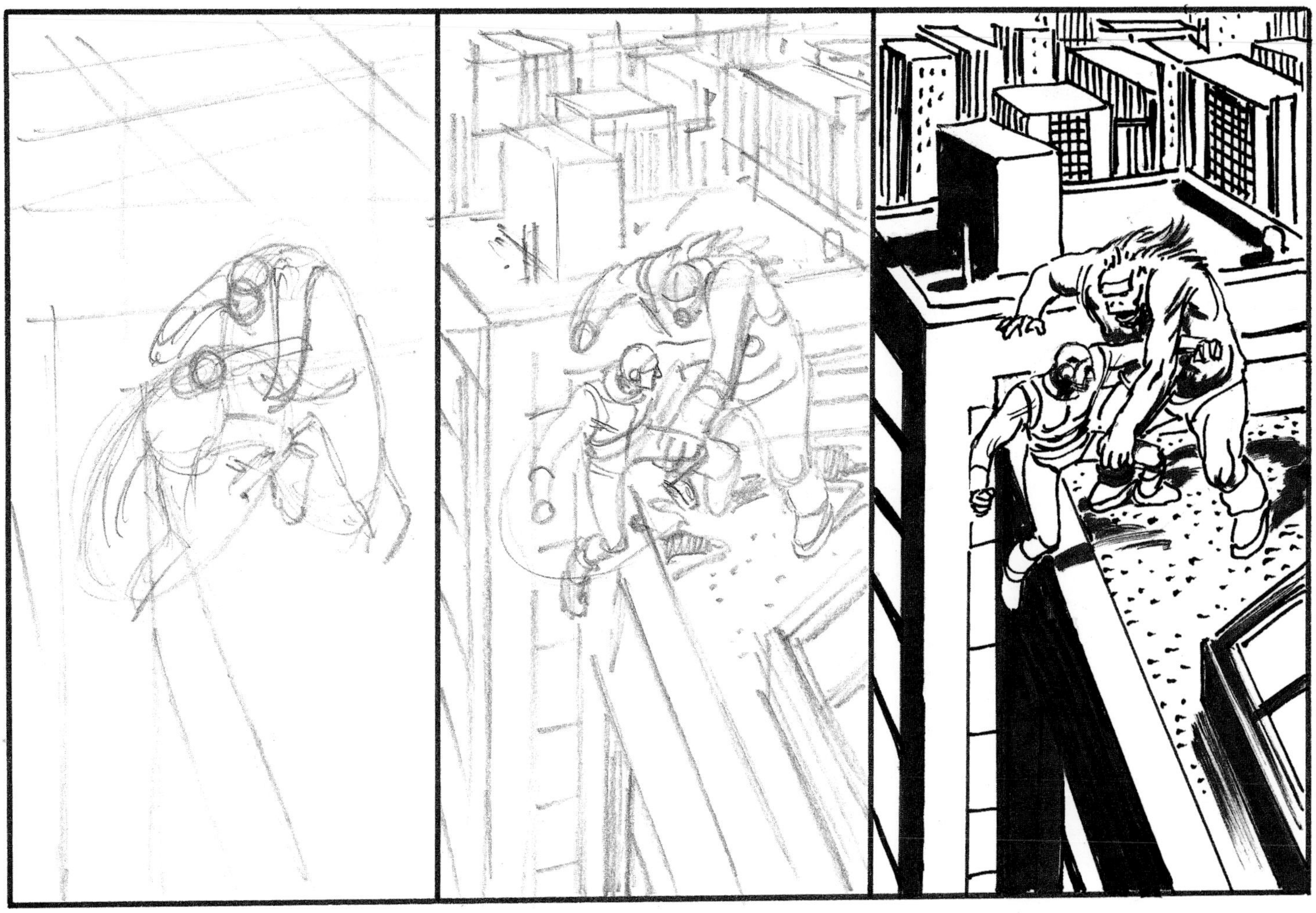

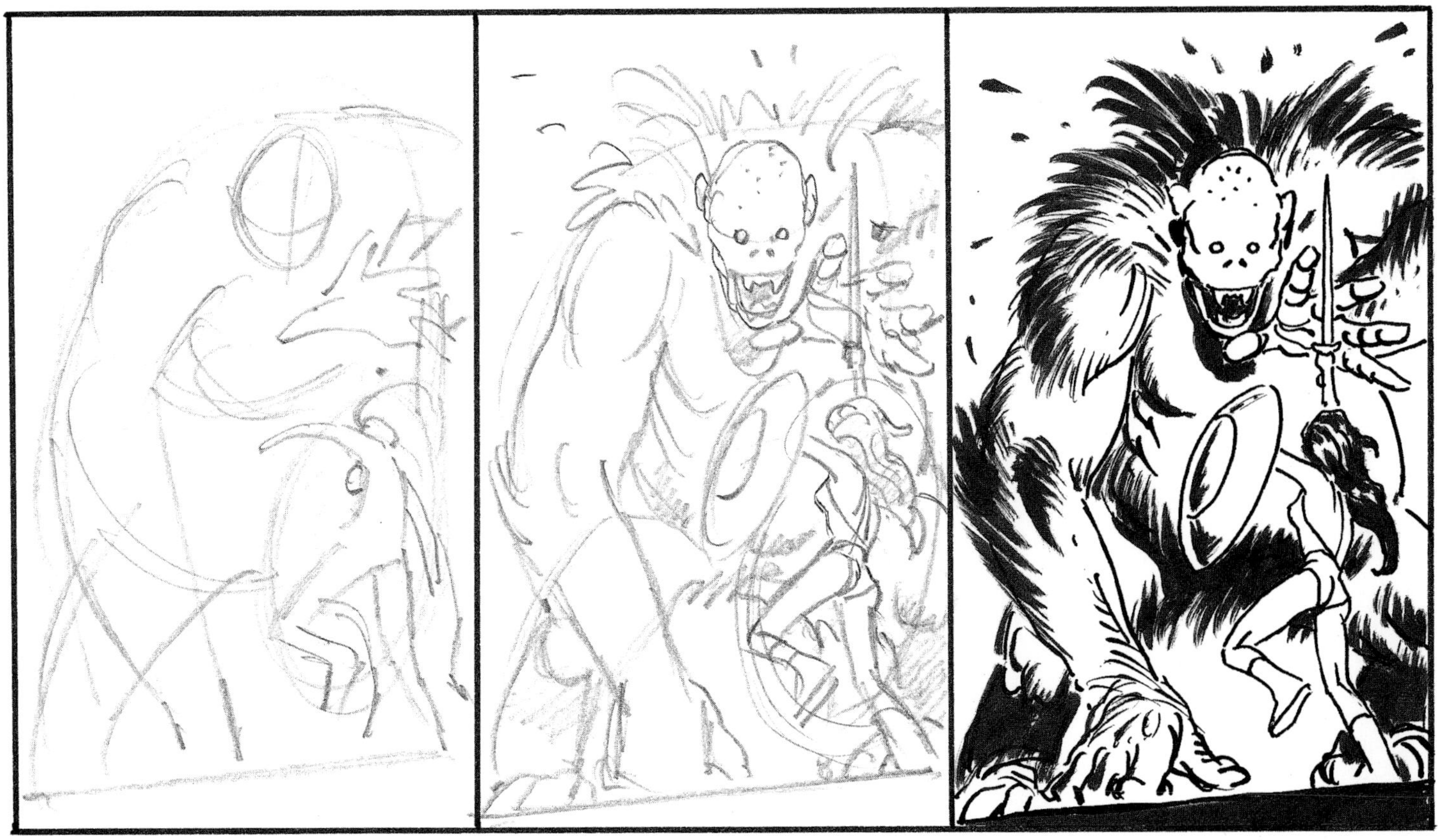

CREATING CHARACTERS WITH STYLE

Now that you've got some of the basics down, you're ready to create your own gallery of superheroes—in your own drawing style. Using the characters in this section as a starting point, give free rein to your imagination. Come up with some far-out concepts, collect your references, and start drawing!

The earliest superheroes had impenetrable skin and enormous strength. Skin-tight costumes were designed to show oversize muscles to advantage, and when a cape was part of the outfit, the character usually had the ability to fly. Fourteen years after the comic book debut of superhero number one, the first superheroine joined the growing number of action heroes with prodigious powers.

Many superheroes, both old and new, got their strange powers as a result of scientific experimentation gone awry. They may have the ability to run at incredible speed, to fly, to breathe underwater, or to stretch their super-elastic bodies around a city block. Characters who periodically turn into giant nonhuman alter egos with superpowers often look more like villains than heros.

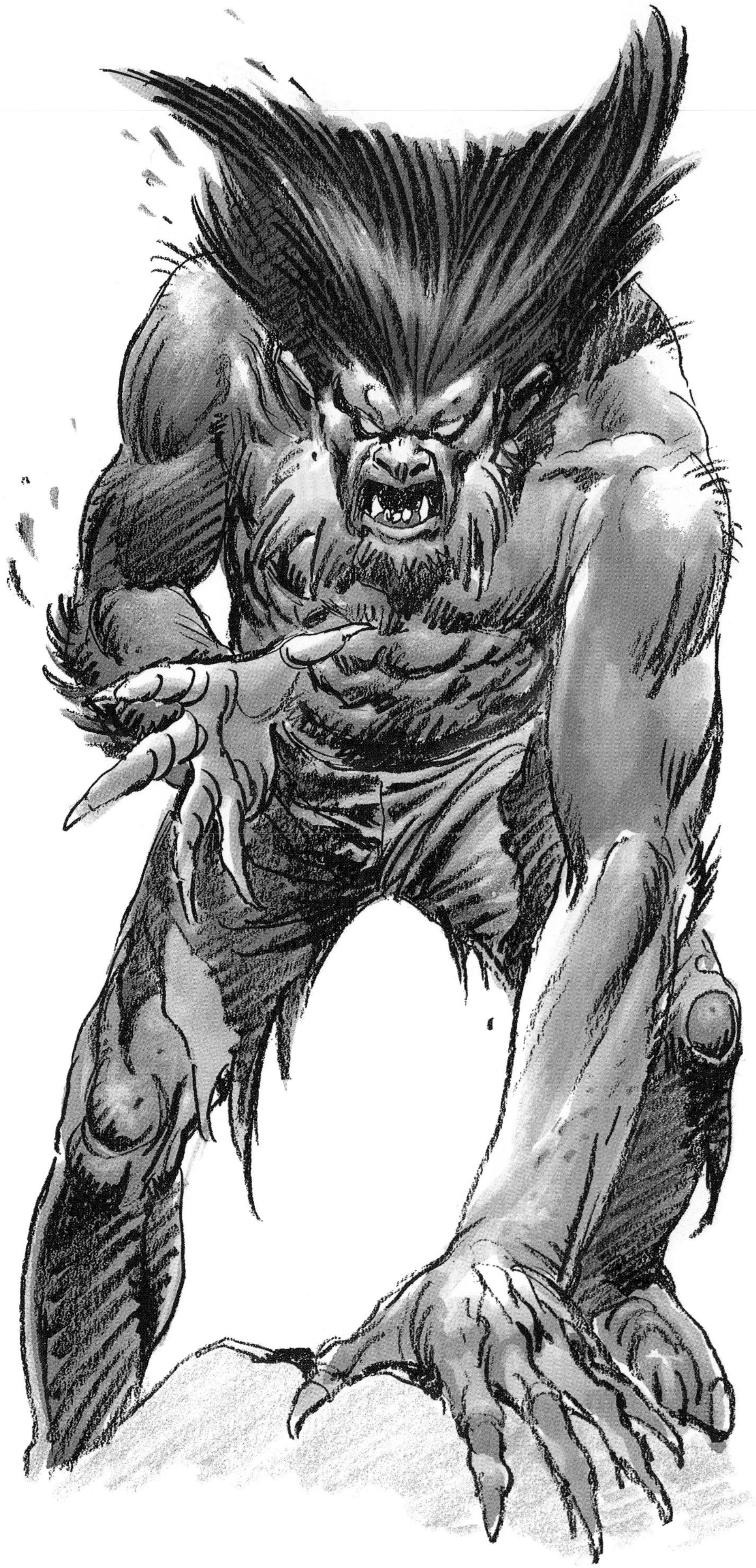

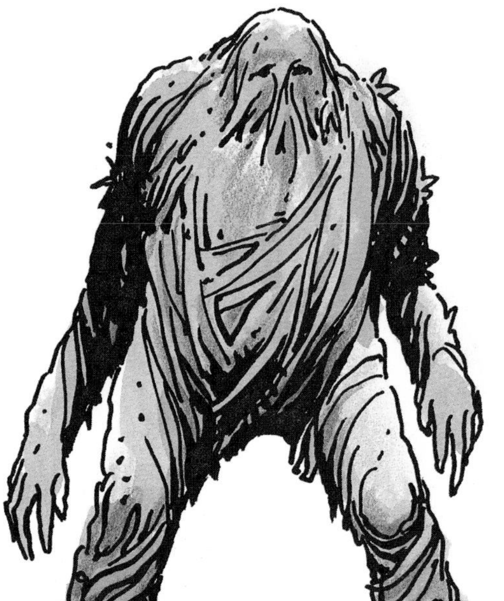

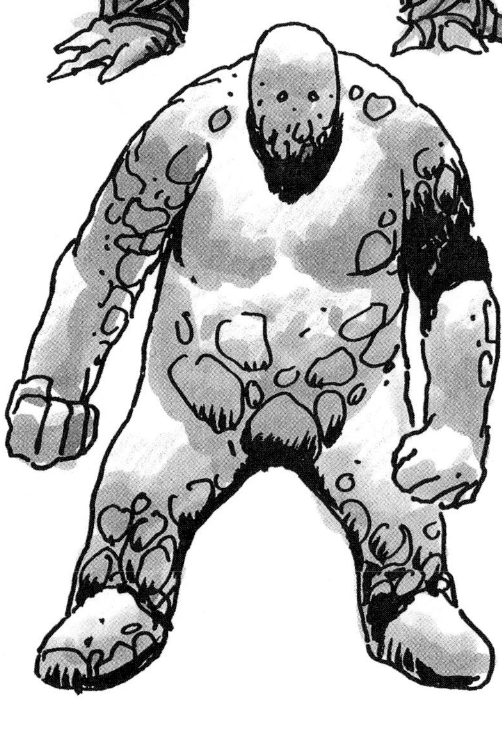

APPRECIATING STYLE

There are as many varieties of cartoon styles as there are cartoonists. In fact, no two cartoonists draw exactly the same way, even when one is trying to copy another. The term *style* refers to how we graphically interpret what we see and imagine. A cartoonist's style is always changing and evolving.

All styles are valid, but a person's preference for one style over another is quite subjective. And even if you like the way a comic strip is drawn, you may not like the way the story is told. Style, character, and story—all are essential for creating a successful superhero series.

The creators of comic book superheroes consistently attempt to outdistance the ideas of science fiction writers. Some of the more successful superheroes have not made their debut in comic books at all, but in animated films and computer games. The envelope is being pushed further and further. But no matter how far-fetched the character, if the drawing is believable the character will be believable.

Manga, which refers to Japanese comic book stories and art, and *anime,* animated films featuring many of the same characters and appealing drawing styles found in manga, are extremely popular all over the world. But the legions of kids and adults who have embraced manga are responding not simply to excellence of drawing style, but to the well-crafted stories featuring clearly defined characters whose personalities develop over time.

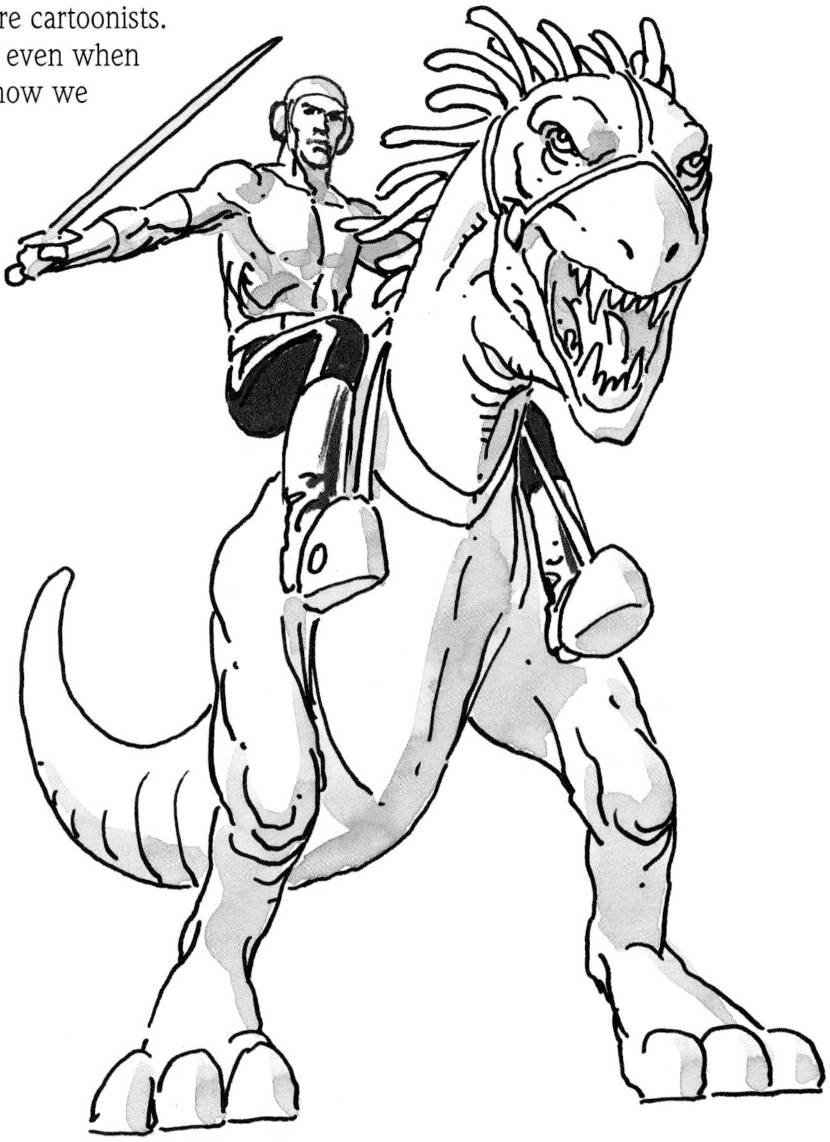

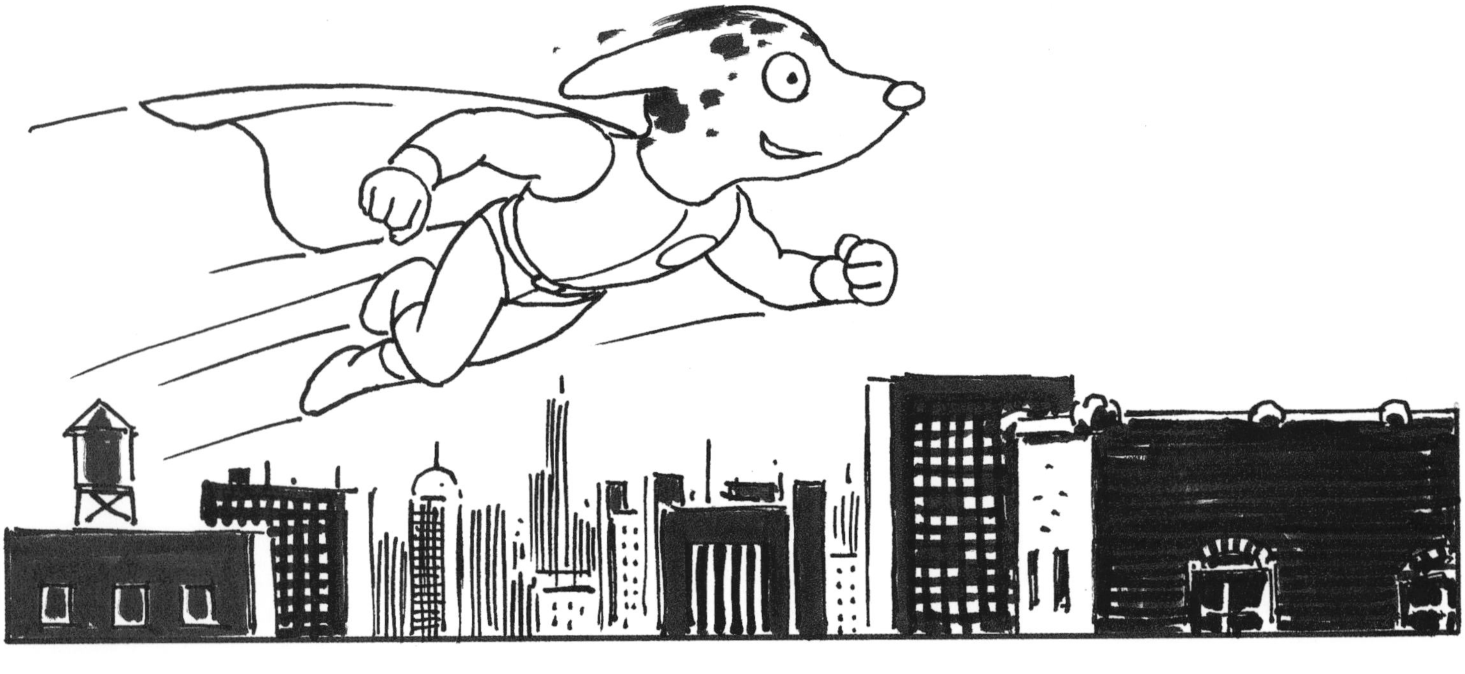

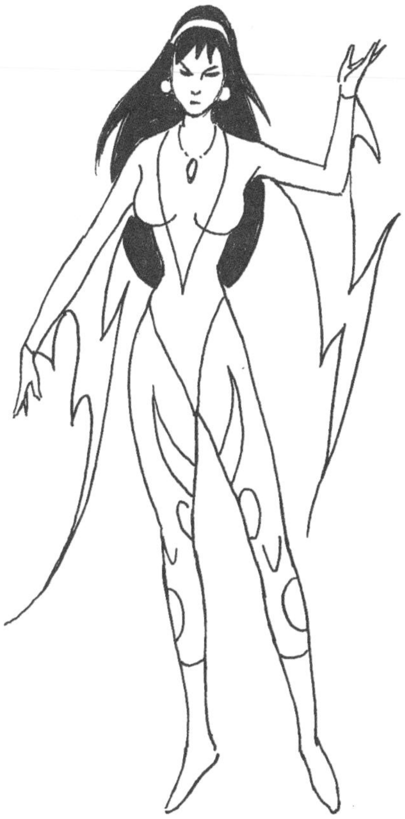

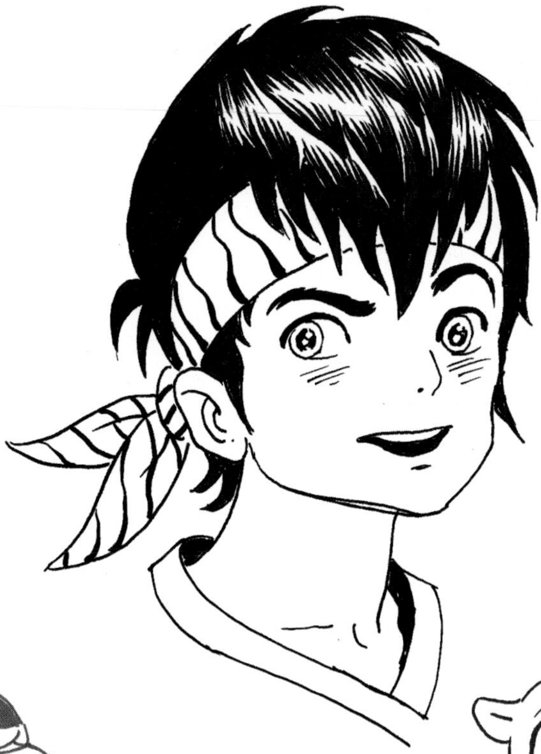

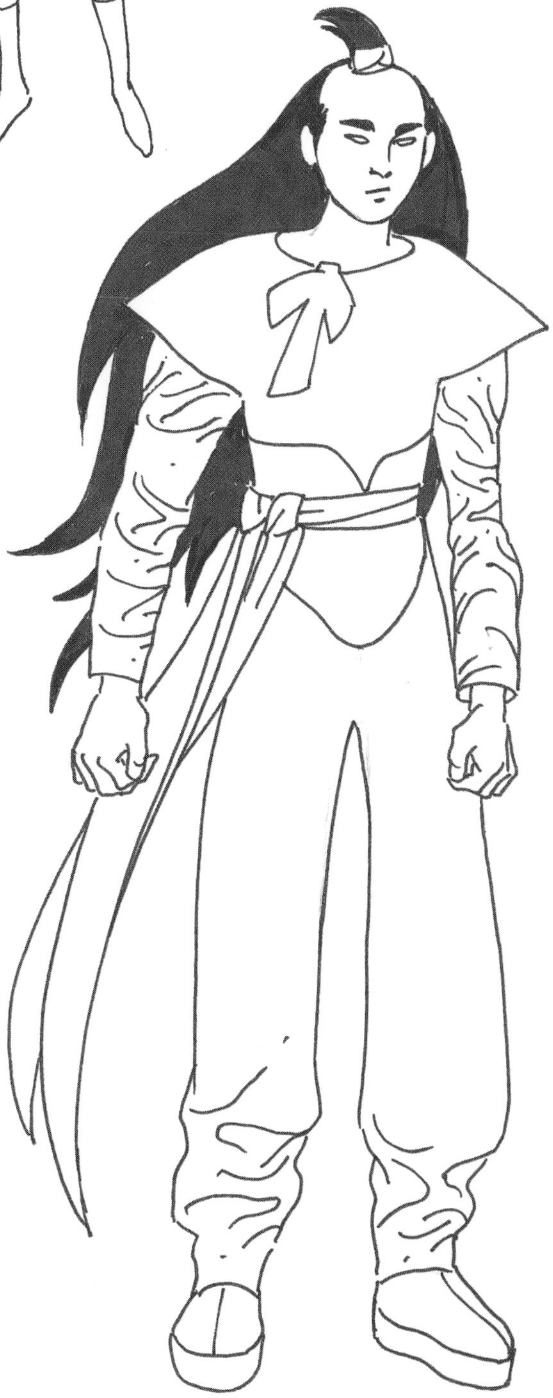

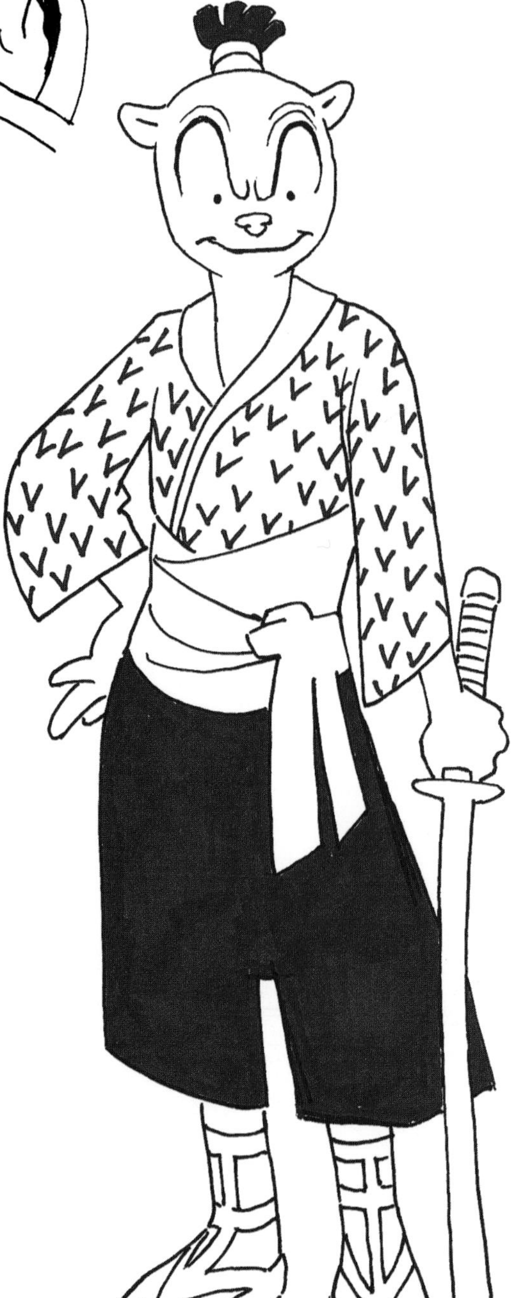

GETTING AGES RIGHT

One way to vary your cast of superhero characters is to create stories involving people of different ages. If you follow a few simple rules, it's not difficult to draw infants, teenagers, and senior citizens—all of whom look their age.

As human beings, both male and female, progress from infancy to adulthood to old age, the dome of the skull undergoes surprisingly little growth. The most dramatic changes occur between eyes and chin. As the teeth come in, the jaw elongates and increases in mass, and the proportion of the head from eyes to chin increases dramatically. At the same time, the nose becomes longer and broader.

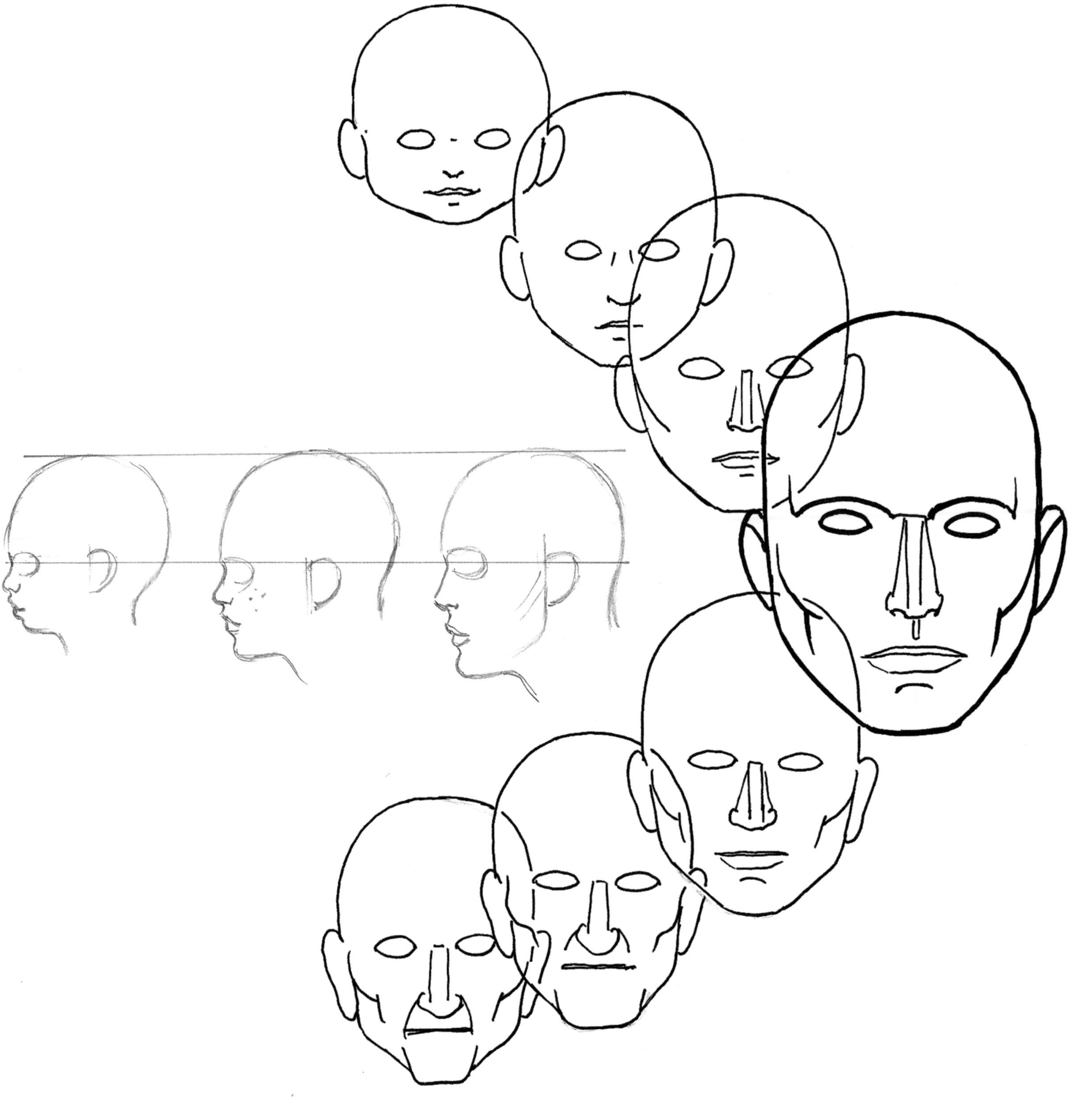

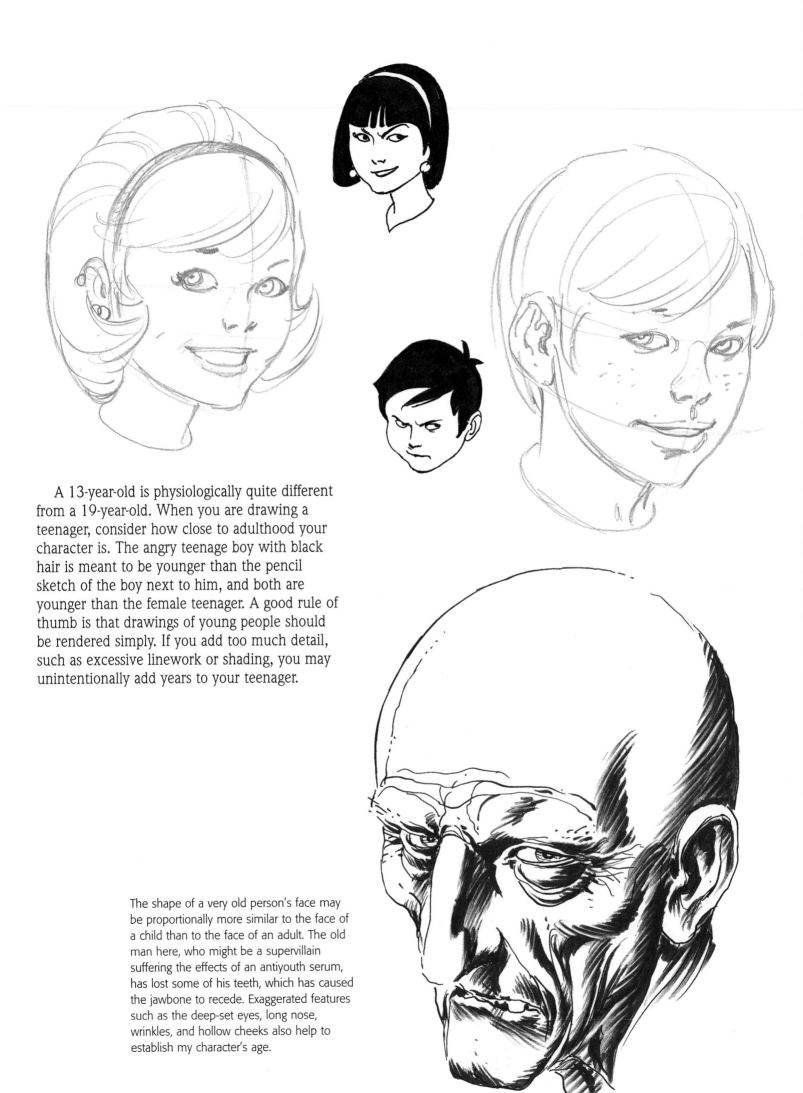

A 13-year-old is physiologically quite different from a 19-year-old. When you are drawing a teenager, consider how close to adulthood your character is. The angry teenage boy with black hair is meant to be younger than the pencil sketch of the boy next to him, and both are younger than the female teenager. A good rule of thumb is that drawings of young people should be rendered simply. If you add too much detail, such as excessive linework or shading, you may unintentionally add years to your teenager.

The shape of a very old person's face may be proportionally more similar to the face of a child than to the face of an adult. The old man here, who might be a supervillain suffering the effects of an antiyouth serum, has lost some of his teeth, which has caused the jawbone to recede. Exaggerated features such as the deep-set eyes, long nose, wrinkles, and hollow cheeks also help to establish my character's age.

AVOIDING STEREOTYPES: CREATING CHARACTERS WHO ARE DIFFERENT

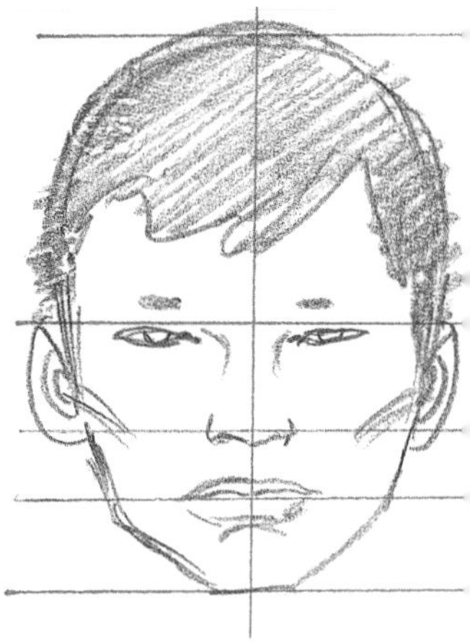

Most comic book superheroes are young, handsome (or beautiful), clean-cut, and physically perfect. Consider creating characters who are older, more experienced and worldly, who can be identified as father (or uncle) figures. As aunts or older sisters. The development of this type of superhero is an exercise in sensitivity. The character cannot be too young or too old. Attractive but not spectacularly beautiful. Think about their personalities. Perhaps they are more emphathetic, less self-centered than younger characters. They are likely to be more intense. Usually, the mature superhero has dark hair (the better to contrast with those bits of gray). The man may have a moustache, even a goatee; the mature superheroine is likely to have close-cropped hair, not long, flowing locks halfway down her back.

Once you've decided on what you want your characters to look like, draw them from many different angles, so you become well acquainted with them. Focus on the features which make them unique.

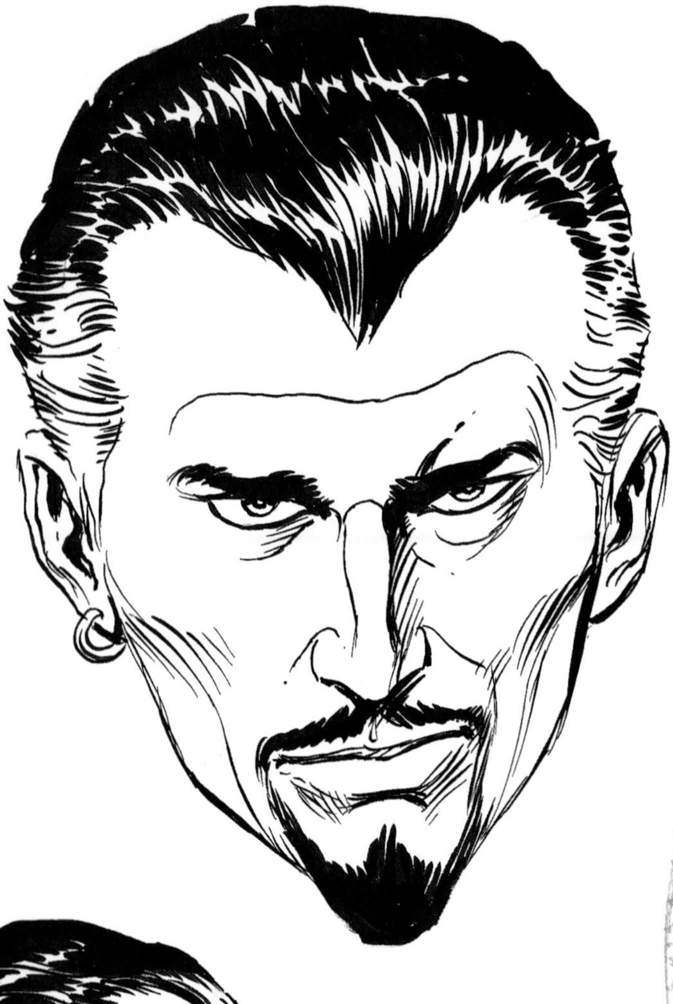

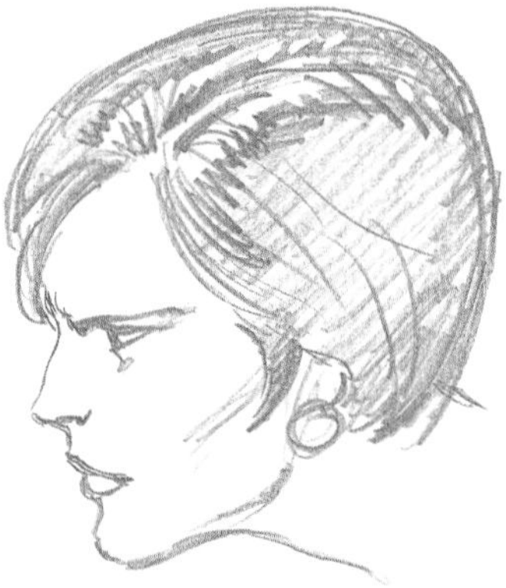

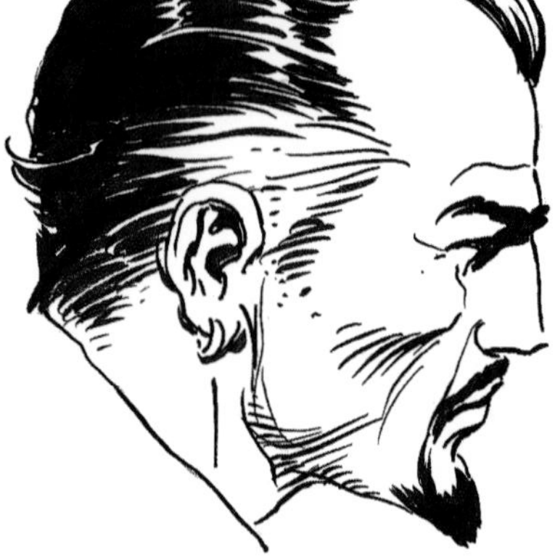

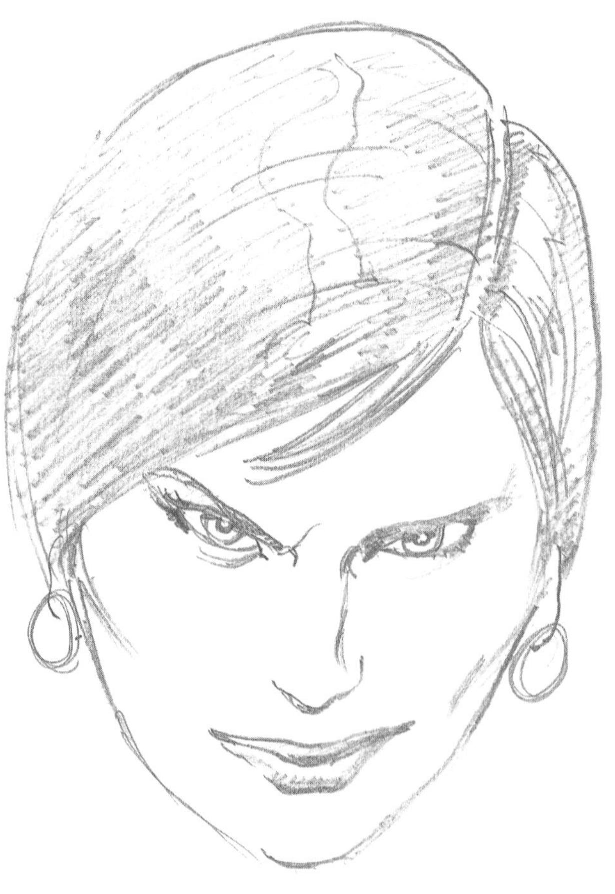

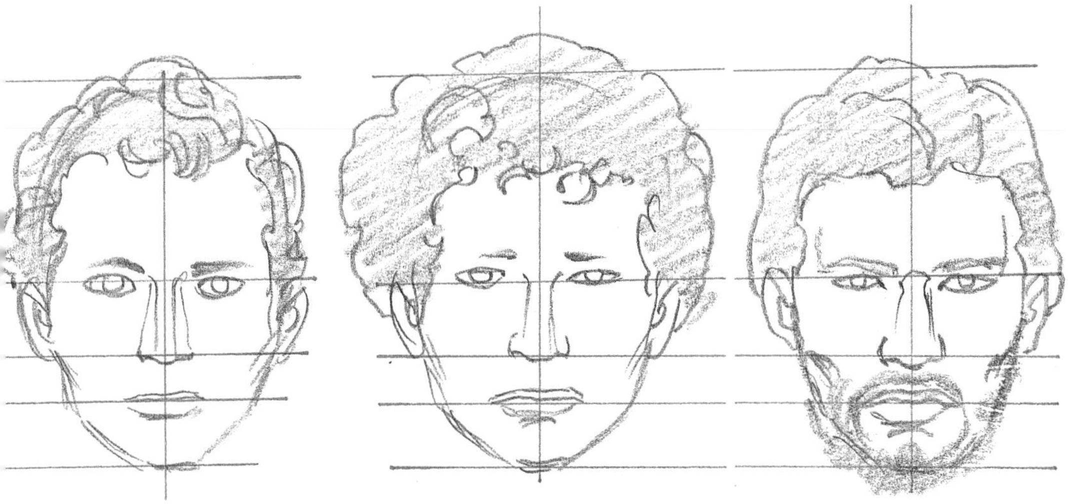

Once upon a time, the pages of U.S. comic books of the hero and superhero variety were populated mainly by white males. No longer. Superheroines abound, as do male and female superheroes of many different ethnic types. And it is no longer acceptable to draw a black character by coloring a typically white European face brown, or an Asian character by penciling in exaggeratedly slanted eyes, then coloring the whole face yellow.

If you decide to draw characters of different ethnic backgrounds—and you should, since it will make your stories more interesting—do your homework. Use your powers of observation. Collect photographs. Sketch from life. Think difference!

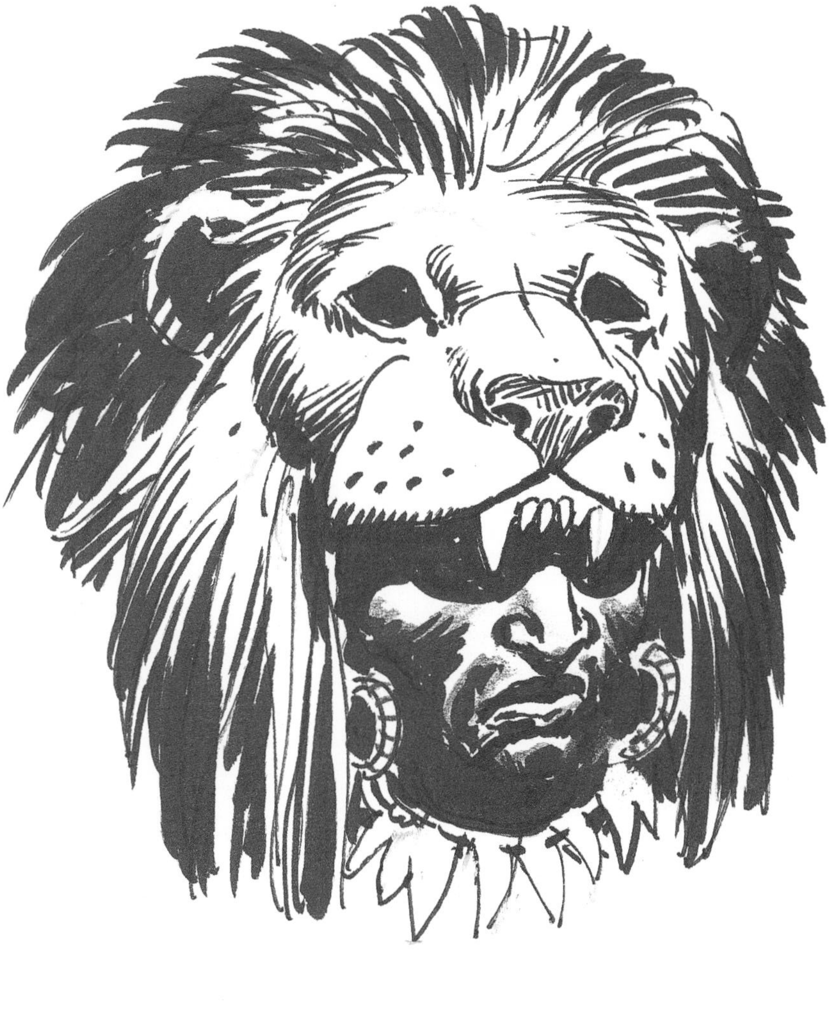

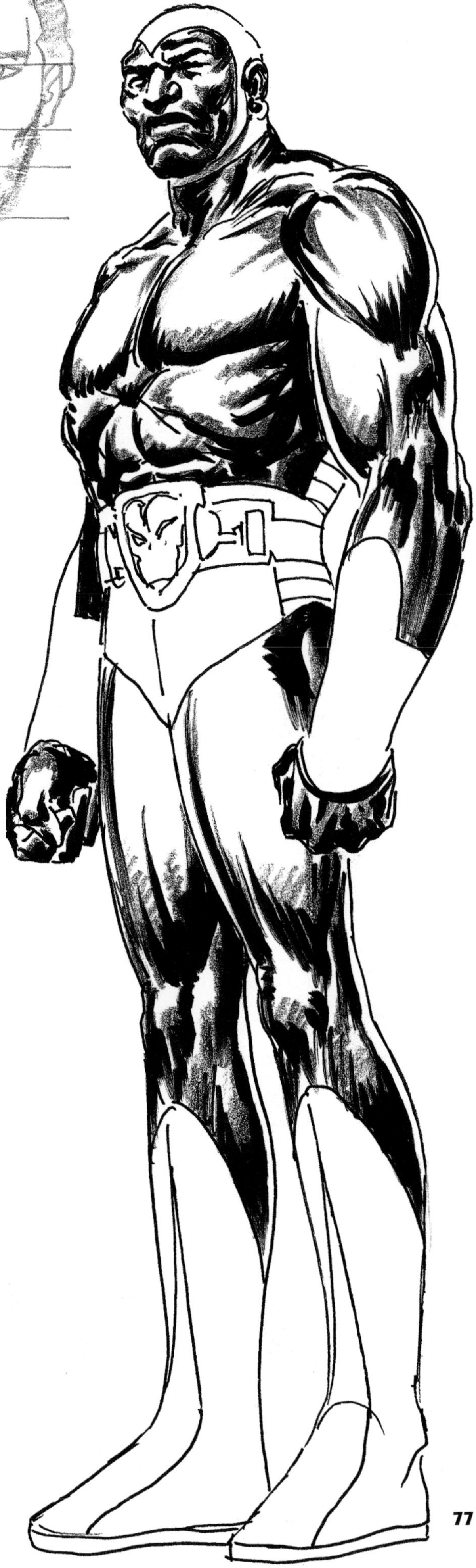

ANIMAL, MINERAL, VEGETABLE, OR . . . ?

Superheroes have been depicted in almost every imaginable guise other than human, and made of almost every imaginable material: vegetable matter, minerals, plastic and electronic circuits, or any combination of these. The artist's ability to be convincing with these representations is dependent on knowledge, research, and (again) pictorial reference.

As you look at the characters on the next few pages, don't forget that audience acceptance of tomorrow's superheroes depends not only on how good they would look as posters but also on how well they play in a story context. So use these drawings as inspiration for your own ideas, but try always to imagine your character inhabiting a believable world, playing a role in a believable story.

A superhero composed of ice must look the part. The cartoonist needs to consider if (and how) ice crystals would form around eyes and nose. Where would icicles appear? The surface of an iceman's skin would not be soft and pliable, but hard and crystalline.

Perhaps our superhero has been encased in ice for millennia. The ice block, too, must be credible. Reflections indicate a transparent solid. Variable translucence shows the effect of water freezing.

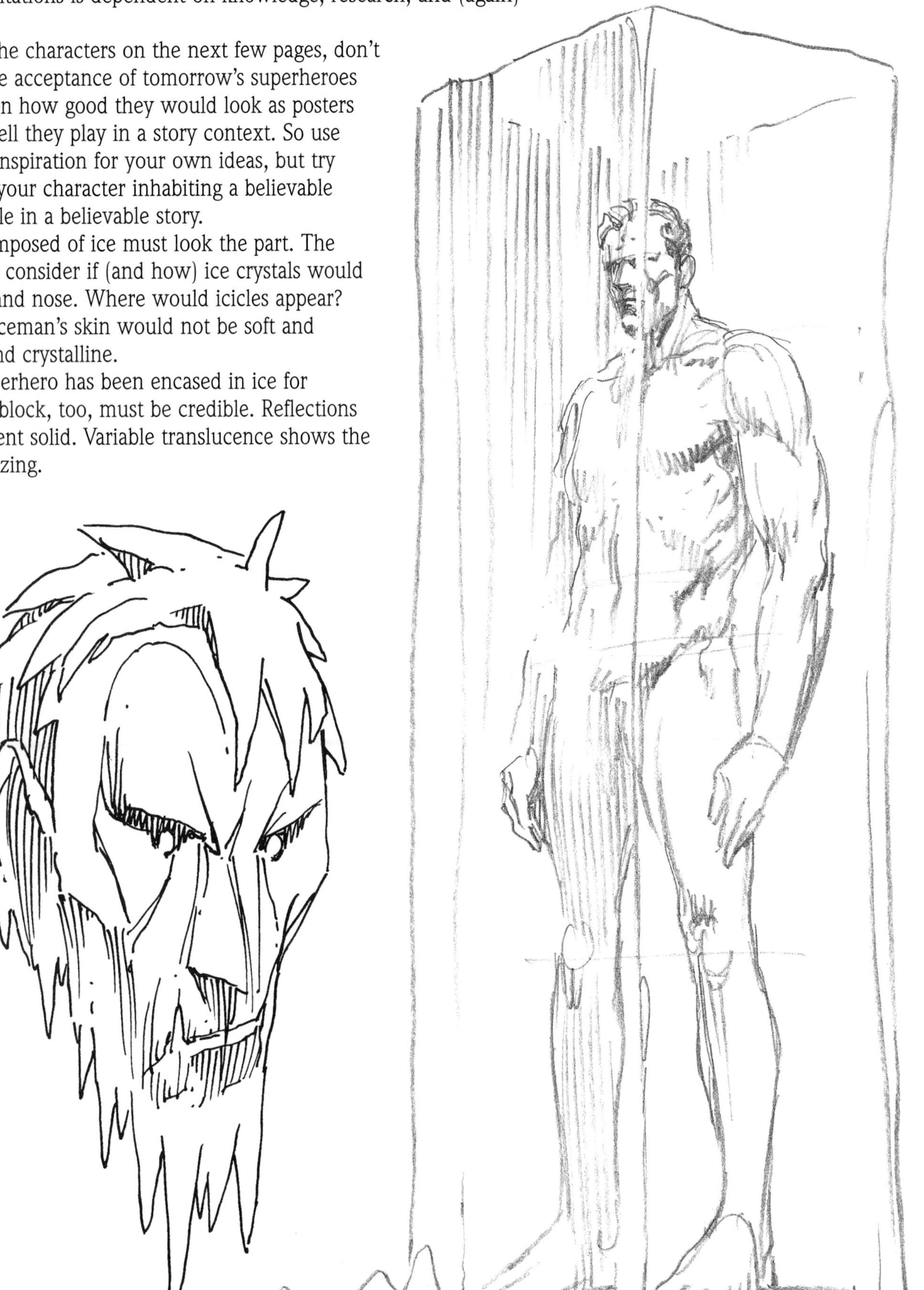

Your superhero can be an android, a robot, a ghost, or any out-of-this world concept your fertile imagination comes up with.

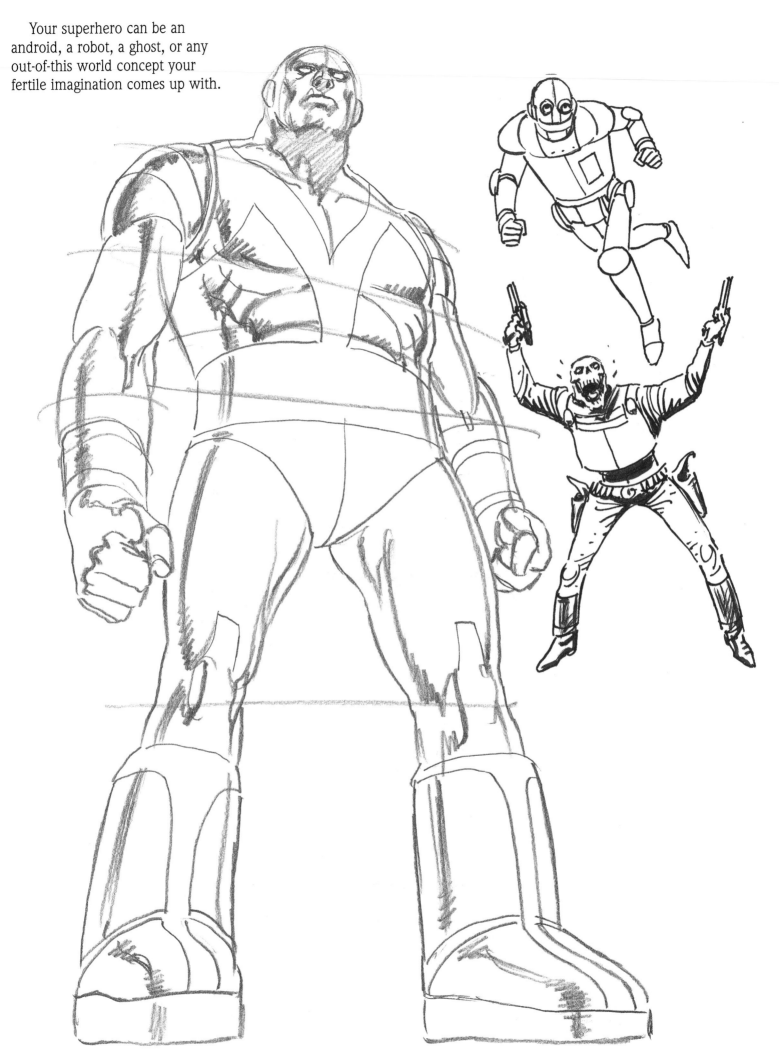

CYBORGS

Many of the superheroes featured in contemporary comic books are a physiological combination of human and mechanical parts. A human brain with a robotic body. Or a human body with a mechanical arm, forged in a supersecret laboratory, with the potential power of a nuclear weapon. These are cyborgs, and the cartoonist should have some knowledge of science and mechanics in order to give the impression that the robotic contraptions really work.

The female cyborg. Now there's a subject that should unleash any comic book or fantasy artist's creative imagination. Whatever mechanical or robotic contrivances you decide to bestow on your female cyborg, she should be quintessentially feminine and at the same time convey a sense of primal menace. Putting an insect- or medusa-like head on her may be just the added dimension you need to create an unforgettable character.

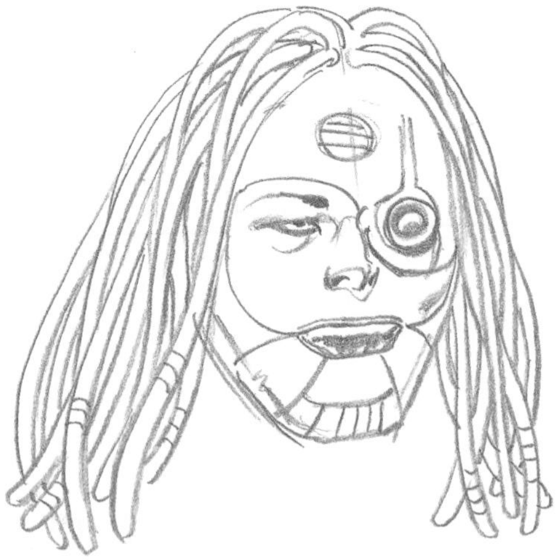

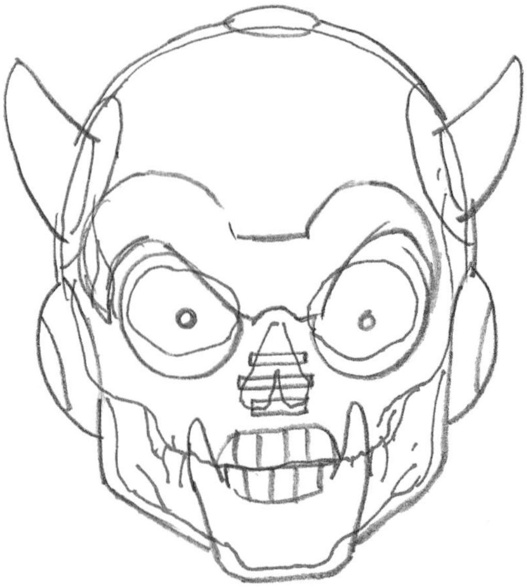

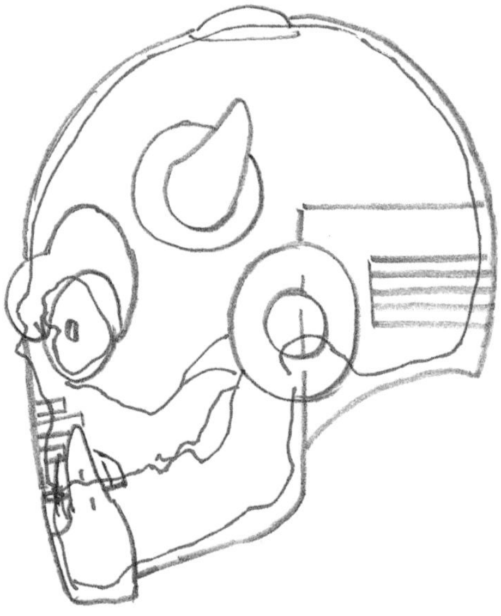

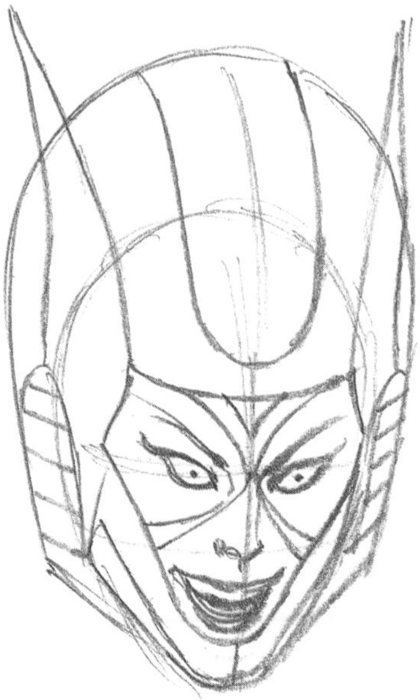

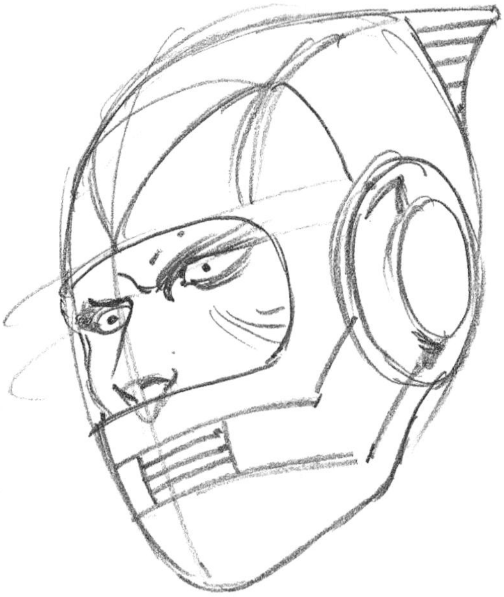

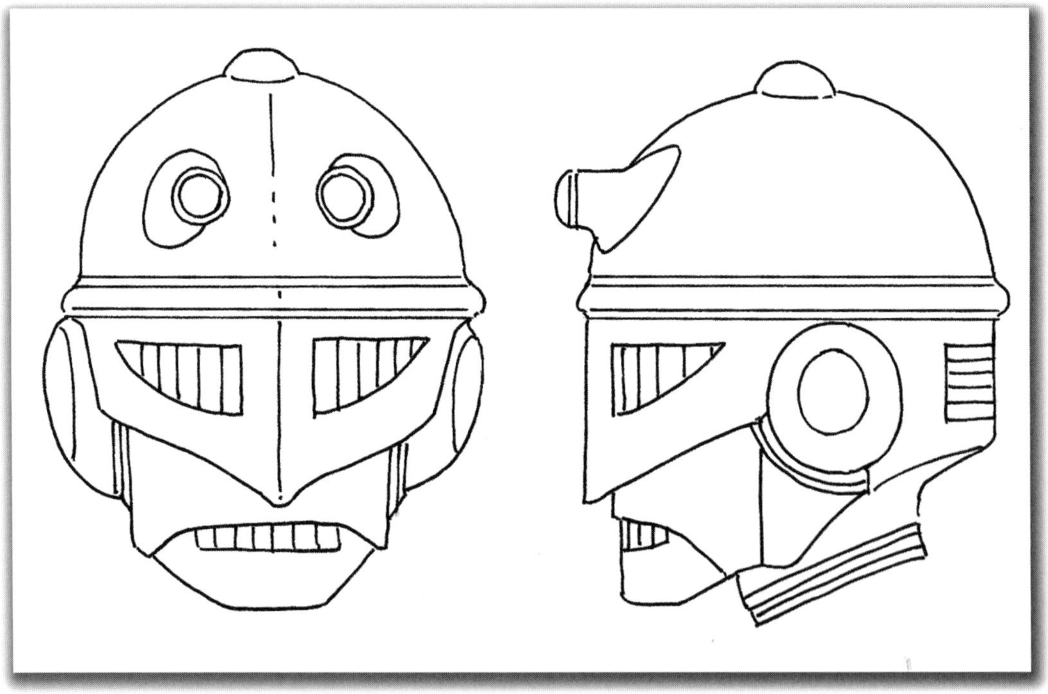

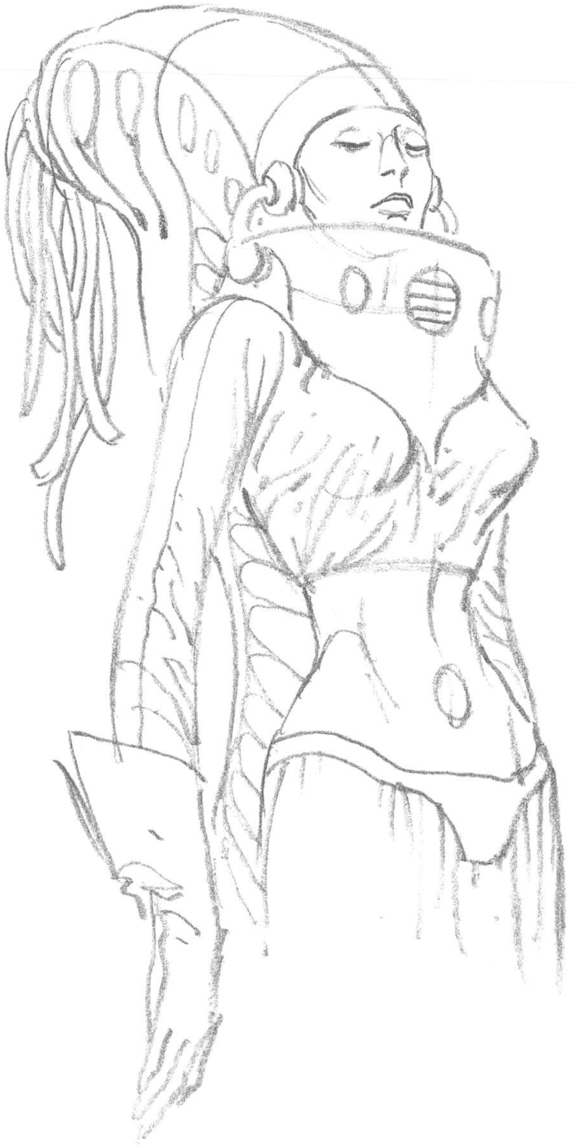
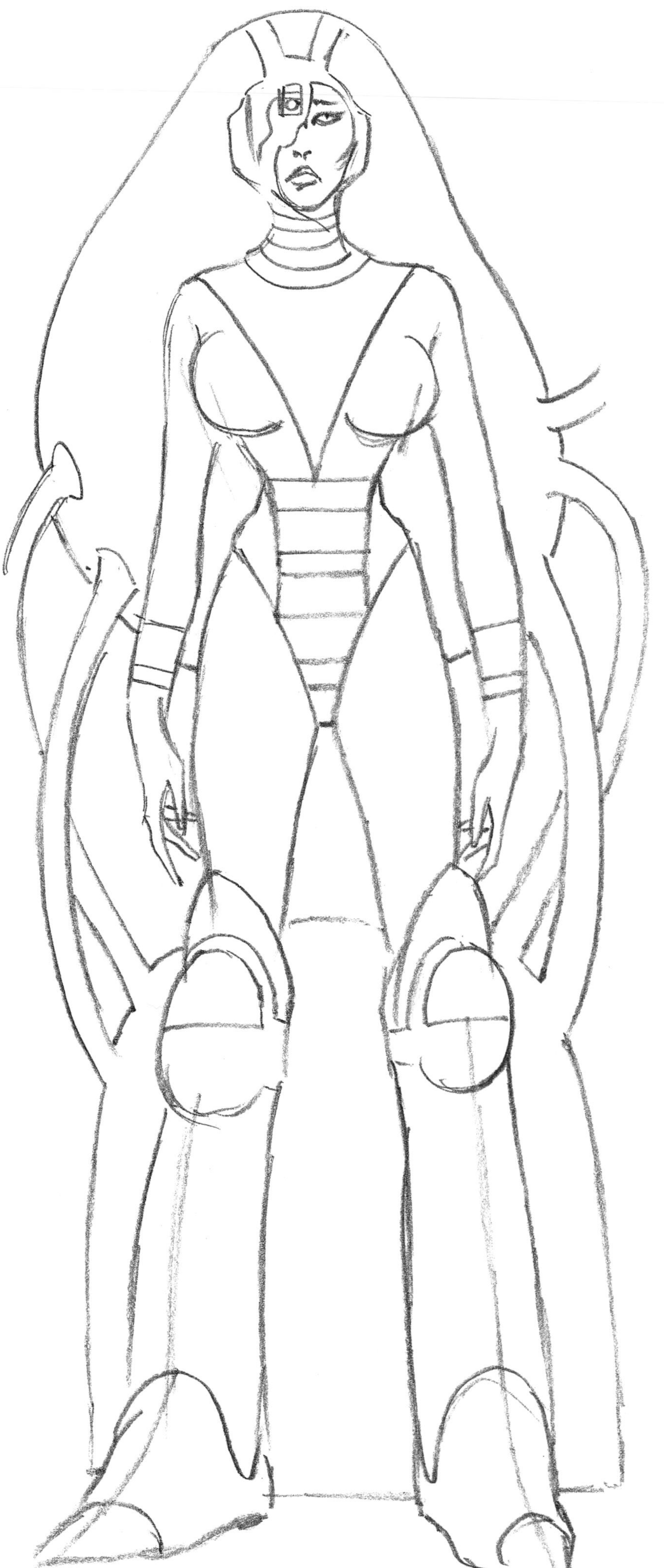
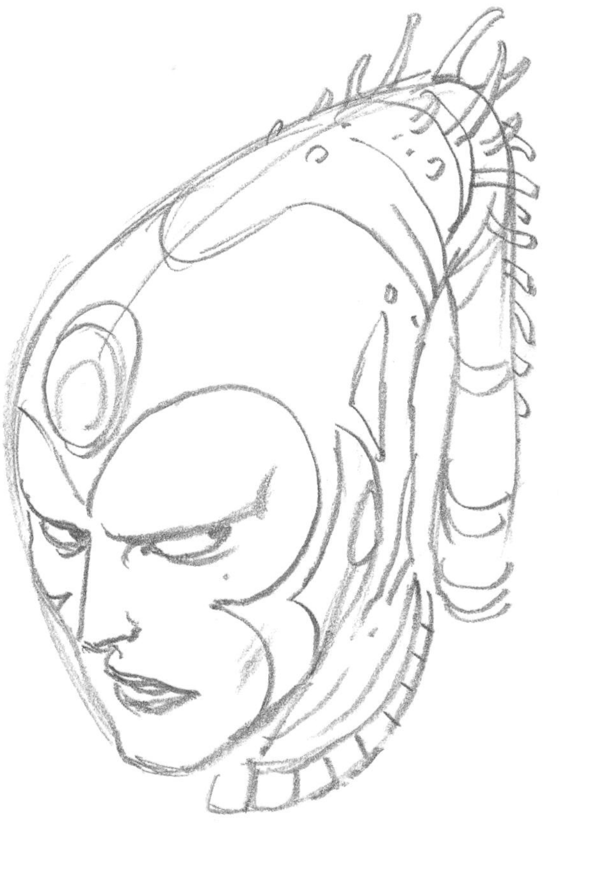

SUPERVILLAINS

Villains encountered by superheroes must be worthy opponents. Only by vanquishing powerful enemies can superheroes prove their own strength, sagacity, and motivation. If the "bad guy" is smaller, weaker, and dumber, the "good guy" has accomplished very little. In fact, beating a lesser adversary gives the hero an appearance of being a bully.

The villain may look bigger and stronger, and be seemingly invincible, but eventually be beaten only because the hero is smarter and pure of heart. (Of course it also helps if the hero has some additional superpowers.)

Villains come in all shapes, sizes, and ages, and not all of them have superpowerful bodies. Perhaps they are endowed with the powers of black magic and can summon evil forces from the netherworld to do their bidding. These characters must be illustrated so that a sense of evil is pervasive.

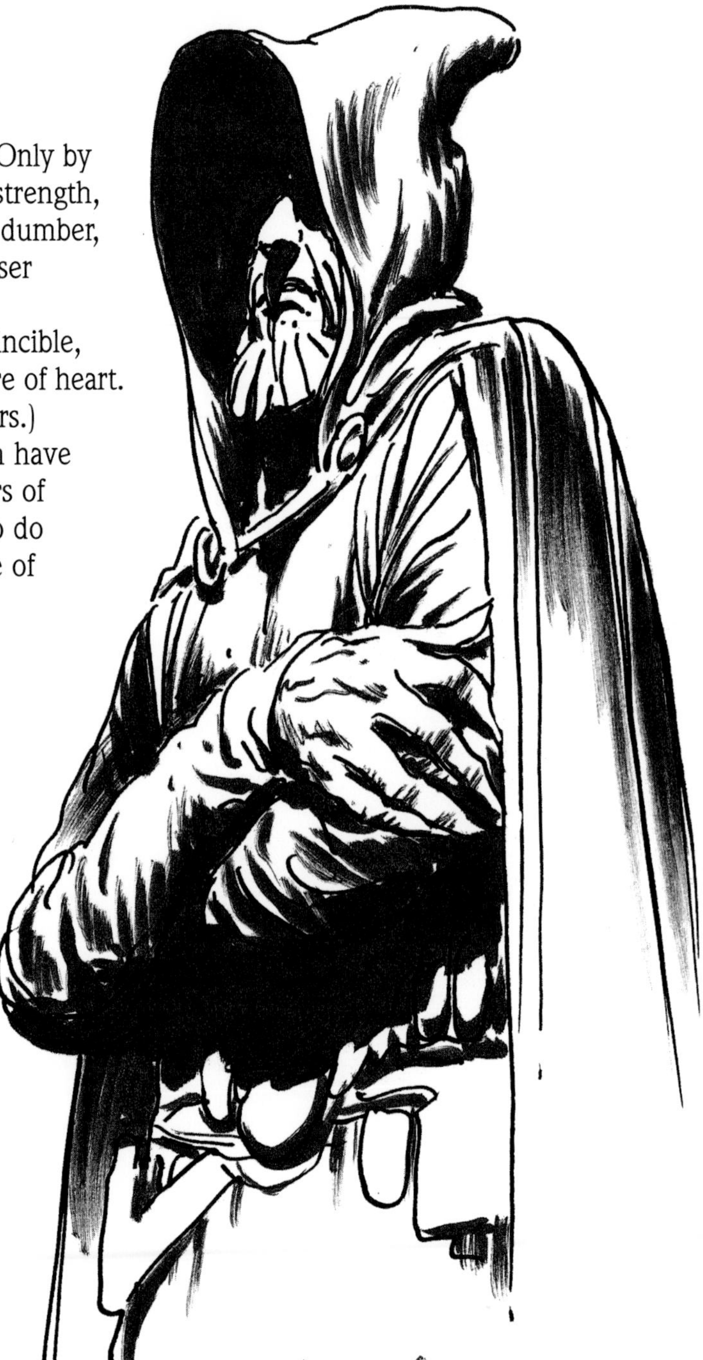

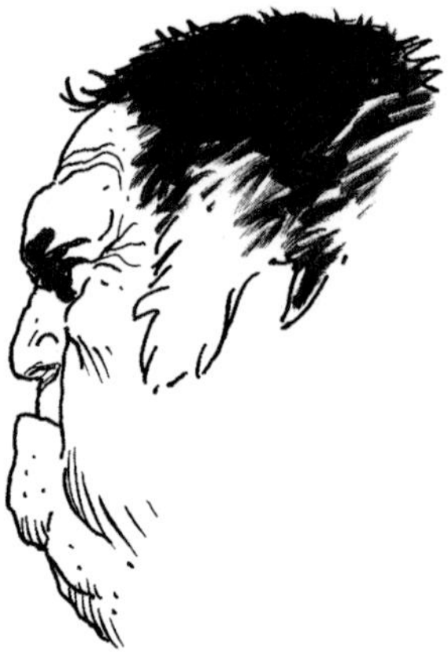

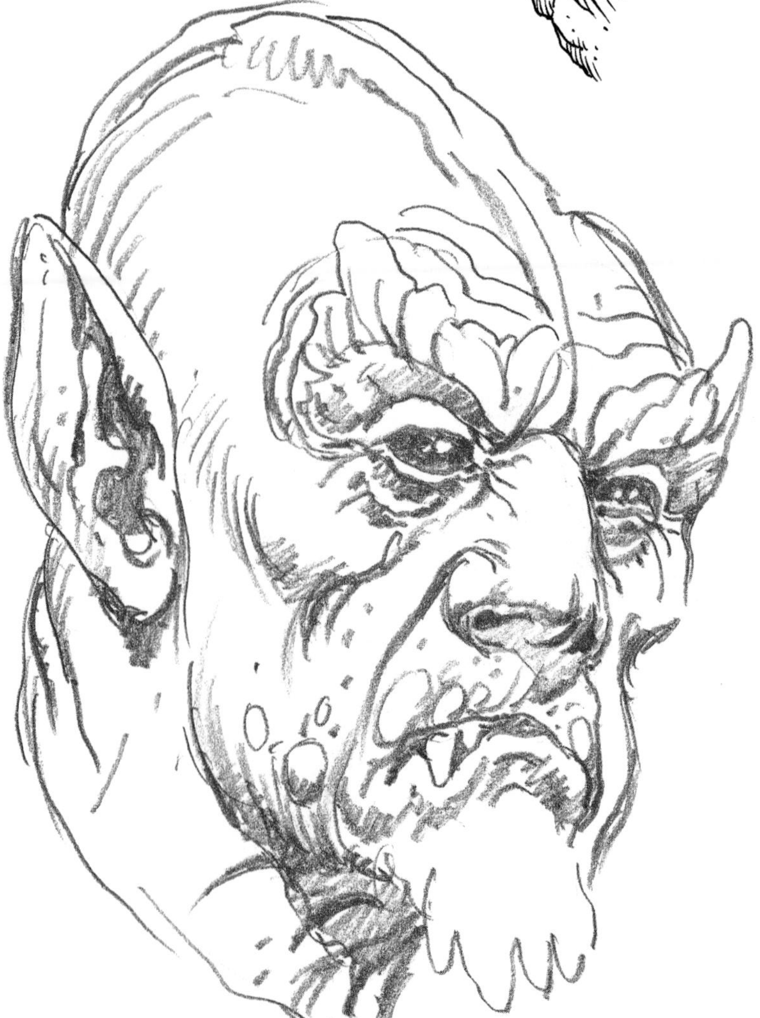

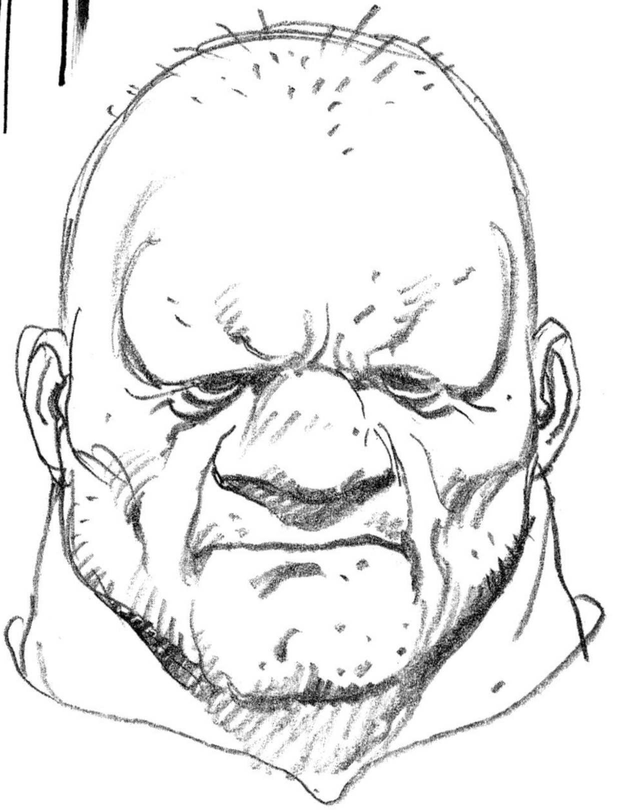

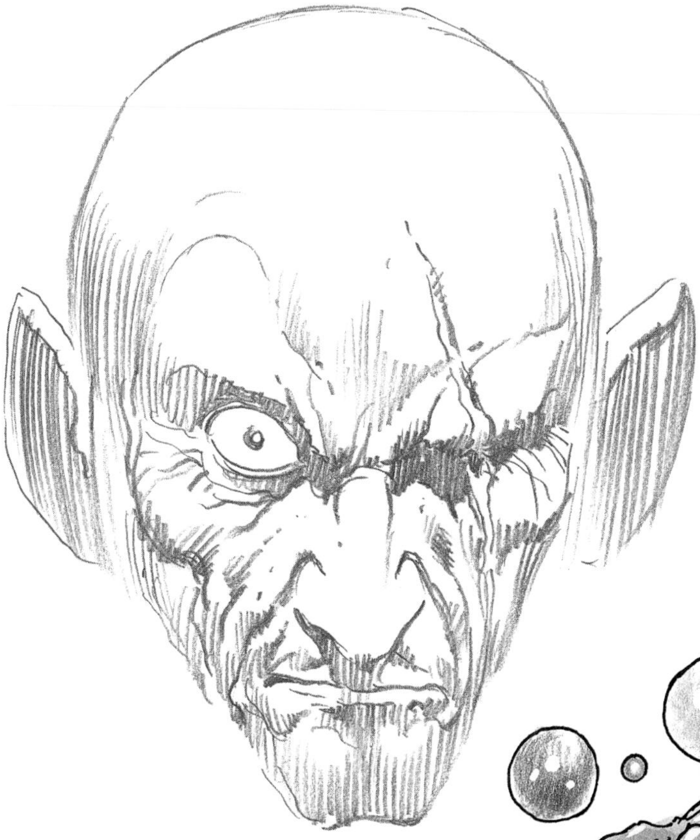
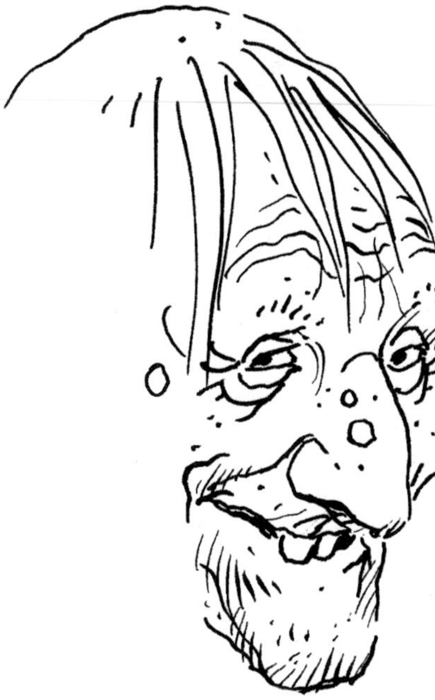
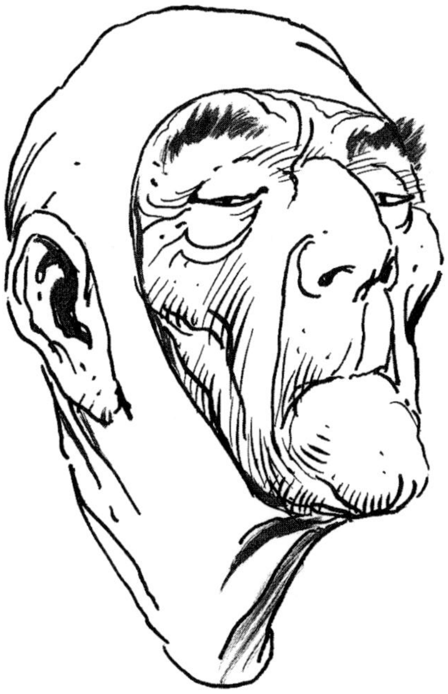
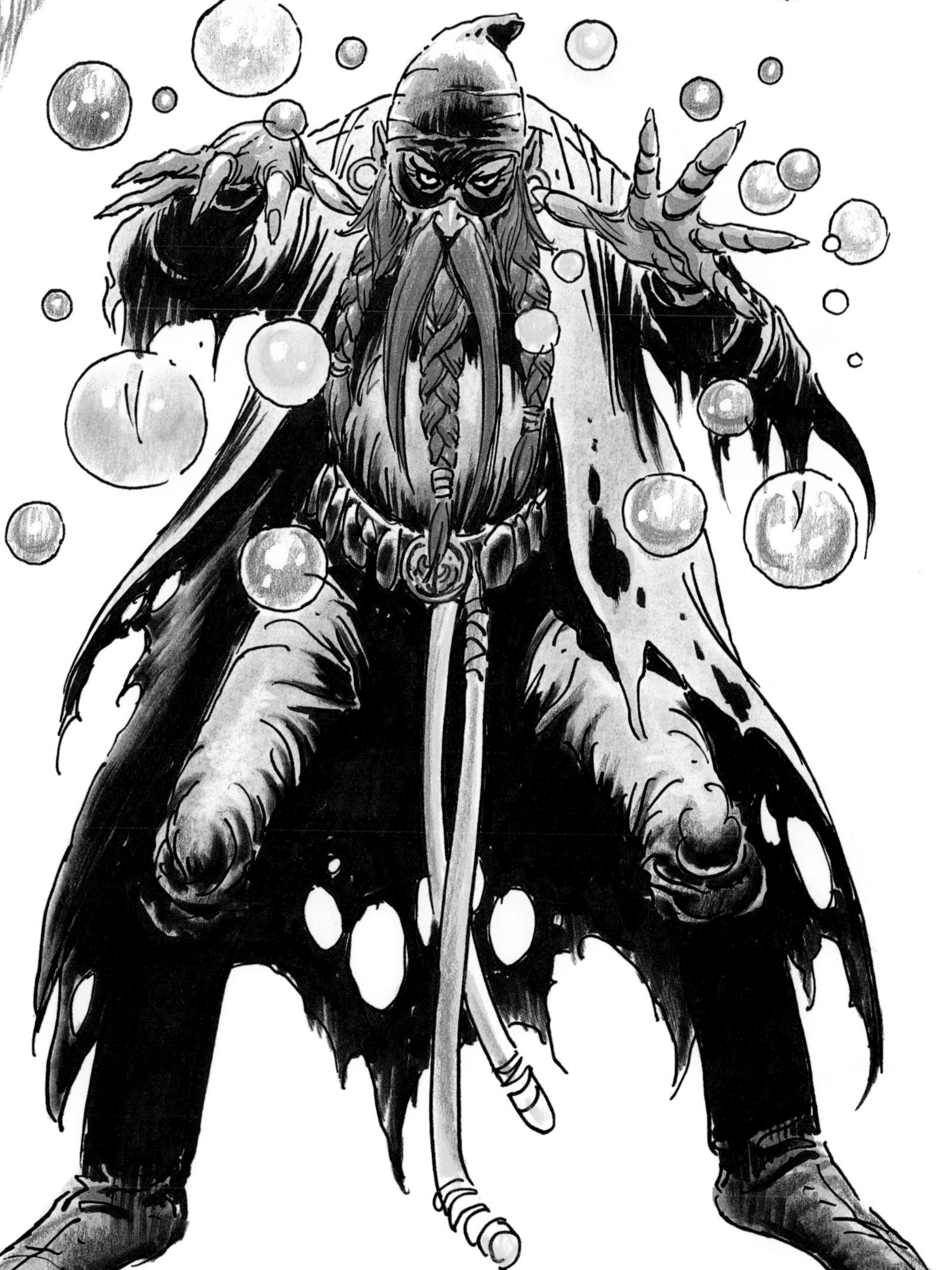

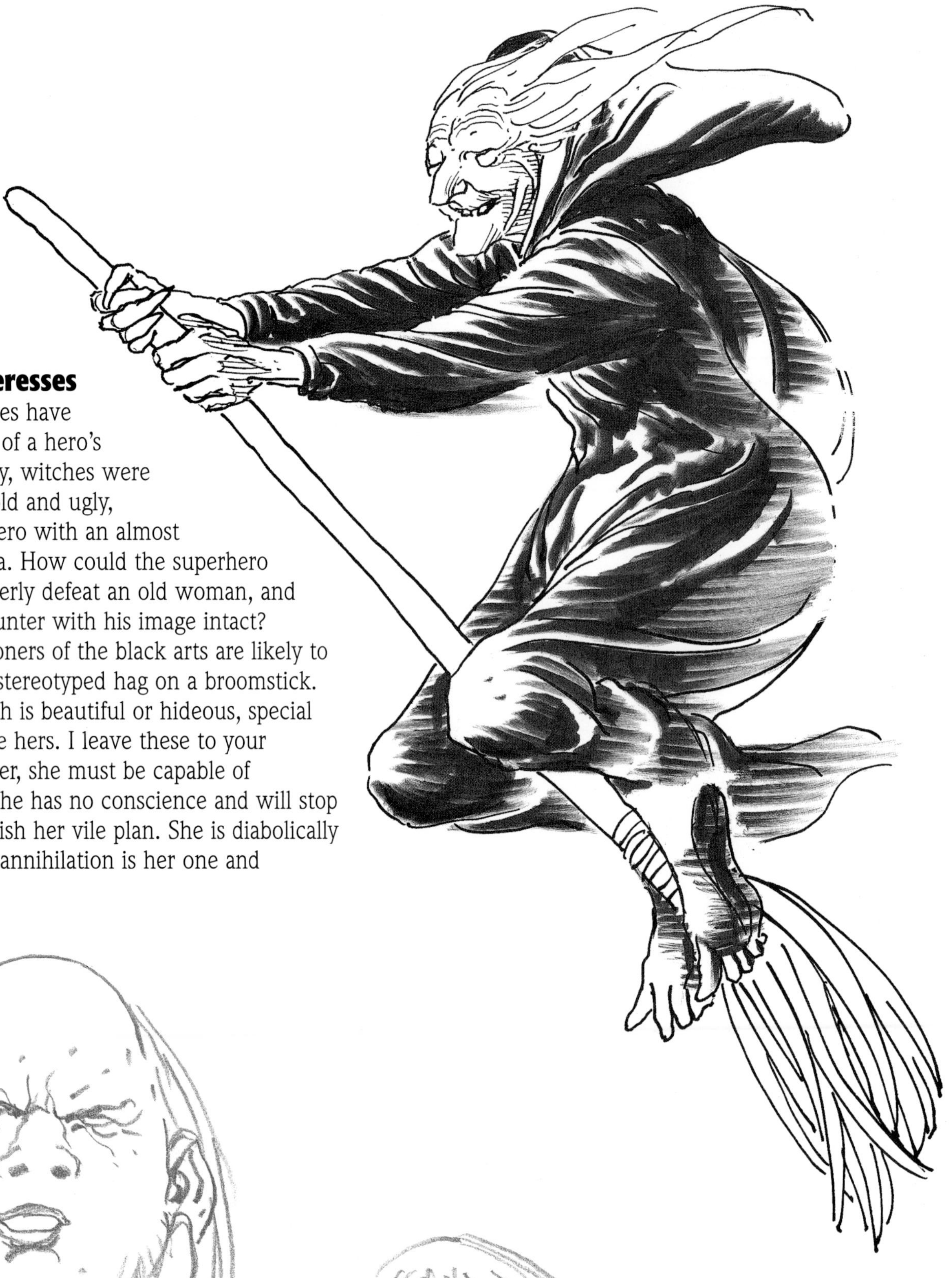

Witches and Sorceresses

Witches and sorceresses have always been the bane of a hero's existence. Traditionally, witches were not only female, but old and ugly, presenting the superhero with an almost unimaginable dilemma. How could the superhero do battle with and utterly defeat an old woman, and come out of the encounter with his image intact? Today, female practitioners of the black arts are likely to look nothing like the stereotyped hag on a broomstick.

Whether your witch is beautiful or hideous, special powers of evil must be hers. I leave these to your imagination. Remember, she must be capable of destroying the hero. She has no conscience and will stop at nothing to accomplish her vile plan. She is diabolically clever, and the hero's annihilation is her one and ultimate goal.

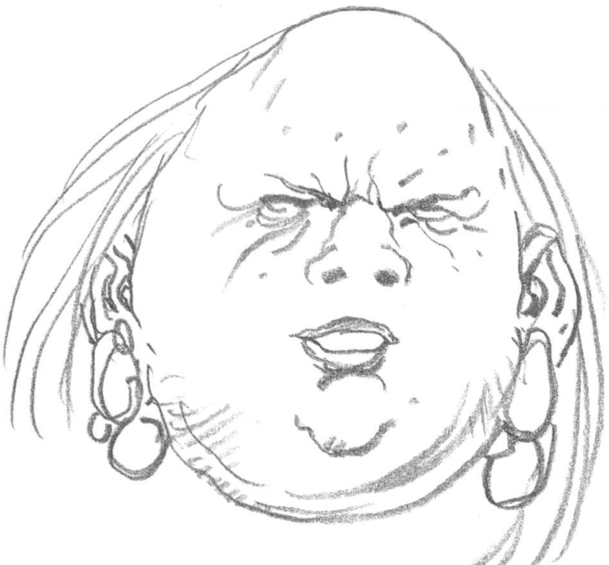

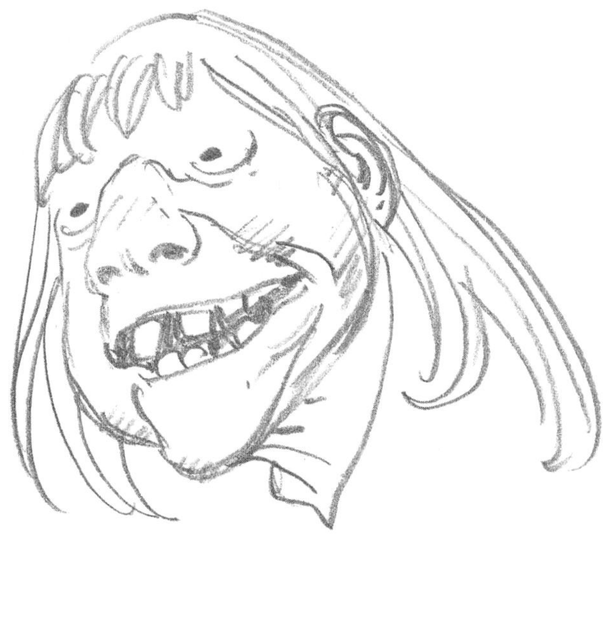

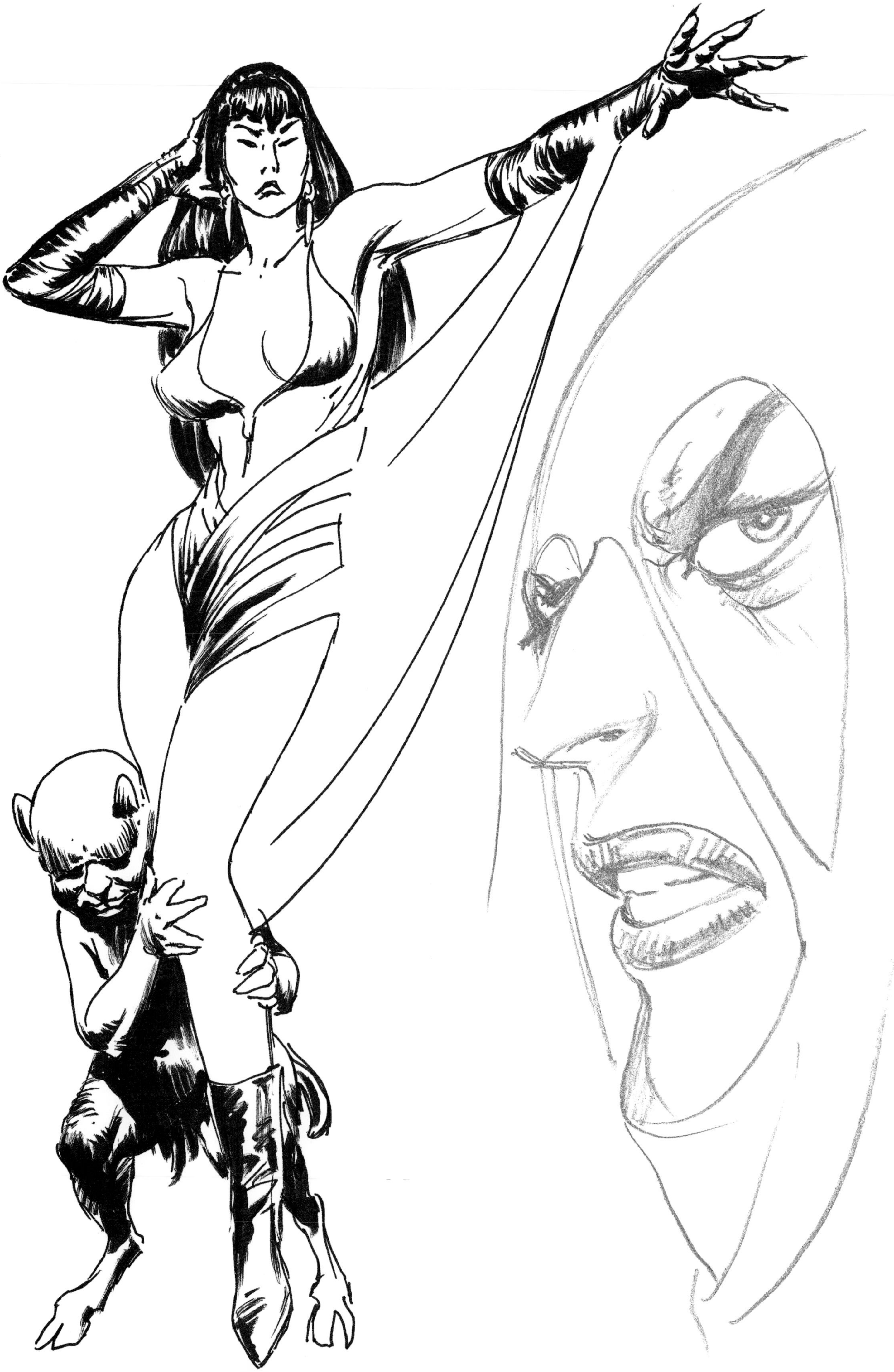

Robots

So far, we have been talking about villains with at least some human qualities. But imagine a powerful adversary completely devoid of emotion, one that attacks without anger or fear, one that cannot feel pain and so will continue its onslaught until every atom of its nonhuman being has been destroyed.

The drawings on these pages are only two of the many possibilities for robotic villains. If you want to create a credible adversary for your superhero, begin with a rough sketch of the human face and figure in proper proportion. Although cartoonists and special effects experts have certainly come up with some nonhumanoid robots, most readers of comic books expect robotic villains to be based on real human anatomy.

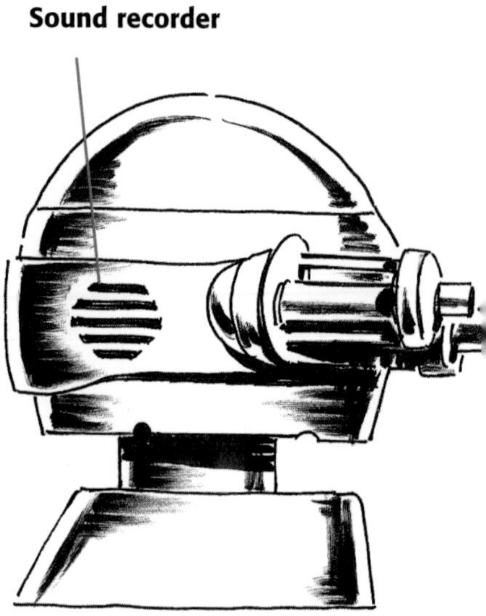
Sound recorder

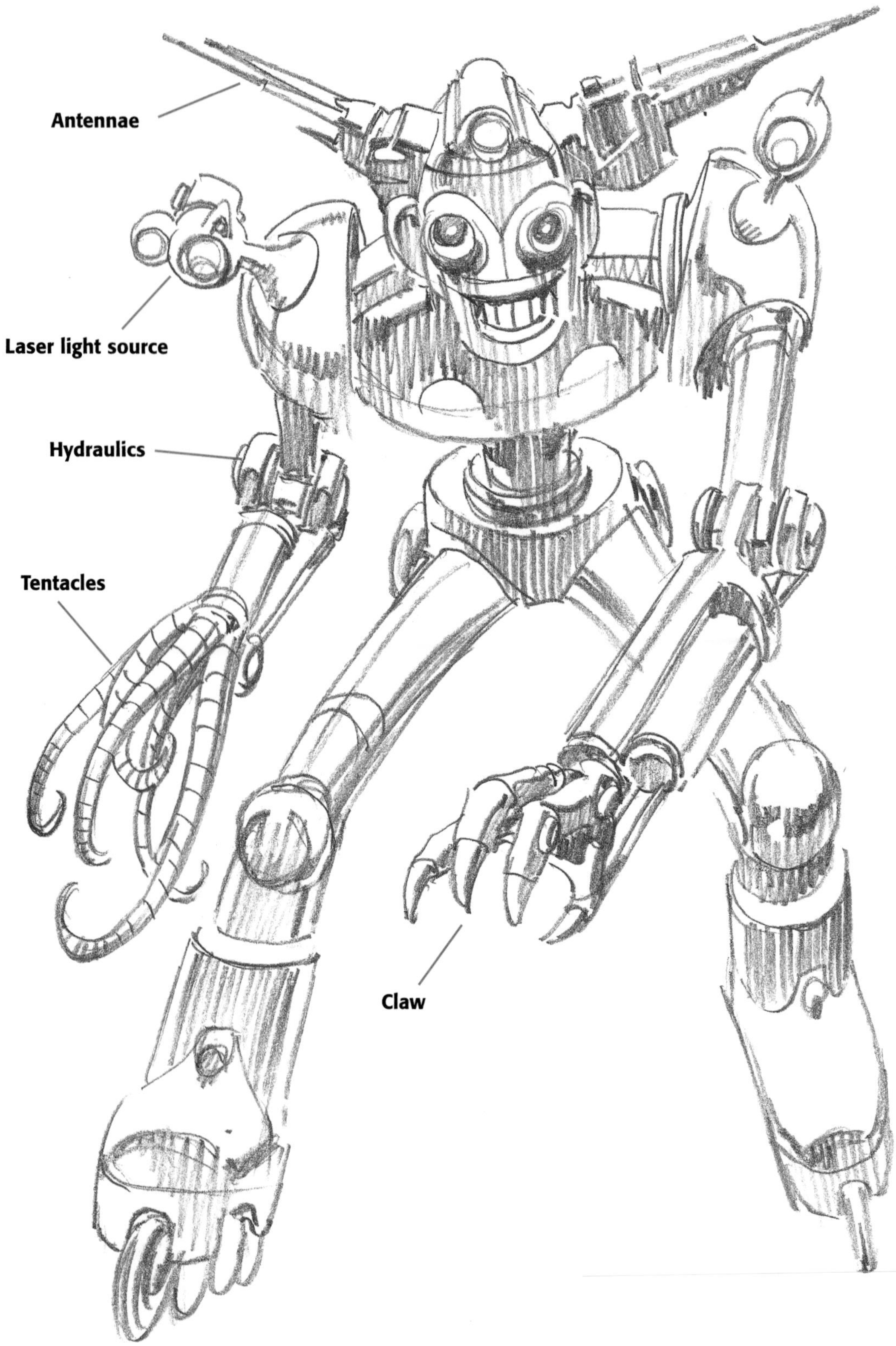
Antennae
Laser light source
Hydraulics
Tentacles
Claw

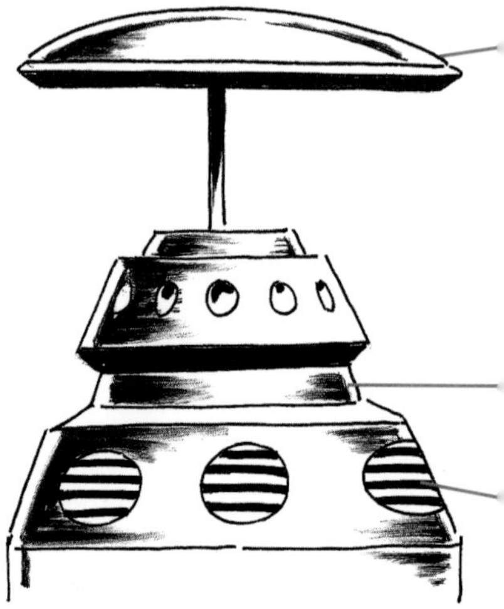

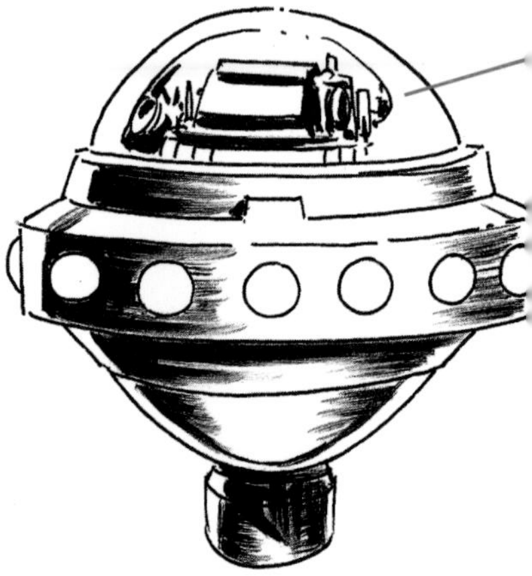

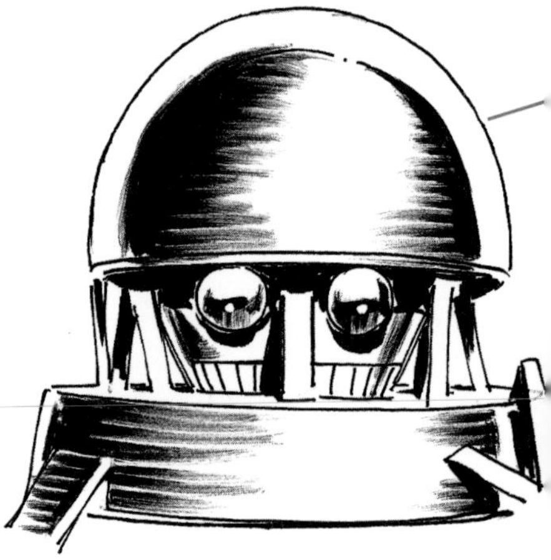

Long-distance vision and aiming device

Neck turns 360º

Antenna dish

Sight bar

Speech device

Transparent top

Multiple "eyes"

Protective dome

Heavy armor

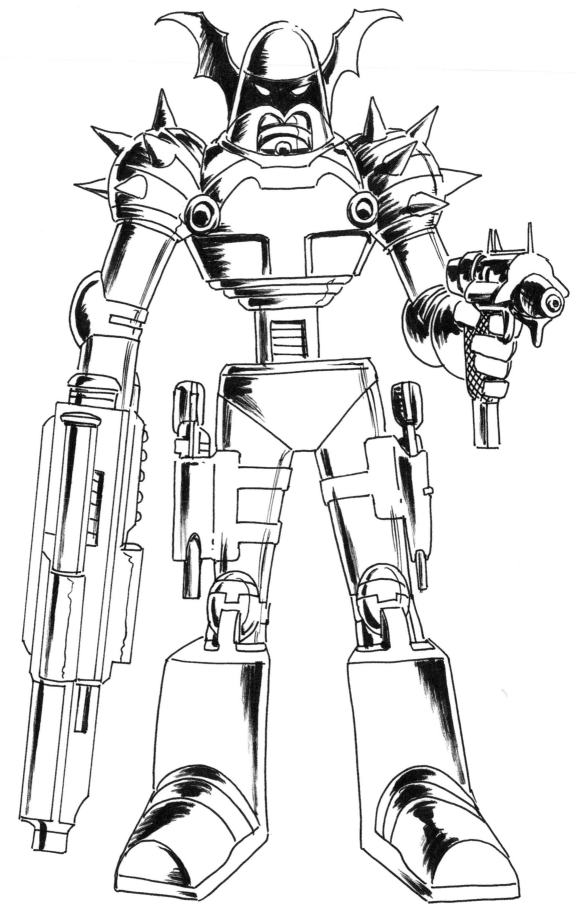

The design possibilities for your mechanical villain are endless. Consider some superpowers a robot villain might have: multiple eyes to see in all directions at once; telescopic vision; feet equipped with retractable in-line skate wheels that can accelerate to high speed; claws that grip, tentacles that grasp, or both at once; a computer-controlled antenna dish that can access secret files of governments and corporations. *The key is to think before you draw.*

Superhero From the Sea

If you were called upon by an editor or publisher to create a superhero that lives and breathes in water, what would he (or she) look like? Would the character be part fish and part human? Would he be able to navigate on land as well as water, an amphibian of sorts?

What kind of powers does he have? How did he get them? Does he have any weaknesses, an Achilles' heel?

My Fish Man has large round eyes, a flattened nose, gills, and finlike adornments on his head. There is a hint of scales on his body, but mostly tight skin over bone. (A bit fishy, isn't it?) His head, on the other hand, is a mass of scales, a sort of armor or protective element. The fins on his body help propel him swiftly through the water. I haven't made up my mind as to whether he'll be able to lay eggs or not—like the seahorse.

He's powerfully muscled and extremely agile. Anatomically, he resembles a man, but he's as comfortable in water as any fish. And he has a liking for worms, especially night crawlers. Well, that's my undersea superhero.

Use your pencil and paper and sketch your own undersea superhero. Try different combinations of things, like the tentacles of a giant squid, and the fins of a shark. Or the suckers of an octopus and the claws of a lobster. Maybe he lives in a Pleistocene sea. Whatever you decide, be sure to collect references.

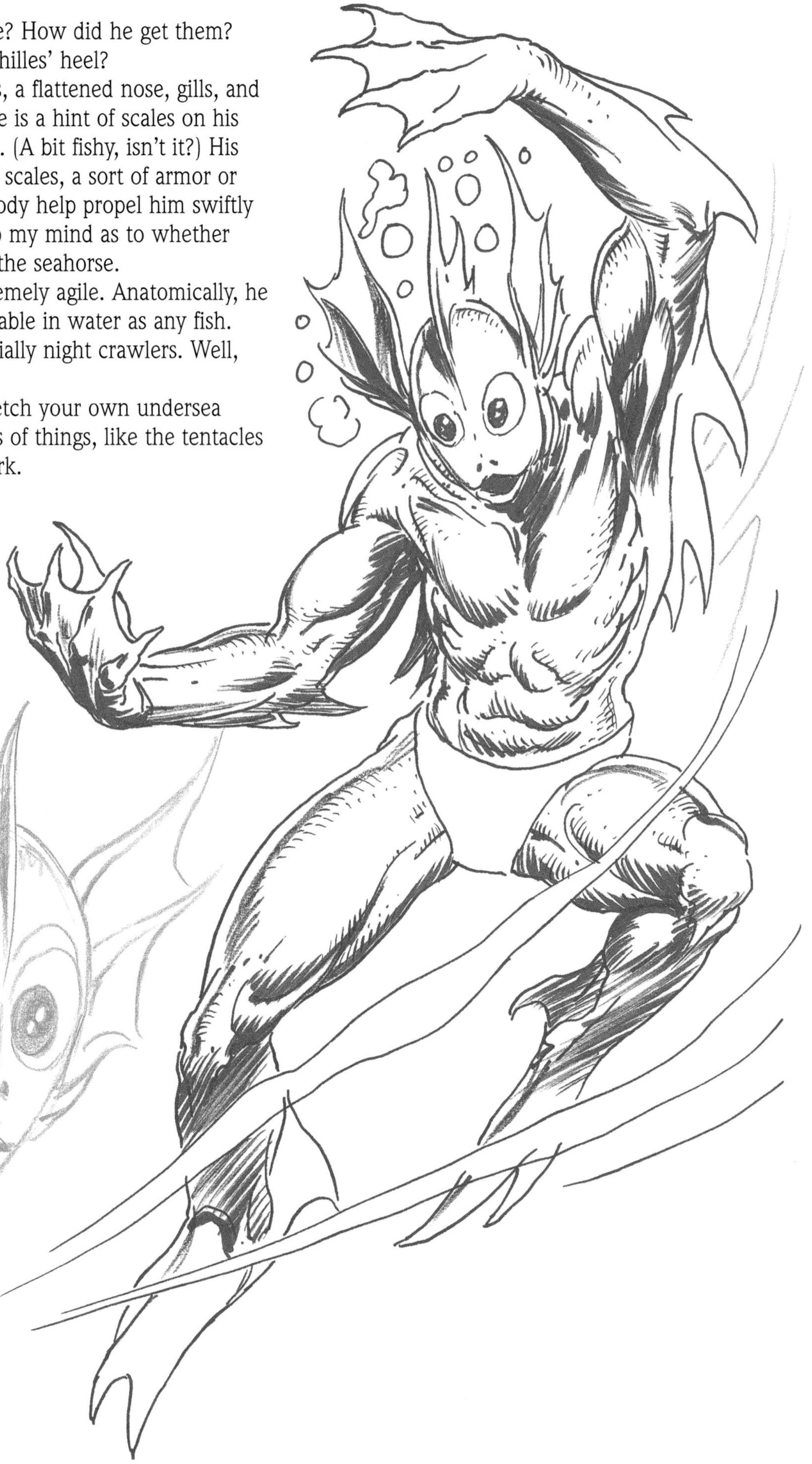

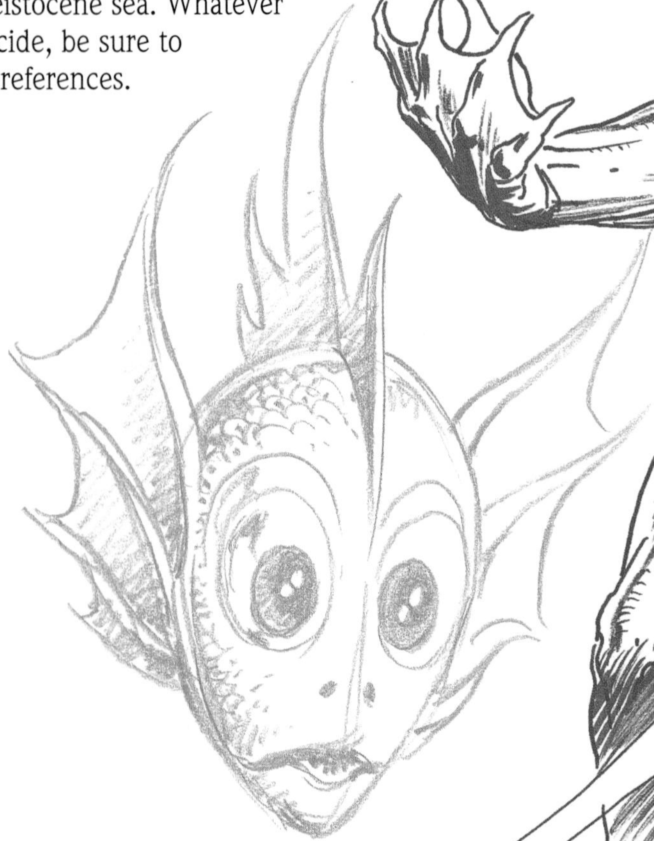

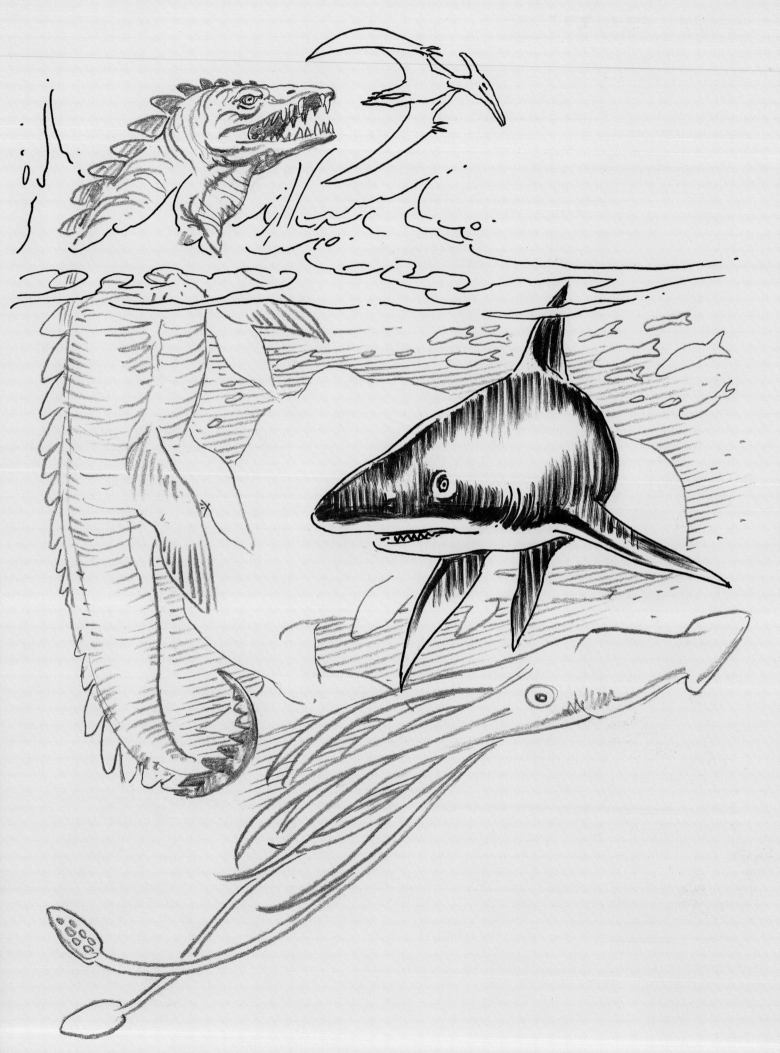

SUPER CREATURES

Check out the animals in the wonderful world of my teenage superhero Ilgom, where great apes, wolves, lions, tigers, and bears coexist with fierce prehistoric reptiles.

Practice by copying the animals shown here, then create your own. *Remember:* Don't start with details. When drawing an animal in motion, roughly sketch the entire form, concentrating on position, proportion, and line of action. When you are satisfied that the proportions and perspective are right, add the details—stripes, fur or scales, expression.

And before you start drawing any kind of animal, do your homework. With animals as with humans, there is no substitute for drawing from life. Visit the local zoo with your sketchbook in hand. Study the details of fur texture, stripe patterns, paw size and shape, and overall anatomy.

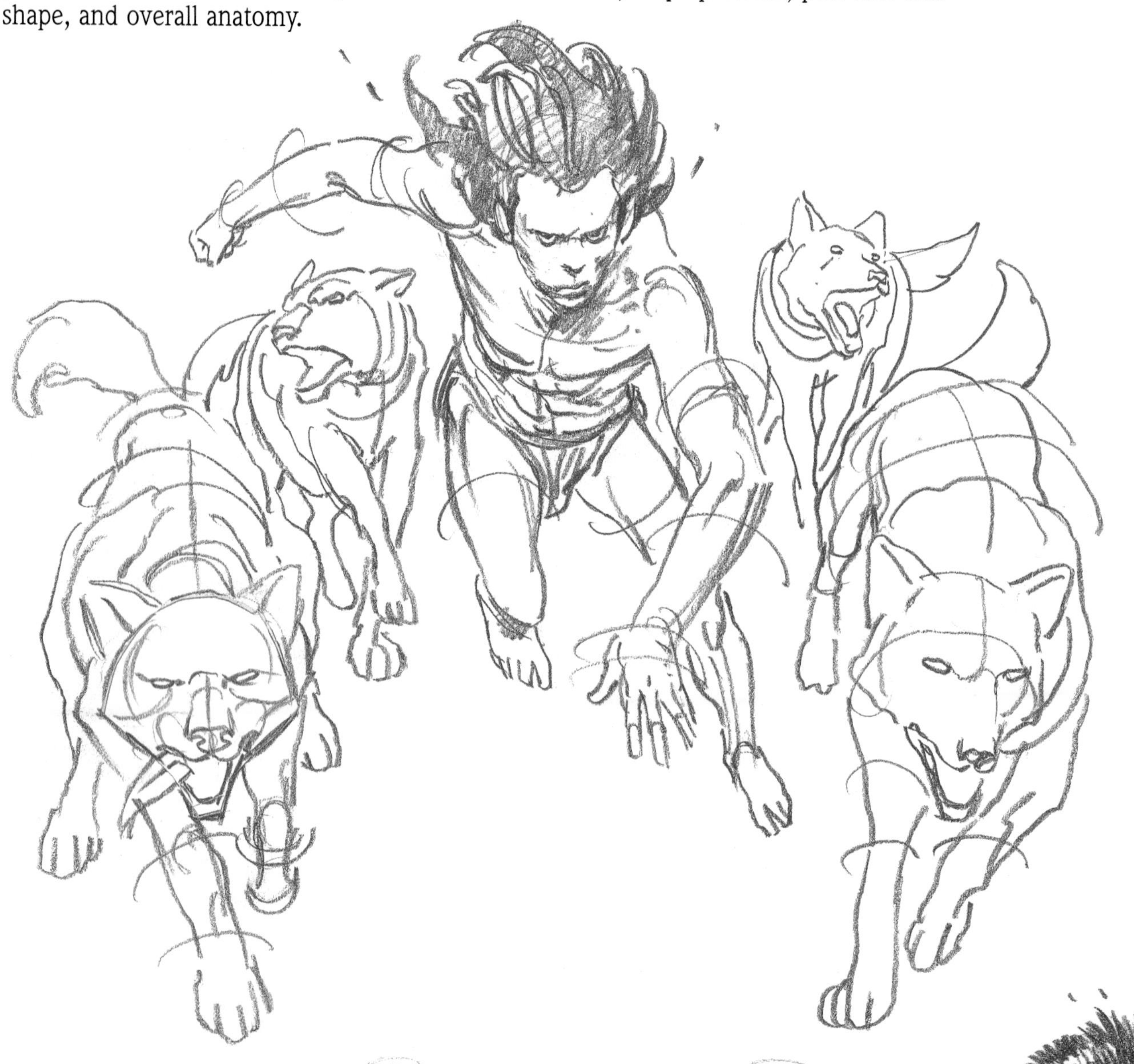

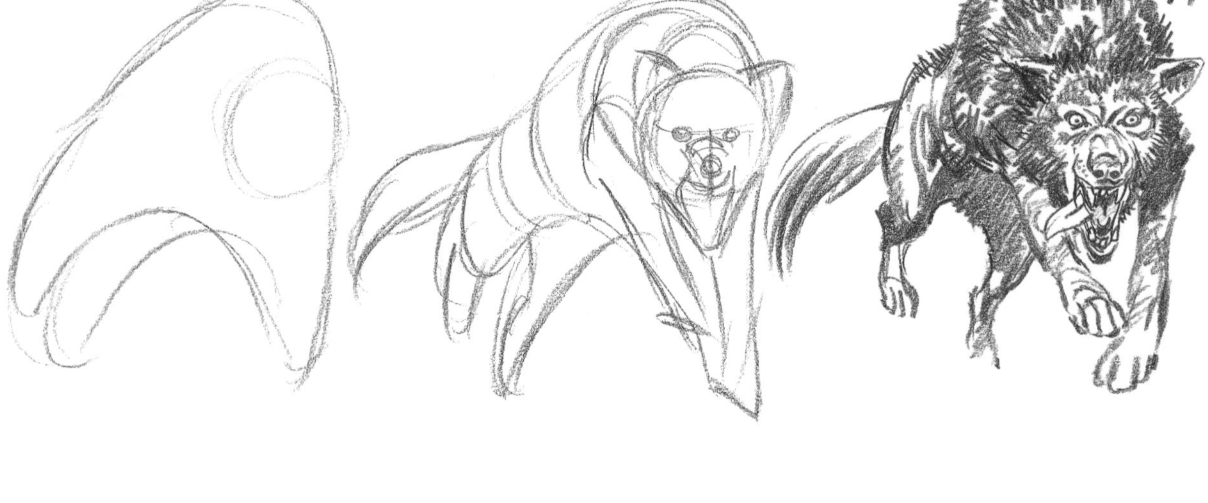

Apes and gorillas look more like human beings than do any other living creatures. However, there are obvious anatomical differences between human and gorilla. Male gorillas can reach a height of 6 feet, and their arms and hands and torsos are much longer and much larger than the average man's. Looking at the male gorilla's huge head, powerful shoulders, and long, thick, solid torso, it is easy to see why they are so heavy—an average weight of 400 plus pounds. Apes walk with the rolling gait of a sailor because their hip sockets and thigh bones are not structured to sustain upright bipedal walking. Actually, their gait is more like a waddle.

In profile, the gorilla's facial features are relatively flat, with a projecting brow and extended rear skull. The dimensions of the gorilla's leathery fingers are several times those of the average human's, and those huge hands exude incredible power.

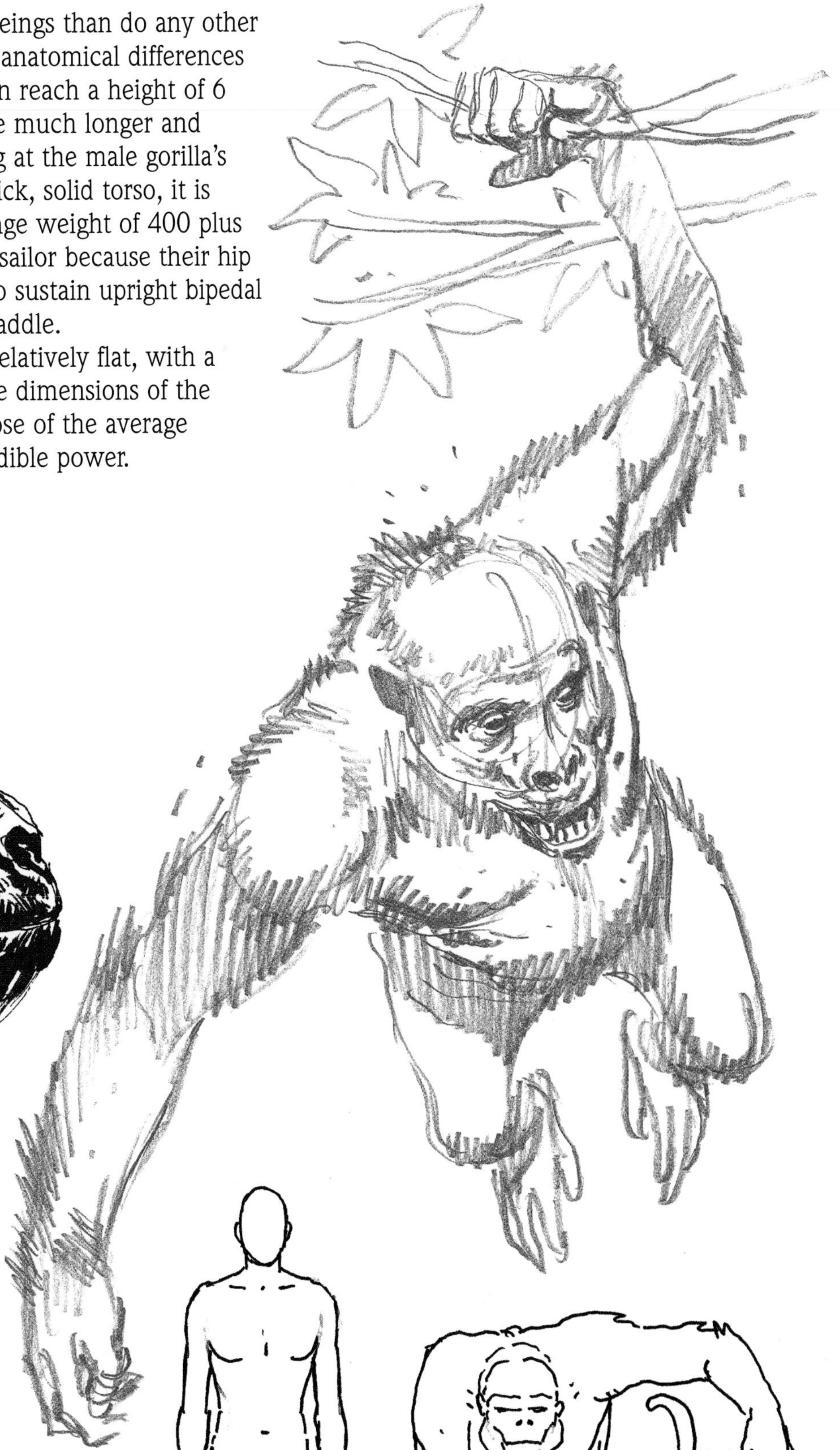

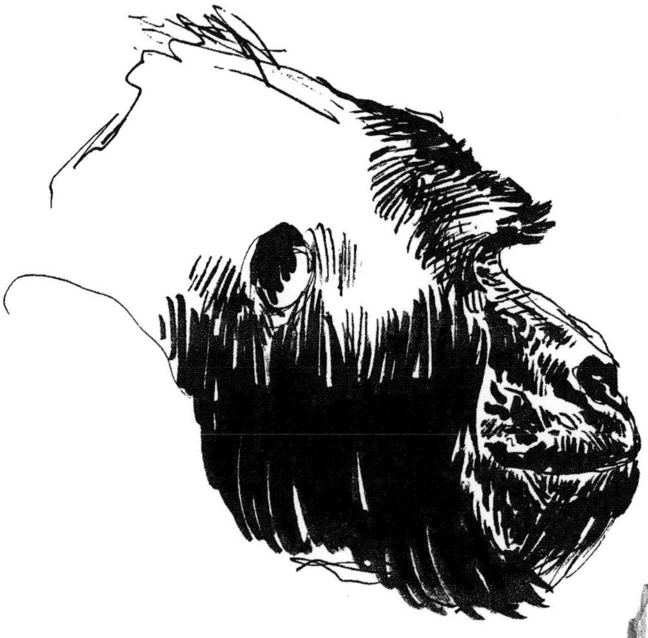

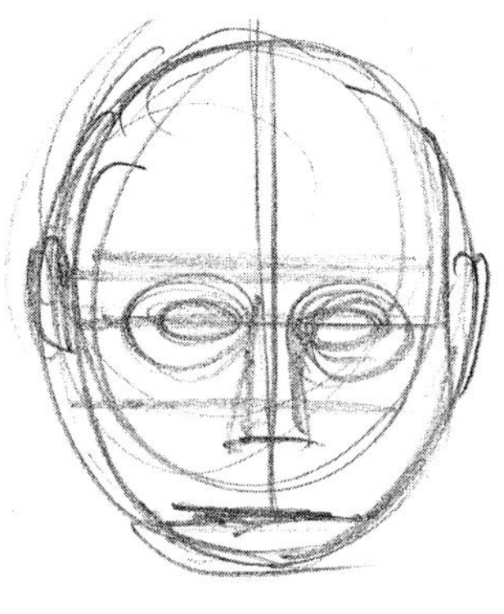

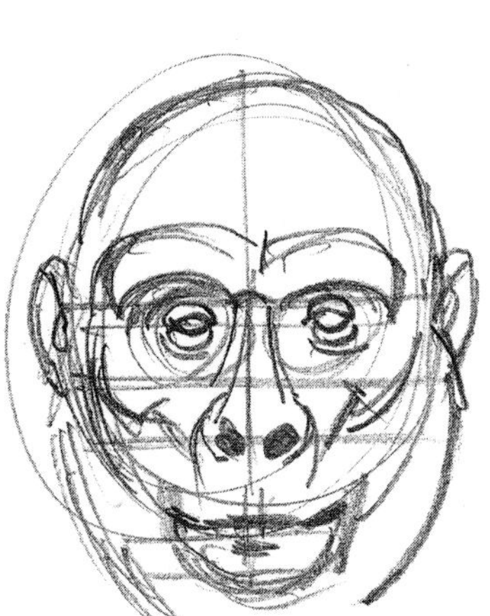

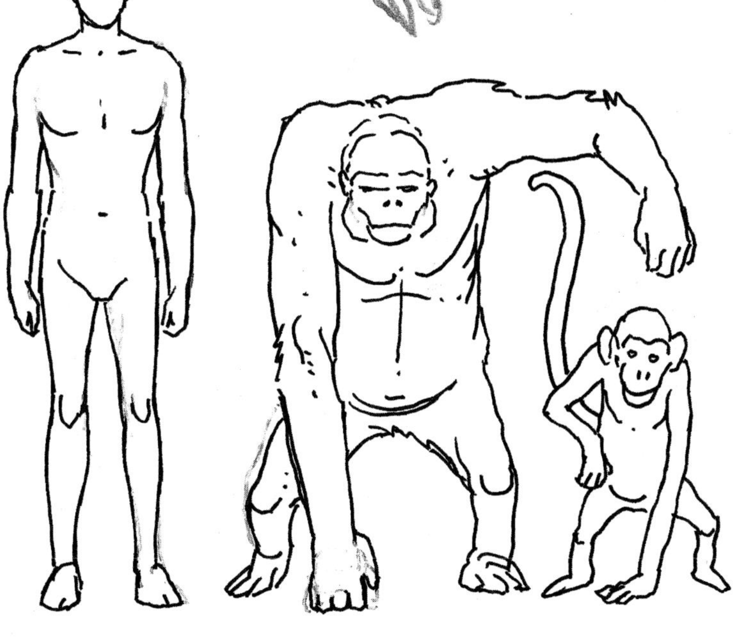

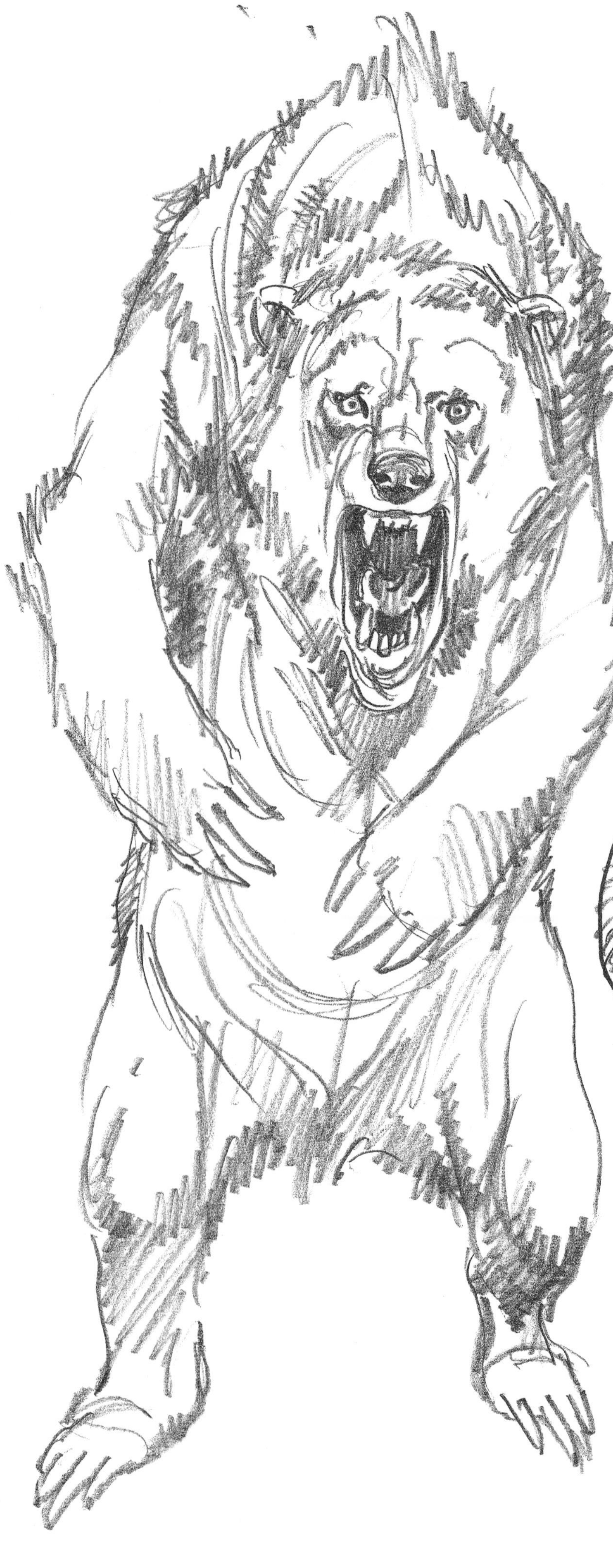

The grizzly bear often attacks on its hind legs, head lowered with mouth agape. Its claws can rip and tear like miniature sabers and are not retractable. The grizzly stands 8 to 10 feet tall and is considered among the Earth's largest carnivores. I find this information essential for me to draw this animal with the feeling and likeness necessary.

Notice the similarity of expression between T. rex, grizzly, and the charging lion on the next page. There is no doubt that all three are in full attack mode.

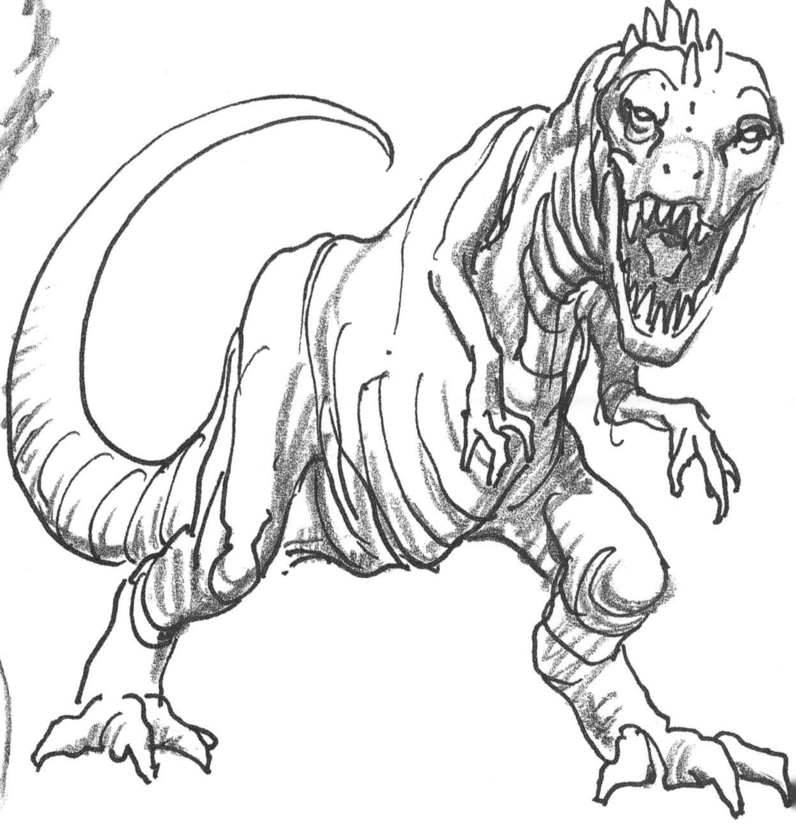

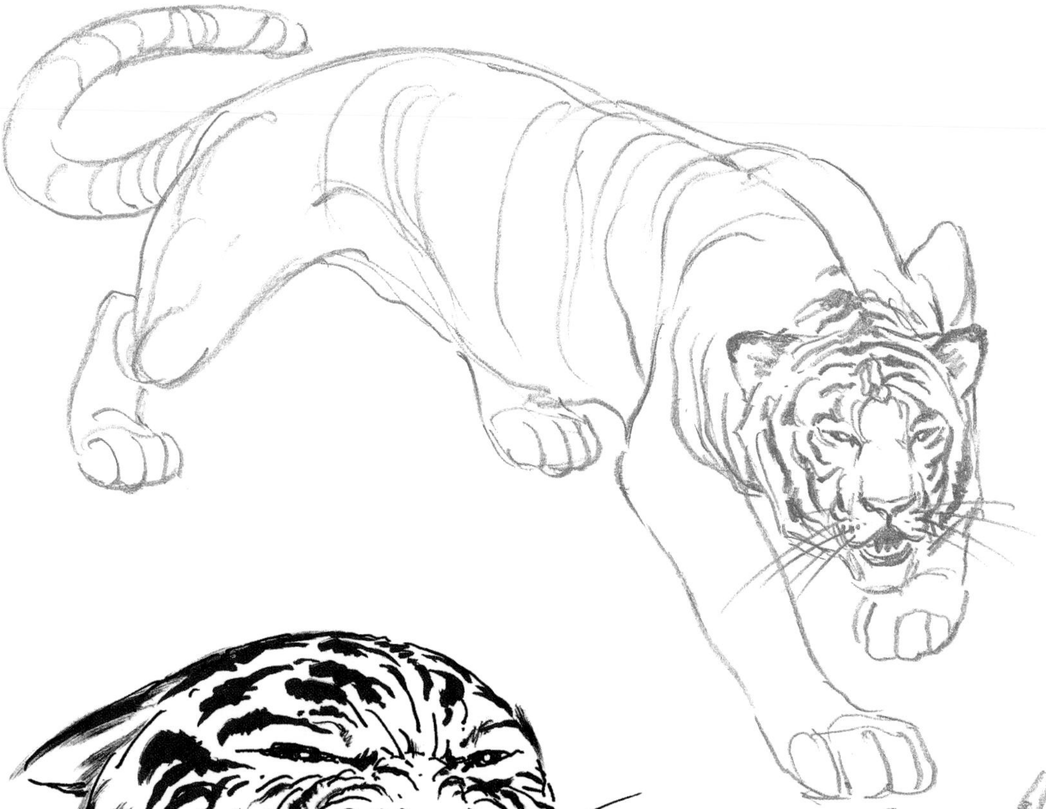

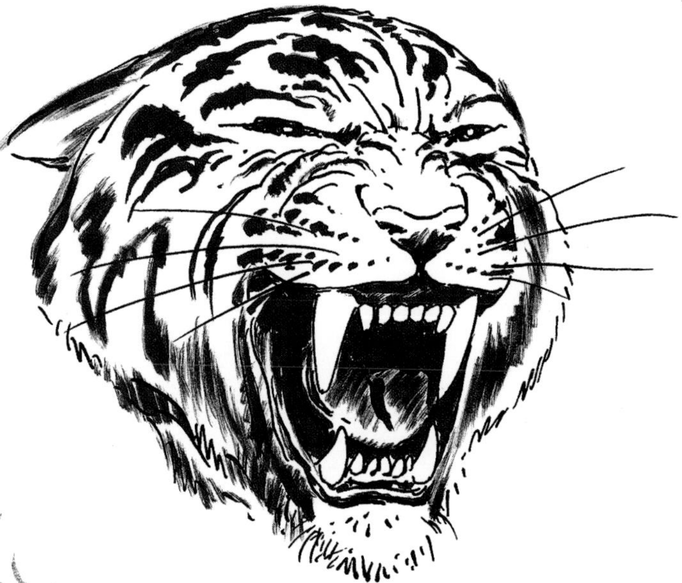

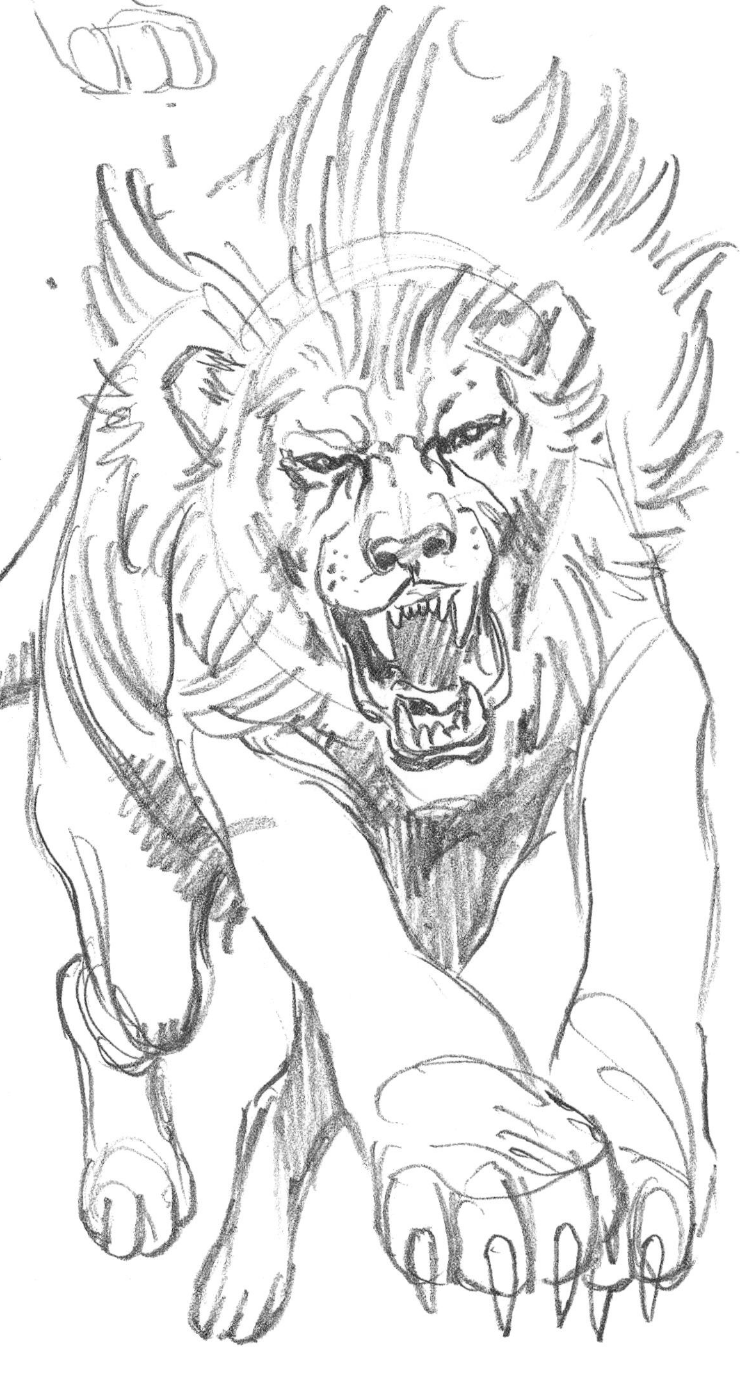

A stalking tiger moves with the fluid sinuosity of all members of the cat family. An angry tiger rivets its eyes on the object of its rage. The ears flatten down and the lips go back, baring razor-sharp teeth. Flip back to page 56. I can draw any enraged animal—man, bear, tiger, dinosaur (or, for that matter, domestic cat, domestic dog, or sewer rat)—using what I have learned, from observation, study, and analysis, about what happens to an angry animal's face.

BACKGROUNDS

The term *background,* used to refer to a panel in a comic book story, refers to everything *other than* the characters performing the action: cityscape, landscape, seascape, interiors (including chairs, tables, T.V. sets, computers, etc.), vehicles, and weapons. Credible backgrounds are an integral part of the overall credibility of any story line you come up with. It may take longer to find good references for a background detail than it does to do the drawing. However, the gratification derived from doing a really good drawing, rather than one that is merely adequate, makes it well worth the time and effort. Besides, the drawings in this section should give you a big head start on your reference collection.

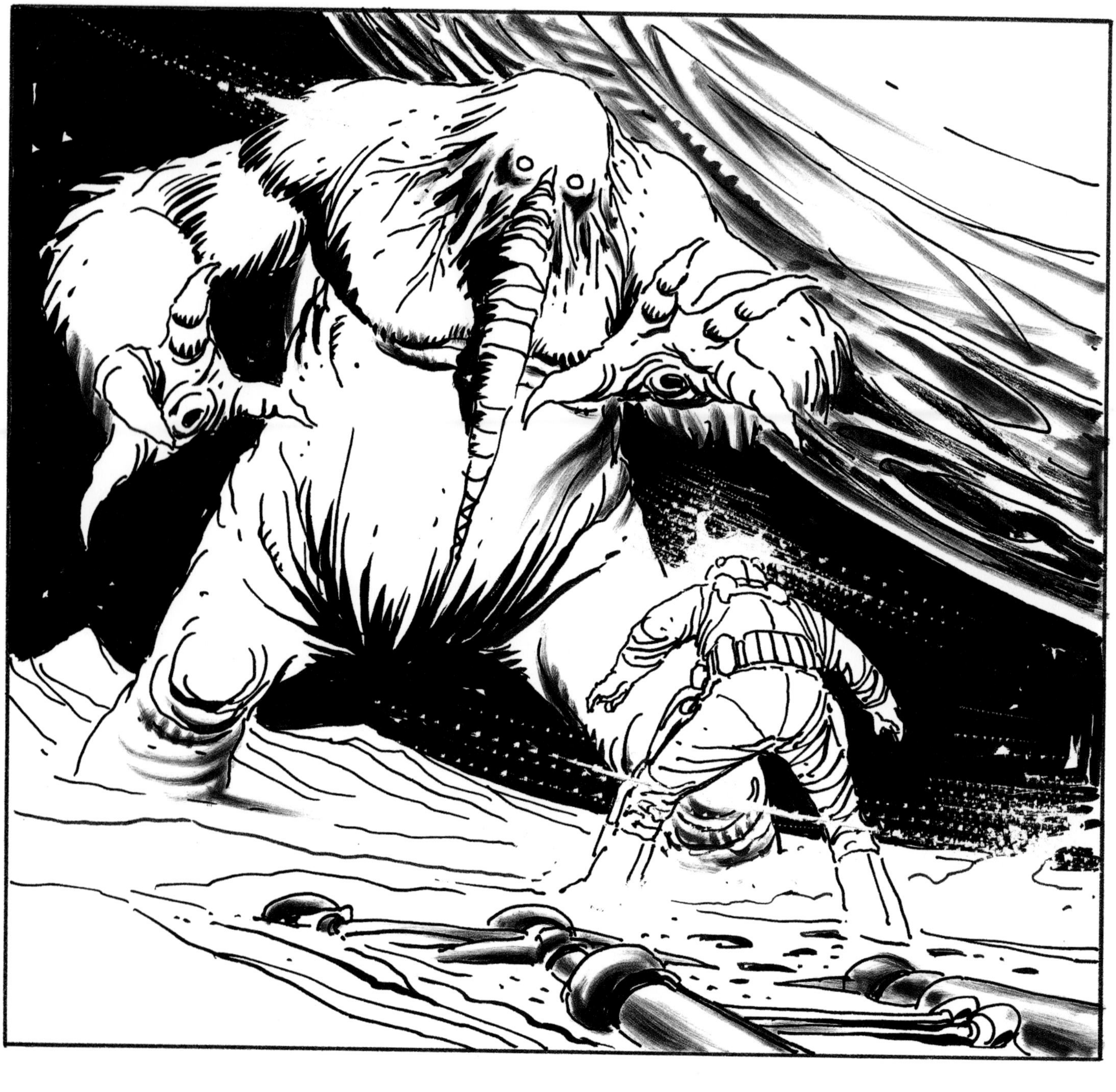

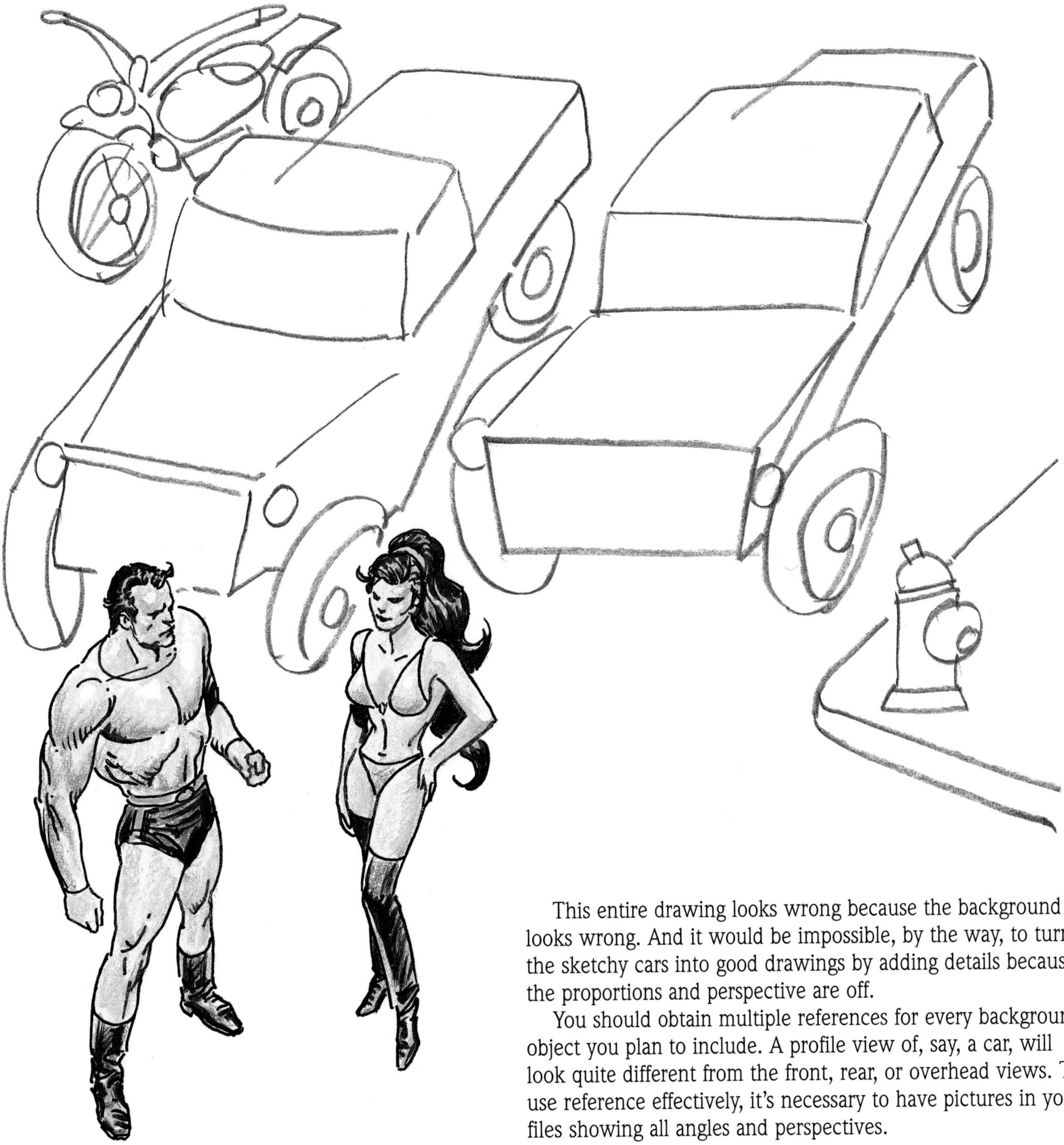

This entire drawing looks wrong because the background looks wrong. And it would be impossible, by the way, to turn the sketchy cars into good drawings by adding details because the proportions and perspective are off.

You should obtain multiple references for every background object you plan to include. A profile view of, say, a car, will look quite different from the front, rear, or overhead views. To use reference effectively, it's necessary to have pictures in your files showing all angles and perspectives.

SKETCH, SKETCH . . . AND SKETCH SOME MORE

I take a sketchbook wherever I go. Zoos, museums, airports, city streets, subways—you name it, it's probably in my illustrated diary. Cameras are okay but I find that my sketches are much better than snapshots at capturing the essence of what I am looking at. Anyway, I love to draw. For me, the concentration needed for drawing is a form of utter relaxation. These sketches are my personal recollection in graphic form. I don't seek approval or recognition. Later, sometimes years later, if I'm called upon to illustrate a story involving subject matter that is contained in my sketchbook, the work becomes more meaningful and enjoyable.

Get a small sketchbook and keep it with you at all times. Draw with pencil, pen, marker, or all three. The tools are relatively unimportant. It's the drawing that counts. And, remember, these sketches are for you.

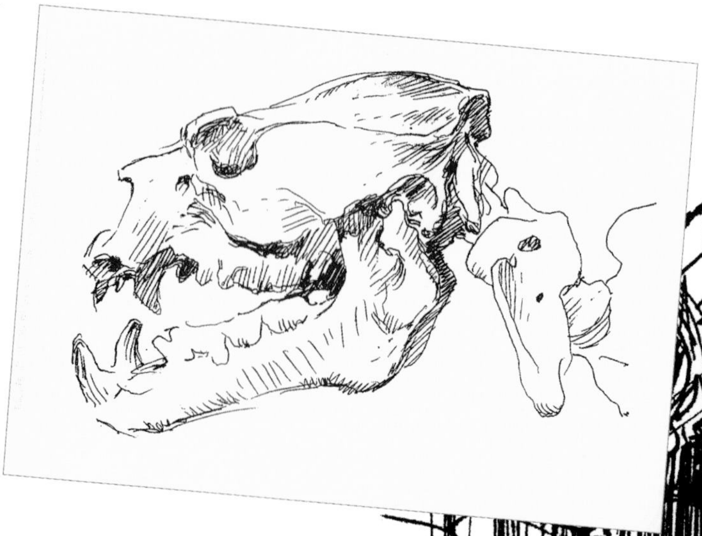

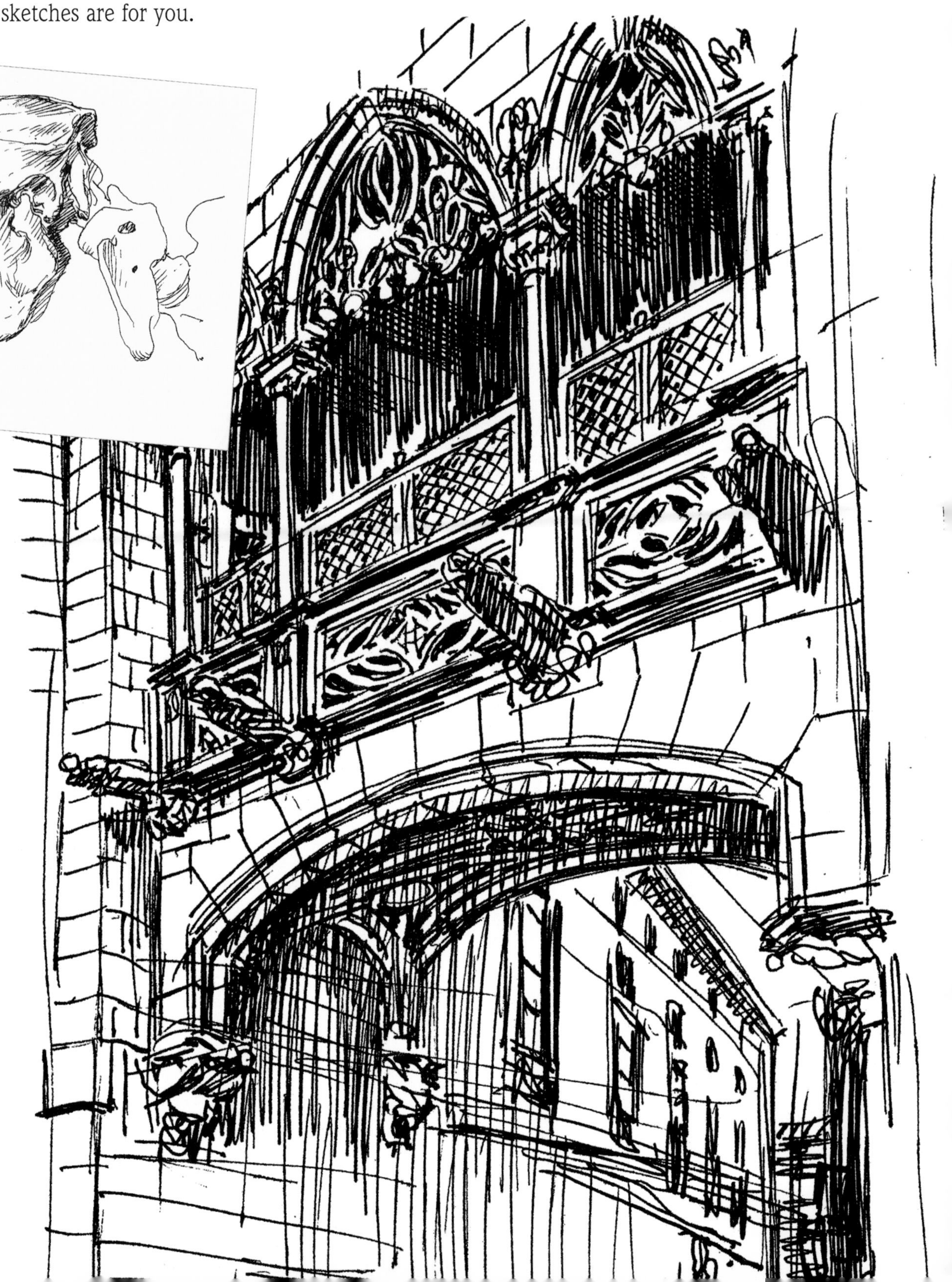

Above is a sketch I did at the Museum of Natural History in New York City in late November 1983. The subject: the skull of an extinct semiaquatic rhino, a metamynodon. It wasn't difficult to draw because the subject hardly moved at all. To the right is a 1990 sketch I did in a small alleyway in the old-town section of Barcelona, Spain, called "Barcelonita."

Landscapes

When you want to draw landscapes for stories taking place on Earth, imagine, if possible, precise geographic locations, then get some references for the backgrounds you have chosen. Rock formations in the western United States bear little resemblance to the great snow-capped mountains of the Alps.

The destructive capacity of the molten runoffs of an erupting volcano will not come across if you draw mere outlines and color them red. Jagged outlines for craggy rocks, or smooth dome shapes for mountains, like the sketches in the insets, won't do the job. A poorly done background or location can destroy the illusion you are attempting to create. The art of art—and that includes comic book art—is in the details.

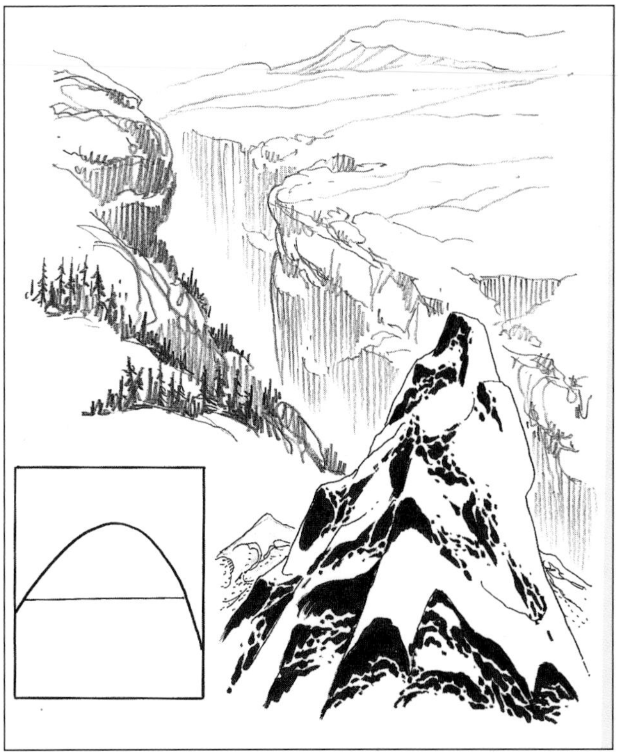

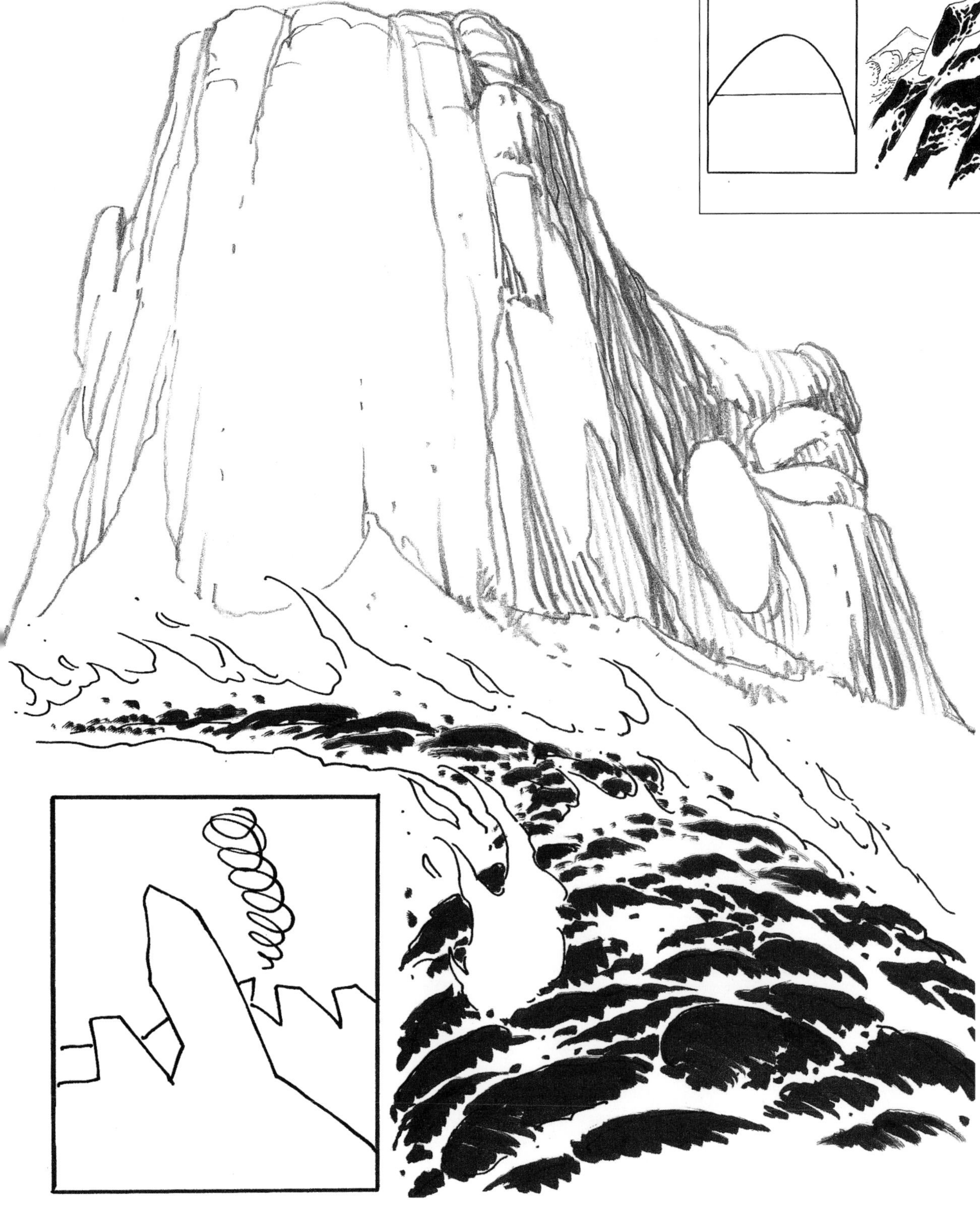

Seascapes

When doing an illustration in which the ocean is the background, conceptualize your subject as a living thing, one that is perpetually in motion. You might think of the water as an entity capable of an emotional response to wind and weather, and therefore a character in the story you are telling.

In the first three drawings, a sense of distance (depth perspective) was achieved by depicting the biggest waves (or, in the first, undulations) in the foreground; the waves diminish in size as they recede into the distance. Also notice that the foreground of these three drawings is relatively darker than the background, another way to create the illusion of distance. The boat, which is clearly a large military vessel, is dwarfed by the vast waters of the ocean and, in the final drawing, by a single towering storm wave. Use objects in your land- and seascapes to provide a sense of proportion and relative size. Once again, reference is important. If you need to draw an object that viewers will perceive as large, yet the object itself must be drawn on a small scale, you've got to have your details right! If my boat looked like a bathtub toy, the drawing wouldn't work.

A peaceful, calm ocean surface may show some undulation, but is basically smooth, like a small lake or pond.

The surface is "irritated" by a series of wavelets that give the water a choppy texture.

Larger waves and deeper troughs, especially in the foreground, are evidence of turbulence.

The whitecaps have developed into huge, curling waves crowned with spray and foam. An ocean storm in all its fury.

Meanwhile, Beneath the Waves, A Titanic Battle Rages

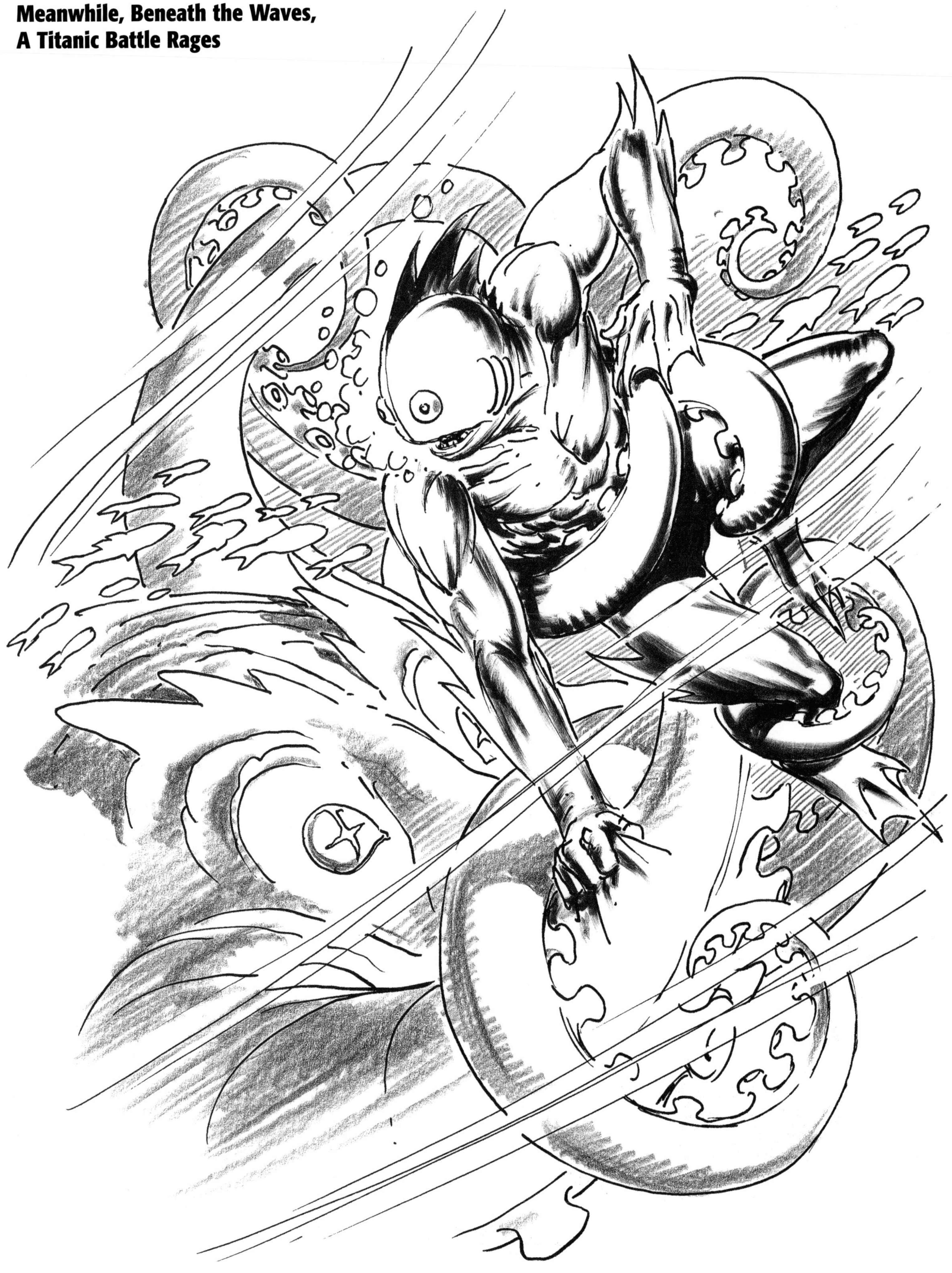

Landscapes and Seasons

A good comic book artist needs to be able to draw anything and everything. I'm often called upon to design a landscape to fit a specific story, like this drawing of a cabin hideout near a tranquil lake. My composition may be a combination of places I've seen, sketches I've made, and references I've found.

A few relatively uncomplicated changes can transform the look and mood of a landscape without altering the basic composition or relative proportions. The mountain does not become larger and the house does not move from its location. But now the evergreens are heavy with snow, and the surface of the frozen lake is mirror-like, with no hint of the movement of water.

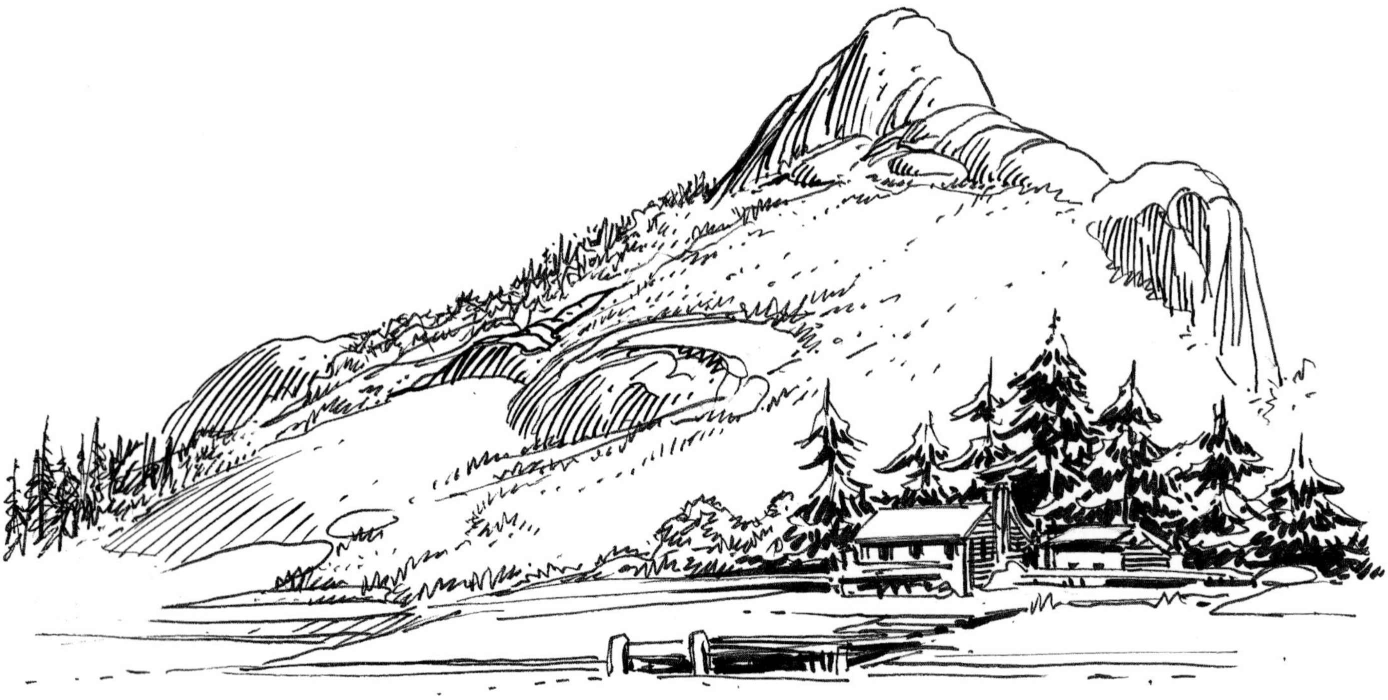

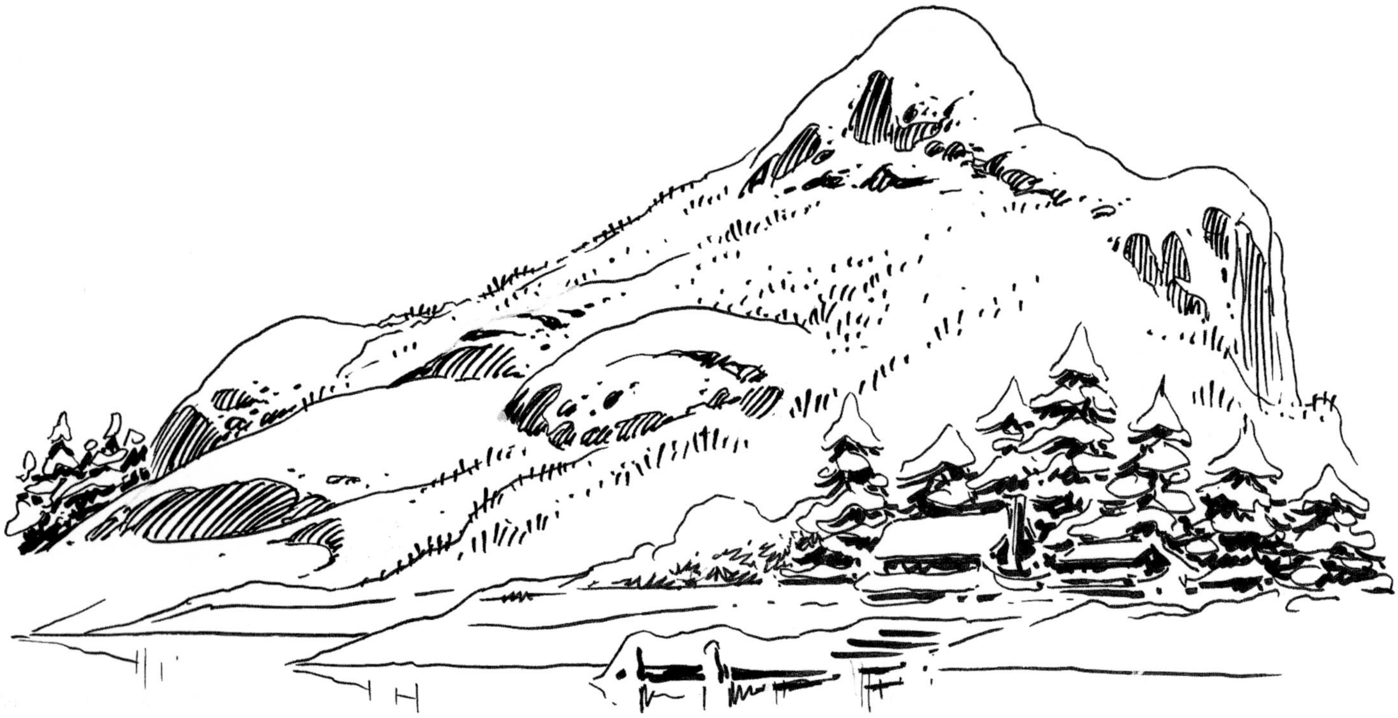

Trees

For drawings like the cabin landscape, you don't really have to know a lot of details about trees and leaves. You just need to know how a generic evergreen is shaped. But if you were asked to illustrate a comic book story in which trees, specific kinds of trees, were important to the story line, how would you go about doing it?

If you are like most aspiring comic book artists, you may be surprised to find that it's not so easy to draw some very familiar things, things you see every day, like trees. For practice, use your sketchbook and draw the trees in your own vicinity. What is the general shape of the tree? What is the texture of the bark? How do the roots form at the trunk's base? What do the leaves look like? Include all those details in your sketches.

Also be aware that the difference between species of trees from different parts of the world is enormous. The northern oak and maple are nothing like the tropical cypress and palm. What you can't find within walking or reasonable driving distance from your home, you'll have to look up—at the library, in nature magazines, in department store catalogs, on the Internet.

Cypress roots.

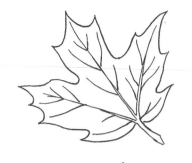

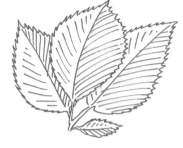

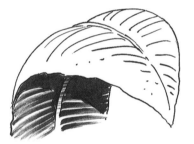

Top to bottom: maple, elm, pine, and palm.

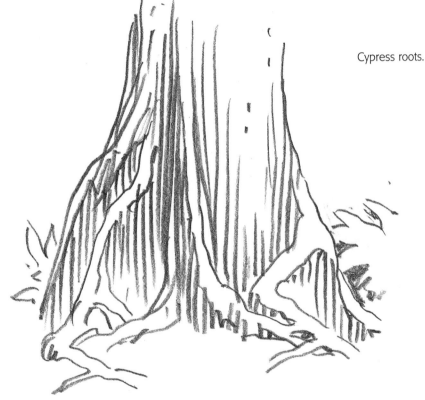

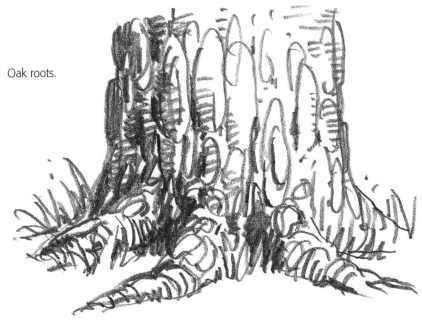

Oak roots.

Materials and Texture

Comic book artists are called upon to draw objects made of many different materials (metal, plastic, wood, rubber, leather, etc.) and with surfaces of very different textures (smooth, rough, serrated, basket-weave, etc.). The only way to become proficient in rendering all the combinations of shape, material, and texture seen in ordinary household objects is—you guessed it—to draw them! Use any drawing material with which you feel most comfortable: pencil, ball-point pen, india ink, wash. Or try combinations of these. The intent is to analyze and duplicate texture and form, not to stylize.

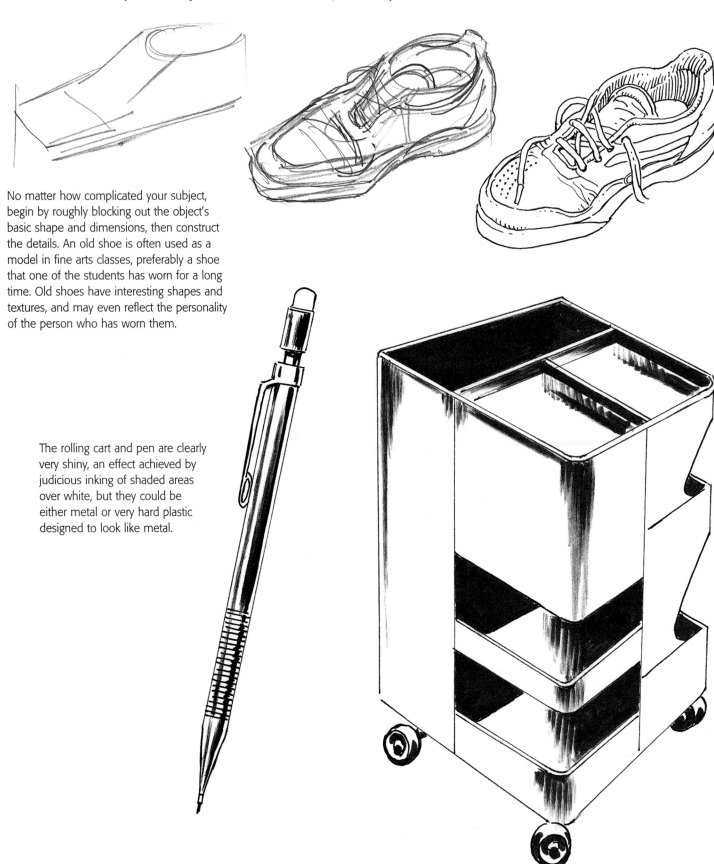

No matter how complicated your subject, begin by roughly blocking out the object's basic shape and dimensions, then construct the details. An old shoe is often used as a model in fine arts classes, preferably a shoe that one of the students has worn for a long time. Old shoes have interesting shapes and textures, and may even reflect the personality of the person who has worn them.

The rolling cart and pen are clearly very shiny, an effect achieved by judicious inking of shaded areas over white, but they could be either metal or very hard plastic designed to look like metal.

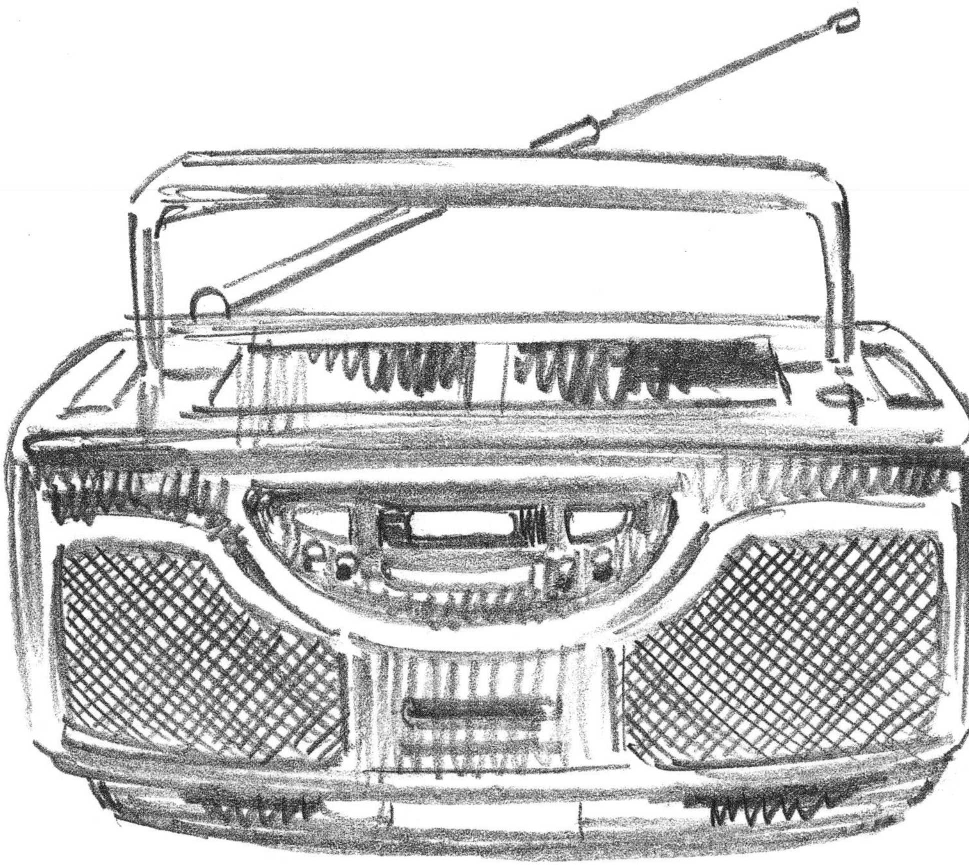

I used pencil, rather than pen and ink, to draw the rubber tire and plastic telephone and boom box. Plastic objects definitely have a lustre of their own, but I didn't want either to be shiny. To convey the relative softness of rubber I worked to make the tread realistic and highlighted the tire part surrounding the hubcap.

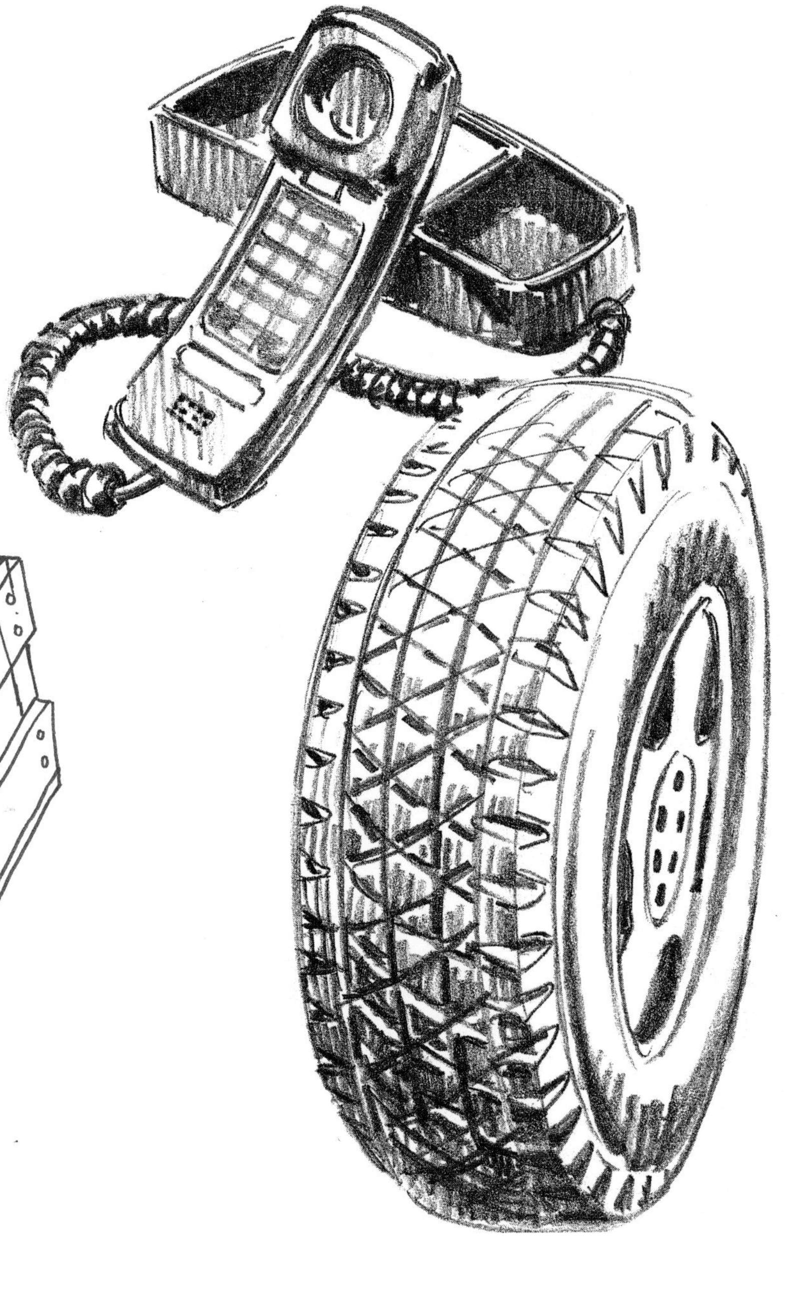

A wooden crate holds together because it is constructed in a logical manner. The end pieces are made of thicker wood so they won't split when the long side slats are nailed in. To maintain consistency of perspective, it helps to draw through solid or opaque areas to show where connections occur, even if they will not be seen in the final drawing.

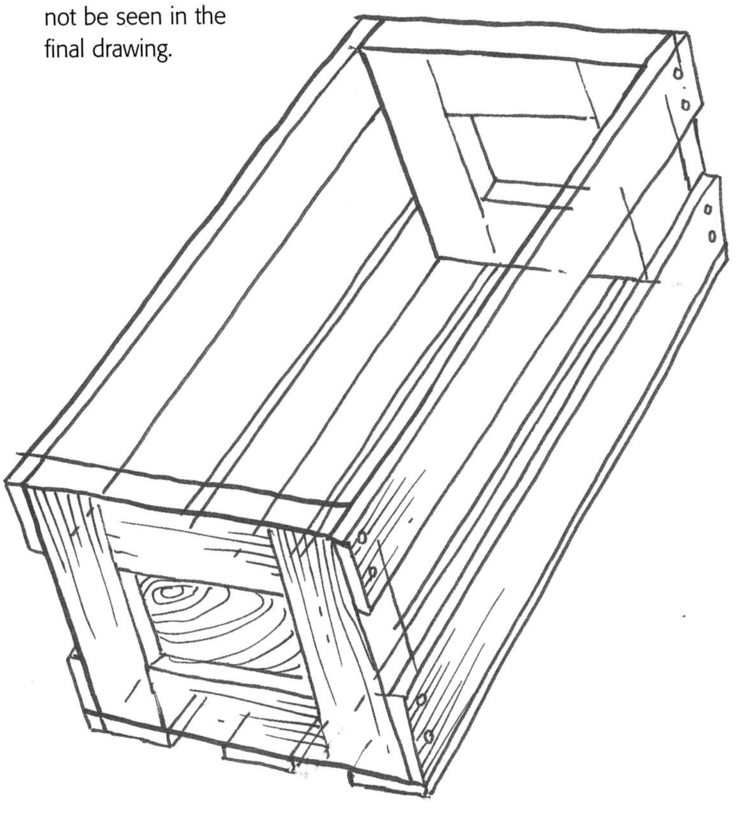

Weapons

Weapons are ubiquitous in comic books stories dealing with good versus evil, superhero versus villain. And, like all the other background details in a story, weapons must be drawn correctly. Historically, the two types of weapons featured most often in action-adventure stories have been guns and knifes. As always, practice drawing weapons by first acquiring proper reference. There are a number of magazines featuring pictures and information for gun collectors on both ancient and current weaponry, and many Internet sites also feature illustrated gun and knife catalogs. Use the pictures as models. Copy them and concentrate on the details. Check for pictures of people firing these weapons.

The selection of which kind of knife or gun to illustrate is dependent on the story's location and the specific situation. An artist wouldn't draw an Uzi in the hands of a superhero from the future, or a medieval saber hanging from the belt of a modern urban crimefighter.

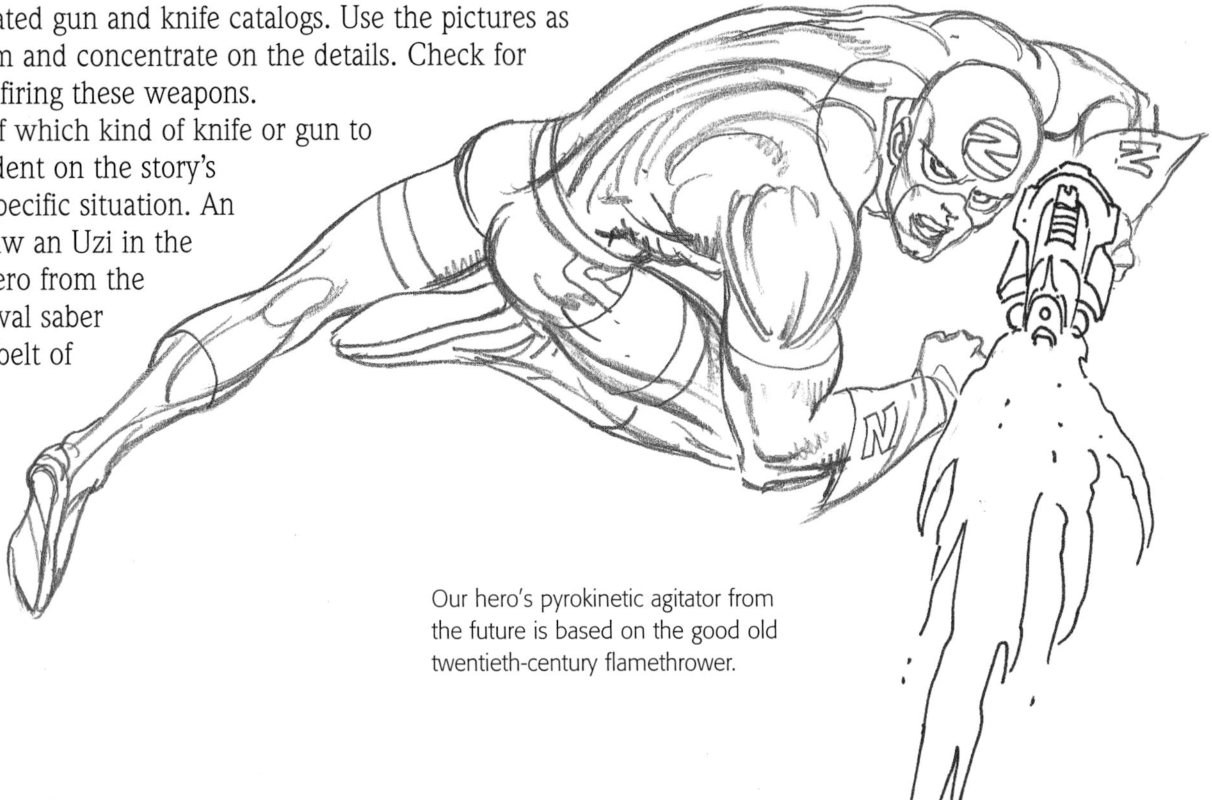

Our hero's pyrokinetic agitator from the future is based on the good old twentieth-century flamethrower.

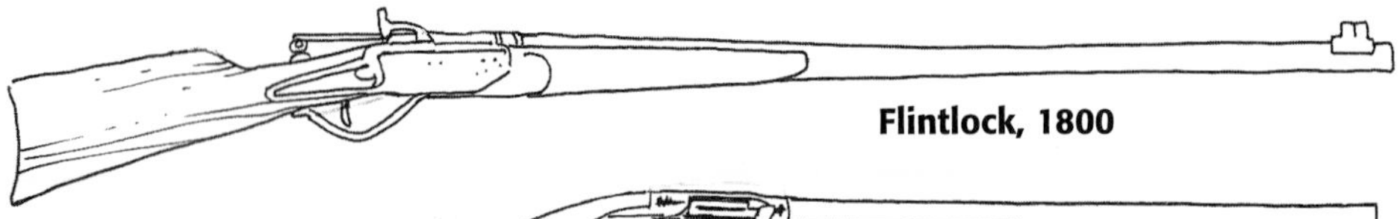

Flintlock, 1800

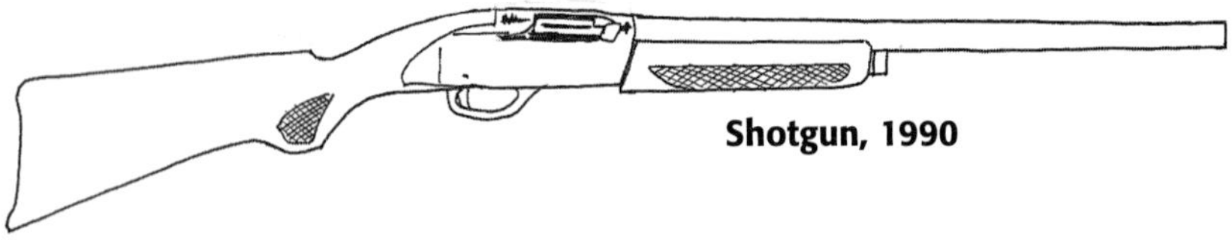

Shotgun, 1990

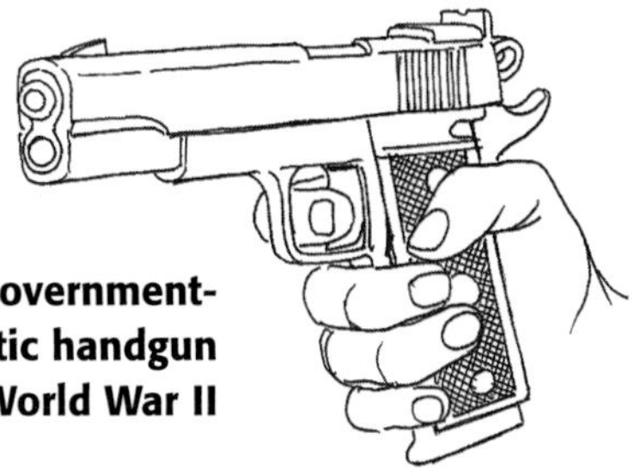

45-caliber government-issue automatic handgun used during World War II

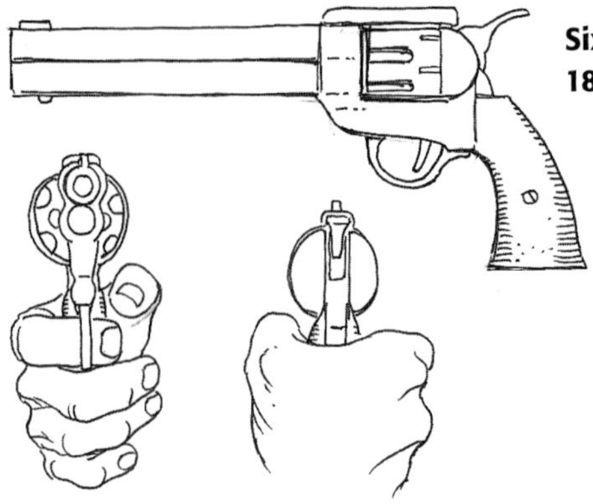

Six-shooter, 1860

It's important for the artist to be able to draw front, back, top, and bottom angles of guns. Notice how a hand fits around a gun both from the front and from the back.

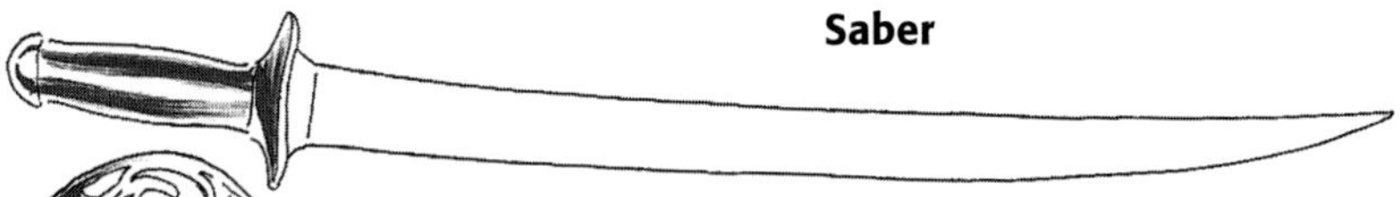

Saber

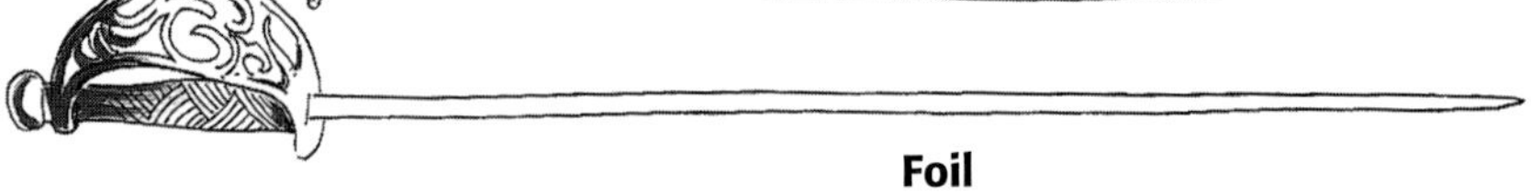

Foil

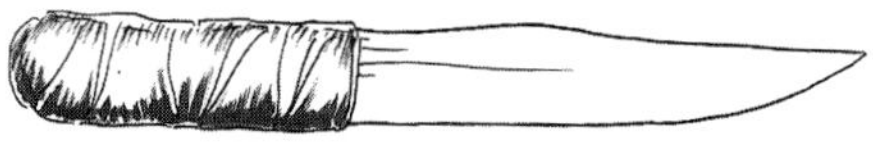

Bone blade

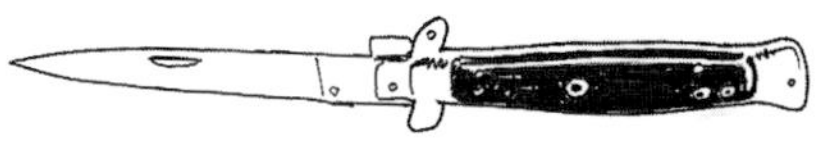

Switchblade

Vehicles

Cars, trucks, motorcycles, and buses are prominent in many comic book stories. This is another instance when picture reference plays an extremely important part in generating credibility. Keep an extensive vehicles file. Don't just collect pictures of exteriors, but of interiors. Practice drawing details—dashboard, steering wheel, shift levers, pedals, headlights, tail lights. Don't try to make them up or draw them from memory. Automobile references are easy to find—in newspaper ads, magazines, and the Internet.

Henry Ford would find it hard to believe the advancements made since his Model T. What will cars look like 100 years from now? For visions of the more immediate future, check out an automobile show—and take your sketchbook.

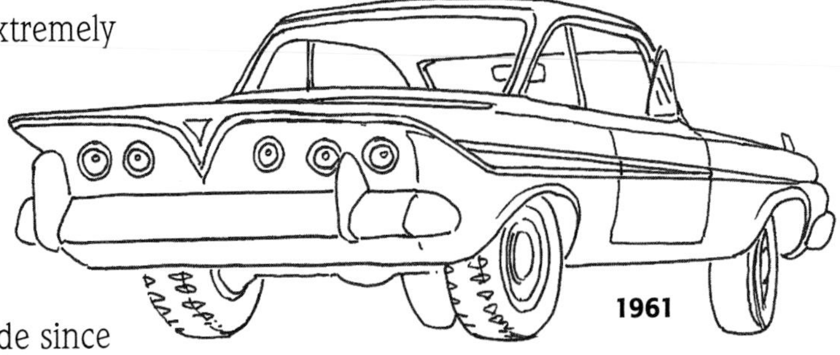

1961

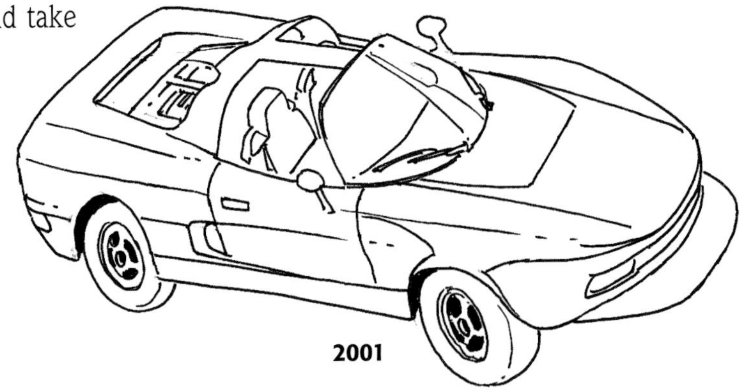

2001

1991

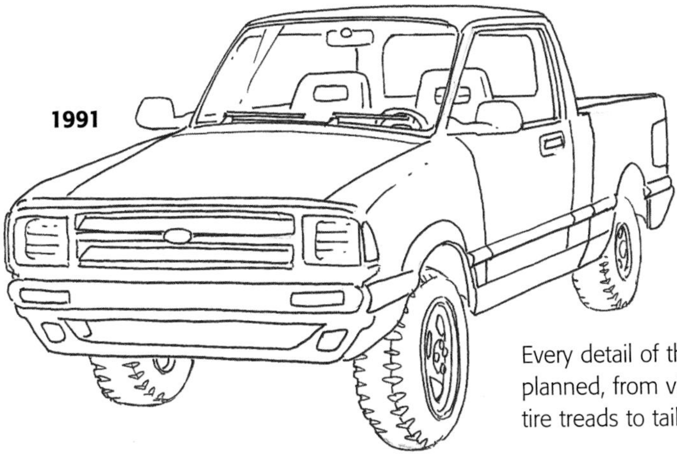

Every detail of this truck exterior was planned, from viewing mirrors to heavy-duty tire treads to tail lights to headlights.

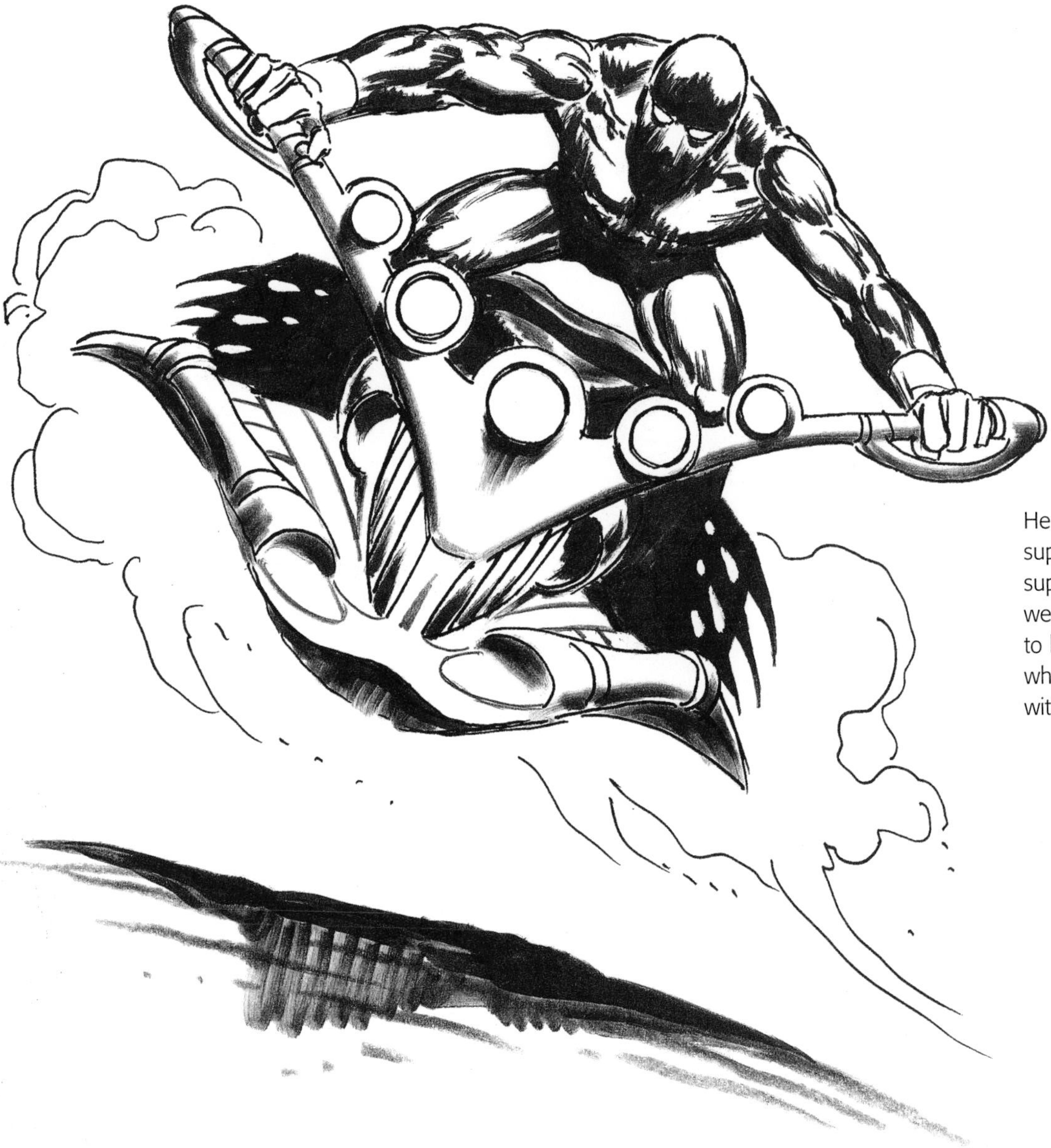

Here I wanted both the superhero's costume and his supercool cycle to look like they were made out of materials yet to be invented. It's amazing what effects you can achieve with ink and brush!

Getting the Details Right: Drawing From a Script

Being able to draw different objects accurately is not something you need to learn simply for your own sense of accomplishment. Often comic book artists draw from scripts written by other people. The scriptwriters do not simply outline action sequences, they describe the background and objects they want drawn in each panel. We'll get into panel descriptions and scripts in more detail later, but this example is typical.

Panel description: A room furnished with a desk and chair. One or two books are on the desk, along with a calendar, pens, a framed picture, etc. The desk itself is wood with drawers on both sides of the leg space. The chair is leather, with arm rests and casters. Near the desk are a T.V. and a fax machine. Holding onto the desk is a man "morphing" into a monster.

If a staff cartoonist asked to do this panel turned in the drawing on the left, he (or she) wouldn't have the job for long. I repeat: If cartoonists draw furniture and appliances in a credible manner, the action taking place will also be believed. It is an essential part of graphic storytelling. If a desk looks like a poorly constructed box, or a T.V. is hastily drawn, the story suffers.

The inking here leaves no doubt that the top part of this superhero's costume is made of metal and the rest is fabric. (And please don't send me letters asking how he puts that megasword in a scabbard. A firm squeeze on the skull sends our hero's mighty blade back to Shirat the Weapon Master, until it is needed once again.)

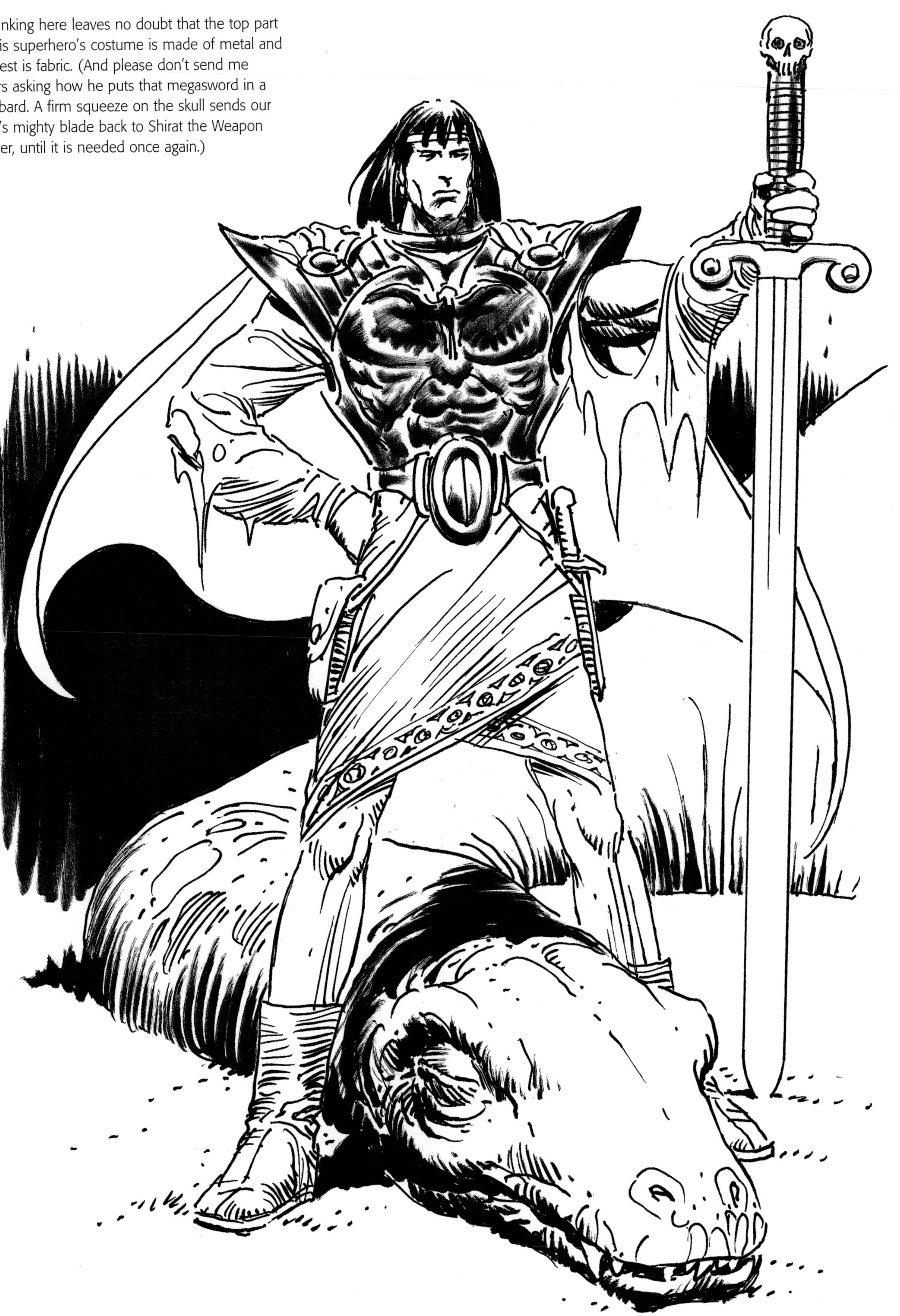

CITYSCAPES AND INTERIORS

If our superhero flies over a city, the city must look real. Basically, a city is a nest of boxes piled one on top of the other. Details are added based on careful reference, not to be made up or from memory.

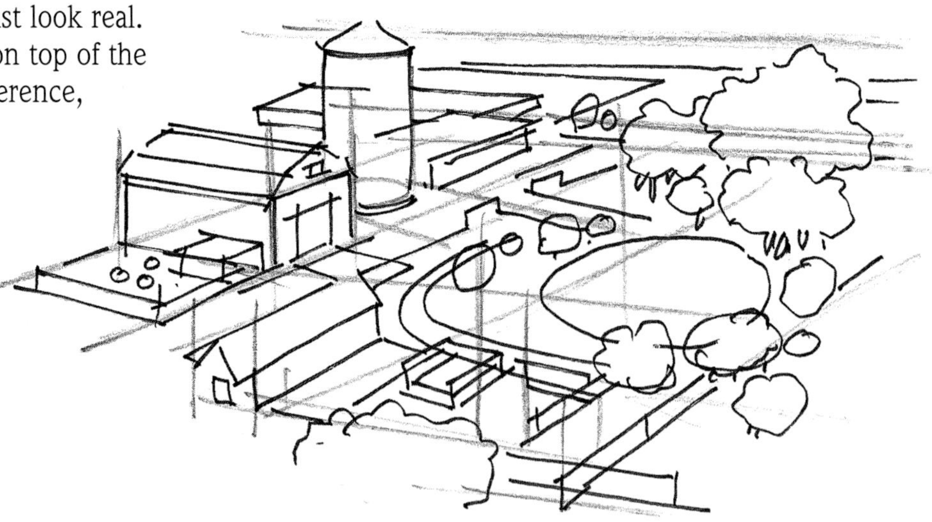

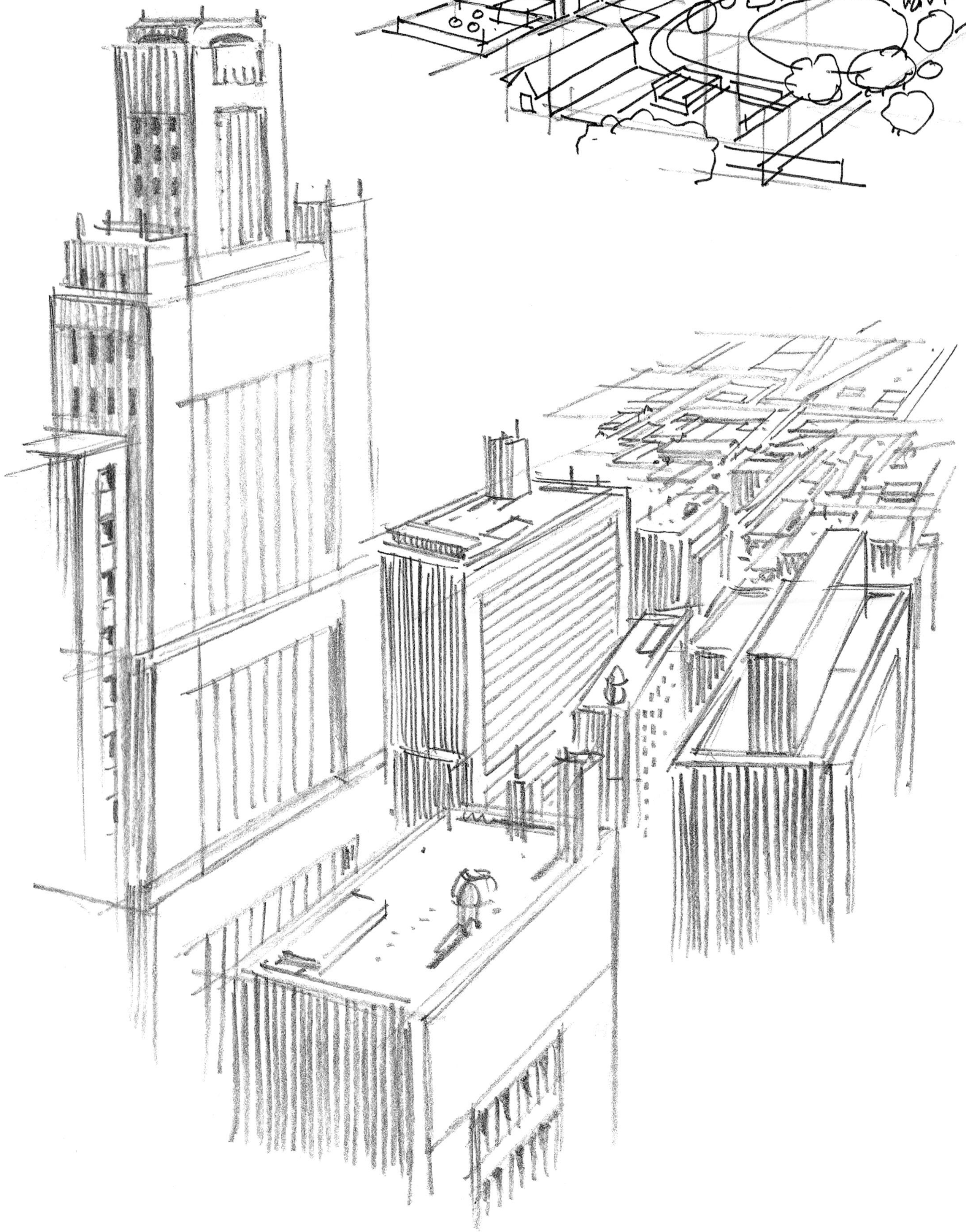

If our superhero is walking down a city street, the street must look real. A helpful approach is to use a checkerboard graph to establish overall perspective. Then draw rough outlines of cars, trees, sidewalk, steps, and other objects using the checkerboard as a guide. This procedure works for a single building or an entire city.

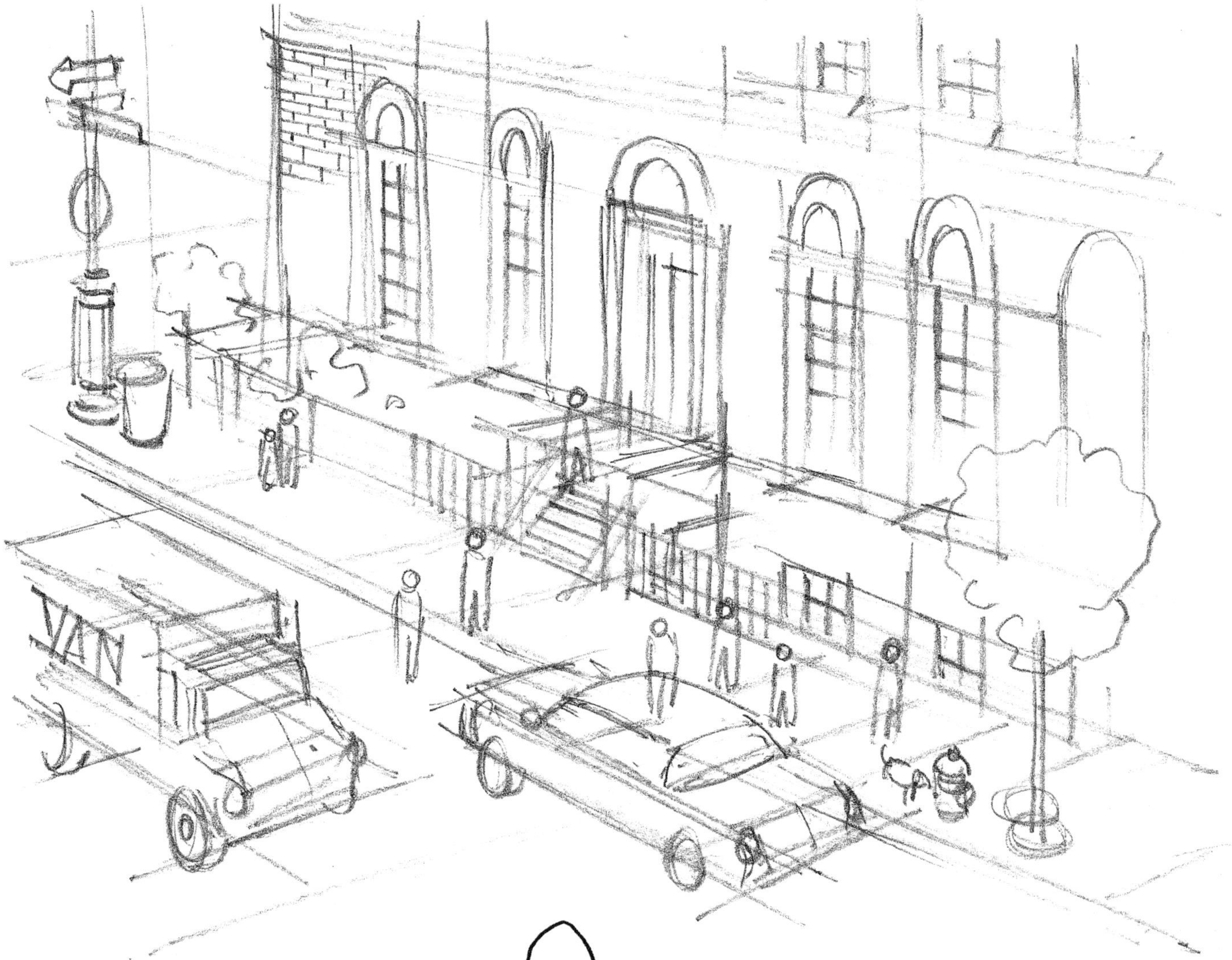
VAN

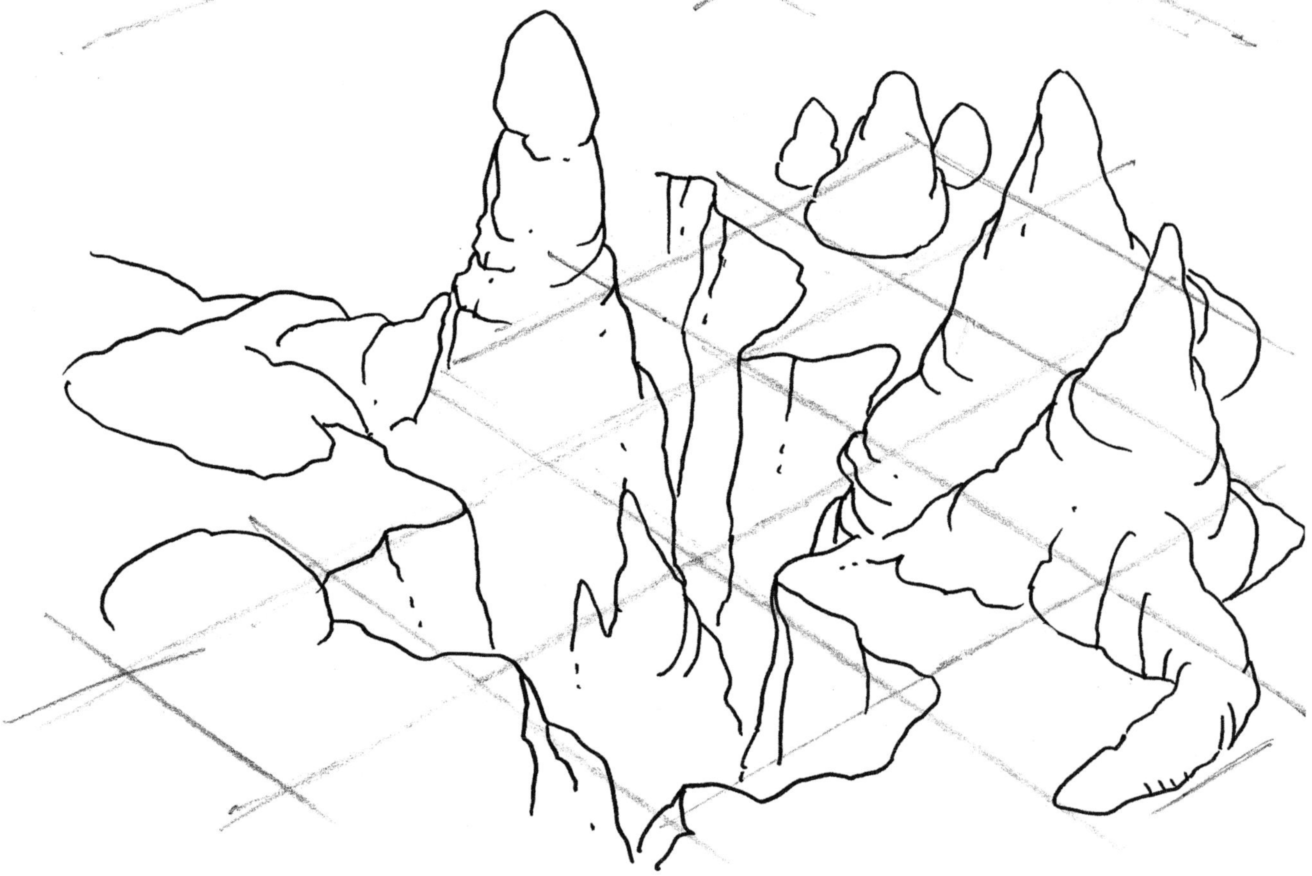

One way to become familiar with the interior space that will be occupied by a story's characters is to draw some rough sketches of different rooms. These are much like the designers' layouts for film scenes, which help the director and the camera operator to visualize a room and its contents before blocking out the actual moves of the actors.

You can start with the checkerboard method shown previously. Consider how large the room must be to hold all the objects you want to be in it. What is the style of the furniture and where will each piece be placed?

It's unnecessary to do a perfect architectural rendering. The purpose of these drawings is to give you, the cartoonist, a clear idea of a room's dimensions and the relative sizes of objects in the room so that you will be better able to plan where your characters will first be seen and where and how the action will take place.

Although you may want to use a ruler at first to create your checkerboard, eventually you will be able to draw your interiors by eye alone. One good reason not to continue to rely on ruler and checkerboard with perfectly straight lines is that exaggeration, or deviation from "true" perspective, is often more effective than a drawing that follows all the rules.

You may notice that the objects in the overhead view are not exactly the same as they are in the interior schematic. The differences are irrelevant. The only really important objects are the ones that will play a part in the development of the plot line.

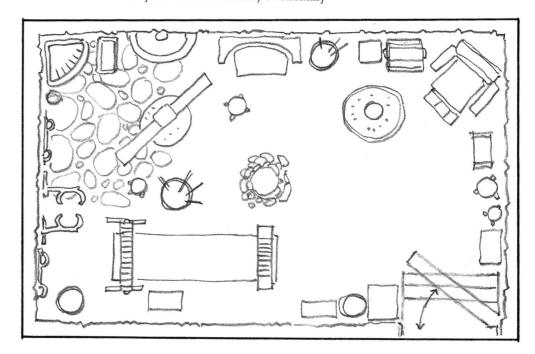

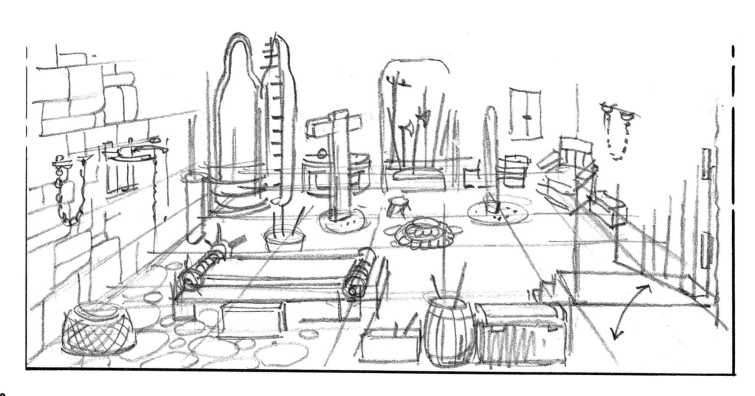

It's a lot easier to plan a page or panel illustration when you are familiar with the parameters of the settings in which the different sequences will take place. Armed with specific site information, you will find that the problems of deciding on angles and perspective, foreground vs. background, longshot vs. closeup, etc. are much less difficult to solve.

The scene shown here takes place in the torture chamber sketched on the opposite page. I included only a small portion of the setting, but a clear picture of the room helped me work out the dynamics of the composition.

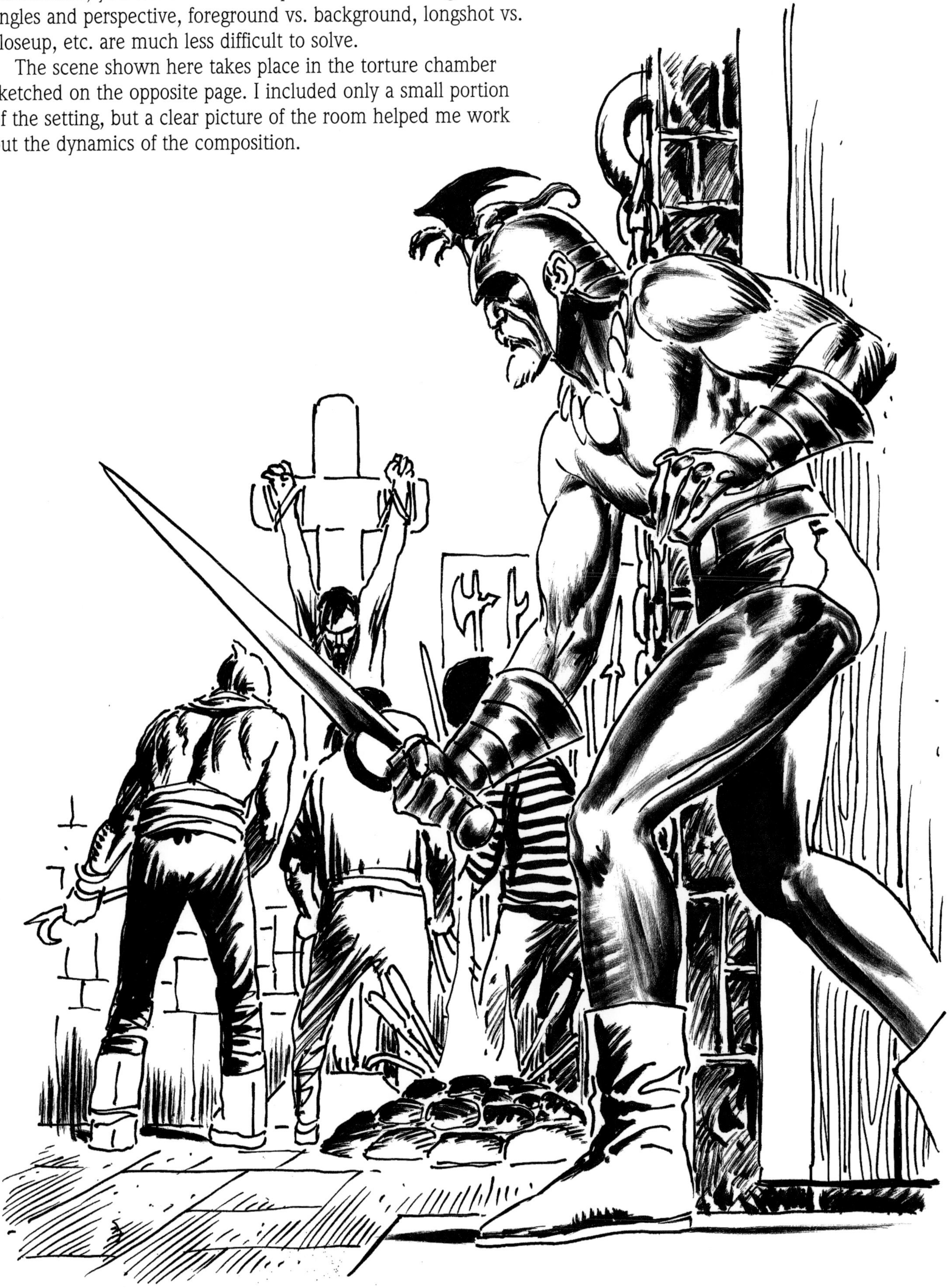

TELLING THE STORY
PROCEDURE AND TOOLS

Every superhero comic starts with the story. The comic book artist's responsibility is to *tell* the entire story graphically, using the most effective layouts, the best compositions, and the most exciting action sequences possible. A few beautifully rendered drawings will not compensate for a poorly told story. Once you have the first draft of your script, you can begin the process of turning your story into inked, lettered, and illustrated comic book panels.

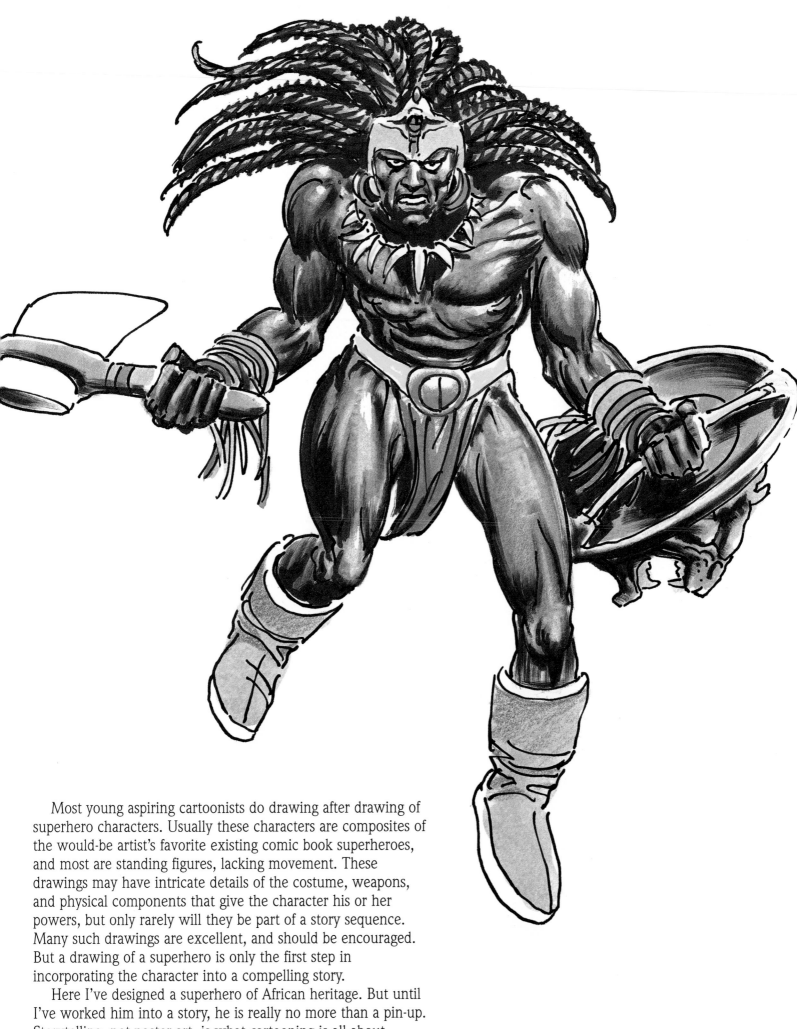

Most young aspiring cartoonists do drawing after drawing of superhero characters. Usually these characters are composites of the would-be artist's favorite existing comic book superheroes, and most are standing figures, lacking movement. These drawings may have intricate details of the costume, weapons, and physical components that give the character his or her powers, but only rarely will they be part of a story sequence. Many such drawings are excellent, and should be encouraged. But a drawing of a superhero is only the first step in incorporating the character into a compelling story.

Here I've designed a superhero of African heritage. But until I've worked him into a story, he is really no more than a pin-up. Storytelling, not poster art, is what cartooning is all about.

SCRIPTS AND SKETCHES

This sample script, an excerpt from a longer narrative, is an example of a form often used by comic book writers. It is very similar to a "shooting script" for a film. This script also includes suggestions for the layout of the panels. The scriptwriter has envisioned a two-thirds-page "splash" drawing (a *splash panel,* the one that opens a given sequence, must hook the reader) of outer space as seen from the ship, with an inset of the spaceship's interior.

1.

THE SCRIPT — PAGE ONE

TITLE / "THE POWER"

(SPLASH) PANEL 1.

AT LEAST 2/3 OF PAGE

DESCRIPTION:

LONGSHOT OF OUTER SPACE, FILLED WITH STAR CLUSTERS AND DISTANT SOLAR SYSTEM MILKY WAYS. FOCUS ON ONE PLANET COMPOSED OF A STRANGE ALIEN LANDSCAPE, SIMILAR TO THE ROCK FORMATIONS IN THE GRAND CANYON. A LONE SPACECRAFT IS NEAR THE PLANET, SEEMINGLY ATTRACTED, BUT STILL QUITE A DISTANCE AWAY.

CAPTION:

THE YEAR IS 2067. SPACE TRAVEL IS NOW A COMMON MEANS OF TRANSPORT... BUT... THE UNEXPECTED STILL OCCURS...

BALLOON (FROM SPACESHIP):

WE'RE... IN... TROUBLE!

PANEL 2. (INSET PANEL IN SPLASH)

DESCRIPTION:

INTERIOR OF SPACESHIP. CLOSEUP OF PILOT AND CO-PILOT AT CONTROLS. GAIL (WHO IS THE CHIEF PILOT) IS YOUNG, ATTRACTIVE. JIM (CO-PILOT), IN HIS LATE TWENTIES. HE IS GOOD-LOOKING. RUGGED. THEY ARE BOTH BENT OVER THE SHIP'S CONTROLS, TENSE AND WORRIED. THEY ARE BOTH ATTIRED IN FLIGHT GEAR. SPACESUIT, HELMET, ETC.

GAIL: ① WE'RE BEING PULLED TOWARDS THAT PLANETOID... SOME SORT OF MAGNETIC BEAM...

② KICK THE POWER, JIM!

JIM: AYE, CAP'N.

(MORE)

2.

THE SCRIPT

TITLE: "THE POWER" (CONT'D)

PAGE ONE

PANEL 3.

DESCRIPTION:

ANGLE FROM SURFACE OF PLANETOID TOWARDS APPROACHING SPACECRAFT. THE SHIP'S TRAJECTORY IS ERRATIC, SEEMING TO COME IN SIDEWAYS.

BALLOON (FROM SHIP):

I-I CAN'T CONTROL IT, JIM! WE'RE GOING... DOWN...

PANEL 4.

DESCRIPTION:

THE SPACESHIP SKIMS ONTO THE PLANETOID'S SURFACE, CRASHING INTO HUGE ROCKS AND BOULDERS. THE SHIP WILL BE DAMAGED. CRIPPLED. BUT NOT DESTROYED.

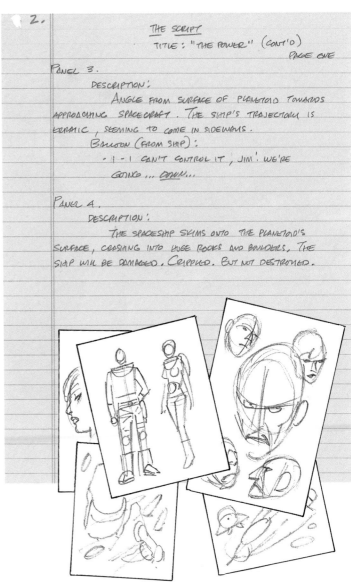

Now you are ready to do rough sketches of some key scenes based on the script. As you do your sketches, you will become aware of areas for which you need references. For example, how credibly can you draw the control panel of a spaceship? Collect all necessary references before you start to do final layout and drawings.

It's a good idea to organize all your reference materials so that you can find what you need quickly. Maintain an up-to-date filing system, with the folders labeled by subject. As you collection grows, you will need to spend less and less time searching for references before you start your actual drawing. Your reference files should be right next to your workstation.

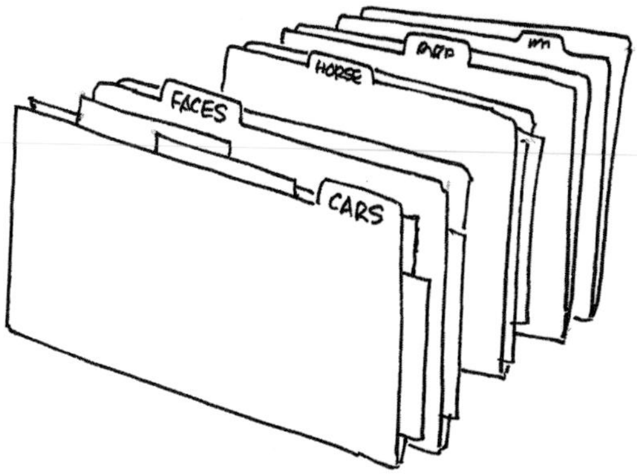
HORSE
FACES
CARS

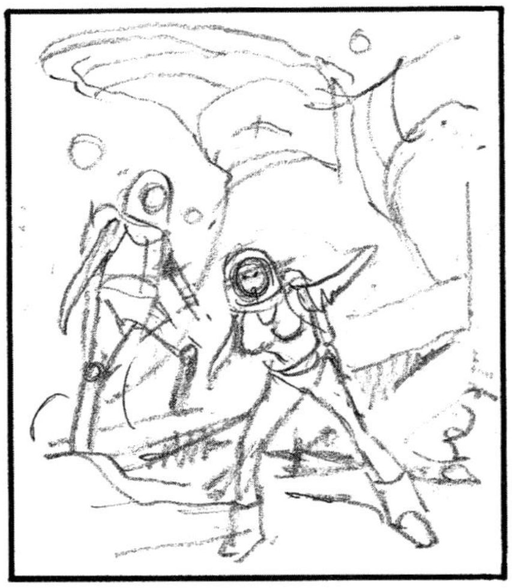

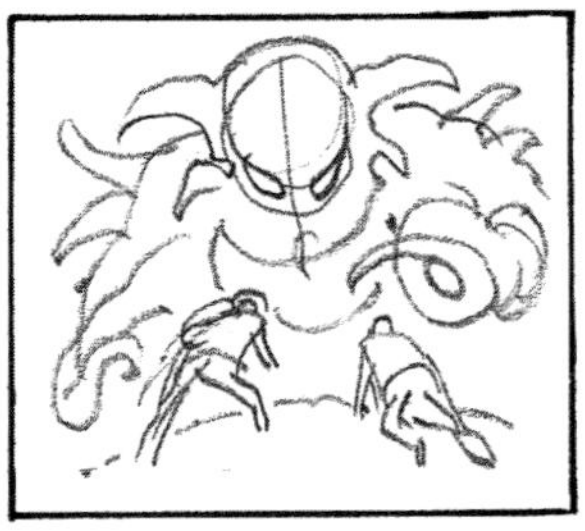

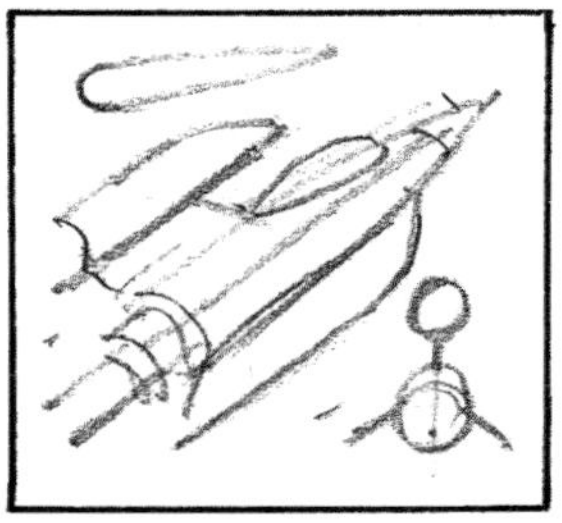

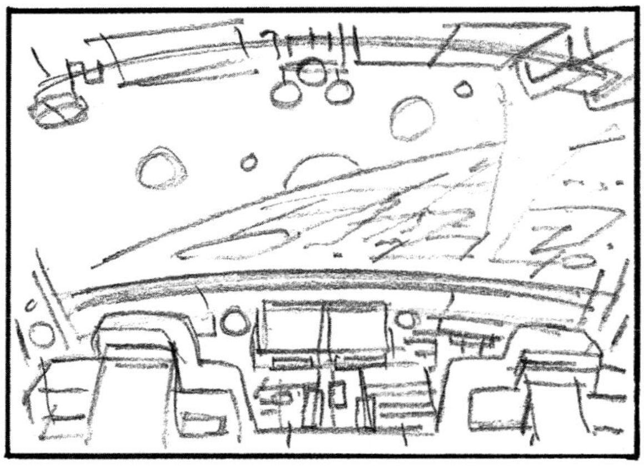

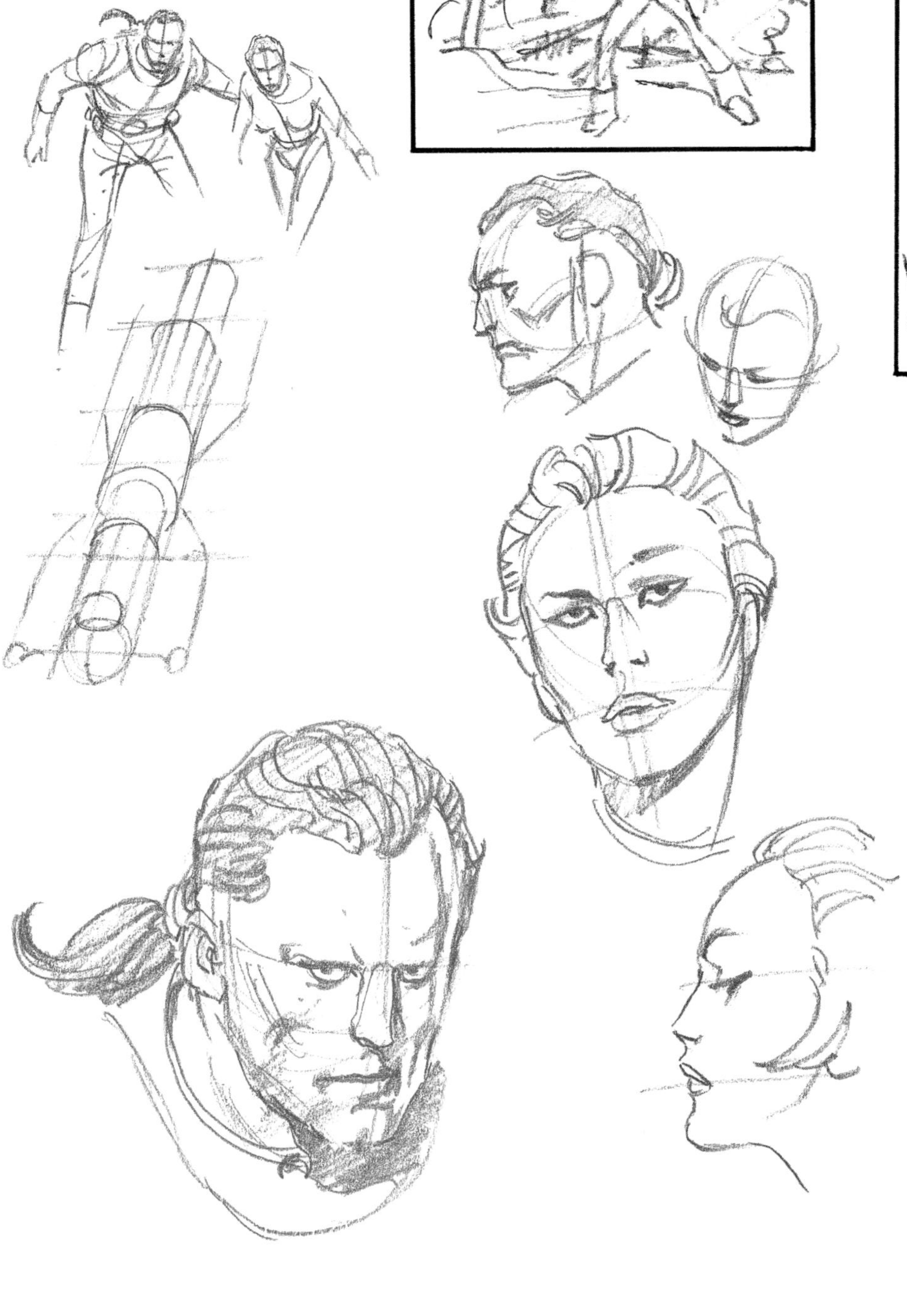

A FEW BASICS

My love for comic books goes way back. I remember the debut of Superman, in Action Comics #1. No, the printing plates weren't carved in stone. But the printing was coarse, the colors were flat, and the paper was rough. I even remember the smell of the ink. I loved comics. I still do.

As a kid, I had no idea of the processes by which comic books were published or printed. I assumed that the cartoonists drew their originals the same size as the printed material, that the black lines were pencil or ink, and that color was applied on top of the original black lines. All those assumptions were wrong!

Most comic books are about 6 inches by 9 inches. Original comic artwork, however, is usually 10 inches by 15 inches. The larger size allows the artist to include more details, and when the drawing is reduced (to approximately 60% of its original size), the printed image is sharper.

Different artists use different types of paper. I generally use smooth, two-ply drawing paper, but some artists prefer a slightly textured surface. Whatever paper is chosen must accept pen, brush, and india ink without "bleeding." (See the Supplies section, page 138, for more information.) Thin stationery sheets and computer paper are not acceptable because they are too easily creased or torn.

Original artwork is first done in pencil, then inked. Color is usually not added until the drawing has been reduced. Most of the the color in comic books is added by professional colorists, and not by the artists who do the black-and-white drawings. (There are exceptions, of course. I did all the color for the superheroes in this book!)

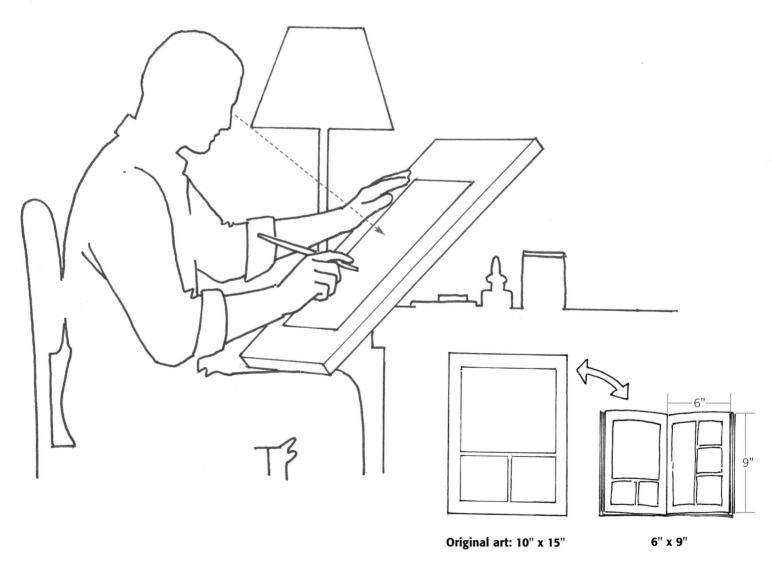

Original art: 10" x 15"   **6" x 9"**

THUMBNAILS

Before you begin actually drawing on your 10- by 15-inch page, you need to make a final decision on what page layout you will use. Experiment by sketching a few alternative layouts, called thumbnails. Making the thumbnails much smaller than the page you will be drawing on allows you to compare the alternatives side by side. (For all your rough sketches, by the way, you can use any kind of paper you have handy.) Deciding on layout design is very subjective.

Which layout works best in terms of the flow of the story? Keep in mind that the largest panel should, in general, be reserved for the most dynamic scene, or the one with the most action. A fight scene is more effective in a large space than it would be squeezed into a small square. Conversely, two people talking, or one person walking, can be placed in a smaller panel.

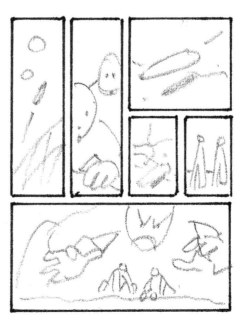

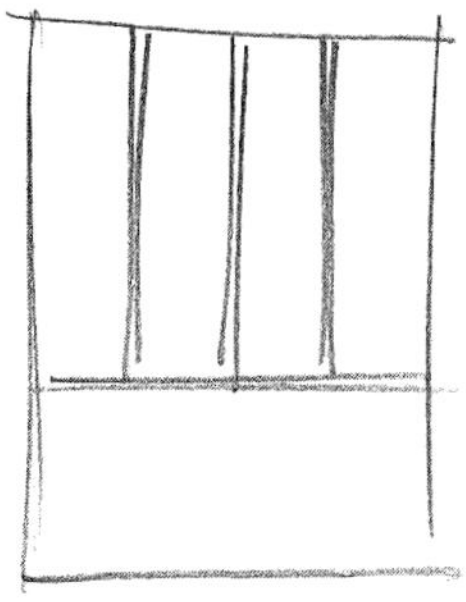

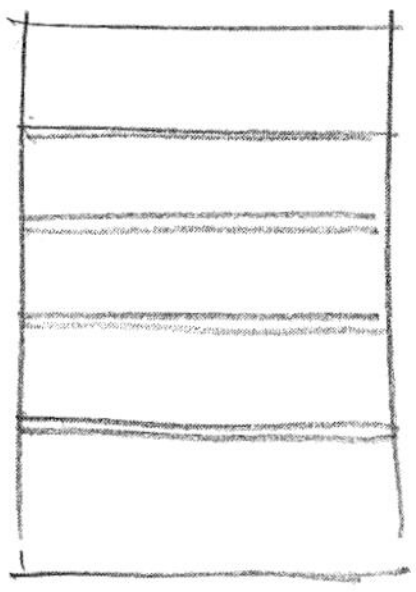

It sometimes helps to add very rough sketches to your thumbnails. The dramatic effect of the two examples shown here would be very different when the drawings were finished. They are both versions of a sequence in which a spaceship makes an emergency landing on a strange planet. Exploring the terrain, two of the ship's passsengers find several strange eggs. What they *do not see* is mama space monster, intent on protecting her unhatched progeny.

PENCILING

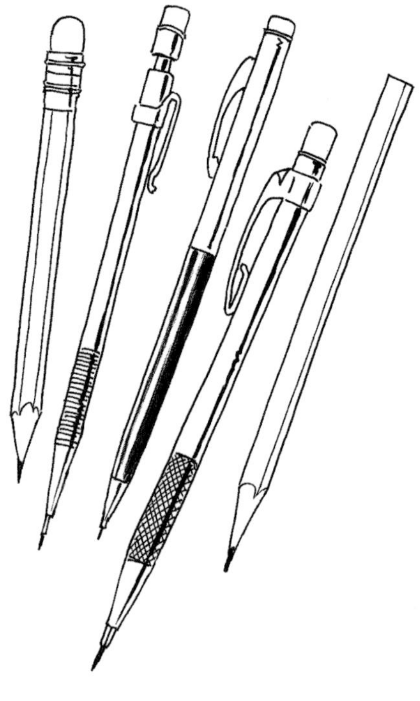

The pencil drawing is the first stage of creating the art for a comic book page. Pencils come in a wide variety of shapes and forms. Some artists use only mechanical pencils; other prefer those made of wood. Test some different kinds and decide for yourself which works best for you.

Pencil leads also vary widely. The hardest and thinnest are H series pencils, which range from 9H (the hardest) to H; the HB is a transition between the harder leads and the softer leads, the B series. For doing your rough drawings I recommend that you have 3H, 2H, and HB pencils. If you like, you can experiment with the B pencils, which give a thicker line but are hard to erase or paint over.

Be sure you have a supply of good-quality erasers of different kinds. It can be terribly frustrating to finish a pencil drawing, then not be able to make a minor correction because the eraser you are using smears the penciling rather than removing the error. Before you use an eraser on your actual drawing, test it on another piece of paper with the same surface and the same thickness of pencil line.

Check out the Supplies section on page 138 for more information on pencils and erasers.

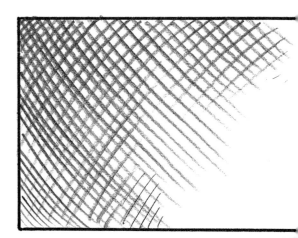

These four types of line work, designed for dark areas and for rendering textures, can be done with pencil or ink. Clockwise from top left: line; crosshatch, dark to light; crosshatch, double and triple lines; basketweave, straight and curved.

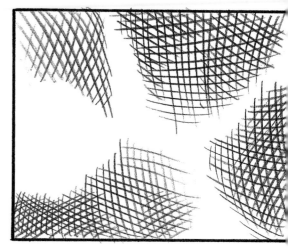

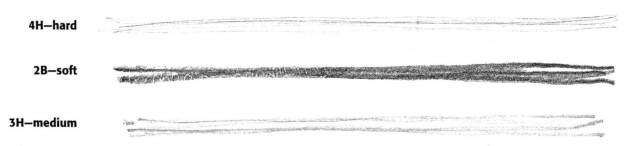

4H—hard

2B—soft

3H—medium

As a general rule, begin your penciling with a semihard 3H lead. Don't press too hard on the paper at this or any other stage. Too much pressure will create impressions and dents in your paper, making it difficult to erase or ink over. Do not include details at this stage.

Begin to add details with a 2H or HB lead. You can also suggest light sources and shadows. If the lead is too soft, or too much pressure is applied, erasing the pencil (to change a detail, such as the bird's right wing, or after inking) may become a problem.

On a piece of scrap paper or fine sandpaper, flatten the point of the lead to a wider stroke, then finish the shading and lining in the darkest parts. Using a softer lead may leave an excessive residue of graphite, causing erasure smears or poor absorption of ink to paper.

FROM THUMBNAILS TO FULL-SIZE LAYOUTS

Comic books are a combination of text and illustrations. Words and pictures. Text is, of course, an important element of telling the story. It is also an integral part of the panel composition. It is critically important to plan the placement of balloons, captions, and sound effects before you start your final drawings. If your initial rough layouts do not include space for text, you will have to squeeze or crowd your lettering or, even worse, find you have to cover an important part of your drawing to get the text in.

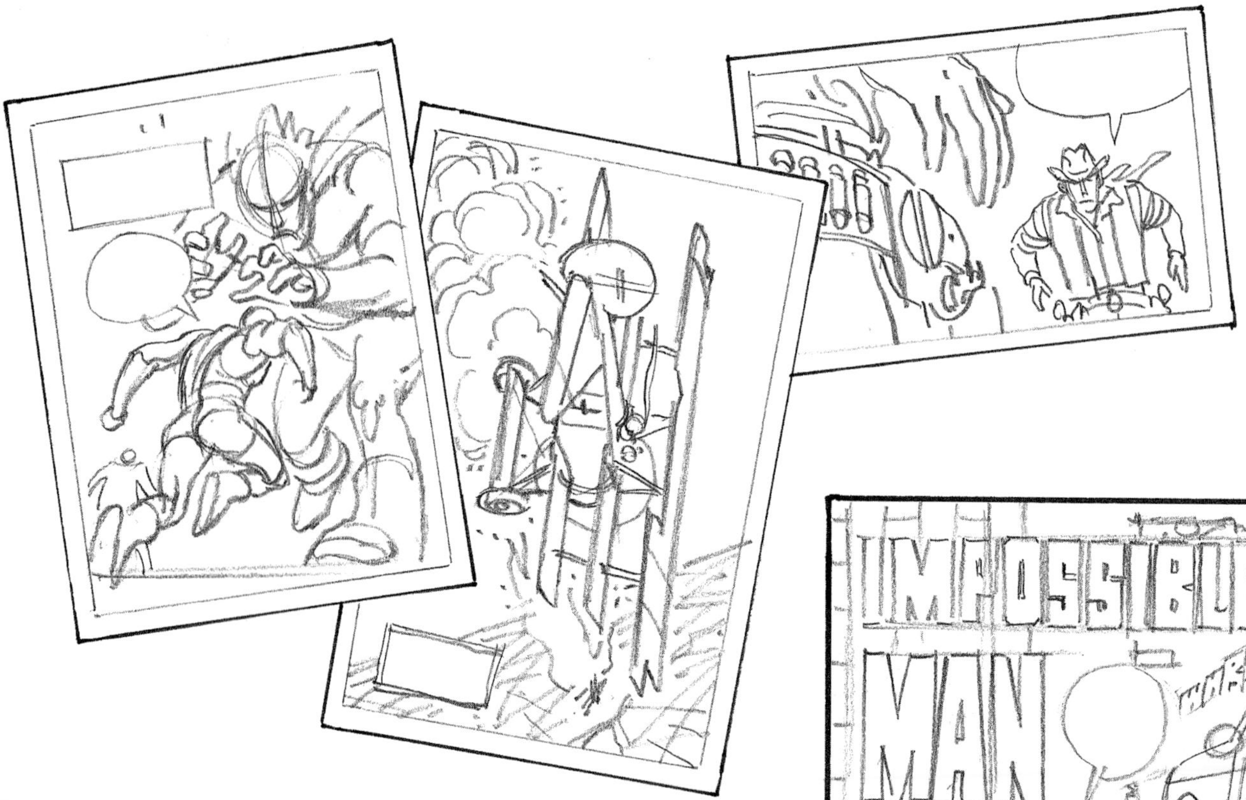

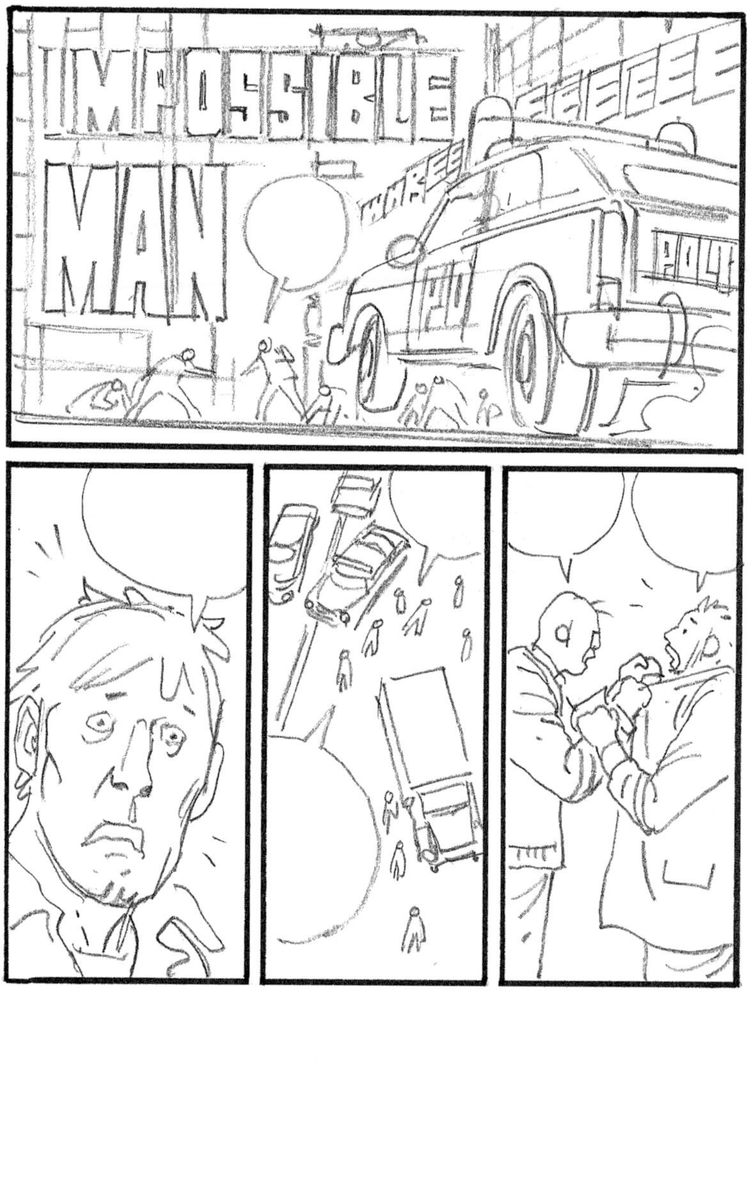
IMPOSSIBLE
MAN

Armed with your preliminary thumbnails, character sketches, and reference pictures, draw layout roughs, with approximate spaces for text, on 8½- by 11-inch sheets. (Doing adequate layout roughs is *not* as easy as it may sound. The last eight pages of this section show how detailed the layout process can be when an artist has a complex script to follow.) Once you have made final decisions about layout and basic composition, you are ready to start your full-size drawing.

In their enthusiasm to get into the "real" drawing, novices often attempt to bypass some of the preliminary stages. But there are no shortcuts. In order to do a proper job, the comic book artist must exercise discipline and patience. Drawing a complete, effectively told story is a building process. Without the proper foundation, the story will literally fall apart.

Although your overall drawing size should be 10 by 15 inches, be sure to leave a ½-inch border around the artwork, a sort of protective frame which you can use to handle the drawing. If you use 11- by 17-inch paper, it's easy to get the dimensions right.

Use a 3H pencil to rule the drawing areas. Make the gutters between panels ¼-inch wide. Now block out all the panels on the page, including space for text. *The drawings at this stage should still be quite rough.*

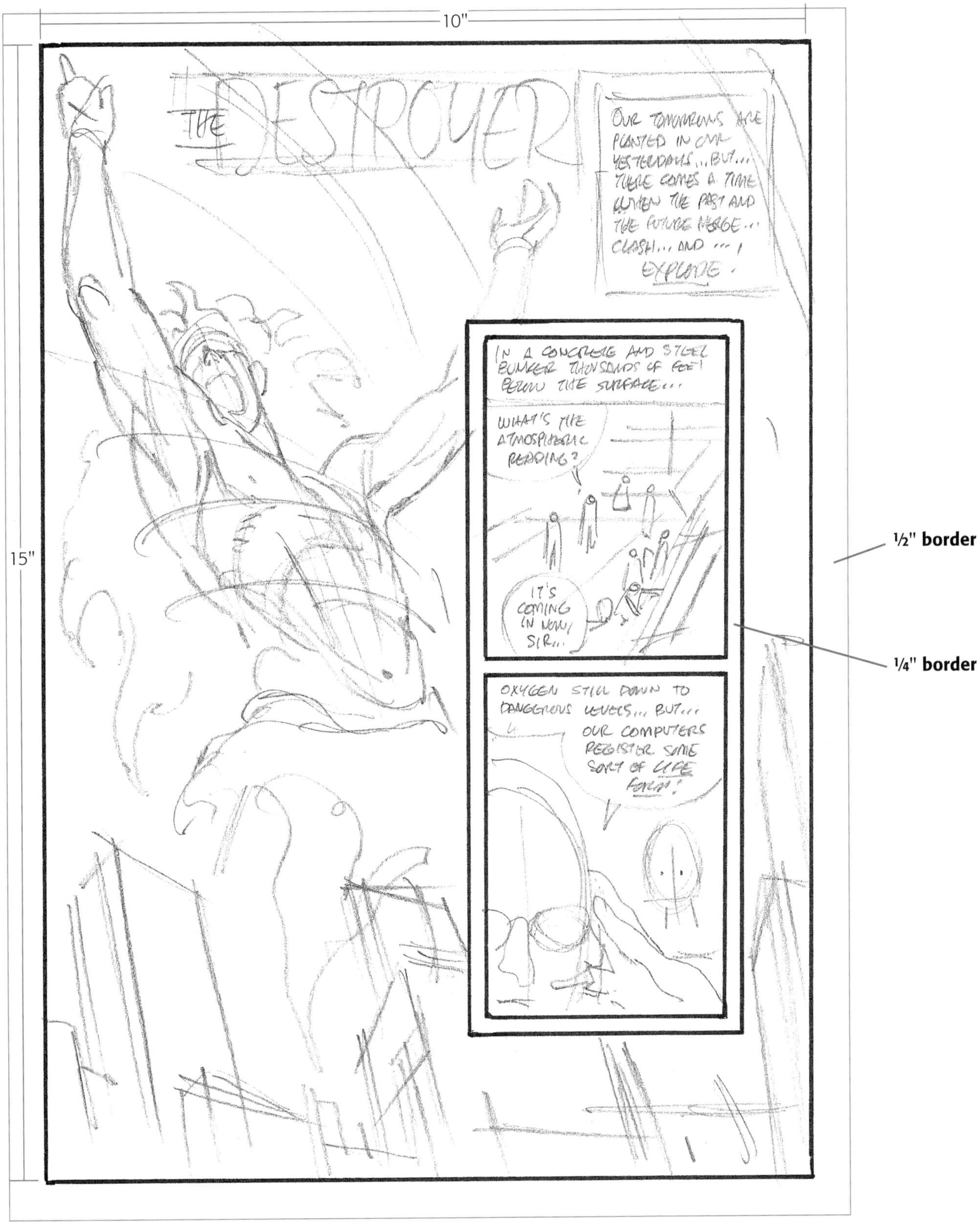
10"
15"
THE DESTROYER
OUR TOMORROWS ARE PLANTED IN OUR YESTERDAYS... BUT... THERE COMES A TIME WHEN THE PAST AND THE FUTURE MERGE... CLASH... AND... EXPLODE!
IN A CONCRETE AND STEEL BUNKER THOUSANDS OF FEET BELOW THE SURFACE...
WHAT'S THE ATMOSPHERIC READING?
IT'S COMING IN NOW, SIR...
OXYGEN STILL DOWN TO DANGEROUS LEVELS... BUT...
OUR COMPUTERS REGISTER SOME SORT OF LIFE FORM!
½" border
¼" border

Now you are ready to add details. Use a 2H or HB pencil to draw them in. Keep your reference pictures by your side as you work, to make sure your details are grounded in reality. Do not press down too hard with your pencil. You are bound to want to make changes, and a light touch in penciling makes erasing a lot easier. Add guidelines in pencil for the lettering.

Visualize where the light in your picture will be coming from, and shade the drawing so that the light and shadows in every part of the composition are consistent with emanation from the light source you have chosen.

Remember that after your drawing is inked, all penciling will be erased. If your pencil rendering is too dark or done with a too-soft lead, erasing will be a problem.

You should be completely satisfied with your pencil drawing before you get to the next stage, inking in the lettering, figures, and background details.

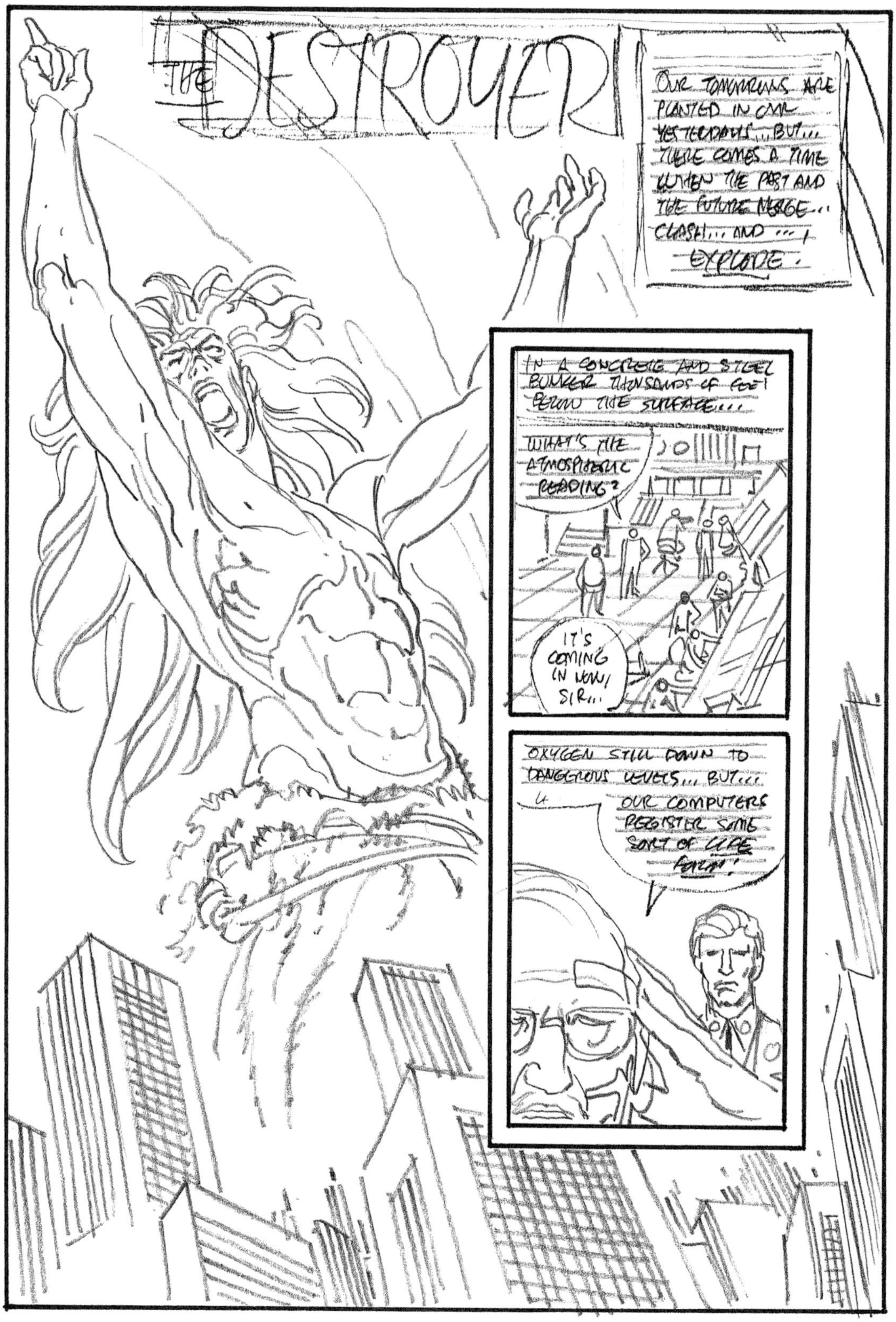
THE DESTROYER
OUR TOMORROWS ARE PLANTED IN OUR YESTERDAYS... BUT... THERE COMES A TIME WHEN THE PAST AND THE FUTURE MERGE... CLASH... AND... EXPLODE.
IN A CONCRETE AND STEEL BUNKER THOUSANDS OF FEET BELOW THE SURFACE...
WHAT'S THE ATMOSPHERIC READING?
IT'S COMING IN NOW, SIR...
OXYGEN STILL DOWN TO DANGEROUS LEVELS... BUT...
OUR COMPUTERS REGISTER SOME SORT OF LIFE FORM!

LETTERING

Lettering is a very important part of any comic book story. It must be both legible and appealing, and the ubiquitous oversize BAMs, POWs, VROOMs, etc. (*sound effects,* or SE for short), need to make a design statement of their own. Although the lettering in comic book stories today is often done via computer programs, many comic books are still lettered by hand. And you should know that the computer fonts (type styles) used for comic book text are designed by human beings, the top letterers in the business.

All lettering is done with waterproof India-type ink of top quality, but professional letterers use many different types of of nibs.

You can use a ruler and a 3H pencil to draw guidelines for lettering. The size of the lettering is 3/16 of an inch with 1/16 of an inch space between lines. It's a good idea to tape the artwork down. Draw the guidelines lightly, since they will be erased after the lettering is inked.

For perfectly spaced guidelines you can use a T-square and Ames Lettering Guide. The Ames guide is a small plastic device with a wheel that rotates inside a frame. Both frame and disk have a number of evenly spaced holes in which you can put a pencil point. By placing your T-square against the edge of your drawing surface as shown here, you can put your pencil in the hole that will give you the right line spacing and slide the guide and pencil across the paper.

Before attempting to letter with ink on your artwork, I suggest that you practice on another piece of paper first. First do the entire alphabet, then cluster letters into words. Lettering well is simply a matter of practice.

TELL ME WHO DID IT?
TELL ME WHO DID IT?
TELL ME WHO DID IT?
TELL ME WHO DID IT?

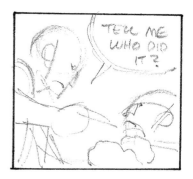

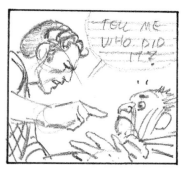

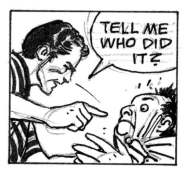

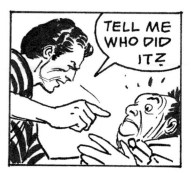

The four-step procedure for completing a panel: (1) do a rough layout, (2) pencil in the details, (3) ink and letter, and (4) erase and clean.

THE PUNCH HIT THE MAN IN A VULNERABLE SPOT... HIS CHIN.
POW

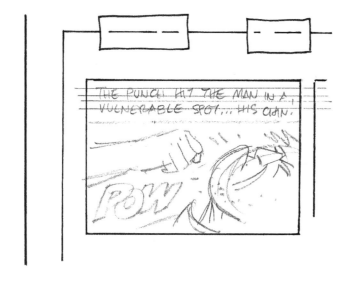

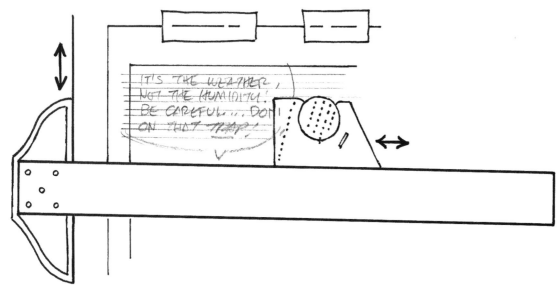

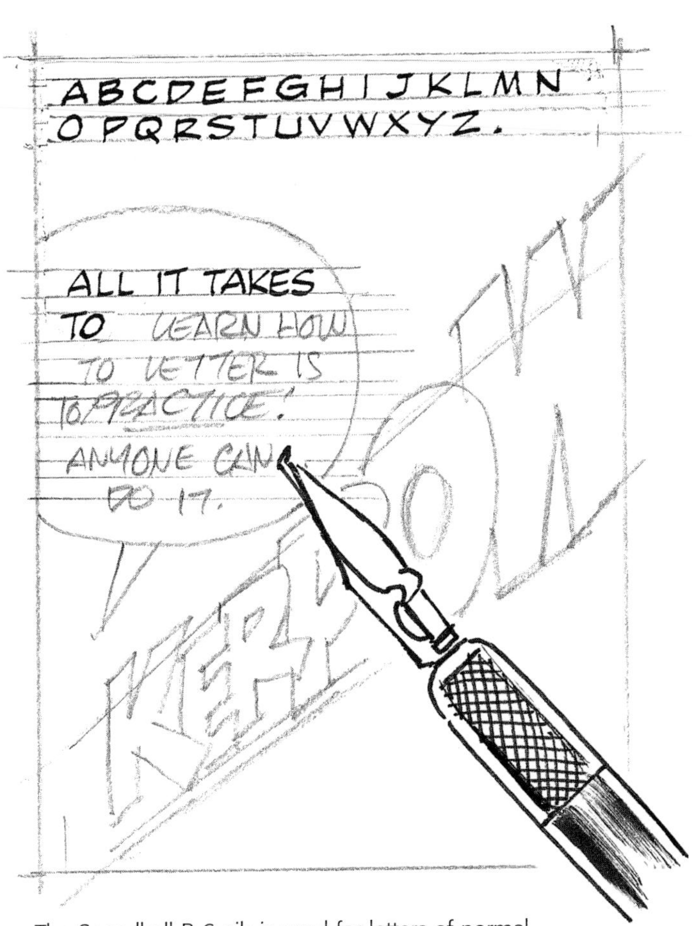
ABCDEFGHIJKLMN
OPQRSTUVWXYZ.
ALL IT TAKES TO LEARN HOW TO LETTER IS TO PRACTICE! ANYONE CAN DO IT.

The Speedball B-6 nib is used for letters of normal weight, for outlining sound effects, and for inking panel borders and caption outlines.

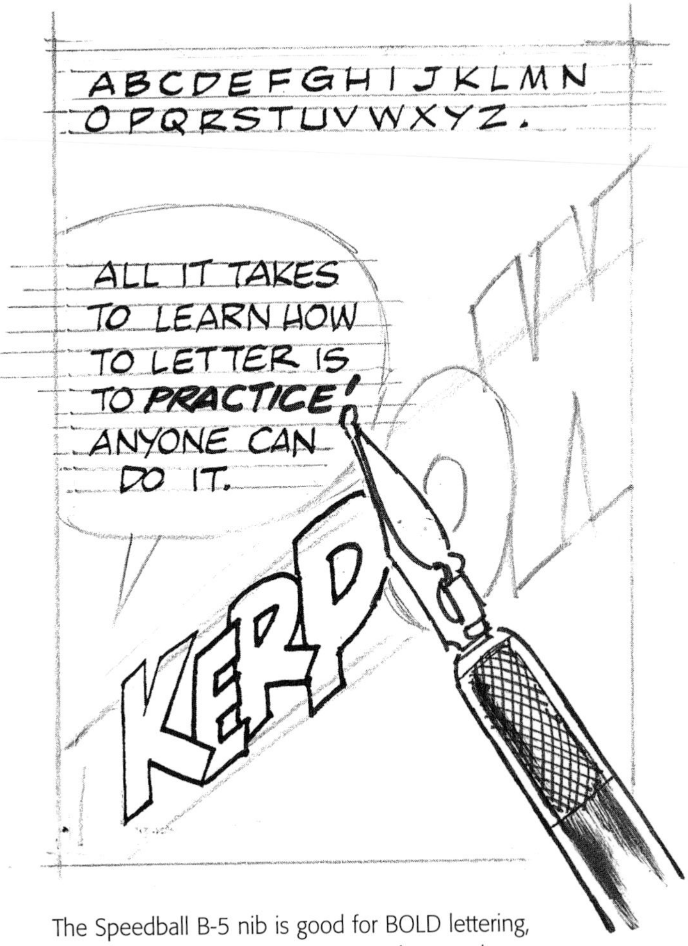
ABCDEFGHIJKLMN
OPQRSTUVWXYZ.
ALL IT TAKES TO LEARN HOW TO LETTER IS TO PRACTICE! ANYONE CAN DO IT.
KERPOW

The Speedball B-5 nib is good for BOLD lettering, when you need to emphasis a word or words, and can be used in combination with the B-6 for outlining sound effects.

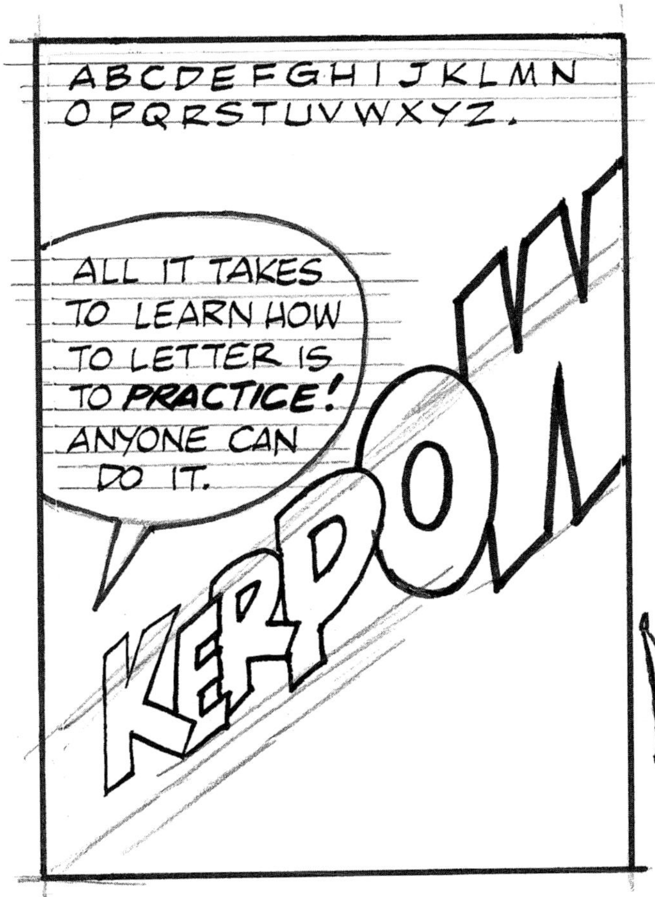
ABCDEFGHIJKLMN
OPQRSTUVWXYZ.
ALL IT TAKES TO LEARN HOW TO LETTER IS TO PRACTICE! ANYONE CAN DO IT.
KERPOW

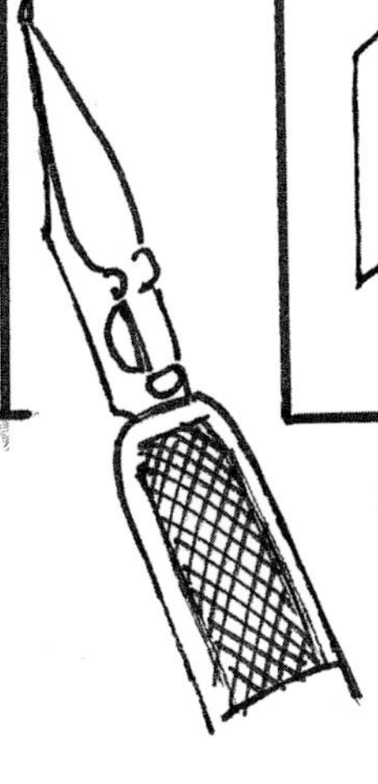

Balloon outlines are often done with a Hunt 512 nib (not shown here). The Speedball B-6 is used for inking borders.

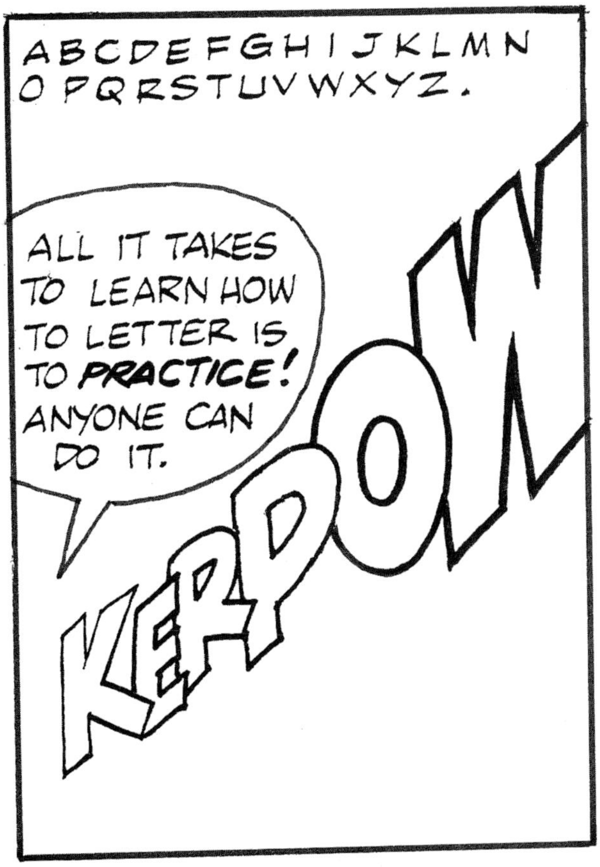
ABCDEFGHIJKLMN
OPQRSTUVWXYZ.
ALL IT TAKES TO LEARN HOW TO LETTER IS TO PRACTICE! ANYONE CAN DO IT.
KERPOW

After the ink has dried, erase all lettering pencil marks.

INKING

Inking is the final stage in completing a piece of black-and-white artwork to be used in a comic book. Pens, brushes, and waterproof India ink of good quality are the tools of choice.

There are a huge variety of pens available, and you should experiment with as many as possible. I use pens with metal nibs which are dipped into an ink source, rather than technical pens, which have their own ink reservoirs. Different nibs may perform quite differently in the hands of different artists. You can find the ones that work best for you only by trying them out.

I use a fine crow-quill nib for fine lines and a thicker nib for heavier lines. All the lines on this page were done with crow-quill nibs. Crow-quill nibs can also be used to render textures.

Once you have finished inking all the fine and medium lines, you will begin your brushwork. Inking with a brush is a skill that requires practice, but once you have learned the techniques, you will be amazed at the effects you can achieve. Brushes can be used to thicken lines, to cover large dark areas, and to create a variety of textures.

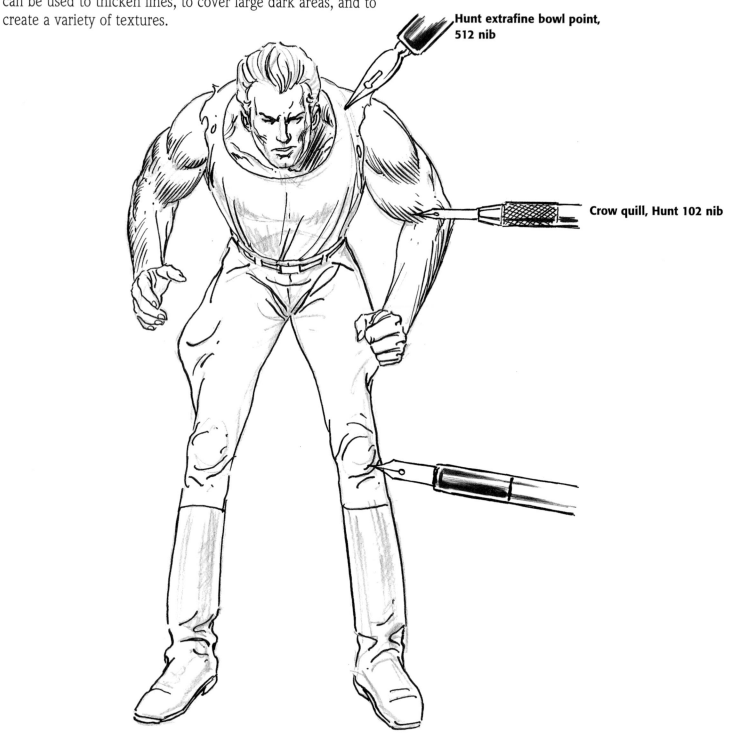

Hunt extrafine bowl point, 512 nib

Crow quill, Hunt 102 nib

Like inking pens, brushes appropriate for cartooning come in a range of sizes, from #1 to #4, with #4 being the largest. I recommend sable brushes, sizes #2 and #3. Even with these larger sizes, you can draw relatively fine lines by using only the tapered point of the brush hairs. A little pressure creates a thicker line. The bigger the brush, the thicker the line.

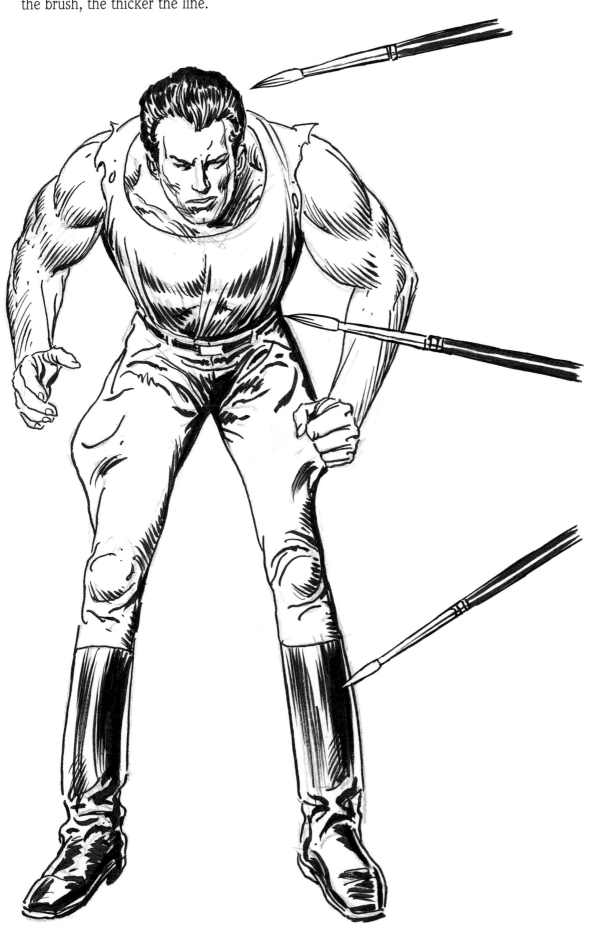

CLEAN-UP

After the penciling, lettering, and inking are completed, finish your page by performing a final clean-up step. First, erase all pencil marks from the art carefully. Test your eraser to make certain that it will not affect the ink. Many erasers are abrasive enough to lighten the inking.

Smears, extended lines, blots, and pencil lines that cannot be erased should be eliminated with white opaque paint. *Use different brushes for white paint from those you use for inking.* White paint will ruin your ink brush and ink will discolor the white paint brush.

Get into the habit of maintaining your art tools properly. Good art materials are expensive. Clean your brush and pen nibs in clear water. Never leave your brushes or nibs in water. Dry the pen nibs completely. Roll your brushes to a slightly damp point on a soft cloth or paper towel; that way they will hold the point even when they are completely dry.

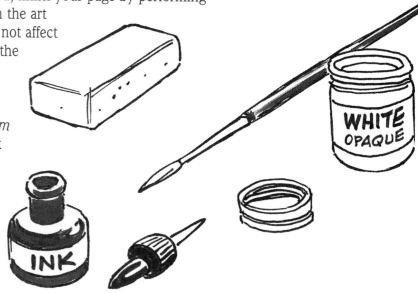

COLORING

As previously mentioned, coloring is not done on the original black and white art, but on reduced copies. Professional colorists use transparent dyes or transparent marker colors or a combination of coloring materials to create what are known as *color guides*. The colors must be transparent so that the inking underneath will show.

These colorized reductions (usually 6 by 9 inches) are used as guides by the people responsible for creating the digital computer files and film used in printing the actual comic books.

THE CREATIVE PROCESS: RAGMAN STORYBOARDS

In the early 1970s, Robert Kanigher and I created Ragman, aka Rory Regan, who has been cited by comic book historians as the first Jewish superhero. After Regan, the son of a junkman on the Lower East Side of New York City, learned that his father had been killed by gangsters, he put on a costume made out of rags and discovered that wearing it gave him superpowers. Although the original series for DC Comics was short-lived, Ragman made guest appearances in other DC comics over the next two decades.

In December of 1991, DC published the first issue in a Ragman miniseries (not written or drawn by Kanigher and me), which emphasized Regan's Jewish background. In Ragman Miniseries #1, "A Folk Tale," a rabbi explains that a golem had been created using rags that conferred superpowers (superstrength, agility, speed, and the power to float on air currents) on the human agent who wore them. The last Ragman, before Rory, was his father, whose real name was Jerzy Reganiewicz and who fought against the Nazis in the Warsaw Ghetto.

The script and storyboards on the next six pages are from Ragman's 1970s incarnation. Take the time to read each page of the script and and then look at the rough layout that corresponds to that part of the script. After Bob submitted the typescript to me (I was editor of the book), I penciled in some changes,* then started in on the roughs. As you will see, the process of translating a story into graphic form is a complex one. And remember: These drawings were "roughs," an apt term for this stage of the process. After I was satisfied that I had the proper pacing, dramatics, basic layouts, and backgrounds I wanted, the next steps, first lettering and then creating the finished inked drawings, lay ahead.

**Editor's note:* It was impossible for us to show you exactly what changes Mr. Kubert made in the first draft of the script because he blacked out the words he was replacing and the original words were not legible. The script that follows, then, is in reality a second draft.

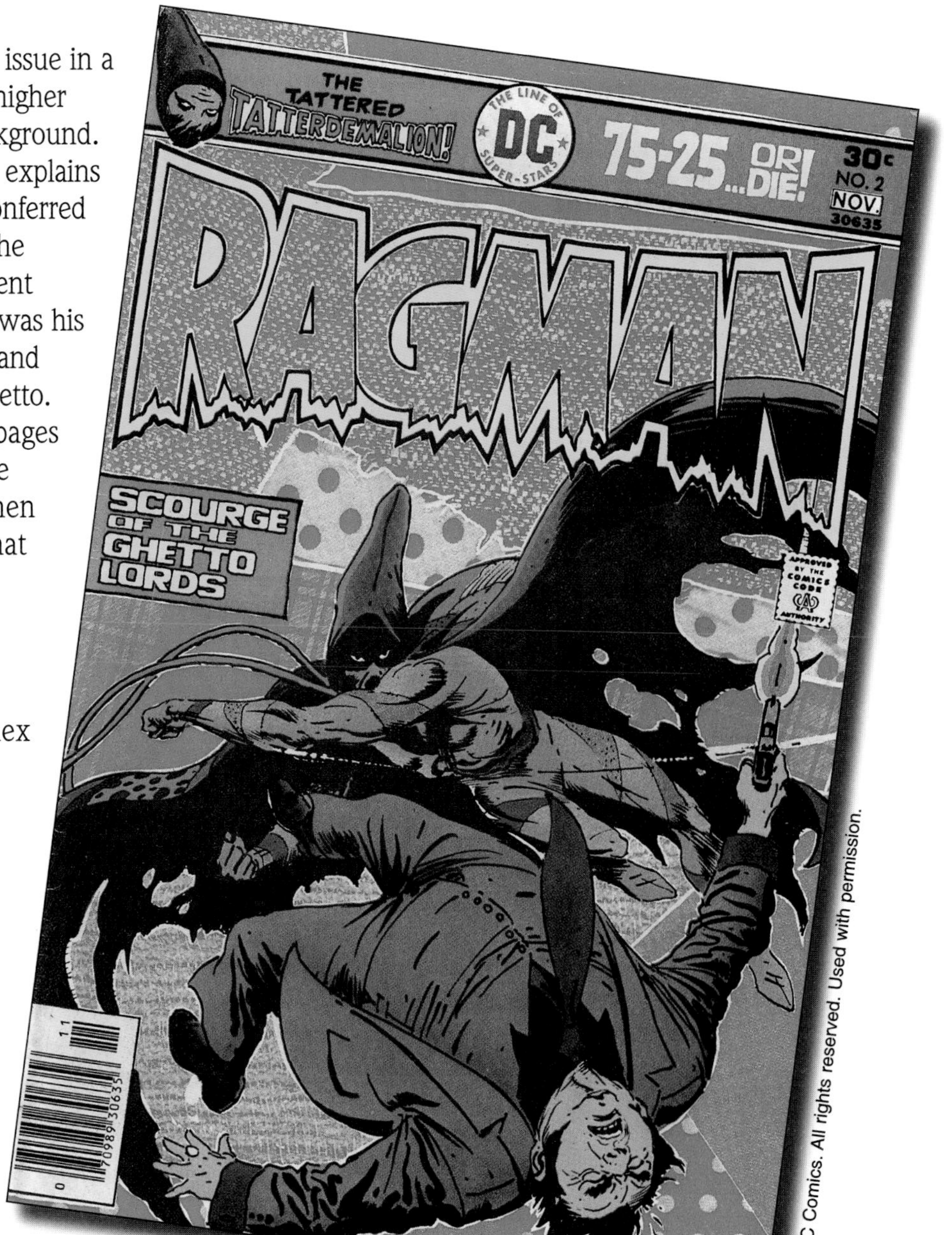
THE TATTERED TATTERDEMALION!
THE LINE OF DC SUPER-STARS
75-25 ...OR! DIE!
30¢ NO. 2 NOV. 30635
RAGMAN
SCOURGE OF THE GHETTO LORDS

READING THE SCRIPT

Numbers refer to individual panels

Circled letters refer to balloons in the panel

```
PAGES 2 AND 3

1. (INSIDE THE CAR, NOW HALTED. LUKA
AS OPAL LISTENS TERRIFIEDLY.)

Lukas: (A)Why'd ya have to run that r
          fuzz are onto us! (B)Just whe
          mint findin' the loot that
          junkyard!
```

Page 1 of the script has been lost, so we pick up our story from page 2. A car chase is in process. Two police officers in hot pursuit of two crazed gunmen (Kinky and Lukas) who are holding a woman (Opal) hostage. The gunmen's car has just crashed through a fence into a junkyard in New York City's Lower East Side. But not just any junkyard. It's Ragman's junkyard!

PAGES 2 AND 3

1. (INSIDE THE CAR, NOW HALTED. LUKAS COMPLAINING TO KINKY, AS OPAL LISTENS TERRIFIEDLY.)

Lukas: Ⓐ Why'd ya have to run that red light, Kinky? Now the fuzz are onto us! Ⓑ Just when we could've made a <u>mint</u> findin' the loot that got stashed in this junkyard!

Kinky: Ⓐ The cops don't bother me, Lukas! This broad gives me <u>bargainin' power</u>! Ⓑ Slide behind the wheel... while I take her out with me!

2. (MALE AND FEMALE COP, WITH GUNS DRAWN, GET OUT OF THEIR PATROL CAR, PARKED 50 FEET BEHIND THE GUNMEN'S CAR. KINKY IS GETTING OUT WITH OPAL, HIS PISTOL AT HER HEAD.)

Kinky: Ⓐ <u>Drop your hardware, pigs</u> Ⓑ <u>or...I'll blow this doll's brains away like</u> sawdust!

3. (MALE AND FEMALE COP SPEAKING APPEASINGLY TO KINKY HOLD-ING PISTOL AT OPAL'S HEAD.)

Male: Hey...Take it easy! Let's talk!

Female: Ⓐ What your're into so far is <u>nothing</u>...compared to <u>Murder One</u>! Ⓑ We don't want anyone to get hurt!

4. (FROM BEHIND LUCAS, AT WHEEL OF CAR, WE SEE COPS APPROACHING IN REAR-VIEW MIRROR.)

5. CAP: Suddenly, the car screeches backwards.

(GUNMAN'S CAR BACKING AT FULL SPEED, RAMS THE TWO COPS, SENDING THEM FLYING.)

SE: K-WHHRUMPPP--

6. (CLOSEUP, INSET, STARTLED KINKY YELLING, STARTLED OPAL.)

Kinky: You got 'em, Lucas...They're out!

Lucas: Hurry up and get into the c___

(SPLASH) CAP: A dark, multi-colored form appears on the car's hood! Is it <u>shadow</u>...or <u>substance</u>? <u>Illusion</u>...or <u>real-ity</u>? <u>Creature</u>...or <u>wraith</u>? The startling figure of the <u>Rag Man</u> seems to materialize like the haunting memory of a nightmare!

(DOUBLE-PAGE SPLASH) "75-25...OR DIE!"

TITLE: **RAGMAN:** *TATTERDEMALION OF JUSTICE*

Created by Kubert & Kanigher
Written by Bob Kanigher   Art by_____

↑ USE PLENTY
GET FEELING
& MYSTERY

②

KINKY –
HAS BLACK, KINKY
HAIR – ALMOST 'AFRO–

LUCAS – BIG,
TOUGH LOOKING –
BULL-LIKE

OPAL –
BEAUTIFUL,
WEARING A LOW
SEXY GOWN &
FUR STOLE

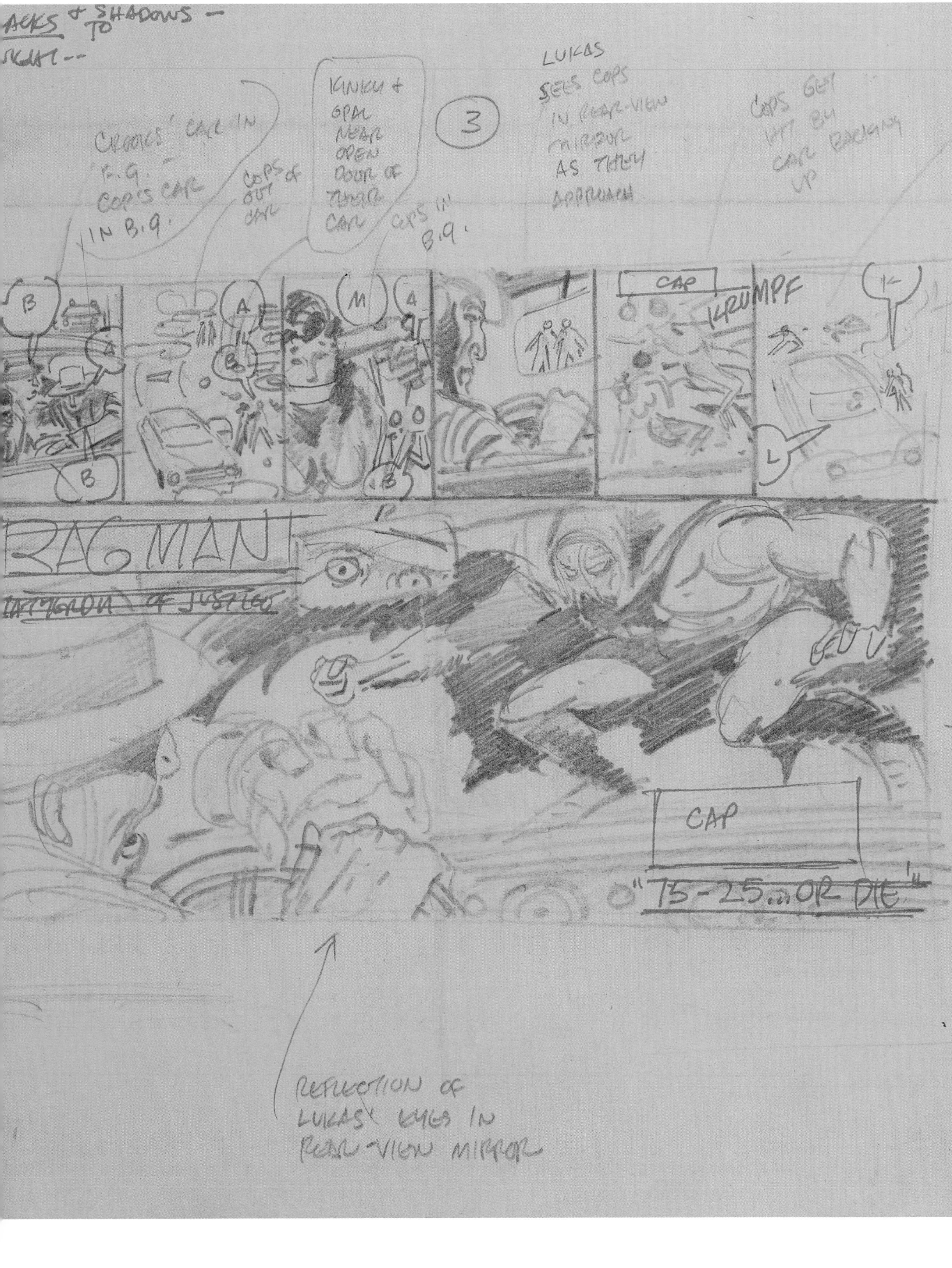

CROOKS' CAR IN F.G. COP'S CAR IN B.G.
COPS OUT OF CAR
KINKY & OPAL NEAR OPEN DOOR OF THEIR CAR
3
COPS IN B.G.
LUKAS SEES COPS IN REAR-VIEW MIRROR AS THEY APPROACH
COPS GET HIT BY CAR BACKING UP
CAP
KRUMPF
RAGMAN
CAP
"75-25...OR DIE"
REFLECTION OF LUKAS' EYES IN REAR-VIEW MIRROR

PAGE 4

CAP (2 ACROSS): The Gunman at the wheel tries to hurl off the Ragman ...

1-3. (LUCAS YELLING AS HE DRIVES, UNABLE TO SEE, BECAUSE RM IS STANDING ON THE HOOD IN FRONT OF HIS WINDSHIELD.)

Lucas: (A)Kinky--SHOOT HIM! HIM! (B)I can't see where I'm drivin'! (C)GET HIM OFF...GET HIM OFF!

4. (HOLDING OPAL WITH ONE HAND, KINKY FIRES AT THE BACK OF RM, WHO IS STANDING ON THE HOOD OF THE CAR LUCAS IS DRIVING, SWERVING FROM SIDE TO SIDE. HEADING IN KINKY'S DIRECTION, BUT STILL ABOUT 50 FEET AWAY.)

Kinky: Hold the wheel steady, Lucas...so I can get a bead on that freak!

SE: K-POWW--POWW--POWW--

5. CAP: The killer's bullets hit home as they smash through the windshield . . .

(BULLETS PIERCING THROUGH SWIRLING BLACK CLOAK, SMASHING THROUGH WINDSHIELD, HITTING LUKAS. HIS HEAD SLUMPS DOWN AGAINST THE WHEEL.)

Lucas: UNGHH!

SE: VIPP--BEEEOW--TZIIING

6. CAP: Like a whirling wraith The Ragman leaps from the car as it careens out of of control . . .

(RM WIRLING AROUND THROUGH THE AIR, OFF THE RUNAWAY CAR, WHICH SKIDS TOWARDS THE SIDE, ON TWO WHEELS, TOWARDS A BIG PILE OF HEAVY METAL JUNK, WHICH WILL SET IT AFIRE IN NEXT PANEL.)

SE: SKREEEEEE--

4
RAGMAN OF HOOD OF CAR
KINKY WITH GIRL, GUN IN HAND
CAP
B
LUKAS IN CAR YELLING
K-POW POW
CAP
CAP
SKREEEEEEE
IN CAR, LUKAS IS HIT AS BULLETS COME THRU WINDSHIELD

PAGE 5

1. CAP: Rolling over, the car smashes into a pile of scrap metal and bursts into flame.

(RM DIVING THROUGH THE AIR AS BEHIND HIM, LUKAS'S CAR BURSTS INTO FLAME AS IT RAMS AND TURNS OVER AGAINST THE METAL JUNKPILE. ANGLE FROM CAR CRASH IN FOREGROUND; TOWARDS RM IN BACKGROUND.)

SE: K-RANNNGG

SE: FROOOSH (fire)

2. CAP: The Ragman looks up to find himself within point-blank range of a frenzied gunman!

(RM IN FOREGROUND, AS THE FRENZIED KINKY, HOLDING ONTO OPAL WITH ONE HAND, IS ABOUT TO FIRE A POINT-BLANK RANGE AT RM.)

Kinky: I'm going to KILL you...Whatever you are!

3. CAP: The Tatterdemalion's legs shoot out...tripping the gunman!

(OVERHEAD LONGSHOT--RM ON GROUND, KICKS OUT AT KINKY, KINKY FALLS AWAY FROM GIRL.)

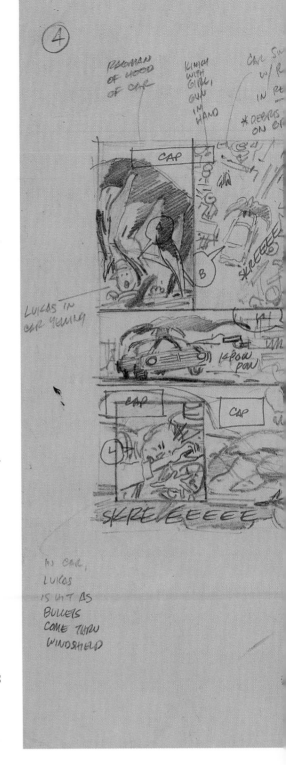

4. (KINKY ON GROUND, FIRING UP.)

SE: POW, KPOW, POW

5. CAP: The Ragman's cloak unfurls between the killer and his victim like a protective curtain.

(WITH HIS LEFT HAND, RM FLAPS THE LEFT SIDE OF HIS CLOAK IN BETWEEN OPAL AND KINKY, SO SHE'S SAFE FROM KINKY, AS KINKY ENRAGEDLY CONTINUES FIRING AT HIM.)

6. (CLOSEUP OF ENRAGED FIRING KINKY.)

Kinky: I'll get that big-mouthed doll...soon as I plant a slug between <u>your</u> eyes!

SE: K-POWWPOWPOW--

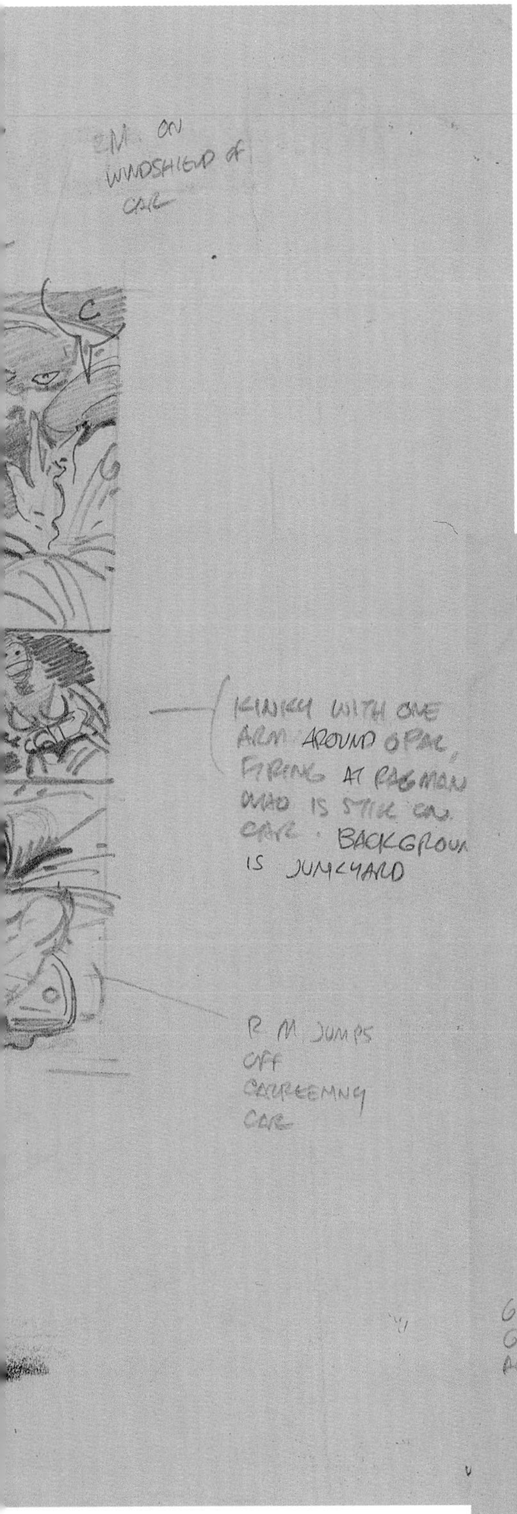

RM. ON WINDSHIELD OF CAR
KINKY WITH ONE ARM AROUND OPAL, FIRING AT RAGMAN WHO IS STILL ON CAR. BACKGROUND IS JUNKYARD

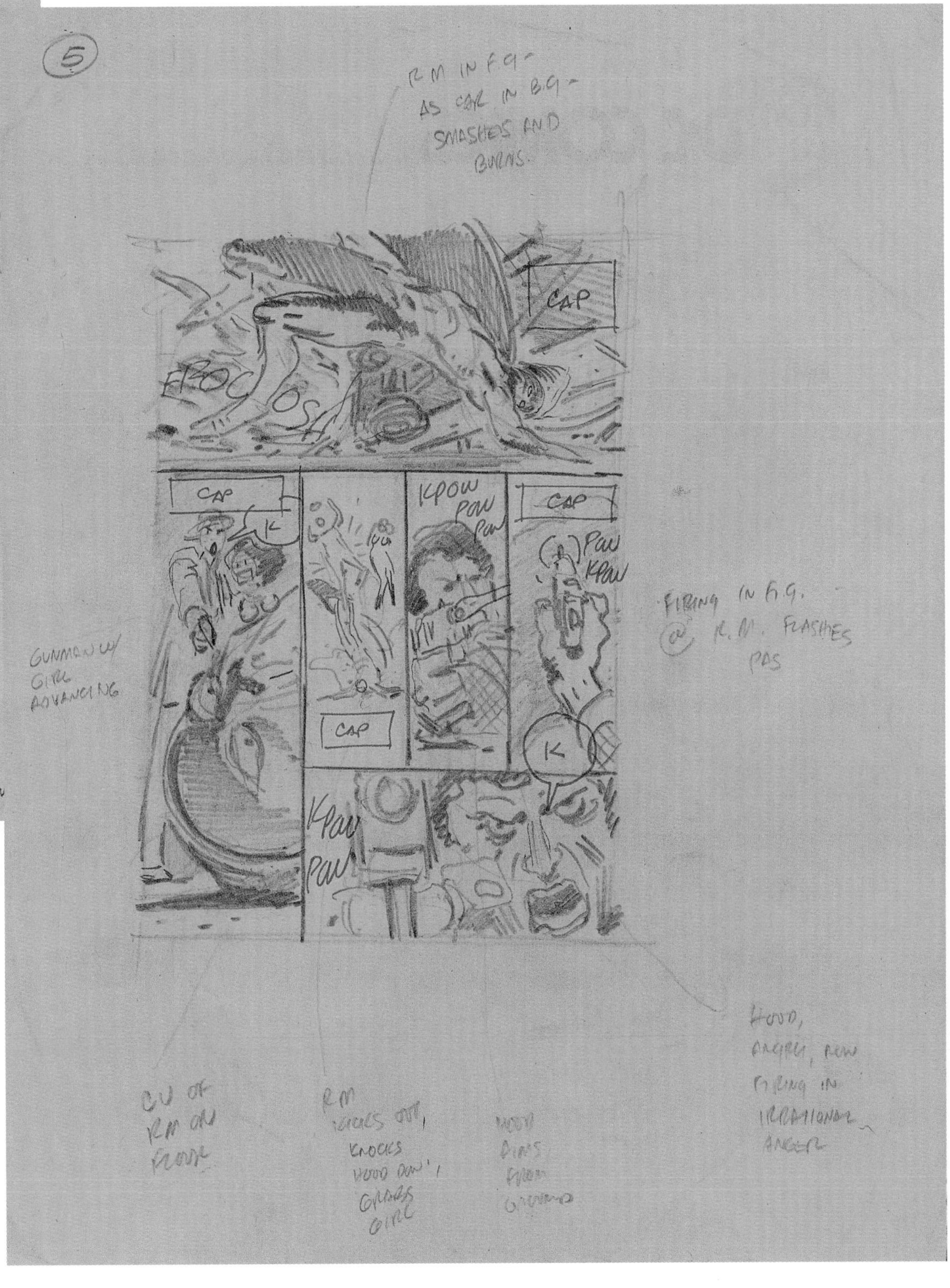

5
R M IN F.G - AS CAR IN B.G - SMASHES AND BURNS
CAP
CAP
K
CAP
KPOW POW POW
CAP
PAW KPAW
K
KPAW PAW
GUNMAN W/ GIRL ADVANCING
FIRING IN F.G. @ R.M. FLASHES PAS
CU OF RM ON FLOOR
RM KICKS OUT, KNOCKS HOOD DOWN, GRABS GIRL
HOOD AIMS FROM GROUND
HOOD, ANGRY, NOW FIRING IN IRRATIONAL ANGER

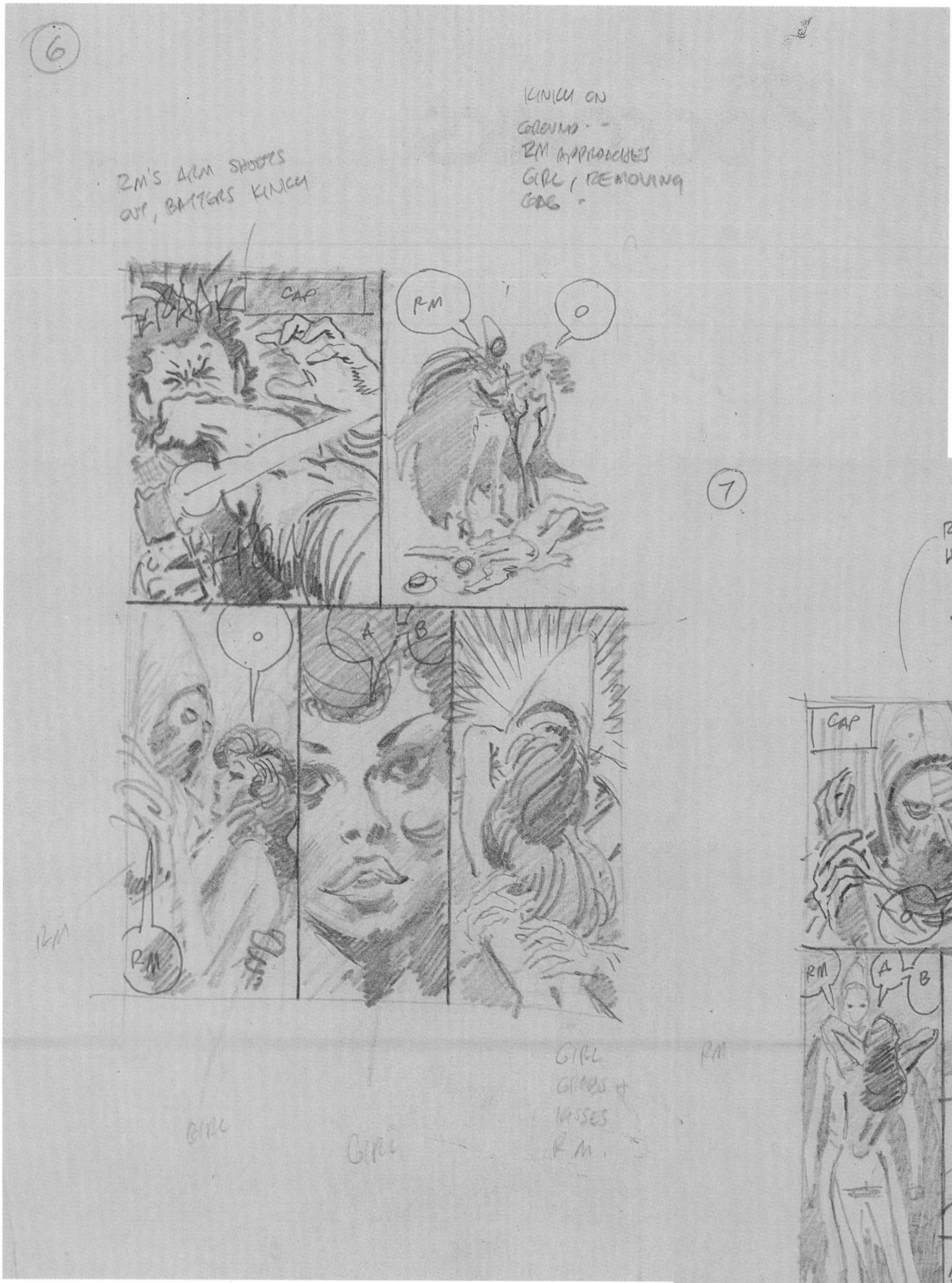
6
KINKY ON GROUND -- RM APPROACHES GIRL, REMOVING GAG -
RM'S ARM SHOOTS OUT, BATTERS KINKY
CAP
RM
O
O
A
B
RM
GIRL GRABS + KISSES R.M.

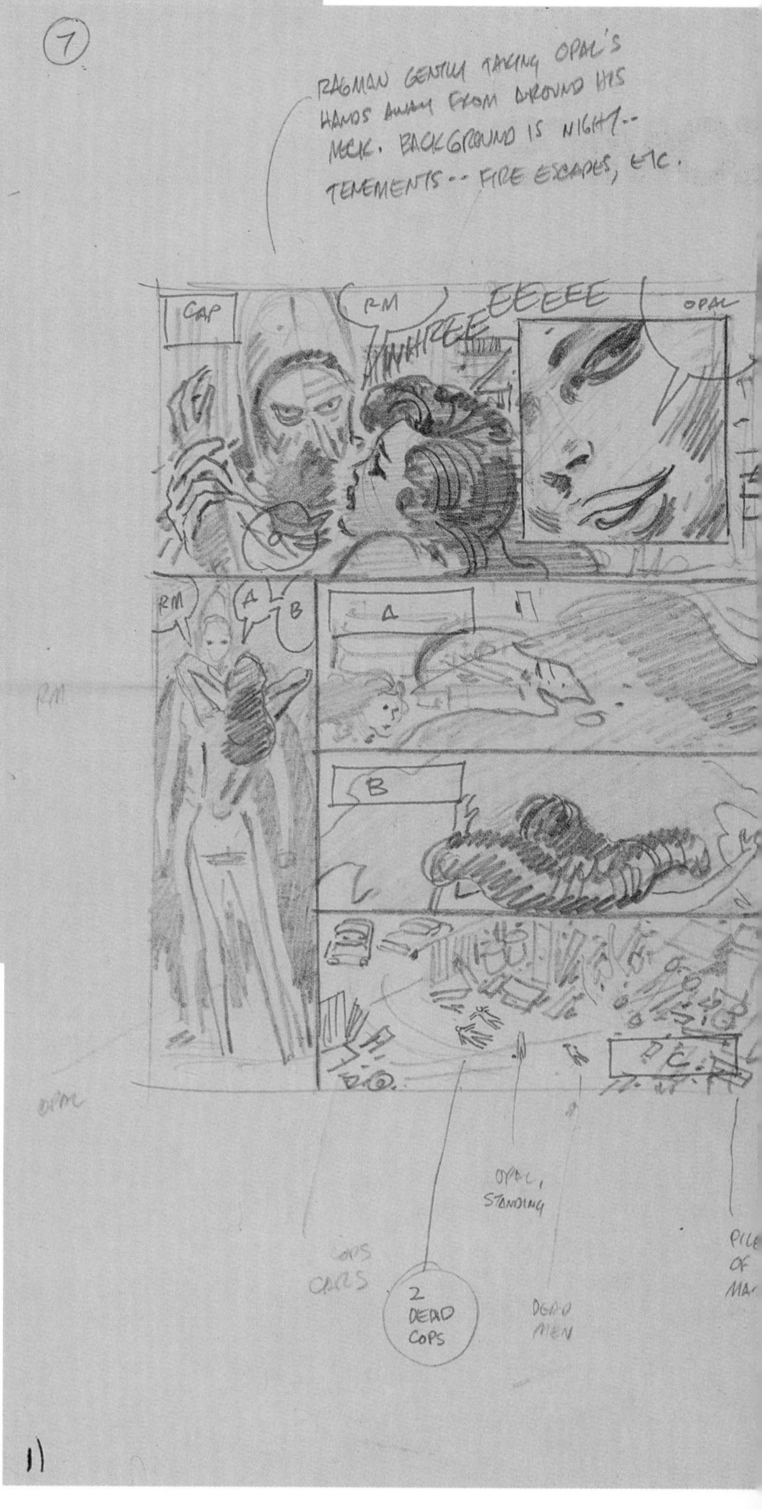
7
RAGMAN GENTLY TAKING OPAL'S HANDS AWAY FROM AROUND HIS NECK. BACKGROUND IS NIGHT -- TENEMENTS -- FIRE ESCAPES, ETC.
CAP
RM
EEEEE
OPAL
RM
A
B
A
B
C
OPAL, STANDING
COPS CARS
2 DEAD COPS
DEAD MEN
11

PAGE 6

1. CAP:A sledgehammer fist flashes out with devastating force . . .

(EXTREME FORESHORTENING OF RM'S FIST STRIKING KINKY'S JAW. UPPERCUT. KINKY FIRES GUN.)

SE: KARAAK-

2. (RAGMAN IS REMOVING OPAL'S GAG. RAGMAN AND OPAL STANDING OVER UNCONSCIOUS KINKY, FLAT ON HIS BACK.)

Ragman: Take it easy, now . . . No one's going to hurt you!

Opal: I . . . can't . . . stop shaking . . .

3. (OPAL LOOKING SEXILY AT RM, VERY CLOSE.)

Opal: Y-you saved my life! Who are you?

RM: . . . Just . . . a rag man!

4. (CLOSEUP OF OPAL.)

Opal: Ⓐ I'm Opal.! Ⓑ I dig you . . . Rag Man!

5. (KISS!)

PAGE 7

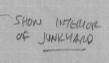

SHOW INTERIOR OF JUNKYARD

1. CAP: The wail of approaching sirens shatters the moment . . .

(RM GENTLY LOOSENS OPAL'S ARMS.)

OPAL STARING IN AMAZEMENT.

SE: WHREEEEEeeeee–

RM: The police are coming, Opal! You can tell them what happened!

RAGMAN'S SWIRLING CAPE — JUNK IN B.G.

Opal: What about . . . what happened between us?

Opal (inset): We set off enough vibes to melt an iceberg! When will I see you again?

2. (RM ANSWERS BEAUTIFUL, SEXY OPAL.)

FROM BEHIND OPAL, SHADOWY FORM ALMOST ENVELOPES HER

RM: Forget me, Opal!

Opal: Ⓐ Can you? Ⓑ You can't forget me . . . anymore than Adam forgot Eve!

3, 4, 5. CAP: Ⓐ Before the beautiful girl's startled gaze, the Rag Man seems to merge with the air . . . Ⓑ . . . the shadows . . . the stuff that dreams are made of . . . Ⓒ . . . as the second police car arrives at the scene of havoc and death.

(BEFORE OPAL'S STARTLED GAZE, THE RUNNING RM, RUNNING AWAY FROM HER, CHANGES FROM A SOLID, TO A SILHOUETTE, TO THAT SPECKLED EFFECT WE SPOKE ABOUT.)

(PANEL 5 IS OVERHEAD LONGSHOT OF JUNKYARD SCENE—CAR BURNING—SECOND POLICE CAR ARRIVING, ETC.)

PAGE 8

1. CAP: Amidst the jumble of relics in the living quarters in the rear of RAGS 'N' TATTERS . . . the unique costume is hung behind a closet door.

(RORY'S HANDS HANGING UP RAGMAN COSTUME ON HOOK IN BACK OF CLOSET DOOR.)

2. CAP: The somber mask with bottomless sockets of anguish . . .

(CLOSEUP OF RM'S MASK)

3. CAP:. . . stares at the man behind the mask.

(ANGLE FROM INSIDE THE MASK, THOUGH EYEHOLDS, AT BACK OF RORY. BANDAGE AROUND RORY'S CHEST FROM BACK TO FRONT. BLOOD SEEPING THROUGH THE BANDAGE.)

Rory: ⒶBlood coming through the bandage! ⒷI'd better change it!

4. (NOW WE SEE RORY'S FACE, AS HE CHANGES TO FRESH BANDAGE, WRAPPING IT AROUND HIS ARM AND SHOULDER IN FRONT OF BATHROOM MIRROR.)

Rory: ⒶThat slug I got in the fight on the roof only grazed me— ⒷWhen I jumped off the car, it must've opened the clot!

BOTTOM CAP: From *Ragman* #1.

5. (CLOSEUP OF RORY)

Rory (thought): Opal . . . A strange name . . . a beautiful girl! I-I can't get her out of my thoughts!

6. (RORY ENTERS THE JUNKSHOP—ALL KINDS ARE PARAPHERNALIA ARE AROUND.)

Rory (thought): I'd better put my mind to work!

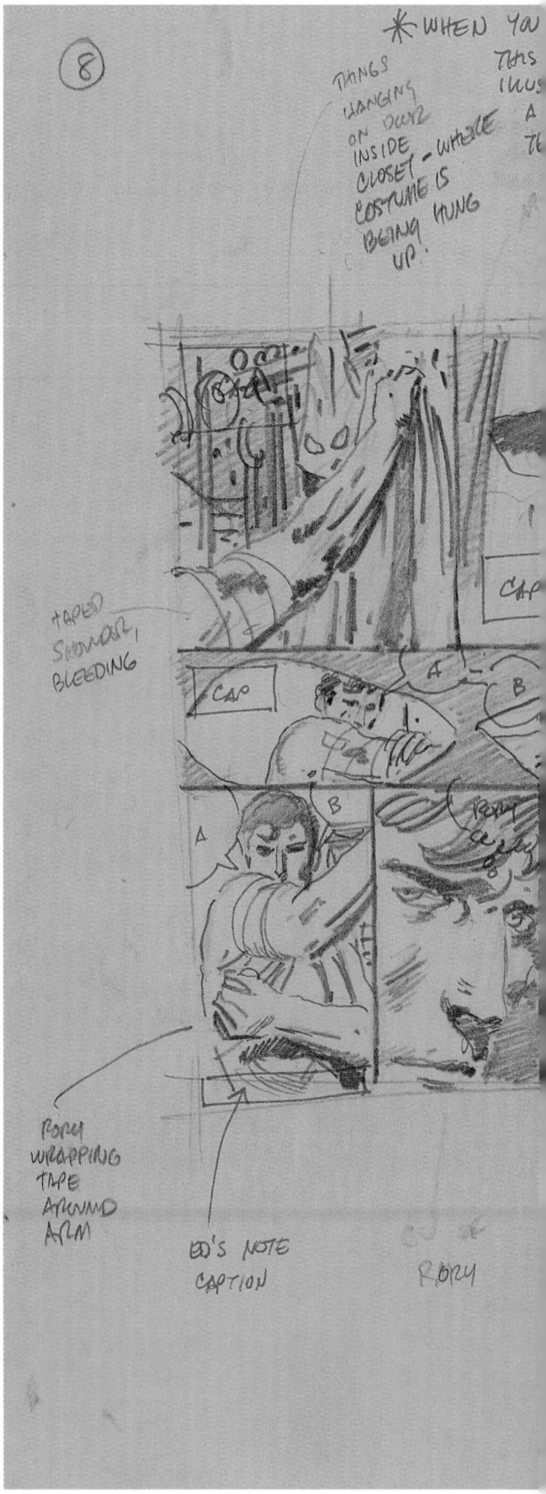
8
THINGS HANGING ON DOOR INSIDE CLOSET - WHERE COSTUME IS BEING HUNG UP.
TAPED SHOULDER, BLEEDING
CAP
A
B
RORY WRAPPING TAPE AROUND ARM
ED'S NOTE CAPTION
RORY

PAGE 9

1. CAP: Deep in thought, ripples of the past fade from Rory Regan, son of a junkman . . . as he stares at the yellowing photo of his dead father.

(RORY STARING AT HIS FATHER'S PHOTO.)

Rory: Poor Pop . . .

2. (LONGSHOT OF BIG JUNKYARD IN REAR, WITH MATTRESS CONTAINING MONEY, ON TOP OF A HEAP OF OTHER MATTRESSES.)

Rory's Voice: . . . You must've been out of your senses . . . just before you died. . .

3. (CLOSEUP OF MATTRESS, SHOWING THE $1000 BILLS AS IF YOU CAN SEE THROUGH THE COVERING OF THE NATTRESS.)

Rory's Voice: . . Raving that you kept your promise to make me a multimillionaire!

4. (LONGSHOT OF JUNKSHOP.)

Rory's Voice: Ⓐ But . . .the truth is, that I've inherited <u>nothing</u>! Ⓑ Nothing but the junk you bought . . . from people who came to you with their last bit of hope!

Ⓐ But Rory doesn't know that the <u>Fates</u> play with a <u>stacked deck</u>! For hidden more deeply than a needle in a haystack is over $2 million dollars from an armored truck robbery cached inside a mattress within a heap of mattresses in the junkyard. Ⓑ Rory's father, for his son's sake, refused to reveal its location, and he and three of his cronies went to their deaths with silent lips and locked hands. But the gang ceaselessly hunts for their lost loot, vowing death to anyone who stands in their way.

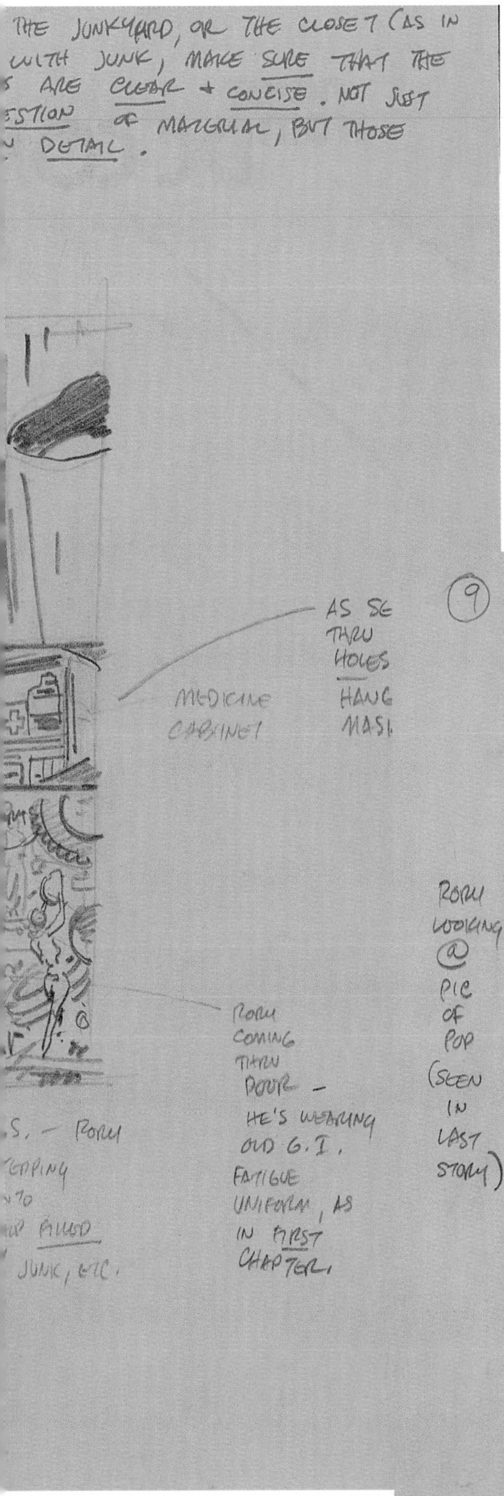
THE JUNKYARD, OR THE CLOSET (AS IN
WITH JUNK, MAKE SURE THAT THE
ARE CLEAR + CONCISE. NOT JUST
OF MATERIAL, BUT THOSE
DETAIL.
AS SE
THRU
HOLES
MEDICINE
CABINET
HANG
RORY
COMING
THRU
DOOR -
HE'S WEARING
OLD G.I.
FATIGUE
UNIFORM, AS
IN FIRST
CHAPTER.
JUNK, ETC.

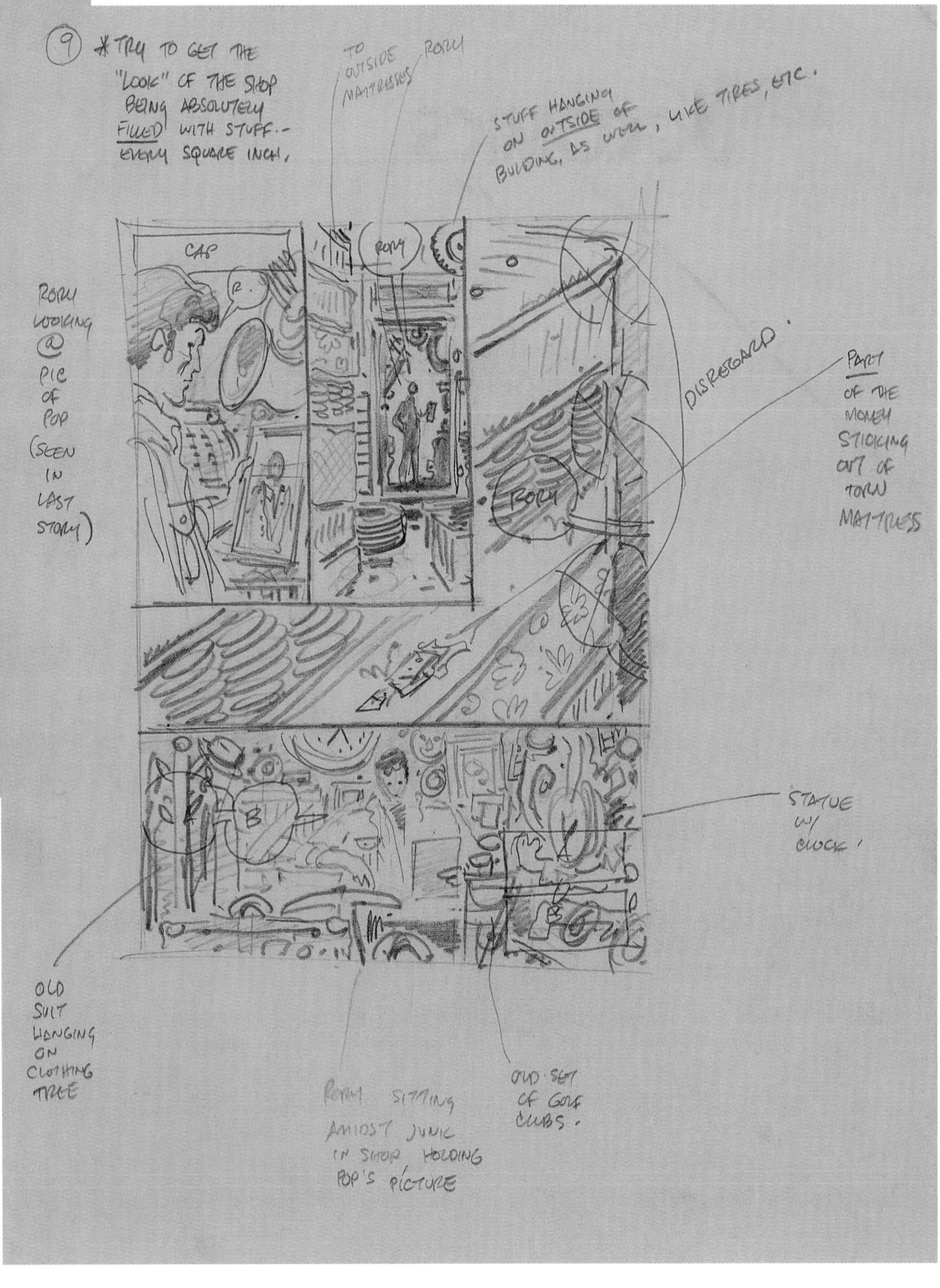
9
*TRY TO GET THE "LOOK" OF THE SHOP BEING ABSOLUTELY FILLED WITH STUFF.- EVERY SQUARE INCH,
TO OUTSIDE MATTRESSES
RORY
STUFF HANGING ON OUTSIDE OF BUILDING, AS WELL, LIKE TIRES, ETC.
CAP
R.
RORY
RORY LOOKING @ PIC OF POP (SEEN IN LAST STORY)
DISREGARD.
PART OF THE MONEY STICKING OUT OF TORN MATTRESS
RORY
B
STATUE W/ CLOCK!
OLD SUIT HANGING ON CLOTHING TREE
RORY SITTING AMIDST JUNK IN SHOP HOLDING POP'S PICTURE
OLD SET OF GOLF CLUBS.

SUPPLIES

The tools and supplies described here (except for the Miscellaneous category) are listed in order of when they are used in creating a page of artwork. The first step for most cartoonists, whether they are creating a new character or illustrating a story featuring a currently existing character such as Spiderman or Superman, is to do some preliminary sketches.

Paper

Any *unlined* 8½- by 11-inch notepaper or stationery can be used for preliminary sketches. White is best, but any pale color will do.

For finished drawings, you need a high-quality surface that will take erasures well and will not blot, bleed, or skip when the drawings and lettering are inked. Two generic names for paper made especially for drawing and inking are bristol board and illustration board. Illustration boards come in different thicknesses. One-ply sheets are the thinnest. Thicker sheets are made by bonding two or more plies together.

Illustration board also comes in different surfaces: kid, which is slightly rough; smooth; and plate, which is a highly polished surface. I use Strathmore 500 two-ply smooth paper. It takes both pencil and ink exceptionally well.

Pencils and Erasers

I work with both mechanical pencils and old-fashioned "woodies." For doing your preliminary sketches, you can use any pencil that suits you, but once you start working on the illustration board, you'll need a relatively hard point. I start by roughing out my page with a 3H lead. Whatever your choice of pencil, don't press down too hard, or you'll dent the paper's surface and make it difficult to erase mistakes. I prefer a 2H for refining and finishing my pencil drawings. The B series pencils all have softer leads than the H series and make darker lines. Although some artists like to use a 2B point for certain effects and for shading, I find that lines drawn with a 2B lead are hard to erase without smearing. A word of caution: The mark a particular pencil makes on paper will vary depending on the manufacturer. It's a good idea to try different brands, in different hardnesses, and test them by doing some actual drawings—including erasures—before settling on your personal choices.

It is very important to have an eraser that does a clean job of removing pencil marks without leaving a lot of residue. My personal choice is the Magic Rub, which is made of plastic. Another good plastic eraser is the Staedtler Mars. The old-fashioned pink rubber erasers are good for difficult-to-remove lines, but they can be hard on paper surfaces. Kneaded erasers are better for charcoal and pastels than for pencil.

Pens

Ask ten different artists what their favorite pens are and you'll probably get ten different lists. My own preferences are listed on pages 125 and 126. For lettering, I use the Speedball B-6 nib for normal text and panel borders; the B-5 for bold letters; and either the B-6 or the B-5 for sound effects and titles. For drawing, I use crow-quill nibs, which all have sharp points but which produce lines of very different character, depending on the nib. The Hunt 106, the Hunt 102, and the Hunt 512 are the three I use most often. Gillott also makes a line of crow-quill nibs suitable for pen-and-ink drawing, including the 290, the 404, the 659, and the 850.

Some cartoonists use technical pens, which come with their own ink reservoirs, such as the Koh-I-Noor Rapidograph line and the Rotring ArtPen series. These pens have no flexibility, however, and therefore no line variation. A product that has improved in recent years is the so-called brush pen, such as the Pigma brush pen made by Sakura. In my opinion, however, neither technical pens nor brush pens (or any of the other alternatives) offer nearly the versatility and durability obtainable with a carefully chosen selection of dipping pens used with the highest-quality ink. It may take some practice to learn how to use dipping pens to best advantage, but the effort definitely pays off.

Brushes

My choice of brush—and the choice of many other cartoonists—is the Raphael Series 8404 Kolinsky. (Kolinsky is the type of mink which provides the fur used for this brush.) It provides consistent results and, when properly cared for, lasts for three or four months. Like all quality art material, brushes are expensive. Some of the pros do use lesser-quality brushes, at least for some effects, but if you are just learning brushwork, you will not get the effects you want with a cheap brush.

For details, I use a Raphael #2; for filling in dark areas I use a larger size (#3 or #4). Some artists find the Winsor Newton Series 7 Sable line an acceptable alternative.

When a brush becomes so worn that it can no longer be used for fluid line effects, you can use it for drybrushing.

Never use the same brush for inking that you use for white paint.

Ink

Pelikan India Ink works best for me, although Higgins Black Magic is preferred by some cartoonists. Ink that is kept too long may become "stale," and will not flow properly from pen or brush.

White Paint

Dr. Martin's Bleed Proof White is my choice for clean-ups and corrections. It is water-soluble, which means you should not apply ink over this paint, even after it dries. Some alternatives are Winsor and Newton Process White, Pro-White opaque water color, and white titanium acrylic. For corrections over which I intend to ink, I use non-water-soluble Liquid Paper Bond White. Some cartoonists say that Pelikan Graphic White can be inked over once it is thoroughly dry.

Miscellaneous

Use of the T-square–Ames Lettering Guide combination—indispensable if you are doing your own lettering—was discussed on page 124. Two other important pieces of equipment are the good old-fashioned straightedge and a single-edge safety razor blade no. 9. I find the single-edge blades easier to use and more durable than utility knives, and they do double duty—as a way of correcting minor mistakes without using white paint and as a means of achieving scratchy art effects. Some other items often found in the cartoonist's studio are (in no particular order):

French curves

Templates (e.g., circle, oval, ellipse), with beveled edges

Triangles

Q-tips (can be used instead of brushes for inking in some areas, then thrown away)

Toothbrush (for spatter effect)

Sponge (for special effects)

Most of the supplies mentioned here (and much more) can be ordered and purchased from the Joe Kubert Art Supply Store. Catalogs and price lists are available upon request. For information, contact:

The Joe Kubert Art Supply Store
37A Myrtle Avenue
Dover, NJ 07801
1-800-343-4792 or 1-973-328-3266
www.kubertsworld.com/depot.html

CAREER PATHS

The paths that one can take to become a working cartoonist are numerous and varied. The one thing that all the professional comic book artists with whom I am acquainted have in common is motivation. Whatever their personal experience, every one of them was strongly motivated to become and succeed as a cartoonist.

Remember, though, that "artist" is just one of the possible career paths open to anyone interested in the wonderful world of comic art. Within the general field, one can specialize in any one of many specific sectors, for example, layout, design, penciling, inking, coloring, lettering, and cover illustration. In the beginning, however, I recommend mastering as many skills as you can, including computer-aided design and the use of advanced applications such as Photoshop. The more abilities you have, the more likely it is that you will maintain gainful employment over an extended period of time. If the work in one specialty is not sufficient to keep you busy, you can supplement your income by working in another area. The more one learns about all art areas, the more one brings to one's specialty. To take just one example, an inker who did not have good basic skills as an artist would almost certainly produce second-rate inked panels.

The best cartoonists are brilliant storytellers, people who can come up with original, imaginative plots and unforgettable characters. Where do they get their stories? Experience and observation are important, of course, but most great comic book artists are ominvorous readers, addicted film buffs, or both. The more you read, the more you learn and the more you bring to your art. The next time you read a work of fiction, try visualizing the characters and text in graphic form. Make some sketches.

After you have seen a movie that you thought was particularly well done, rent the video and analyze the film—frame by frame if you can find the time. There is a close relationship between such cinematic techniques as editing for effective scene transitions and laying out comic book panels, pages, and hooks leading to the next episode.

Finally, haunt comic book stores and check out the new offerings as they hit the stands. *Read* comic books—hundreds of 'em—and read all different types, from superhero vehicles to manga to the Vertigo line of "adult" comics. What you learn will not only help you decide exactly what you'd most like to do but will be helpful during job interviews.

Getting a Job

The physical steps to be taken if one is serious about becoming a professional comic book artist are relatively straightforward. Always, a good amount of tenacity and commitment are essential.

A good portfolio is a must. Your portfolio should be a sampling of what you feel is the best of your current original artwork. It should also include work that relates directly to the kind of artwork the editor or art director who will be looking at your portfolio publishes. If you are concentrating on trying to get a job for a company that publishes mainly superhero comics, you'll need to include some superhero samples— either your invention or a variation on one of that company's own characters. But don't be afraid to show that oddball piece that you feel is really, truly good. Evidence of versatility can't hurt.

Portfolios may be submitted in person or by mail. Obviously, an in-person submission is desirable, so the editor can discuss and answer directly any questions pertaining to your portfolio. However, appointments with editors are hard to come by. If you know anyone in the business, maybe he or she can put in a good word for you. In any case, never try to see an editor without calling first for an appointment. Editors are (usually) very busy people.

If you are submitting your portfolio by mail, be sure to send copies only, no originals. And if you want your work back, include a stamped, self-addressed envelope in the package. Comic book editors receive hundreds of submissions each week. Often, an assistant will go through the submissions pile to do a preliminary weeding out before submitting the most promising to the editor.

If your work is rejected, draw another set of samples and continue to submit your work. A new submission, especially when it comes closer to a particular publisher's requirements than the previous sample, is evidence of your serious intent.

Whether you are offered a job depends on three factors: You've got to be at the right place, at the right time, with the right stuff. If any one of these elements is missing, a job will not be forthcoming. And here is a crucial bit of advice: Once you get a job, if you don't maintain strict deadlines you won't have the job for long. A professional *attitude* is as important as professional *artwork*.

Conventions

Comic book cons are held in virtually every one of the United States, as well as in Europe, South America, Australia, Mexico, and Asia. Every week of the year a comic book convention is being held somewhere in the world. Many publishers, editors, and cartoonists attend these conventions. If you don't live near any publishers' offices, the right convention may give you the opportunity to gain an interview with a publisher or editor and show your portfolio.

Schedules for comic book conventions are listed in various comic book–related publications, such as *Wizard* magazine and *Cartoonist PROfiles*. There are also numerous Web sites devoted to comic books and animation, and many of them feature up-to-date lists of comic book cons, with direct links to the biggest of the conventions.

Apprenticeships

Some young cartoonists are lucky enough to get a job as an assistant to a working cartoonist. This form of apprenticeship can be very rewarding in terms of experience. Apprentice opportunities are scarce, but they do exist. Again, conventions are a good place to get information about this possibility of employment.

Education

You don't need a postgraduate degree from an art school to be a comic book artist, but many of the best artists do have formal art education, in specialities such as drafting, graphic arts and design, illustration, and animation. Short of signing on for a full post–high school or postcollege art curriculum, you can, and probably should, enroll in individual classes. As I have repeatedly stressed throughout the book, drawing from life is the best way to learn to draw the human body—superhuman or normal—and there are a lot of life drawing classes out there. All you have to do is find one and sign up. In addition, many art academies offer individual courses in cartooning and/or animation. A good source for locating such courses is the official Web site of the National Cartoonists Society: http://www.reuben.org/main.asp.

Unfortunately, there are very few schools that offer a complete curriculum designed to prepare a young artist for employment as a working cartoonist in comic books. Here, I must blow my own horn.

The Joe Kubert School of Cartoon and Graphic Art, Inc., founded over 20 years ago, is the only school that offers the diverse courses needed to become a professional comic book cartoonist. It is a full-time, three-year institution. Our purpose is to train aspiring cartoonists. Graduates from the Joe Kubert School are currently employed by all the major comic book companies. I am very proud of our graduates' achievements. The high quality of their work is testimony to the excellence of our instructors and the unstinting dedication and efforts of the students.

For additional information, visit our Web site, call, write, or e-mail:

The Joe Kubert School of Cartoon and Graphic Art, Inc.
37 Myrtle Avenue
Dover, NJ 07801
1-973-361-1327
www.kubertsworld.com
e-mail: kubert@intrepid.net

The Kubert School also offers a series of correspondence courses in various specialities and subspecialties of comic book cartooning, Joe Kubert's World of Cartooning. For more information, write, phone, or e-mail:

Joe Kubert's World of Cartooning
37 Myrtle Avenue
Dover, NJ 07801
1-800-JKWORLD (559-6753) or 1-973-537-7760
www.kubertsworld.com
e-mail: kubert@intrepid.net

INDEX

Senior editor: Candace Raney
Editor: Sylvia Warren
Designer: Jay Anning, Thumb Print
Production Manager: Hector Campbell